Human Adaptive Strategies
Ecology, Culture, and Politics

DANIEL G. BATES

HUNTER COLLEGE,
THE CITY UNIVERSITY OF NEW YORK

Allyn and Bacon

Boston • London • Toronto • Sydney • Tokyo • Singapore

Series Editor: Sarah Dunbar
Editor-in-Chief: Karen Hanson
Series Editorial Assistant: Elissa V. Schaen
Executive Marketing Manager: Suzy Spivey
Consulting Editor: Sylvia Shepard
Composition and Prepress Buyer: Linda Cox
Manufacturing Buyer: Suzanne Lareau
Editorial-Production Service: The Book Company

Copyright © 1998 by Allyn & Bacon
A Viacom Company
Needham Heights, Massachusetts 02194

Internet: www.abacon.com
America Online: keyword:College Online

Portions of this material appeared first in *Cultural Anthropology* by Daniel G. Bates, copyright © 1996 by Allyn & Bacon.

Library of Congress Cataloging-in-Publication Data
Bates, Daniel G.
    Human adaptive strategies : culture, ecology, and politics /
Daniel G. Bates.
        p.   cm.
    Includes bibliographical references and index.
    ISBN 0-205-26998-2
    1. Human ecology.   2. Social ecology.   3. Ethnology.   I. Title.
GF50.B37   1997
304.2--dc21   97-36032
                                                  CIP

Printed in the United States of America.

10 9 8 7 6 5 4 3 2 1   02 01 00 99 98 97

For Judith

Contents

Chapter 7
Beyond Industrialism: Cultural Change and Economic Development   *136*

Preface

A NUMBER OF INSTRUCTORS USING *Cultural Anthropology* (Allyn & Bacon, 1996) have urged that the sections of that book that deal with human ecology, cultural change and economic development, and with case studies of diverse societies as they respond to their environmental settings, be adapted for classroom use as a free-standing work. *Human Adaptive Strategies: Ecology, Culture, and Politics* is the result of this idea. It is designed to be used either alone or with other textbooks or case material in a variety of courses that consider human behavior and environmental relationships cross-culturally. These courses include cultural anthropology, cultural or political ecology, cultural geography, development studies, and human ecology.

A central theme of this book is that individuals are active decision makers, continually involved in creating and using their cultural and material environments, however misguided their creations may sometimes be. Hence, the reference to ecology, culture, and politics in the title. Faced with new problems and new situations, people will often attempt to find solutions that go beyond traditional cultural solutions or customary behaviors and received prescriptions. In other words, behavioral innovation and variation constantly exist within as well as between societies. Those variations that are proven to be advantageous are often passed on to new generations; they become part of the cultural matrix. Some ways of doing things that are useful in one context may prove otherwise in other situations; cultural innovation and transmission are not patterns of cumulative "progress" but processes of continual intergenerational experiment, "filtering," and change that affect all peoples. Every generation, ideas, technologies, social usages, and even modes of speech pass through what might be seen as a filter or screen. Generally, what is transmitted is what seems to work in a particular context. Processes of innovation, the adoption of new ideas and their transmission to others, lie at the heart of cultural variation and are part of broader ecological and evolutionary processes.

"Change" is the word that most accurately captures what is distinctive about humans. Our brief history on earth is one of unparalleled expansion as the early representatives of our species spilled out of Africa to inhabit virtually every region of the globe. This expansion required altering behavior in all domains to meet the demands of very different habitats; in short, continual interplay between learned behavior and ever-changing environments. Decisions arrived at by individuals, the adaptive strategies of people and societies, and the evolutionary processes of which these are a part are central themes of this book. The approach, then, is essentially ecological and evolutionary. However, we cannot ignore what might be called the ideational or symbolic aspects of social life; ways of behaving and believing that validate our behavior, form our social identities, and satisfy our aesthetic needs. Nor can we ignore the extent to which individual and group behavior is played out in environments in which the most striking features are other people and other groups. This is, of course, true across the evolutionary spectrum, but it is particularly notable for humans.

In this sense any understanding of human ecology has to consider the politics of group life—factors that determine who gets what, and when. Human populations are often socially far more differentiated than are other social animals. We not only engage in division of labor beyond that associated with age and role in sexual reproduction, but we also create systems of perpetuated inequality, such as caste, class, and other differences in economic and political access across age and gender lines. Such inequality has major ramifications for the ways in which we interact with our environments. The fact that there are no physical limits on the accumulation of wealth in a market or capitalist economy, for example, has important consequences for the way that natural resources are exploited. And the fact that the nominal "owners" of resources and the means of exploiting them do not necessarily live and work near them, has important consequences for other people who do. Thus, local people may be powerless to prevent their central government from granting rights to a foreign company to cut down the forest they live in. The impact of cultural diversity, exchange, and inequality on humans and on the ways that humans interact with environments has grown with time and with changes in human social organization since the earliest *homo sapiens* developed tool technology in the Paleolithic period.

Also, we cannot ignore the pitfalls inherent in the concept of adaptation which, all too easily, can be employed to explain everything and hence nothing. The record of human evolution contains much that is due simply to chance, misadventure, and error. Further, the ecological and evolutionary perspective includes much more than simply the material aspects of life. Religious and political beliefs and practices, even kinship systems, are as much a part of human adaptation as are subsistence strategies and economic practices. I will attempt to show this throughout the text and, in so doing, show how the many topics customarily treated as basic to an understanding of human society are integrated rather than separate aspects of culture: politics, economics, and religion are closely intertwined in the adaptive process. I hope that I convey some of the excitement and controversy that are part of the contemporary sciences of human ecology and behavior.

The book consists of seven chapters. Four of the chapters focus on ethnographic case studies and discussions relating to distinctive forms of human food procurement or subsistence: hunting and gathering, horticulture or low-energy farming, pastoralism, and intensive agriculture and industrial society. While this organization reflects a very general evolutionary or historical scheme, it is not offered as a rigid typology or simple sequence of stages of development. Rather, it provides a closer look at the anthropological perspective in action. I use a number of case studies to illustrate how anthropologists view long-term cultural change, analyze cultural adaptation, and attempt to understand diverse aspects of social behavior. Populations whose ways of life and livelihood are as diverse as the San People of Southern Africa and the farmers of Central California are

viewed similarly as people responding to, and usually coping successfully with, the problems facing them. What is emphasized are the costs and rewards of different ways of providing for necessities of life and the relationship of settlement system, mobility, and economic and political organization to other aspects of adaptation. A distinctive feature of all these chapters is that they describe not only different societies but also a wide range of methods and techniques of studying them. This organization is intended to draw the student into interesting ethnographic material and give an insight into methodological concerns. With some modification and revision, the bulk of the material comes from *Cultural Anthropology*. New discussion on issues related to human ecology and evolution, as well as planned and unplanned change, is presented in Chapters 1, 2 and 7.

The first chapter introduces general concepts in the study of human social behavior, the concept of culture, and establishes the organization of the book. Chapter 2 outlines the ecological framework on which subsequent chapters build. It offers an extended discussion of adaptation, politics, decision making, and behavioral variation. The importance of gender is stressed. The final chapter deals with planned and unplanned cultural change, development, and environmental implications of human activities; it concludes with suggestions for risk assessment as we plan for the future. Students are introduced to basic concepts and methods in the course of reading about particular people and places. Each of the four case study chapters, Chapters 3 to 6, presents at least two ethnographic cases. Together these illustrate topics such as kinship and marriage, economic process, politics and leadership, social control, religion, and cultural change. The case study material is, I hope, lively, timely, and jargon-free; the discussion accompanying it draws attention to important issues, including the importance of energy in human society, responding to problems or hazards, innovation and entrepreneurship, and short- and long-term processes of change. The book will show anthropological scholarship in action as it addresses important and immediate human concerns such as the costs and consequences of human energy requirements, environmental degradation, population pressure, social and economic equity in a changing world, and planned and unplanned social change.

This book contains a number of unique features, among which are the following:

Each case study is presented in a contemporary setting, showing people coping with issues and problems to which the reader can easily relate.

Each case is tied to larger issues of cultural evolution and change.

Cases exemplify a variety of research methods and theoretical approaches.

Each chapter begins with a parallel discussion of energy requirements, environmental hazards and special problems, the development and significance of the adaptive strategy in human history, and the social organizational component.

Each chapter has a list of key terms, suggested readings, and illustrations.

Each chapter has boxed inserts that either present recent technical reports in summary form or delve more deeply into specialized topics than does the text.

Readers who are interested in pursuing in greater depth the topics and problems raised in these chapters are urged to use the vast resources of the World Wide Web or Internet (see Chapter 7 for a discussion of this vast and expanding computer network). One easy was to begin such a search, of course, is by using a conventional search engine to explore the web. A more anthropologically focused and often more expeditious way to find out about current research is to begin with a particularly well-constructed home page of an academic or research department, which typically has an array of research-related resources. The home page of the Department of Anthropology at Hunter College, City University of New York (http://www.maxweber.hunter.cuny.edu/anthro/), for example, has links to several hundred departments of anthropology and museums around the world, enabling one to see what thousands of individual scholars are doing and, when appropriate, to make contact with them. Further, it contains links or gateways to numerous libraries, research facilities, professional organizations, scientific publications, news sources, and some on-line courses and tutorials. A recent article by Brian Schwimmer details what is available on the Internet for anthro-

pologists (1996). Readers are welcome to communicate with me by e-mail at the following address:

dbates@shiva.hunter.cuny.edu

Acknowledgments

This book was undertaken using material largely derived from *Cultural Anthropology*, published by Allyn & Bacon—itself my revision of a previous work published by McGraw Hill that I coauthored with Fred Plog. The responsibility for the present content rests with me. Some of the new material in Chapter 2 draws heavily on papers I coauthored with Susan Lees. Judith Tucker worked on the project from the earliest stages to completion and made numerous recommendations as to reorganization, style, and presentation. She also made a substantial contribution to the boxes in this book. Other academic critics, consultants, and reviewers include David Cleveland, Center for People, Food, and Environment; Josh DeWind, CUNY-Hunter College; Alan Duben, CUNY-Hunter College; Gerald Creed, CUNY-Hunter College; Elliot Fratkin, Smith College; Nancy Flowers, CUNY-Hunter College; David Gilmore, SUNY at Stony Brook; William Irons, Northwestern University; Patricia Johnson, Pennsylvania State University; Susan Lees, CUNY-Hunter College; Louise Lennihan, CUNY-Hunter College; Mike Little, SUNY at Binghamton; Tom McGovern, CUNY-Hunter College; Patrick McKim, California Polytechnic State University; Warren Morrill, Pennsylvania State University; Tom Painter, The Social Science Research Council; William Parry, CUNY-Hunter College; Burt Pasternak, CUNY-Hunter College; Ida Susser, CUNY-Hunter College. I greatly appreciate their generous help. I was, as with other projects, immeasurably assisted in numerous ways by many other people; at the head of this list is my consulting editor Sylvia Shepard.

Daniel G. Bates

Chapter 1

The Study of Human Behavior

By at least some biological criteria, humans are an extremely successful species. Homo sapiens, to give the formal description, are the most widespread and numerous of the large animals, are distributed throughout the world, and live under the most diverse and extreme conditions. Despite the enormous variety of local problems and hazards that humans must deal with to survive, all of the world's peoples are very similar in biological makeup and physique. In comparison with many other animals we are remarkably homogeneous and even rather a dull lot, lacking plumage and other specialized survival equipment. What accounts for the success of our species, and what can we surmise about our future? Why is it that humans vary considerably in social life and customs while differing only in small degree biologically? Such concerns underlie much research in anthropology, human ecology, cultural geography, and other fields.

These fields emphasize the connections between human society and the larger web of life. Only by appreciating the fact that we are subject to the same forces that affect all other living organisms can we come to understand those many aspects of human behavior that distinguish us from other species. And if we more fully appreciate the extraordinary diversity evident in the ways of life of the world's peoples, we may come to a better understanding of our own society.

The Anthropological Perspective

A perspective on humankind encompassing non-human life forms is relatively recent in European thought. For millennia Europeans were accustomed to thinking of the world, its peoples, and all other living things as eternally fixed and unchanging. Although similarities among species were widely noted, these similarities were not thought to represent the outcome of a shared and ongoing process of change—the process we call evolution. Instead each species was seen as a unique entity with its own unique characteristics. No such group was related to another or to anything else. Obviously, the world existed for humans—in particular, for those favored to be participants in European civilization.

However, by the mid-nineteenth century the idea of evolutionary change had become respectable in European scholarly circles, and soon became familiar to the public, in large part as a result of the tremendous impact of Charles Darwin's famous book, *On the Origin of Species by Means of Natural Selection*, published in 1859. The thesis of this book is that species are related to one another by descent, with modifications, from common ancestors. Darwin postulated that such modifications occur primarily through differential reproduction, or the ability of some members of a species to produce more surviving offspring than others. These favored individuals pass on their traits to the next generation, whereas the less favored do not do so to the same degree. Darwin called this process **natural selection** and demonstrated that it can change the characteristics of an entire species over time, or even give rise to new species. We will return to this in greater detail in Chapter 2.

The idea that humans also may be a product of a long sequence of ongoing change received support of a rather startling variety: the discovery of human-like fossils in association with stone tools. Fossils are the naturally mineralized remains of organic matter—earlier forms of plant and animal life turned to stone and thus preserved—very often lying underground for thousands of years until chance discovery brings them to light. During the seventeenth and eighteenth centuries, many such fossil remains of extinct plants and animals were collected and classified and the similarities and differences between them and living species were duly noted. These discoveries, along with Charles Darwin's theory of natural selection, established the idea that not only human beings themselves, but also societies, were the products of evolution—that is, they developed from earlier forms. Over millions of years the human body and human societies had emerged from earlier human and prehuman forms, through a combination of physical evolution (cumulative changes in biological makeup) and cultural evolution (cumulative changes in thought and behavior). The study of contemporary peoples and their social behavior offered here is closely tied to this view of the world: the evolutionary view.

All science is an effort to describe and explain natural phenomena. The aim of the social sciences, including anthropology, economics, cultural geography, political science, history, sociology, and psychology, is to describe and explain one particular natural phenomenon: **Homo sapiens**, the human species. Much of what anthropologists and other social scientists study in their investigation of the human species lies in the broad domain we call "culture." **Culture** is a system of shared beliefs, values, customs, behaviors, and artifacts that the members of a society use to cope with their world and with

one another, and that are transmitted from generation to generation through learning. This definition includes not only patterns of behavior but also patterns of thought (shared meanings that the members of a society attach to various phenomena, natural and intellectual, including religion and ideologies), artifacts (tools, pottery, houses, machines, works of art), and the culturally transmitted skills and techniques used to make the artifacts. In short, culture includes almost any form of behavior that is learned rather than instinctive. We will leave until later the difficulties that may arise in attempts to apply this distinction.

Holism

All scientists tend to specialize, to reduce their subject matter to manageable proportions. But when anthropologists apply themselves to specific questions, they try to retain a breadth of view that is unique to the profession. **Holism** is the philosophical view that no complex entity can be considered to be only the sum of its parts. This is not to say that all organic or inorganic matter does not have concrete attributes that can be measured and quantified. As a principle guiding social research, holism is the assumption that any given aspect of human life is to be studied with an eye to its relation to other aspects of human life. Anthropologists, for example, attempt to understand specific problems or questions of interest within a wider context. Carol Laderman, who has worked with rural Malaysian women in an effort to understand traditional medicine and childbearing and midwife practices, writes:

> The strength of anthropology lies within a paradox. The broad philosophical and theoretical concerns of anthropology must be approached through studies of a particular people, living in a particular place and time. But in order to understand the particular, we must approach it from a generalist viewpoint. The specific nature of our inquiries cannot be allowed to limit our field of investigation. Data must be collected even in those areas which at first glance seem to impinge only peripherally upon the problem. For example, understanding a people's dietary habits requires a knowledge of their economy and ecology, as well as their religious, social and aesthetic ideologies. An analysis of childbirth practices must include an investigation into sex roles, rules of marriage and divorce, and the status and training of childbirth attendants, as well as the medical system of which these practices are a part. [Laderman, 1983, p. 1]

Thus a researcher studying child nutrition in Brazil will probably consider how the occupations of parents affect family diet, and then how differences in nutrition arise and what causes them to persist. The political implications of nutritional differences among ethnic groups also may be explored. The biological anthropologist studying the evolution of the human brain will take into consideration not only the shape and size of fossil skulls, but also evidence in regard to the evolution of language, tool-making, social organization, and of hunting and gathering techniques, all of which are related to the growth of the brain. Likewise, the archaeologist studying prehistoric stone tools and the linguist investigating the origins of language will take all these matters (and more) into account. Scientists in other disciplines are consulted as well. Geologists, paleontologists, botanists, zoologists, geneticists, physicists, geographers, and specialists in other fields all provide information relevant to these concerns.

Cultural Relativism

The second important principle in the study of cultural diversity is **cultural relativism**—the ability to view the beliefs and customs of other peoples within the context of their cultural matrix rather than one's own. This ability does not necessarily come naturally. Our perceptions are obviously adjusted to our own cultures. So, at first sight, an African man with ritual scars on his face or a Middle Eastern woman in *purdah* (that is, with her face and body largely covered), is likely to appear strange to us. Unfamiliar food preferences may seem revolting. When the practice in question is one that we consider a matter of morality rather than simply one of taste—as, for example, the ritual homosexuality found in some New Guinea tribes, or the infanticide practiced by the Yanomamö of Venezuela—our reactions can be far stronger.

Such cultural self-centeredness, the tendency to judge the customs of other societies by the standards of one's own, is called **ethnocentrism**. It is by no means a phenomenon exclusive to Western societies. People in every society tend to view outsiders and their customs with suspicion and often condemnation. If we consider infanticide cruel and unnatural, those peoples who practice it may consider our own custom of shutting old people away in homes for the aged to be equally appalling.

Adopting a perspective of cultural relativism aids understanding; it allows the observer to see the customs of other societies as ways of solving problems—problems that all societies share to some extent. Throughout the world, for example, people have a desire for sexual activity that outstrips their desire for babies or their ability to support them.

Americans tend to solve this problem by artificial birth control mechanisms and, in some cases, abortion; other societies solve it by enforced sexual abstinence or late marriage; others by infanticide, which, when understood in its cultural context, is seen to be most often an extreme measure taken by parents who, in times of food shortage, sacrifice a newborn infant to secure the well-being of another child. Even so, the concept of cultural relativism does not imply that one condones or justifies any particular behavior just because it occurs; rather, it is a means for understanding why it does occur and its significance for the society in question.

When we can see cultural differences through the prism of cultural relativism, we approach other cultures with open minds and an appreciation for human diversity. We need not and we should not surrender our own values and our own ethical or moral standards. We simply adopt an approach that fosters scientific objectivity and at the same time encourages empathy with other peoples: an ability to see things, to some degree, as they see them. These products of cultural relativism—objectivity, empathy, and informed judgment—are indispensable to the anthropologist, as they are to anyone who tries to understand the customs of another society.

There is, however, a troubling dilemma inherent in cultural relativism—one that is increasingly central in discussions of universal human rights. Can we use cultural relativism to justify the violation of basic civil and human rights? Eugene Hammel has written, with respect to the bloody war in Bosnia and Croatia, that when a society with which one is familiar is consumed by the flames of war, the anthropologist must speak out against war crimes, as would any moral person. These crimes, such as politically motivated rape, massacre of civilians, and torture, cannot be justified even if such behavior is considered justified by those carrying it out and expected by those on the receiving end (Hammel, 1994). The dilemma is that in extending our own society's value system (for example, concepts of universal civil and human rights), we are, in fact, imposing our own moral standards on other societies.

As the impact of development threatens to destroy the cultures of indigenous peoples that have traditionally been of concern to anthropologists, more and more action-oriented anthropologists are questioning the notions that a detached, objective stance is possible and that silence on social issues equals neutrality. According to these anthropologists, failure to speak out and refusal to become involved is tantamount to supporting the status quo. These anthropologists see the fieldworker's role as making resources available to the people being studied and

helping them to understand possible alternatives and articulate their own views. They support cultural relativism—so long as it does not become an excuse for inaction in the face of exploitation.

The Science of Anthropology

Anthropological investigation involves comparisons of contemporary cultures and investigations of cultural and biological changes. Anthropology takes, as its object of study, all human peoples, across the globe and across time, treating subjects as varied as their teeth, their diseases, their ways of getting food and shelter and rearing children, and their ideas about their place in the world. Consider the investigations of the ethnographers Teresa and John Hart (1996), who carefully determined the caloric and nutritional values of food resources in the Ituri rain forest of Zaire. Their findings indicated that the Mbuti Pygmies—hunters and gatherers in the forest—could not live independently of the farmers with whom they trade. Elliot Fratkin and Eric A. Roth, working in Kenya among the Ariaal (see Chapter 5), found that the key to Ariaal pastoral subsistence was herd diversity combined with mobility. Families who had different varieties of livestock could cope with drought far better than those who focused on one. Further, wealthy herders with large numbers of animals were better able to recover from periodic disas-

ters, a fact that amplifies wealth differentials. Paul Stoller studied the kaleidoscope of cultures on New York City's West 125th Street, where an informal West African street market had sprung up and persisted, in spite of the city's efforts to close it (1996). On examination, what appeared to be a mass of disorganization, turned out to be very structured—just as in West Africa, where many of the traders originate. Space is allocated along regional and ethnic lines, with traders selling similar things grouped together (1996). It is this breadth of inquiry that gives anthropology its vitality. Anthropologists continually probe the essence of human existence, asking philosophical as well as pragmatic questions.

The Role of Theory

The kind of questions the researcher asks depends largely on the theoretical perspective in which the individual is trained. Theories are the backbone of scientific research. A **scientific theory** is a statement that postulates ordered relationships among natural phenomena and explains some aspect of the world. The theoretical model chosen by researchers leads them to ask certain kinds of questions and helps them formulate some questions as specific hypotheses. For example, a functionalist theory of politics that stresses social stability and integration will direct a researcher to gather data on institutions that adjudicate disputes, release tension, and promote group solidarity. A Marxist theory of politics that emphasizes conflict and competition among those who control the means of production and those who supply the labor will direct a researcher to study instances of conflict reflecting class or economic divisions.

This is not to say that researchers see only what they are looking for and block out everything else. Still, perception is always selective and tends to be shaped by one's assumptions—in this case, by what one expects or hopes to find. To prevent this issue from becoming a problem, anthropologists should be careful to spell out their theoretical assumptions when they write the plans for their research and later when they report their findings. Thus their biases, if indeed they have influenced the research, are at least not hidden.

A theory is never tested directly; one tests theoretical expectations by testing specific hypotheses. A **hypothesis** is a statement about relationships that can possibly be shown to be untrue. The statement, "Cigarette smoking is bad," is not a hypothesis because it does not define "bad" or specify the relationship between smoking and anything else. It seems like a valid or logical statement, but a skeptic might well argue that the economic, social, or psychological benefits of smoking outweigh the physical harm it causes. The similar statement, "Cigarette smoking increases the risk of lung cancer," is a hypothesis because the risk of lung cancer can be measured among smokers and nonsmokers and a causal relationship between exposure to specific carcinogens in tobacco and smoking can be established. This distinction is important because unless a statement is logically falsifiable by appeal to relevant facts (or subjected to the appropriate test), it cannot enhance our knowledge of the world. If the actual results or observations are consistent with the hypothesis in a significant number of cases, the theory that generated the hypothesis is strengthened and perhaps expanded. But if the observed results of hypothesis testing repeatedly contradict theoretical expectations, the theory is eventually altered or abandoned. In short, theories survive as long as they continue to suggest useful approaches to the phenomena that scientists are trying to explain.

A theory may be the product of decades of diligent research. Or, as in the case of Darwin, it may be the product of a young scientist capable of seeing through the preconceptions that block the insights of others. Every theory has its blind spots: aspects of a subject that are underemphasized or disregarded in favor of other aspects. And new theories often displace the old by redirecting attention to those neglected areas. Through this dynamic process—the constant challenging and retesting of ideas—the discipline's theoretical framework is refined and developed over time.

Objectivity in Anthropology

Some anthropologists argue that, as scientists, they have an obligation to strive for the objectivity generally associated with the sciences. This position is based on the belief that it is possible to suspend one's cultural and theoretical biases in the field and to observe and report, with detachment, what one sees. A researcher's cultural background, academic training, and personality influence both what is perceived and what is reported. Some therefore argue that it is impossible to "go backstage," or, as Vincent Crapanzano puts it, "We were told not to ask leading questions; as if there were such a thing as a non-leading question" (quoted in Berreby, 1995, p. 46). By pretending to objectivity, it is argued, anthropologists are deceiving themselves. A recent article in the *New York Times Magazine* describes Clifford Geertz as having done much to turn anthropology away from thinking of itself as an "objective science"(Berreby, 1995, pp. 44–47).

While there are many complex issues involved, they all turn on two interrelated questions. What is science? Can anthropology contribute to it? While usually one contrasts art and science, Steven Reyna, in a provocative critique of contemporary efforts to move anthropology away from its scientific tradition, points out their similarities: "Art, among other things, is a creative, imaginative representation of experience. Science is an art. Like other art forms it is a manner of representing experience. The experience it represents is reality" (Reyna, 1994, p. 556). In order to understand how reality is constituted, basic science is explanation; in order to determine how well we are explaining reality, science is validation. Science is not a quest for absolute truths or the collection of concrete facts. If it were, then anthropologists would be justified in not engaging in the endeavor—in fact this form of "science" would have little utility for anyone. Science is simply a quest for information about the world.

Anthropology can and does contribute to this quest, even if the researcher is faced with the challenges of cultural diversity. If there are doubts, one only has to look at the state of knowledge about human behavior today in comparison to forty years ago, when anthropology in Europe and America moved into the post–World War II era. The methods of anthropology—indeed, the methods of science in general—are strikingly similar to processes in nature where individuals (and the populations of which

Box 1.1

Ethnography and Ethnology from Other Times, Other Places

ANTHROPOLOGICAL THEORY IS the product of a long tradition of scholarly inquiry in the West. Beyond this tradition, however, anthropology is, in its essentials, as old as human society itself. There is a universal nature to the spirit of inquiry and description that lies behind the discipline.

The historian Jonathan Spence describes the adventures and misadventures of a would-be Chinese ethnographer, one John Hu. In 1722 a Jesuit missionary and noted scholar of Chinese literature, living in China, was granted permission to return to France with a collection of books for the king's library. Since he needed a Chinese calligrapher and secretary, he engaged Hu, the mission gatekeeper. Hu was semi-educated, a Christian convert, and eager to see the West. "Hu also believes," his employer noted, "he will be able to write up his travels in the form of a book that will make him famous among his countrymen when he returns" (Spence, 1988, p. 25).

After a lengthy and difficult voyage, in itself sufficient to cure the average person of any desire to see the world, Hu and his mentor reached Port Louis, France. Once on land, Hu set out to investigate the customs of the natives. But, making errors that modern ethnographers know all too well, he shocked then outraged his companions: He could not sleep in a proper bed and insisted on the floor, with an open window (unconcerned about the natives' beliefs in noxious nighttime vapors); he repeatedly wandered into kitchens, sampling the food uninvited; he borrowed a horse, left unattended for a moment by its owner, for a gallop of exploration through the city. Scolded, he was not contrite, asking "Why, if a horse is being left unused, may someone else not use it?" (Spence, 1988, p. 51).

When Hu decided he wanted to walk across France, which would have exposed him to great danger, he was packed unceremoniously into a coach to Paris. Nevertheless, his inquisitive spirit led to trouble: Hu stopped the coach to explore windmills, he jumped out to sample fruit in passing orchards, and one night at an inn he gave his best jacket to a beggar. His companions began to suspect that he was mad. Once in Paris, continuing his frantic explorations and still having learned very little French, he indeed gave local people every appearance of having lost his mind. Not content to observe and experience, he began to preach that men and women should be kept apart in church, as was the custom in China. Eventually his mentor and companions had him committed to a madhouse, where he remained in near-naked misery for over two years. Finally, through the help of a priest, he was repatriated, and concluded his days answering such requests as, "Uncle Hu, Uncle Hu, tell us what it's like over there, in the West."

An Arab ambassador, Ibn Fadlan, was sent through Russia by his caliph in 922 A.D. and was rather more successful in his effort to describe another culture. He provides the only first-hand account we have of a Viking encampment on the Volga. Ibn Fadlan, like missionaries of many faiths, sometimes colored his observations with unfavorable judgments about "barbaric" customs. He nevertheless contributed a vivid portrait of the

---

they are a part) respond to experience. Survival, cultural and otherwise, depends on successful responses to experience. Science is not concerned with what is universally true, but with what is approximately true—that is, explanations that are useful until new ones offer improvements. The methods of science are diverse but all rely on some form of validation—the encounter of explanation and experience. "If one rejects science, one rejects the art of explaining, and validating the explanation, of the experience of reality" (Reyna, 1994, p. 557).

Perhaps what is called for is a matter less of objectivity than of rigor. By using the most rigorous methods possible to evaluate their conclusions, anthropologists guarantee, if not absolute objectivity, at least comparability in the evaluation of theories and ideas. By any criteria, in the forty years following World War II, anthropology has contributed a great deal to the understanding of human behavior, origins, language, and cultural history. By any measure, anthropological scholarship meets the test of experience.

The unifying belief among anthropologists who subscribe to the natural science approach is that there are important regularities in human behavior across cultures, as well as diversity, and that these can be accounted for through empirical methods. **Empiricism** refers to the direct experiencing of the reality being described or explained. Obviously there are limits to direct experience, but direct observation

political hierarchy, costumes, trading ventures, and life of the Vikings in their great wooden houses. His inquisitive spirit led him to record their funeral rites:

Finally, the news was brought me that a prominent man among them had died. They laid him in a grave and covered it with a roof over it for ten days until they were through with the cutting out and sewing together of his garments. Thus it is: if the deceased is a poor man, they make for him a small bark, put him in it and burn the bark; if he is a rich man, they gather his possessions together and divide them in three parts: one third remains for his family; with the second third they cut garments out for him, and with the third part they brew nabid *(beer) for themselves which they drink on the day when his slave girl kills herself and is cremated with her master. They drink the* nabid *to insensibility day and night. It often happens that one of them dies with his beaker in his hand. When a high chief dies, his family says to his slave girls and servants, "Which one of you wishes to die with him?" Then one of them answers, "I." When he has said this, he is bound. He can in no way be allowed to withdraw his word. If he wishes it, it is not permitted. For the most part, this self-sacrifice is made by the maidens.*

While there are many examples of early, non-Western ethnography, it is not only the ethnographic spirit that is universal. The need to systematize or generate theories about the cultural world also has a long tradition. Ibn Khaldun, born in Tunis in 1332, was an influential statesman and philosopher—one whose works still are read and valued today. While he traveled, as governor to Islamic provinces and as ambassador to Christian courts in Spain, he carefully recorded what he saw. But he was not content with observation. A highly educated individual, he wanted to understand the reasons why dynasties rise and fall, why great empires expand and die, and why people organize themselves in groups and live in tents, towns, and villages. He felt that "behind the external data is an internal, rational structure which, if understood, could explain the whys and wherefores, and render the external intelligible" (cited in Mahdi, 1971, p. 48).

Ibn Khaldun's theory of cultural evolution and what he saw as the laws of history are quite complex, but not dissimilar to much contemporary theorizing. For example, he saw dynasties and empires as usually passing through five distinct stages: (1) the overthrow of an existing regime, (2) initial consolidation of the new regime in a period

of recruiting and integration, (3) conquest and expansion, (4) a period of imperial glory and contentment, and (5) corruption and decline. What makes this particularly interesting is that he postulates the mechanisms by which each phase leads to the next, something that any adequate theory of change must do:

The fifth stage is one of waste and squandering. In this stage, the ruler wastes on pleasures and amusements [the treasures] accumulated by his ancestors, through [excessive] generosity to his inner circle and at their parties. Also, he acquires bad, low-class followers to whom he entrusts the most important matters [of state], which they are not qualified to handle by themselves, not knowing which of them they should tackle and which they should leave alone. [In addition,] the ruler seeks to destroy the great clients of his people and followers of his predecessors. Thus, they come to hate him and conspire to refuse support to him. [Furthermore] he loses a number of soldiers by spending their allowances on his pleasures [instead of paying them] and by refusing them access to his person and not supervising them [properly]. Thus, he ruins the foundations his ancestors had laid and tears down what they had built up.

and measurement, implicit in the empirical approach, is central to the idea of anthropology as a scientific endeavor (see also Barth, 1994, p. 76; Brown, 1991; Rappaport, 1993, p. 76).

Aspects of Culture

The most distinctive single attribute of our species is that complex but elusive trait we call culture. It is complex in that it encompasses behaviors as diverse as tool-making, bridal customs, funerary rites, farming, religious practices, art—in short anything that is based on learning and that is passed on among individuals. Culture is elusive because, while it seems easy to distinguish what is learned from what is innate (for example, how to start a fire as opposed to the emotion of fear we experience when threatened by a fire), in practice it is very difficult. This because all behaviors, learned or otherwise, have a basis in the human brain. Learning English as we grow up—as opposed to Arabic—is clearly a cultural phenomenon, but the ability to learn a language at all is a unique biological property of our species. Since culture encompasses all that we acquire through learning as we proceed through life, it can and does regularly change; after all, we do not think and behave as do our parents. Cultural behavior also varies greatly among individuals in the same society; not everyone has the same preferences in food and dress or even practices the same forms of sex. Nevertheless, there are apparent limitations to cultural plasticity; human sensory mechanisms, intelligence, emotions, reproductive systems, color recognition, and linguistic ability are universally shared. Even aspects of social life fall into very familiar patterns among very diverse cultures: notions of human beauty, the importance of family or kin ties, the importance of "reputation," the importance of religion and art are part of every human society. Thus while human culture appears as a wonderfully colorful collage, it has an underlying structure expressing our common humanity. This chapter explores some aspects of this commonality together with the nature of language itself. Our common humanity is rooted in our unique ability to acquire and use language and, despite the many biological traits we share with other species, only humans possess the neurological infrastructure that allows for true language and, hence, culture.

Culture Gives Meaning to Reality

Culture encompasses not only social behaviors but also ways of thinking. From our cultural training we learn what meanings to attach to the events of our world, and especially to the behavior of others, so that we can make some sense of those events and know how to respond to them. The meanings of specific actions can vary with the cultural context in which they are interpreted.

Because meaning is supplied by cultural context and because such contexts differ, people of various societies can view the world in quite different ways. For example, members of societies that speak different languages and follow different religious traditions may well make very different distinctions between the natural and the supernatural. For the Australian aborigines, certain rocks, animals, and places have souls that are very much a part of them. The sacred sites of Christianity, Islam, and Judaism have meanings for their adherents that are not shared by outsiders. The beliefs and values of a society are a cultural reality. Whether marrying more than one spouse is treated as a crime or as a preferred form of marriage depends on culturally defined rules of behavior.

Even so, we cannot regard our ability to define reality and to make rules for appropriate behavior as completely open or arbitrary. While different systems of marriage, mating, or cohabiting are practiced by societies around the world, we can easily think of variations that no society has adopted or condoned. There appear to be universal constraints on sex roles,

as on other areas of human behavior, within which variation occurs (Brown, 1991). As David Gilmore points out, "All societies distinguish between male and female, providing institutionalized sex-appropriate roles for adult men and women. Most societies also hold consensual ideals—guiding or admonitory images—for adult masculinity and femininity by which individuals are judged as worthy members of their sex and are evaluated more generally as moral actors" (Gilmore, 1990, pp. 1–2).

Culture Is Integrated

The religious, political, and economic institutions of a society are shaped by common adaptive forces operating over long periods of time, and as a consequence they tend to "fit" with each other. The "fit" is often supplied by language or, at least, verbally expressed models of the world. We use language to signify the legitimacy of a given political order or religious institution. The language used to justify equality or, on occasion, to justify a revolution is expressed symbolically in special terminology: for example, the words of the U.S. Constitution, the Bible, or the Bill of Rights. We also rely on social rules and symbols such as the shape of stop signs and the colors of traffic lights to provide order to our daily lives.

The many ways in which cultural practices are interrelated gives stability and continuity to cultural evolution; changes are incremental and often occur very slowly. We do not wake up each morning with a burning need to reconfirm the existence of institutions on which we depend or the symbols through which we interpret our reality. It is probably just because stability and continuity are so important to our survival that change and innovation are usually so conservative. It is as though humans were generally guided by the maxim "If it ain't broke, don't fix it." Sometimes we see this tendency toward stability and continuity most dramatically when it is violated by the cataclysmic events of war or other disasters; people who are suddenly cut off from their customary practices and familiar ways of doing things experience stress not unlike what is sometimes called "culture shock"—the feeling of disorientation one may experience when thrust into an unfamiliar cultural setting. In many respects, when an individual is born into a particular society and grows up learning its language, social rules, and expectations, it is analogous to a new employee coming into a long-established corporation. The established ways of doing things is the environment in which the new employee must find his or her way; for the most of the employee's career, conformity will be the rule and experimentation the exception. Nevertheless, people do innovate, and, out of individual shifts in behavior, major cultural shifts or trends occur.

Culture Is Adaptive

Cultural adaptation encompasses all of the learned or socially acquired responses and behaviors that affect reproduction, provisioning, shelter—in short, survival. Like many other species, humans adapt by learning new ways of doing things. The swelling human population is testimony to just how rapidly we can adjust our systems of food production and other technologies. Our ability to learn rapidly and to communicate learning is, in large measure, due to our ability to use language. These abilities have enabled us to develop technologies that allow us to occupy most areas of the earth—something no other large animal can do. In the long run, of course, these technologies may also prove to be maladaptive; we may be a species with a relatively short history. Cultural adaptation involves changes of all sorts that continually affect our relationship to our environment. It results in changes that can never be ideal, as the environment is itself constantly changing. No adaptation or response is a perfect or final solution; each carries with it certain costs and hazards.

Adaptation is always opportunistic: We take advantage of whatever resources are available to us at a particular time (including available genetic and cultural materials), often with little regard for future consequences. For example, industrialized societies began to use oil as a fuel at the beginning of the twentieth century in an initially very limited way. This adaptation soon solved the problem of furnishing an effective, cheap fuel to power modern machinery. Its use was opportunistic in the sense that the oil was there to be tapped and our technology happened to have developed to the point that allowed us to make use of it. In adapting to oil fuel, we made numerous commitments that have altered the structure of our society: We rely on food produced with oil-fueled machinery; we grow crops dependent on fertilizers and pesticides derived from the petrochemical industry; we use rapid transport, cheap electricity, and productive systems too numerous to mention. All these activities are fueled by oil. In recent years, the environment has been changing in unexpected ways. We are faced with declining reserves of oil, with the toxic consequences of a highly developed industrial society, and perhaps with long-term changes in the atmosphere—all consequences of heavy oil use. It is also certain that whatever other energy sources we turn to next will

Rituals such as circumcision must be understood in terms of the particular cultural environment of which they are a part. For the young Masai male, the year of circumcision, the most important of his life, marks his emergence into manhood.

(George Rodger/Magnum)

be imperfect solutions and will generate a host of new and unforeseen difficulties as well. Adaptation is at once the solution to a particular problem and the source of unanticipated changes and, inevitably, new problems.

Behavior, Language, and Learning

As we have seen, animal behavior (including, of course, human behavior) is seen in terms of a basic distinction: It may be instinctive—that is, genetically controlled—or it may be learned. This is especially true when looking at human social behavior. Learned ways of behaving constitute a very large percentage of human activity, probably far outweighing instinctive behavior. We might visualize this situation by thinking of the difference between the behavior of a very young child and that of an adult in the same family. All animals have some capacity to learn, and learning is important to the survival of most species. But no other animal learns, can learn, or needs to learn as much as the human animal. In order to function as independent members of our societies, we require not only a long period of physical care but also a long period of training in how to use language, to think and behave; in other words, training in a society's system of behaviors—its culture.

A child born into any society begins to learn behavior, language, and skills appropriate to that culture from the day of birth. The child's toilet training and feeding habits, the encouragement (or discouragement) given its first experiments in interacting socially with others, the rewards offered for correct deportment—all amount to an intensive training course in how to be a proper person. The child goes on to learn social roles specific to the appropriate sex, useful technical skills, and his or her people's religion and moral codes. This training in one's own culture is sometimes called **socialization** or **enculturation**, and what we become is greatly influenced by the persons who carry out that enculturation and the way they do it. In many societies a fairly narrow circle of people, primarily parents and kin and community elders, are responsible for the bulk of an individual's socialization. In other societies, as in our own, much of this training is provided by specialists outside the family or immediate community; we send our children to schools, churches, summer camps, and universities. To a considerable extent our behavior as men and women, our conduct as parents, our expectations, and our attitudes are shaped by this process.

Socialization is by no means uniform for all members of a society. In our own society, for example, some parents raise their children quite strictly, setting clear rules and clear punishments for violations. Others take a more permissive approach, making large allowances for experimentation and failure on the child's part. Nor are the parents the only socializing influences. Each child has a unique constellation of friends, relatives, and neighbors, and hence each learns a somewhat distinctive version of the culture. Moreover, the exact content of the socialization process varies along gender, ethnic, socioeconomic, religious, and regional lines.

For example, Yanomamö boys are encouraged by their parents to be aggressive and to display anger and rage. Their sisters are not encouraged to behave in this way, although we may assume that their capacity for anger and rage is as great as that of boys. Among the Yomut Turkmen of northeastern Iran,

young men are brought up with a high regard for physical prowess and the necessity of defending one's kin and community, by force if necessary. One tribe or descent group among the Yomut, however, is considered holy, and the men do not fight. In fact, it is considered a serious religious offense to strike a member of this holy tribe or to steal their property. Boys in this group are socialized quite differently from those born into other Yomut groups, with little emphasis on fighting or self-defense.

Nevertheless, there are broad similarities in how and what the members of a single society are taught. The members of a given society tend to take such similarities for granted (often marking them up to "human nature") and to notice only the differences. But to the outsider, individual differences in thought and behavior within a society may be less striking than the similarities. Recent research by two biologists from Israel, Eva Jalonka and Eytan Avital, suggests that some learned behavior in animals, including humans, follows the same rules as genes: Parents, especially mothers, pass on behavioral traits to their children much as they do genetic ones (Angier, 1995, pp. 13–22). Thus, children learn at infancy to fancy the behavioral styles of their parents, and these modes of behavior can be passed on over generations. This, they suggest, may account for the fact that there is a decided tendency for people to favor as mates individuals who share characteristics with their parents.

This is not to say that these learned behaviors have no basis in biology; in fact, all behavior is mediated by biological processes and limitations. Our basic physiological requirements—the need for food, water, shelter, sleep, and sexual activity—underlie a good deal of our behavior. Our brains, with their elaborately encoded propensities for liking some things and avoiding others, also channel behavior in ways that are only recently being researched, as we see with the work on parental imprinting noted above. One fact seems clear: Rather than being a sharply distinct alternative to instinct, learned behavior is often guided by information inherent in the genes (see Gould & Marler, 1987, p. 74). Speech learning is a good example. "Human infants innately recognize most or all of the consonant sounds characteristic of human speech, including consonants not present in the language they normally hear" (Gould & Marler, 1987, p. 82). Some cognitive scientists now propose that human brains may be "wired" with a universal program enabling infants to very rapidly learn the subtle and complex patterns of seemingly drastically different languages (Smolensky & Prince, 1997). Learned behavior, quite apart from instinct, serves biological purposes

Box 1.2

Social Learning and Caste Identity: Two Fishing Communities in Southwest India

WHILE CULTURAL BEHAVIOR CAN be seen as adaptive, inasmuch as it is an important factor in determining individual and group success, it also has to be understood as having qualities that transcend immediate material rewards. One striking example comes from two fishing communities of Karnataka, India (Deb, 1996, pp. 109–123). India is famous for social groupings, or castes, that are occupationally specialized and endogamous—that is, marry only among themselves. Two fishing castes, the Ambiga and Harikantra of Karnataka, employ different techniques for throwing nets although they live in in close proximity to one another. Ambigas throw the net from above the head, as opposed to the far easier Harikantra method of throwing at waist level. These different techniques are transmitted from one generation to the next through social learning.

Ecologist Debal Deb argues that each caste persists in its unique method of casting the net because the contrasting techniques have come to take on social significance; that is, they have come to symbolize caste boundaries between groups who share a physical space but not a social one. The Ambiga people identify themselves as the "Water Children" and have, for centuries, specialized in exploiting riverine and marine habitats (p. 112). The Harikantra are not as specialized and cojoin fishing with numerous secondary occupations. They are also viewed as socially and economically superior. As Deb puts it, "Many objects of functional utility tend to be transformed through tradition into objects of socio-religious conventionality, often to the extent of prejudices" (Deb, 1996, p. 117).

This is a point made in a more general way by anthropologist Roy Rappaport with respect to many food and occupational taboos (1971). Even dress, such as uniforms, hats, and shoes, may take on significance as group boundary markers. Deb suggests that when one group's occupational area, or niche, is invaded by other castes, the caste originally occupying the niche is likely to place great symbolic importance on behavior associated with its specialization. "The more difficult a behavior is, the more likely it is to be preferred as a marker for the original occupant of the niche, because that behavior would be the least likely to to be usurped by outsiders" (Deb, 1996, p. 118). To test this proposition, Deb recruited student volunteers from nonfishing castes who had no net throwing experience. He divided these into two groups assigned to either an Ambiga or to a Harikantra fisherman. By various measures the Ambiga technique turned out to be about four times as difficult to learn as the Harikantra technique (p. 116). The near-total conformity among Ambiga fishermen would thus appear to be a socially learned preference or bias rather than a functionally expedient trait. Interestingly, a third population of Moslems has recently come to the region and adopted the easier to learn Harikantra technique but with a new twist: While they throw their nets from the waist, they do so consistently from the right-hand side which is the mirror image of the Harikantra throw. The dynamics of social learning and the importance of group conformity as symbolizing identity has to be considered within the adaptational approach.

because of the practical advantages it confers, advantages that are attested to by our success in reproducing and surviving in virtually every climatic zone on earth. Even our universally shared taste for sweets, fats, and salts, and hence the underlying basis for our dietary systems, is the result of a long evolutionary process. It has been suggested that human systems of knowledge—religion, magic, science, philosophy—are based on a uniquely human, inborn need to impose order on experience. This is not surprising, as pattern recognition (for example, seeing a dangerous situation) is a key means for processing information critical to survival.

The biological basis of human behavior, then, is important. But how we go about satisfying inborn needs and developing successful coping strategies is largely a matter of contextual learning. Whether we feed ourselves by growing yams and hunting wild game or by herding camels and raising wheat, whether we explain a thunderstorm by attributing it to meteorological conditions or to a fight among the gods—such things are determined by what we learn as part of our enculturation. Enculturation prepares us to function as members of a given society—to speak its language, to use its symbols in abstract thought, and so forth. This ability depends in turn

Language is a crucial element in forming individual and group identity. In Bulgaria, the former Communist government attempted to suppress the use of Turkish by over a million of its Moslem minority. Here religious and other leaders meet to demand recognition of their linguistic and religious rights.
(Fevzi Omer)

on genetically inherited physical traits, notably a brain of awesome complexity. But even though cultural behavior may be guided by genetically rooted limitations and propensities, it is obvious that we do not inherit genes for speaking English as opposed to Swahili, or for training as a doctor as opposed to a pilot. It is more difficult to assess the contribution of our biological heritage to the shaping of very basic aspects of social organization, sex roles, aggression, and family, but clearly there are limits to the range of variation found in different societies.

Language, Biology, and Culture

Two areas in the interaction of biology and culture that have been studied intensively are language and gender. Presumably human language began as a call or gesture system. But language as we recognize it differs from such systems in several ways. Animal calls, probably because they are in large part genetically determined, are rigidly stereotyped; the call is always the same in form and meaning. Moreover, animal call systems are closed; that is, elements of one call cannot be combined with elements of another to produce a new message. The calls are unique, limited in number, and mutually exclusive.

Human language is open—the number of messages that can be conveyed is infinite. Indeed, with language people can, and continually do, create entirely new messages—sentences that have never

before been spoken—whereas call systems can generally convey only a very few simple meanings: danger, hostility, sexual excitement, the availability of food, and so on. As Bertrand Russell put it, "No matter how eloquently a dog may bark, he cannot tell you that his parents were poor but honest" (cited in Fromkin & Rodman, 1988, p. 346). Human language can be used to communicate a vast range of meanings, from subtle philosophical abstractions to complex technical information to delicate shades of feeling. This flexibility is made possible by the arbitrariness of human language. Unlike animal calls, the sounds of a language have no fixed meaning. Instead, meaning emerges from the way sounds are combined into words and words arranged to make sentences, in accordance with a complex set of rules (grammar).

Another distinctive feature of human language is that it is stimulus-free. That is, a linguistic utterance need not be evoked by an immediate situation. We do not have to turn a corner and come upon a tiger in order to say the word "tiger" or talk about "danger." We can discuss things that are not present—things experienced in the past, things that may happen in the future, even things that are not true or not real, such as unicorns and utopias. Little of this sort of communication appears to be possible in call systems, which lack the dimensions of time and possibility. While animals have been frequently observed to send false signals, generally the use of call systems for deception is limited. It has been said, with some justice, that hominids became truly human when they became capable of telling a lie.

All animals communicate with one another, using various kinds of cries, calls, gestures, and chemical emissions. Such means of communication are usually genetically determined, however, and therefore are much less flexible than human languages. A bird's danger call may be the only call it can produce in a dangerous situation; the bird cannot add any refinements to the call to indicate, for example, the source of the danger or the direction it is coming from. Bees, however, are known to have very sophisticated systems of communication, and in some species "scouts" are sent out by the hive and return to inform the others of the way to proceed to reach a newly discovered food source. Even so, this pattern is far removed from human language, with its nearly infinite flexibility and capacity to generate new meanings. And though we associate human language with speech, sounds are not a necessary aspect of language; people who cannot hear or speak can acquire and use language. Conversely, when a parrot imitates human utterances, it is not using language the way a human does.

Using language involves structures in the brain that other animals, including closely related nonhuman primates lack; at the same time, apes, in particular, seem to have linguistic ability at the level of what Bickerton calls "protolanguage" (1995). That is, much like human infants prior to age eighteen months or so, they are capable of communicating emotional states, but fall far short of fully developed natural languages.

For many years, it was thought that one barrier to primate language use was simply physiological. In primates the pharynx (a tunnel of muscle connecting the back of the mouth to the larynx, crucial to the production of speech) is smaller in relation to body size and is shaped differently than in humans. As a consequence, the earliest experiments that sought to teach chimpanzees spoken language were not successful. To get around the vocal-tract problem and test intellectual capacity, two psychologists, Alan and Beatrice Gardner (1969), in a now-classic experiment, decided to teach their test chimp, Washoe, American Sign Language (ASL).

In four years Washoe not only learned to use 130 signs. More important, she showed that she could manipulate them creatively. Having learned the signal "more" to persuade the Gardners to resume a pillow fight, she spontaneously used the same signal when she wanted a second helping at dinner. Furthermore, whereas chimpanzee calls are never combined, Washoe spontaneously combined hand signals to make new words. Not knowing the signal for duck, for instance, she dubbed it "water bird."

One of the most successful of the later experiments involved a gorilla named Koko. At age four she was able to use 251 different signs in a single hour. After five years of training in ASL, she scored between 80 and 90 (the equivalent of a five-year-old child) on an IQ test for nonreading children. Like Washoe, Koko could combine words creatively to name new objects. She was also particularly adept at expressing her feelings. Whenever Penny Patterson, her trainer, arrived late at Koko's trailer, the gorilla would sign "sad." On other mornings, when asked how she felt, she would report herself "happy" or sign "I feel good." This was the first clear instance of emotional self-awareness on the part of a nonhuman primate.

There have also been experiments using, not sign language, but lexigrams—symbols that represent common objects, verbs, and moods. Starting in the late 1970s, Sue Savage Rumbaugh trained two chimps, Sherman and Austin, to use a keyboard to produce lexigrams (1994). When they had become fairly fluent, she constructed an experiment that entailed Sherman and Austin having to cooperate to perform various tasks. She found that they spontaneously used the lexigrams to learn from and communicate with each other. Even more interesting is the case of Kanzi, a young pygmy chimpanzee, who surprised the psychologists when he revealed that he had learned to use the keyboard to produce lexigrams entirely on his own by watching his adoptive mother.

It would seem to be incorrect, however, to conclude that these animals used language in the human sense, or even came close (Bickerton, 1995). First, the languages that the test apes learned were in part iconic—the symbols imitated the things they stood for. There is a geometrical relationship between some of the signs and the things they represent. The ASL sign for book, for example, is two palms pressed together, then opened, much like the geometrics of opening a book. Thus, it seems doubtful that apes have the intellectual capacity to handle a totally arbitrary language such as our own. Second, there is still some doubt as to whether the test apes put together sentences spontaneously or simply by rote, although the lexigram experiments with Sherman, Austin, and Kanzi seem to indicate that the chimpanzees were not merely responding to cues from researchers without really understanding their meaning. Third, even if ape language differs from human language only in degree, the distance separating them is vast. The suggestions of subtle reasoning in the apes' verbalizations are quite intriguing, but they are also quite rare. Finally, teaching language to an ape requires immense effort under highly artificial conditions, whereas human children learn it naturally, without training. Apes may share with us certain faculties necessary for language, but it is clear that these faculties have remained relatively undeveloped in their line.

Because sounds leave no trace, researchers investigating the origins of language have to depend on indirect evidence: studies of the way children acquire language, comparisons of human and nonhuman vocalizations, guesses as to what kinds of brains and vocal tracts might have accompanied fossil skulls, and of course cultural evidence of the way our early ancestors lived.

The cultural evidence seems to indicate that at least some aspects of language began to evolve as early as four million years ago (Schick & Toth, 1993). It was probably around that period that our early ancestors made a crucial change in their way of procuring food—from individual foraging for vegetable foods to regular eating of meat and vegetables on a communal basis. The new pattern demanded cooperation and the coordination of hunting and gathering activities, for which at least an advanced call or gesturing system seems to have been required. The cultural evidence, in the form of stone tools, may, some say, suggest a very early date for the first rudimentary language skills (Schick & Toth, 1993). The flakes made by these early hominids are far more sophisticated than anything a chimpanzee can make when taught by trainers to do so. Most importantly, the earliest stone tools indicate by how they were struck that their makers were preferentially right-handed—suggesting that their brains were already lateralized as are modern humans (and unlike other primates).

Of course, there are other perspectives on the same cultural data. Derek Bickerton argues that the relatively slow rate at which technology changed over the first four million or so years of hominid evolution suggests that while an elaborate call system is probable, true language did not appear until approximately 100,000 years ago (1995). For example, he points out that the caverns of Zhoukoudian in northern China were inhabited continuously by hominids from 500,000 years ago until 200,000 years ago, their history of occupation well known, and yet the tiny handful of artifacts produced underwent no change during a period of 300,000 years. "The people of the caves of Zhoukoudian crouched over their smokey fires, eating half-cooked bats" and made no structural improvements in their habitation or elaboration of a very simple material

culture (1995, p. 46). This degree of cultural stasis, he argues, could not be associated with a population possessing full language.

To speak, the early humans had to have more than just the need to communicate. Speech requires physical mechanisms as well, such as certain structures in the brain. These structures allow us to associate incoming auditory messages with remembered messages from other sensory pathways—especially with the memory of the words that we will need to voice our thoughts. They also enable us to signal the muscles of the vocal apparatus to make the movements necessary to produce the appropriate sounds. Current research indicates that these operations are carried out mainly by three specific parts of the brain, all located in the cerebral cortex, the thick rind of gray matter that constitutes the outer layer of the brain. It is also the region of the brain responsible for the processing of visual stimuli.

The cerebellum of the human brain, a fist-sized structure just above the brain stem at the back of the head, is a recent development; it expanded rapidly and quite late in hominid history and is distinct from that of other primates. Around the time of the transition to food sharing and meat eating, the early human brain was less than half the size of ours and its cerebral cortex was smaller still, but still larger than modern nonhuman primates. Thus, while it seems unlikely that the language-producing structures of the cortex were fully developed at this time, it is a fair assumption that the structures underlying the conversion from call system to language had begun about four million years ago.

By about 100,000 years ago, when the Neanderthals lived in Europe and the Middle East, the cerebral cortex had reached approximately its present size. Quite possibly these people had the mental equipment necessary for a complex language. Some of the cultural evidence, sophisticated tool manufacturing and, in particular, the deliberate burial of their dead, suggests abstract reasoning and well-developed modes of communication. Still, until recently it was thought that they may have lacked the physiological equipment necessary for fully human speech.

In addition to the cerebral cortex, as we noted in the discussion of language in other primates, the pharynx is crucial to the production of speech. Until very recently, it was thought that the pharynx developed to the size and shape necessary to produce intelligible sounds only after the Neanderthal period. However, a Neanderthal skeleton excavated in Israel in 1989 with the small bones of the larynx intact appears to have had the physiological capability for human speech. Still, it is possible that truly fluent language is only a very recent achievement in the history of our species.

The use of language is undoubtedly responsible for the archaeologically recent, explosive development of human culture. Groups whose members communicated effectively with one another hunted more successfully, gathered more efficiently, made more sophisticated tools, built stronger shelters, found more suitable locations for habitation, and argued and resolved their differences without necessarily coming to blows. A recent book argues that language is really a form of "verbal grooming" (Dunbar, 1997). Just as our primate cousins, the chimpanzees, spend a large portion of each day in mutual grooming exercises, humans devote a great deal of time to gossip. Perhaps as much as 70 percent of conversation is devoted to sharing observations about others in our social world (Dunbar, 1997). This is so important to our constructing and maintaining cooperative group life that it may well be the impetus for the evolution of language. This point is important because complex social behavior associated with group living and cooperation entails individuals reconciling their immediate self-interest with their long-term prospects. Language greatly facilitates this, as individuals can negotiate long-lasting relationships of mutual trust and assistance that continue beyond any given event. The concomitant growth of language and culture in turn created strong selective pressures for more complex brains, which made possible the development of yet more elaborate language and culture. There arose, in other words, a feedback cycle: Language, culture, and the brain evolved together, each stimulating and reinforcing the development of the others.

Gender, Biology, and Inequality

There is no society that does not recognize, encourage, and even demand behavioral differences between the biologically defined sexes. Anthropologists generally define "sex" as the biological category determined largely by genital structures and secondary sexual characteristics (see Worthman for a good discussion, especially 1995, p. 597 ff). **Gender** is usually taken to be the behavioral or culturally interpreted dimensions of sexual categories, and the term is employed to avoid confusing cultural (and hence "learned" and presumably malleable) aspects of male/female differentiation with biological or inherited characteristics. The issues are rather more complex than implied by this straightforward distinction. Behavior of all varieties and, most par-

ticularly, that associated with sex is mediated or regulated by the body's hormonal systems. Thus our sexual identities are largely fixed during prenatal development (see Angier, 1997). Generally speaking, this basic identity is not subject to simple variation in socialization or childrearing. What does seem clear is that there is no evidence of rigidly dichotomized male/female or sex-linked cognitive or intellectual capabilities (Worthman, 1995, p. 607). Put simply, there is no biological imperative determining or limiting either male or female participation in cultural arrangements.

Gender, as we have seen, refers to the behaviors associated with the biologically defined sexes, and it is this that varies from culture to culture. Parents in all societies begin to train their children at an early age in the social behavior, or gender roles, considered appropriate to their biological sex. Gender identity is one's feeling of being male or female. Gender identity and gender roles usually develop in tandem (Frayser, 1985). Gender roles tend to be defined by the society and establish the kind of behavior that is appropriate and inappropriate for a male and a female. Children are socialized also to respond favorably to what are perceived as the social tasks or jobs appropriate to their gender.

It is impossible to understand any society in the absence of gender as a category of analysis; at the same time, gender itself requires a cultural and historical context (Susser, 1989, p. 343). Although gender is a universal source of individual identity and a pervasive means by which access to resources and political power is structured, generalization in the absence of specific historical or cultural experience is risky. The gender experiences of people vary with historical processes, as reflected in religion, cultural conventions, access to resources, and education—not to mention the fact that within a complex society, gender experience varies with ethnicity, class, and region.

Because gender roles are so intensely socialized and so personal, it is difficult to separate the present from the possible. It is no accident that until recently anthropologists (like other observers of society) largely ignored intercultural variation in gender roles; they simply took it for granted as a biological given that men and women belonged to different spheres of activity and the female domain was domestic while the male domain was everything else: productive, political, ceremonial, and military. Not only was great variability in gender roles overlooked, but so was the fact that even apparent similarities in gender relationships could have very diverse roots. In the West, traditional male power and authority has been largely based in property rights and control of wealth; the classic patriarchy, in Roman law, gave the male head of house final title to almost all property and control over his children (to the exclusion of his wives). Among the Yanomamö, male dominance seems to rest, in part, on the threat of physical violence. Among other Amazonian peoples (the Mundurucu, for example), male social and political precedence rests on their ability to dominate religious and ceremonial life through control of rituals and ritual objects (Murphy & Murphy, 1985).

Anthropologists have become aware of the shortcomings of ignoring gender, in part because of the recent transformation of their own societies. There are three interrelated areas that are of primary concern in analyzing gender: gender socialization, gender and work, and gender and power (Susser, 1986, p. 344).

Gender Socialization. Gender socialization of children begins immediately after birth and generates systematic inequality between the sexes. It is largely in the process of socialization that individuals form their notions of what gender identity means in terms of appropriate or expected and acceptable behavior.

CASE STUDY

Gender Socialization in Yörük Society

In Yörük society (see Chapter 5), the birth of a boy is often celebrated with the sacrifice of an animal and a feast; the birth of a daughter is hardly announced at all. Socialization immediately establishes the very different social worlds the sexes are expected to occupy. The daughter, rarely fussed over, is taught at a very young age to care for her younger siblings, if she has any; to help in collecting firewood and cleaning; and, as her skills develop, to sew and weave. The essence of the training is summed up in the expression, "The sun never shines on a sleeping bride." In order to become a desirable bride, a girl is expected to show her willingness to work from before dawn to after dusk; she watches her mother and older sisters make much fuss over her brothers and other growing male adolescents.

The socialization of a Yörük boy means he is both the center of a great deal of maternal and sisterly attention, and also subject to a great deal of teasing in the form of "Be a man! Be strong! Be

brave!" A boy's economic contributions do not begin until he is old enough to attend to the family herds, a task rarely given to girls since they must be kept where their outdoor activities can be continually supervised. He will routinely accompany his father and older brothers on trips to the market (a rare treat for his sisters), and when he finally marries, his wife will join him in the household while his sisters, upon marriage, move out. He will inherit his share of the family's herds; his sisters will not, even though by law they have equal rights. The girls will have been conditioned to accept this as natural; after all, their own husbands will inherit and look after them. Should they be widowed or divorced, their brothers will be their final security. While attitudes and practices vary and change over time, the irony is that the women themselves have the biggest role in socializing their children into gender expectations that seemingly do not benefit their daughters. ◗

Gender and Work. The organization of work in society is critical for understanding gender. Labor is often valued differently for men and for women, with the work done by women often seen as private or domestic (rather than productive) and hence undervalued. Further, even restricting access to nonproductive sectors such as religious ritual and ceremonial leadership differentiates between the sexes. In most cases, it is women who play a secondary role in ritual and public ceremony. While there are exceptions, when examined more closely it becomes clear that women appearing in prominent ritual, ceremonial, and even political roles are often regarded as honorary men for that purpose. Using gender to create different domains of activity usually contributes to stratification. While gender considerations obviously affect access to resources and contribute to inequality, gender usually has to be viewed along with other sources of identity used to compartmentalize and divide society.

Gender and Power. The third area of concern is closely related to socialization and the organization of the work force: That is, gender, power, and access to the political process. Even family life can be seen as political, in that individuals are contending for resources. Moreover, social control operates quite differently on men and women in many instances. In societies where notions of family honor are important in local politics or public life, this may be linked to male control over female sexuality and, by extension, many aspects of female public behavior. Thus, it might be thought threatening to family honor for female members of the family to be seen with nonfamily males. This puts serious constraints on female behavior, sometimes so as to make it difficult for a woman to accept employment outside the home. Outside the household, gender can be seen as an aspect of stratification, particularly, as we shall see shortly, when taken in conjunction with race, ethnicity, and class. Women from different ethnic groups in the United States, for example, experience very different rates of poverty, childbearing options, and involvement in community mobilization. Class inequality can be greatly amplified by gender expectations regarding housework and childrearing for poor women. However gender is understood, it has to be kept in mind that gender relations can and do change; in the final analysis, gender is shaped in society by the activities, beliefs, and values of both men and women. People are not simply passive respondents.

Summary

THOUGH ANTHROPOLOGISTS TEND TO SPECIALIZE, they maintain a holistic approach: they assume that any given aspect of human life is to be studied with an eye to its relation to other aspects of human life. Of vital importance to the holistic perspective is cultural relativism, or the ability to view the beliefs and customs of other peoples within the context of their culture rather than one's own. Although everyone is somewhat ethnocentric, judging the customs of other societies by the standards of his or her own, anthropology underscores the need to view other cultures with objectivity and empathy.

Applying the concept of culture, anthropologists make certain assumptions about the behavior, beliefs, and experiences of individuals as members of society: that the human species learns rules of behavior and is dependent on learning for survival; that learned rules of behavior and thinking supply meaning to events and the behavior of others, although each society has its own interpretations; that knowledge is transmitted via language and is to a large degree created out of symbols.

A scientific theory is a statement that postulates ordered relationships among natural phenomena. Theory provides a framework for research, directing researchers to certain kinds of questions and leading them to expect certain results, against which they can check the results actually obtained. The many theories that cultural anthropologists have put forth revolve around basic questions: Why do societies differ? How do societies differ? What is the relationship between the individual and society?

Evolution explains the development of all species as the outcome of adaptation to environmental circumstances through the process of natural selection.

All people are born with certain biological traits that account in part for broad similarities in human behavior. Biology also affects us on an individual level by setting limits—through our health, stamina, and body build, for instance—that cannot be overcome. In addition, biological factors affect certain kinds of individual behavior.

Through social learning, members of a society develop their own ways of behaving or perceiving, which differ from the ways of other societies. Social learning occurs primarily through socialization, the process by which the social group and the family, through formal training and unconscious modeling, pass on skills, knowledge, values, attitudes, and behavior to the next generation. Channels of socialization include childrearing, education, gender- and age-role learning, and rites of passage.

Role learning—adapting to a set of behavioral expectations appropriate to one's position—is an important part of education. While roles channel a person in certain prescribed directions, each individual interprets a given role in a somewhat distinctive way. Both gender roles and age roles are affected by socialization. The form and intensity of the set of distinguishable characteristics associated with each sex—a social construct referred to as gender—vary from society to society.

While all animals apparently communicate through call systems—repertoires of sounds, each of which is produced in response to a specific situation—humans are the only animals that use language. Human language presumably began as a call system. Language differs from animal call systems in that it is open—the number of messages that can be conveyed is infinite. This flexibility is made possible by the arbitrariness of human language (sounds have no fixed meaning) and the fact that it is stimulus-free: an utterance need not be evoked by an immediate situation. The training of apes to use limited sign language has convinced some researchers that their linguistic ability differs from ours only in degree; however, while apes may share with us certain faculties that are necessary for language, it is clear that these faculties have remained relatively undeveloped in their line.

Researchers can only speculate on the origins of language. Cultural evidence suggests a very early date for the first language skills; the physical evidence suggests a later date for the full development of language. It seems likely that the change to language from call systems began about four million years ago and proceeded only gradually. It is believed that human language developed through the blending of calls to produce new calls with more complex meanings. This transition is largely responsible for the development of human culture. Language, culture, and the brain evolved together, each stimulating and reinforcing the others.

Languages vary in subtle and complex ways. Human brains may be equipped with a universal program enabling infants to very rapidly learn the patterns of drastically different languages very rapidly.

Gender refers to the behaviors associated with the biologically defined sexes and it is this which varies from culture to culture. There are three interrelated areas that are of primary concern in analyzing gender: gender socialization, gender and work, and gender and power. Gender socialization begins shortly after birth and generates systematic inequalities between the sexes as boys and girls learn gender-specific notions of appropriate behavior. Second, the organization of work in society is critical for understanding gender. Labor is often valued differently for men and for women, with the work done by women often seen as private or domestic (rather than productive) and hence undervalued. Further, even restricting access to nonproductive sectors such as religious ritual and ceremonial leadership differentiates between the sexes. Third, closely related to socialization and the organization of the work force, is access to the political process. Even family life can be seen as political, in that individuals are contending for resources. Moreover, social control operates quite differently on men and women in many instances.

Key Terms

cultural adaptation	holism
cultural relativism	Homo sapiens
culture	hypothesis
empiricism	natural selection
enculturation	scientific theory
ethnocentrism	socialization
gender	

Suggested Readings

Bernard, H. R. (1994). *Research methods in anthropology* (2nd ed.). Thousand Oaks, CA: Sage. A thorough treatment of qualitative and quantitative approaches in ethnographic research.

Brown, D. E. (1991). *Human universals.* New York: McGraw Hill. Explores recent findings on what appear to be universally or widely shared traits among humans of all societies. The author argues that anthropology has overemphasized the plasticity of culture and thus lost sight of what is shared cross-culturally.

Bickerton, D. (1995). *Language and human behavior.* Seattle: University of Washington Press. An important study of the nature of language and its relation to human evolution, behavior, and consciousness.

Fox, R. (1994). *The challenge of anthropology.* New Brunswick, NJ: Transaction. Examines a wide variety of core topics in anthropology in terms of recent challenges to received wisdom.

Fox, R. (1997). *Conjecture and confrontations: Science, evolution, social concern.* New Brunswick, NJ: Transaction. A lively exploration of how biosocial anthropology deals with contemporary social and ethical issues.

Gilmore, D. D. (1990). *Manhood in the making: Cultural concepts of masculinity.* New Haven: Yale University Press. Addresses the question of what it means to be a man in different cultures around the world. The author treats manhood as a status achieved through culturally approved stressful, competitive tests.

Podolefsky, A. & Brown, P. J. (Eds.). (1995). *Applying anthropology.* Mountain View, CA: Mayfield Press. An introductory reader that emphasizes the practical application of research methods in biological anthropology, archaeology, anthropological linguistics, and cultural anthropology. The articles are timely and interesting; they offer a view of anthropology not available in any other reader. A number of these articles are cited throughout this text.

Steward, J. H. (1972). *Theory of culture change: The methodology of multilinear evolution.* Urbana, IL: University of Illinois Press. A collection of Steward's theoretical and substantive essays. These works provided the initial impetus for the development of an ecological tradition within anthropology.

Wolf, E. R. (1982). *Europe and the people without history.* Berkeley: University of California Press. An analytic history of European expansion; the effects of this expansion on the native peoples of Africa, Asia, and the Americas; and how these peoples in turn affected the history of Europe.

Chapter 2

Evolution, Ecology, and Politics

Human ecology is the theoretical orientation that emphasizes the problem-solving significance of culture and behavior, from procurement systems to kinship systems to political and religious life. In this chapter we will explore the rationale for this perspective in greater detail, building on our discussion of evolution in the first chapter. We will discuss what is meant by adaptation, the role of variation and decision making in adaptation, and finally we will place evolutionary processes affecting humans in an ecological context.

The Human Evolutionary Legacy

It is easy to overlook the fact that evolution is an ongoing process. Our species and all of its constituent populations are continually being shaped by evolutionary forces. While most often we speak of natural selection as the major force acting on the genetic compositions of populations, any force that causes the genetic composition of a population to change is an evolutionary force. Interbreeding, or gene flow, is a major source of both unity and change in human populations. Our species, of relatively recent origin, has always contained highly mobile local populations that have continually interbred. As a result, we are relatively homogeneous in terms of genetic material. In fact, most anthropologists feel it is inappropriate, or at best difficult, to speak of biologically distinct races (Rensberger, 1989).

C. Loring Brace has studied skeletal remains from Japan. His results indicate that the present population of Japan is the product of the interbreeding of two genetically distinguishable groups: the Ainu, which he says are the original inhabitants of the islands, and the Yayoi, who migrated from Korea and China only slightly more than 2,000 years ago. He further claims his evidence shows that the famed Samurai warrior class descended from the people of northern Hokkaido (the Ainu), that Japanese royalty and nobility intermarried with them, and that other Japanese were primarily descended from the Yayoi (Brace, C., Brace, M. L., & Leonard, 1989). This view almost completely reverses traditional Japanese thinking about their heritage, in which the Ainu are considered to have no role. Today they in fact suffer from social discrimination. Whether Brace's theories turn out to be true or not, the point is that we have to be wary about considering any population as a fixed entity.

In January 1988, the popular media ran a series of major stories on what was widely described as "The Search for Eve" (see Tierney, Wright, & Springen, 1988). The report that focused national attention was by Rebecca Cann, a biological anthropologist. Her work was based on new techniques of studying the origins, unity, and diversity of our species that do not rely on the examination of fossils or bones, but rather on the cell tissues of infants. By collecting and analyzing mitochondrial DNA from placentas of babies born throughout Asia, Africa, Europe, and the Americas, Cann and her coworkers appeared to have established that about 200,000 years ago all present-day Homo sapiens shared a female ancestress who lived in Africa (Cann, 1988, pp. 127–143).

Since the publication of her original findings, some aspects of the dating techniques have been questioned, as well as the implications that modern humans simply replaced existing hominids throughout the world rather than there being a period of interbreeding and/or coexistence. The notion of a single recent origin for our immediate ancestral line has long been the subject of controversy. A recent origin would imply that many earlier hominids, such as the widespread Neanderthals found in different parts of the Old World, did not directly contribute to our family line. Although the idea of our ultimate African origins is now well-established, it is unclear whether our modern species evolved only there and subsequently spread, or whether our species emerged more or less separately in different parts of the Old World, coexisting in places with our close relatives, the Neanderthals (see Stringer & Brauer, 1994; Frayer et al., 1994, for opposing interpretations). On the other hand, research using different segments of DNA has found renewed support for the out-of-Africa hypothesis (see Tattersal, 1995, and Stringer & McKie, 1997). Regardless of the outcome of this debate, it must be kept in mind that those features we often use to describe different peoples of the world (skin color, eye color and shape, stature, and hair) are all the products of very recent and minor adaptations—adaptations that are continually changing in every population.

Stephen Jay Gould, speaking of these recent research developments, says, "It makes us realize that all humans, despite differences in external appearance, are really members of a single entity that had a very recent origin in one place. There is a kind of biological brotherhood that is much more profound than we had ever realized" (Gould, quoted in Tierney et al., 1988). The major differences we see between human beings are the products of behavioral or cultural adaptation. As Lewis Binford (1989) writes, "Our species had arrived—not as a result of gradual, progressive processes but explosively in a relatively short period of time. Many of us currently speculate that this was the result of the invention of language, our peculiar mode of symbolic communication that makes possible our mode of reasoning and in turn our behavioral flexibility" (p. 30).

Humans are bound to the rest of nature by evolutionary history—that is, by descent from common ancestors. Our species is kin to every other living thing on earth—not just in a metaphorical or sentimental sense but in a strict biological sense, as two cousins are related by virtue of having the same grandparents. Of course, we are related more closely to some species than to others. Chimpanzees are much closer kin to us than are monkeys, not to mention nonprimates. Varying degrees of kinship are reflected in varying degrees of anatomical and behavioral similarity. Ultimately, however, all living things, ourselves included, are descended from the same forebears: minute organisms that lived 4 or 5 billion years ago in a world we would not recognize.

How, from such beginnings, did we and all the other species of the earth come to be what we are? The answer to this question did not become clear until the early twentieth century. In the eighteenth and early nineteenth centuries, some scientists recognized that species could change over time as organisms adapted to their environments. But they could not visualize how or why such changes occurred. Indeed, most of them did not believe that such changes could actually create new species. Natural processes might produce new "races," or strains within a species, but only God could create a new species. It was not until 1859, when Charles Darwin (1809–1882) published his treatise, *On the Origin of Species by Means of Natural Selection*, that the major mechanism of evolution was finally described in a way that accounted both for change within species and for the emergence of new species without divine intervention.

Darwin: Evolution by Natural Selection

Darwin was convinced that new species arose not through acts of divine intervention but rather through a blind and mechanical process. He understood that all species of plants and animals tend to produce more offspring than the environment can support and that this results in intense competition for living space, resources, and mates. Only a favored few survive long enough to reproduce. Darwin noted also that individual members of a species differ from one another physically. In a given population of animals, for example, some may have thicker fur or longer limbs than others. These variations are adaptive if they enhance the animal's chances of survival and therefore enhance its chances of producing offspring that survive to reproduce themselves. Needless to say, this process depends on the nature of the demands placed on the organism by its environment and by the changes that environment is undergoing. (Thick fur, for example, could mean a longer life in an increasingly cold environment, whereas it might be a handicap in an increasingly warm one.) Those individuals whose peculiarities give them a competitive edge in their particular environment produce more offspring, and those offspring inherit their parents' peculiarities, so they in turn survive longer and produce more offspring. Thus with each generation the better-adapted members of a population increase in number at the expense of less well-adapted individuals. In the process, the species as a whole changes.

This is the mechanism that Darwin called "natural selection." It served to explain not only gradual changes within a species, but also the appearance of new species. For as different populations of a species adapted to different environments, they eventually diverged until the differences in their anatomy or behavior became so great that they could no longer interbreed. According to Darwin, this process—adaptation to environmental circumstances—accounted for the great variety of species observable in nature. Speciation is not, in fact, quite as simple a phenomenon as is described here. Many species are "ring species," which means that adjacent populations can interbreed but nonadjacent ones cannot. Also, in studying populations of the past, it is not always possible to determine whether or not separate but fairly similar populations could have interbred. The concept of species, however, remains useful as a standard despite empirical problems in applying it.

Mendel: The Genetics of Natural Selection

A major weakness of Darwin's theory was that he could not explain how favored characteristics were inherited—and such a systematic explanation was needed. The prevailing belief was that each individual inherited a blend of its parents' characteristics, which, if true, implied that advantageous variations would be lost by dilution with less advantageous traits long before natural selection could act on them. It was an obscure Austrian monk named Gregor Mendel (1822–1884) who discovered the hereditary basis of natural selection.

In the garden of his monastery, located in what is now the Czech Republic, Mendel spent years crossbreeding strains of peas and other plants in an effort to find out how traits were transmitted from one generation to the next. He discovered that biological inheritance was not an irreversible blending of parental traits. Rather, individual units of hereditary information, later called "genes," were passed from parent to offspring as discrete particles according to certain regular patterns. In one individual a gene's effect might be blended with the effects of other genes, or even suppressed altogether. But the gene itself remained unchanged, ready to be passed on to the next generation, where it might express itself and thus be available for natural selection.

Mendel's work attracted little attention in the scientific community until both he and Darwin were dead. It was rediscovered in the early 1900s, but its relevance to evolution was not fully appreciated until the next generation. By that time, other apparent discrepancies in Darwin's theory had been resolved and it was finally accepted that the human species, along with every other species, is a product of evolution. Today evolutionary theory is at the very heart of all research in the biological and natural sciences. With the recent breakthroughs in modern genetics, population biology, and biochemistry, the utility of the "evolutionary synthesis," as it is now called, is established beyond doubt.

Evolution and Human Culture

While agreeing with the premise that humans have to be understood as products of a long evolutionary heritage, cultural anthropologists have generally emphasized the importance of learning and cultural plasticity relatively unconstrained by biological factors (apart from obvious physiological requirements). In the 1980s, however, this position was challenged by new theoretical perspectives on evolution that subsequently emerged from the natural and social sciences—in particular from the areas of neurobiology, population genetics, ethology, and cognitive psychology. The main contention is that genetically controlled biological processes are responsible for shaping a good deal more of social behavior than has been generally acknowledged. The arguments are often controversial. As they have focused much attention on the relationship of biology and culture, we will look at them in some detail.

In the last twenty years, new approaches to the study of social or cultural behavior, called variously human behavioral biology, human ethology, evolutionary ecology, and sociobiology, have been propounded (see Cronk, 1991, pp. 25–53, for a review). They share the view, brought most dramatically to popular attention by E. O. Wilson in 1975, that Darwinian models of natural selection apply to aspects of human culture and social behavior as well as to animal social behavior. Researchers found a significant percentage of social behavior in nonhuman animals to be under the direct or indirect influence of genes, and they argued that such behavior has adaptive significance (Chagnon & Irons, 1979; Dyson-Hudson & Little, 1983). These types of behavior included mate selection, parenting, social relations among kin, food sharing and procurement, and mutual assistance and reciprocity. Genetic influence does not imply that a specific gene (or genes) controls a particular behavioral complex (say, the love of a parent for its offspring), nor does it imply determinism, as is sometimes charged. Behavior, where genes are concerned, is best seen as an "open program" whereby a behavioral trait or propensity is shaped by the interactions of genes and environmental influences; thus, genetic material and the environment are inextricably linked. An organism continually tracks environmental changes, a process Irons refers to as "adaptive plasticity" (Chagnon & Irons, 1979, p. 250).

The animal whose mating, defensive, and food-procurement behaviors work best within its given environment is the animal most likely to survive, reproduce, and rear its offspring to maturity. Organisms have a genetically-based propensity to respond to various environmental circumstances in ways that are appropriate—that is, in ways that promote or facilitate individual reproductive success. Some aspects of this approach are well-established and not subject to controversy. Certainly genetically conditioned aspects of animal social behavior are the result of and continually influenced by the forces of natural selection. Much social behavior involves cooperation among close kin (who share much genetic material), as this approach would predict. The genes that control or influence behaviors that contribute to reproductive success are preferentially transmitted through generations, whereas genes that facilitate less adaptive behavior gradually disappear. So well-established is this basic premise that virtually all behavioral research with primates and other social species takes it as a given.

Should this line of reasoning apply also to humans? A variety of studies point to the value of the evolutionary model for an understanding of broad patterns of human behavior: the importance of kinship and family and male-female reproductive strategies. The usual argument for exempting the human species from this line of reasoning is that once humans developed culture (and the behavioral flexibility that accompanies it), they parted ways with the other animals. Our social behavior came to be based primarily on learning, and our ability to learn can produce behavioral changes much more rapidly than natural selection can via specific genetic codes. Our behavioral repertoire has been passed down to us through our culture rather than through our genes. The behaviors that have survived have been of value less to individuals than to groups, for culture is, in this view, the property of groups.

Even granting these points, those who employ the evolutionary model argue that while culture is transmitted by learning, what is inherited is a built-in propensity to learn and pass on some cultural rules and beliefs at the expense of others (see Gould & Marler, 1987). There is no simple resolution to this disagreement. We cannot doubt that lines of continuity run through the behavior of all animals. This line of reasoning has produced a wealth of useful studies (see Cronk, 1991; Smith & Winterhalder, 1992). For example, William G. Irons proposed that in most societies, what is considered "cultural success" (prestige, power, respect), consists of accomplishing things that make biological success probable (1979, p. 258). He tested this on data from the Yomut Turkmen of Iran and found that the wealthier, culturally more successful half of the population had more surviving children. This has been followed up by numerous studies of other populations with results that seem to confirm his hypothesis. Still, there may be other ways to interpret these findings; ways that do not require the assumption that behavior is generally directed to reproductive success (Cronk, 1991, p. 29). Whatever the results of particular studies, we cannot doubt that human capacity for culture adds a unique dimension to human social life. Much of what anthropologists are interested in explaining is not directly addressed by this model; for example, the nature and persistence of inequality, the role of value systems and ideology in social life, and the evolution of contemporary political systems. Nevertheless, any serious inquiry into human behavior will have to consider the complex ways in which cultural and biological processes intersect (Brown, 1991; Fox, 1994). Social scientists in such diverse fields as political science, economics, cognitive science, and psychology increasingly draw on evolutionary theory (see Dennett, 1994; Pinker, 1994, for accessible examples).

Human Ecology

In the social and biological sciences there are a number of themes and interests that bridge disciplines and bring new, often unsuspected, insights to light. Ecology is one example and its broad subfield, human ecology, is another. Human ecology links the disciplines of anthropology, biology, geography, demography, and economics, to name just a few. Ecol-

Social prestige, wealth, and reproduction can be closely related in traditional societies. Among the Turkmen, wealthy men have numerous children. Here, a well-off rural family sponsors a feast with wrestling competitions to celebrate a son's circumcision ceremony.

(Daniel Bates)

ogists, whether concerned with humans or other species, are interested in three very broad questions: How does the environment affect the organism? How does the organism affect its environment? How does an organism affect other organisms in the environments in which it lives? The quest for answers to these questions encompasses almost everything ecologists do. What distinguishes human ecology is not so much the larger questions, but the species that is of prime interest: human beings.

Without ignoring the complexity of the issues involved, it is possible to design strategies for research that are at once empirical and consistent with biological models used in studying behavior in general (Smith & Winterhalder, 1992, pp. 4–5). As the term suggests, **human ecology** combines two approaches: an interest in those features that are unique (or at least distinctive) attributes of humans, and the science of ecology, including evolutionary theory on which it is ultimately based.

Human ecology is distinctive also for theoretical reasons. Ecological models designed to study the interactions of other species are often inadequate to fully accommodate our own. Humans hold an unusual position in nature and their special, if not unique, attributes pose problems for modeling local interactions. As we have noted earlier, humans rely upon and are dramatically affected by our symbolic interpretations and representations of ourselves and other things (White, 1949). Symbols guide the ways that we interact with the organic and inorganic elements of our environments by making them intelligible in ways specific to our cultures—say, by representing what is good to eat and what is not, who may eat what and when and how. Of major importance to humans is the way that we distinguish group differences symbolically, creating cultural diversity among ourselves. This cultural diversity is often an important element of our social environment, affecting the ways we interact with one another and other elements of our environments.

Our propensity to engage in exchanges of goods and services and information among individuals and groups in widely separated territories has the effect of vastly extending the range of our resources and of our impacts upon them. It is rare today for a local population to rely entirely on local resources, or to be uninfluenced by adjacent or even distant populations.

Ecology is the study of the interplay between organisms (or the populations to which they belong) and their environment. Implicit in this definition is the connection between ecology and evolutionary theory. As we said earlier, evolution operates primarily through the mechanism of natural selection. That is, certain characteristics become more and more common within a population because within the context of that population's environment these characteristics give individuals an edge in the competition for survival and reproduction. So a crucial factor in the evolutionary process is an ecological factor—the fit between organisms and their environment.

The Nature of Ecological Systems

Humans, along with every other form of life, can be visualized and studied as part of a single **ecosystem** —the cycle of matter and energy that includes all organic things and links them to the inorganic. All organisms depend on energy and on matter. Unlike plants, most of the energy and matter that animals use are not taken directly from the sun and the earth. Rather, these are produced by other organisms and cycled among species through feeding—"eat and be eaten" is the rule for all. Humans breathe the oxygen emitted by plants, and plants take in carbon dioxide emitted by humans and millions of other species of animals. Such relationships, taken together, constitute a vast network of individuals exchanging the energy, nutrients, and chemicals necessary to life; humans and bacteria alike are involved in the same process.

The usefulness of the ecosystem concept is, first, that it can be applied to any environment. Second, and more important, the ecosystem concept allows us to describe humans in dynamic interaction with one another, with other species, and with the physical environment. We can chart and quantify the flow of energy and nutrients and specify the interactions critical for the maintenance of any local population. Thus the ecosystem concept gives us a way of describing how human populations influence and are influenced by their surroundings (Bates & Lees, 1996).

There is usually considerable order and continuity in natural ecosystems. This is not surprising since, over time, the millions of component species of any ecosystem have come to mutually limit one another as they feed, reproduce, and die. The fact that ecosystems appear to persist through time does not mean, however, that they are static. While most ecosystems are viewed as being in equilibrium or near-equilibrium, in fact relations among the component populations are continually changing. One ecologist, C. S. Holling (1973), employs two concepts to describe continuity and change in ecosystems: resilience and stability.

Resilience is a measure of the degree of change a system can undergo while still maintaining its basic elements or relationships. **Stability** is a measure of the speed with which a system returns to equilibrium after absorbing disturbances. Systems with high resilience but low stability may undergo continual and profound changes but still continue to exist as a system; that is, their constituent parts persist together even though they take a very long time to return to their initial states. Systems with high stability but low resilience, on the other hand, may show little change when suffering some disturbances, but then collapse suddenly.

These concepts have considerable relevance for our study of ecosystems. We often assume that if an ecosystem appears to be in equilibrium or is very stable that it is likely to persist unchanged. As pointed out, this is often not the case. A highly stable system, such as the Arctic terrestrial ecosystem, may in fact be very close to the threshold at which it could collapse. The most resilient ecosystems, are resilient only to a point—beyond which they collapse. We should bear this in mind when we feel that we are having no serious impact on our ecosystems simply because we see little evidence of immediate changes. For example, the seas around us may appear little changed despite the oil and other wastes dumped into them. Thus, they would seem to be quite stable. Yet each new addition of oil or wastes requires the organisms and microorganisms of the sea to respond in some way, and there are limits to their capacities to continue to do so. The resilience of marine ecosystems is limited, even if the threshold for change is obscured by the appearance of stability.

Anthropologist William Abruzzi (1993, 1996) applies ecological models developed from plant and animal research to account for how members of an American religious movement, the Mormons, came to colonize the arid and seemingly inhospitable Little Colorado River Basin in northeastern Arizona. He makes good use of the concepts of stability and resilience as they apply to ecological systems. While his main focus is on environmental variables such as rainfall, floods, and other hazards to farm life, he shows that settlement was closely linked to the nature of the larger organization—the church. Settlers agreed to come to this then-remote region because of their beliefs, their faith in church leadership, and because they feared persecution; they were able to do so because the church hierarchy made resources available (in particular, what was needed to tide settlements over during droughts or other disasters). The settlers were farmers who, in the late nineteenth century, attempted to settle three distinct ecological zones or habitats: the river basin itself, where dams could be built for irrigation; the middle slopes above the rivers, where runoff water was available; and the upper slopes. As it turned out, the middle slope settlements were the most successful over the long term—they had the resiliency to survive most threats to farming. The upper communities found rainfall too unpredictable and died out; the lower-level communities achieved a high level of production through damming rivers but this was often punctuated by disasters, as flooding destroyed dams which then had to be rebuilt. The middle range of settlements were able to construct water storage facilities enabling them to survive both droughts and floods. None of the colonizing would have been possible without the strong, centralized authority of the church, which used members' tithes and contributed skills to assist communities in need.

The Human Ecological Context

The structure of ecological systems—the flow of energy and nutrients—puts fundamental constraints on the way of life of any human population. Applying the ecosystem model to specific human populations, we can address two major questions. First, what is the population's place in its particular ecological system—that is, what are its relationships with the rest of the living world? Second, how are particular behaviors characteristic of this population related to its place in the ecosystem?

Humans hold a rather unusual position in their ecosystems. First, we occupy a remarkable diversity of such systems. This fact becomes strikingly evident when we look at the habitats and the niches that our species occupies. The habitat of a species is the area where it lives—its surroundings. Its niche is its "way of making a living," as defined by what it eats, what eats it, and how it reproduces and rears its young. Most animals are limited to a few habitats and a relatively narrow niche. In contrast, we occupy an exceptionally broad niche (think of the great variety of foods eaten by human beings and the many ways in which they are produced), and we live in an extremely wide range of habitats. Indeed, there are very few habitats, from deserts to Arctic ice sheets to tropical rain forests, where human beings have not found a way to thrive.

Second, once humans enter an ecosystem, they tend to become its dominant species. We strongly affect the life chances and reproductive rates of the other populations. While we are affected by other species, especially by those that threaten our well-being (such as malaria-bearing mosquitoes), our influence on them is far greater than theirs on us. Our dominance is due to the sophistication of our technology. Some other species use tools, but no other species has developed them to the extent we have, and no other species depends on tools for its survival as we do. Our technological expertise has allowed us to transform a vast variety of materials—including some rather unlikely ones—to sources of usable energy. It has also enabled us to be creative in our use of the resources we share with other animals. To use the energy stored in a tree, for example, other animals must drink its sap, seek shelter in it, or eat its leaves and branches. Humans not only eat parts of the tree, but cut it down and use the wood to build houses and furniture. We also use its energy in the form of fire to warm those houses and cook our food. Likewise, we can use the energy stored in animals' muscles, not only by eating them, as other animals do, but also by harnessing them to plows and by putting bits in their mouths and riding them. When a plant or animal is not suited to our needs, we can alter it through selective breeding to make it more useful to us. The use of tools has enabled us to create artificial environments, such as farms and cities, in which we maintain very high human population densities by greatly increasing the inflow and outflow of energy, materials, and information.

Human-dominated ecosystems are considerably less resilient than other ecosystems because they can be maintained only by constant expenditure of human energy and ingenuity. Cities depend on surrounding ecosystems for their food, water, and other necessities. In fact, inhabitants of cities tend to organize the countryside around them since they control the capital, markets, and transportation systems on which the rural farming sector depends. Cities also produce large quantities of waste products that the surrounding ecosystem must absorb. When urban ecosystems become large or numerous, the balance between the cities and the food-producing areas that sustain them may break down. In any event, these ecological arrangements depend on massive and costly inputs of energy. With our recent dependence on fossil fuel for energy, the stability of today's urban systems may be severely limited—not only by future fuel shortages, but by problems of waste disposal.

Ecosystems and Adaptation

Despite all of our technological advances, we are still as deeply enmeshed in our ecosystems as any other group of organisms. What distinguishes humans from other species in their relation to the environment is the rapidity with which we respond through learning. Different human societies may develop wholly different ways of life as they adjust to their environment, and can change rapidly as circumstances require. We can most usefully study the nature of this adaptive process by combining ideas from evolution and ecology.

While evolutionary research is diachronic (that is, through time) by definition, ecological research tends to be synchronic (that is, primarily concerned with the present). However, both focus on the same phenomenon: adaptation—the process whereby organisms or populations of organisms that live together in a defined environment make biological and/or behavioral adjustments that increase their chances for survival and reproduction. An evolutionary study may trace adaptation backward through time in an attempt to understand major causes of change within a given species as an outcome of natural selection and other evolutionary forces. Ecological studies, in contrast, tend to focus on the present and to look at the outcome of the adaptational process by analyzing the totality of relationships among organisms in a given environment. Evolutionary-ecological research unites these two approaches by studying living organisms within the context of their total environment to discover how their evolved characteristics and strategies for survival contribute to their success within that environment—how they have adapted. Still, culture, or aspects of it, has an identity quite distinct from behaviors that are directly acted upon by such evolutionary forces as natural selection. In fact traits adopted and favored by cultures may, for a while at least, work at cross-purposes with individual strategies for adaptive success. People enthusiastically embrace beliefs and adopt behavioral traits that apparently have little immediate relevance, either to their own well-being or to that of a larger group or a community.

Sometimes extreme examples are more useful illustrations than are commonplace ones where costs and benefits are obvious. Consider societies that have stressful initiation rites, including in some instances severe genital mutilation. It is hard to understand just how such practices, with the attendant risk of death or injury, can benefit the individual (or his or her parents), except in the important context of social relations. Traditional practices of female circumcision and female infibulation (sewing the vagina closed), found in the Sudan and East Africa, and male subincision (cutting open the penis and the urethra), found among Australian aborigines, hardly promote the well-being or reproductive success of the individuals who suffer through them, except as they contribute to the initiates' social acceptability. They also may benefit other members of the society at the initiates' expense. For example, female circumcision aids male control of female sexuality and reproduction, and male subincision enhances older men's control of younger men (Irons, 1995). Such practices appear to be related to the nature of the society itself—the way it forms its cultural identity, defines concepts of sexuality and social maturity, and effects social control. Many anthropologists argue for a "dual inheritance" perspective, from which cultural transmission and change are seen as working simultaneously with a parallel process of natural selection (Boyd & Richerson, 1985; Durham, 1991). This means that we should not expect humans to operate within the narrow constraint of immediately perceived costs and benefits, but rather to respond to and solve problems using a wide range of cultural tools. We cannot blame genes for acts of violence, warfare, racism, and similar chilling facets of human social life; what we do know is that we have the biological potential for them to occur, as well as the capacity to limit such behavior (see Wrangham & Peterson, 1996; Gould, 1996).

We have seen that evolution is a process of cumulative change consequent on the responses of organisms to their environments (adaptation). Adaptation can be an elusive concept because it involves processes that seem to operate on several different levels at once. Furthermore, adaptation can only be observed over long periods.

Variation: Human Decisions and the Environment. Variation, whether biological or behavioral, is the key to the process of adaptation. One of the main contributions of recent studies of animal behavior is the recognition that among animals of all sorts, systems of mating, male-female differences, feeding habits, food sharing, social interaction, and the like can be understood as the outcome of behaviors that start as individual strategies. Groups are never homogeneous; all contain individuals who respond somewhat differently to the problems at hand. Seen in this light, patterns of behavior become increasingly interesting. As human culture is elaborated, new solutions that seem to work can be rapidly added to the repertoire of knowledge that is passed on. The acceptance of innovations depends to a great extent on the fact that customary ways of acting are always subject to variation. Individuals constantly make decisions, and decision making gives rise to behavioral variation. There are enough conflicting versions of proper behavior in every society to create some ambiguity, thus allowing for the introduction and acceptance of innovation.

To understand the nature of human decision making or problem solving, we have to consider the environment in which it takes place. We are all too prone to treat the environment as a fixed landscape or static fact, and so fail to consider the nature of variation in all environments. Environments are complex and they constantly fluctuate. The environment of any individual or population consists of all external factors that affect it in any way—not only the obvious features of the habitat (the place where the population lives), but the presence of organisms that transmit disease, competitors, shelter, and climate. It also includes the cultural setting in which the individual must operate. In a society in which male initiation rites are important, for example, this social fact is part of the individual's environment. The environment also includes the demographic structure of the population; often, the most important feature of an individual's environment is the presence of other members of the same population among whom an individual will find both allies and competitors.

Finally, environments are dynamic. One ecologist, Lawrence S. Slobodkin (1968), has argued that four patterns of change underlie the dynamics of all environments: the degree of novelty (how new), frequency (how often), magnitude (how much), and duration (how long) of environmental events of all sorts. The organism with the best chance of success is not necessarily the one most perfectly adapted to its environment at any particular point, but rather the one that maintains its ability to respond to the environment in flexible ways. Generally speaking, the most successful response is the one that involves the minimum sacrifice of flexibility. In other words, choices among alternatives are made to minimize risk, not simply to attempt to make large gains. This seems to be the case with humans, in that people are generally conservative in their behavior and hesitant to change ways of doing things that appear to work.

In general, behavior is fairly predictable and conventional; people tend to arrive at similar decisions under similar circumstances. Were it not so, group life would be impossible. People regularly make major decisions regarding such basic issues of subsistence as whether to plant one crop or another or whether to migrate to new pastures or not; they also make day-to-day decisions such as with whom to socialize or to whom to send a greeting card. The structure of human societies provides the context for, and information concerning, choices among alternatives. As Frederik Barth (1981) has put it:

> Social life [is] generated by actors who go about their activity by pursuing their interests fitfully, often thoughtlessly, and generally conventionally. Yet they are concerned about the outcomes of their efforts in so far as these affect themselves. In this concern their judgments are based on values which serve to organize choice and action by providing standards to compare different alternatives and outcomes, both prospectively and retrospectively. When doing so, people tend to maximize the amounts of value they obtain by pursuing benefits and avoiding losses and drawbacks inasmuch as they see a way to do so. [p. 102]

Adapting Through Innovation. It is important to recognize the very important role that variation in behavior plays in societal change, even when that behavior is termed "deviant." Behavior that is said to be strange or outside the established range of varia-

tion can in time become widely accepted, and, in some cases, the basis for the survival of the group. A farmer may initially be seen as "strange" or abnormal because he adopts a new plant or tries a new system of cultivation—as, for example, in the United States when a few innovative farmers began in the 1980s to farm organically; that is, without chemical fertilizers. While considered eccentric at first, by 1995 organic farming had become widespread because of changed consumer tastes and, importantly, its cost-effectiveness.

In any society, most people know what is appropriate to do in a given situation, but they do not always act according to a rigid formula or set rules. And when we look at the ways in which people break the rules they espouse, an interesting pattern emerges. For one thing, most of us "sin" in more or less the same way our neighbors sin; that is, we deviate in packs. A simple example of this phenomenon is seen in the tendency of drivers to exceed the speed limit, just a little. When the legal limit is 55 miles per hour, most people can be found driving at 60 to 65. In fact, most of us look askance at people who obey all the rules to the letter. The rigid bureaucrat who plods through every inch of red tape, refusing to cut corners, is generally considered a deviant. Likewise, though few Americans would openly condone lying, all would agree that in many social circumstances, telling the complete truth would be a mistake; we tell "white lies" or otherwise manipulate the facts to fit our needs.

People everywhere establish rules for acceptable behavior and then proceed to break the rules in more or less predictable ways. The reasons for this behavior is the necessity of making received rules and values fit the circumstances of the individual. Though most people feel a need to do what is "proper," and though their culture provides time-honored definitions of "proper" for them to fall back on, survival nevertheless depends on the ability to solve problems in the immediate environment and adapt to changing circumstances. Once people develop a new solution, they usually begin to argue not that it is new but that it is good—not expedient but proper.

Changing gender roles in our own society are a case in point. At one time it was not considered desirable for women to work outside the home, and usually only those who had no alternative did so. In time certain kinds of work in offices, hospitals, and schools came to be viewed as quite appropriate for women, and families began to invest in the training of their daughters as secretaries, nurses, and teachers. With the advent of World War I, industry and the civil service needed women to fill jobs left vacant by men who had gone off to war. Following the war, women not only continued to be employed in large numbers but the right of women to vote was secured. Slowly the employment of women in wider and wider sectors of the economy came to be viewed not only as legitimate but desirable by a substantial percentage of the population. In recent years the right of women to be employed in every occupation became established in law, though not necessarily in practice.

Once a new behavior, with its newly acquired moral value, gains enough adherents, it becomes a shared practice that is taught to the next generation as part of "the right way to do things"(Irons, 1991). In time newer solutions will be adopted, but the rule remains the same: Individual ways of coping, if enough people find them useful, will become part of the system of shared behavior.

Procurement Systems, Adaptation, and Food

Of all the problems people face, securing adequate food is the most fundamental. When ecologists note that "you are what you eat," they mean that the source and variety of foods used by any population, human or otherwise, is critical to its maintenance. While a vast array of adaptive patterns can be found throughout the world, if we concentrate on the central issue of the way a population procures and distributes its food, we will note common strategies. The behavioral strategies that a particular group uses to secure foodstuffs is termed its **food procurement system**. Within general patterns, the available strategies are so numerous that no two systems are exactly alike. In fact, it is rare to find two individuals within a society practicing precisely the same strategy. However, there are some important generalizations that can be made about food procurement behavior that will help to explain the nature of adaptation in this context. Five major patterns of food procurement can be identified:

1. **Foraging** (or hunting and gathering): collecting wild vegetable foods, hunting game, and fishing.

2. **Subsistence agriculture**: a simple form of agriculture (sometimes called **horticulture** or extensive agriculture) based on working small plots of land with perhaps some use of draft animals, plows, or irrigation. In contrast to foragers, subsistence farmers produce food by managing domesticated plants and animals.

3. **Pastoralism**: an economy based on herding. Pastoralists maintain herds of animals and use their products (milk, curds, whey, butterfat, meat, blood, hides, bones), both to maintain themselves directly and to trade with other populations. They also often use their animals to gain mobility that can be used for military purposes.

Food procurement is fundamental to all populations. Humans today rely on intensive agriculture for most food; today's populations could not be sustained without the highly industrialized techniques utilized by this American farmer. The agricultural decisions of individuals have implications for the availability and prices of food products in distant countries.

(John Running/Stock, Boston Inc.)

4. **Intensive agriculture**: a form of agriculture that involves the use of draft animals or tractors, plows, and often some form of irrigation. Intensive agriculture produces far greater yields per acre of land with less human labor than can be obtained by subsistence agriculture. Intensive agriculture is often highly specialized, with farmers relying on one or two main crops.

5. **Industrial agriculture**: food production and manufacturing using of machines powered largely by fossil fuels, including modern commercial fishing and marine farming.

The Evolution of Procurement Patterns

As we have stressed, the crucial selective pressures giving rise to the divergence of the human line from that of the apes probably entailed brain-related behavioral changes—the gradual development of a greater commitment to group life and cooperation, and language use. The Australopithecines, from whom the earliest humans evolved, probably ate meat only occasionally; their main food resources were the plants of the East African savanna, which they ate as soon as they found them (Wrangham & Peterson, 1996). From what we can guess, a few populations of Australopithecines, while still relying heavily on vegetable foods, began to supplement their diet with a regular intake of meat that they procured by hunting and scavenging. Further, they probably began sharing their food more extensively, bringing both the vegetables and meat they found to be divided among the whole group. In time, this change in food procurement and consumption patterns produced the behavioral changes and anatomical features unique to the human lineage. One of the behavioral changes was an increased emphasis on learning, as exemplified by the development of tool making and use. Anatomical changes included increased brain size and decreased tooth size (see Wrangham, 1997d).

Foraging, or hunting and gathering, has itself changed greatly since the time of the Australopithecines, some 4 million years ago. However, in one form or another it continued to be the universal human food procurement strategy until relatively recently. Over the centuries, it was gradually refined. Approximately 100,000 years ago with the appearance of anatomically modern hominids (Homo sapiens) almost all of the Old World was occupied by highly successful hunter-gatherer populations utilizing hitherto unknown technologies (see Wrangham & Peterson, 1996). It is likely that this successful adaptive radiation of Homo sapiens was related to the fact that they possessed a fully developed language. We can infer this from the morphology of their brains, from their artistic accomplishments, and indirect evidence of religious beliefs (see Bickerton, 1995). People learned to make containers and digging sticks to help them in gathering, and they developed improved weapons—spears, spear throwers, and eventually bows and arrows—to increase their efficiency as hunters. By 40,000 years ago, different local populations had also learned to be highly specialized in terms of procuring specific kinds of game and plant resources in very different habitats. As early as 20,000 years ago, European and Asian hunters and gatherers (and probably others as well) were making and using textiles and basketry, showing a high degree of technological sophistication (Soffer, Vandiver, & Klima, 1995). Also approximately 20,000 years ago, humans crossed the newly exposed land bridge at the Bering Straits and began their rapid dispersal throughout North and South America.

From specialized hunting and gathering, with skills adapted to the exploitation of particular plant and animal species, it is a relatively short step to systematic planting and herding. Although we do not know precisely how or why, we do know that about 12,000 years ago societies in various parts of the world began experimenting with the domestication of plants and animals. However, another 3,000 or 4,000 years passed between the first appearance of agriculture and its widespread use. Not until 5,000 years ago, in the Near East, are we able to find signs of irrigation and the beginnings of intensive agriculture. (In this period, too, specialized pastoralism probably became important.) Over the next 2,000 years, agricultural practices became more efficient and productive in some areas. Large-scale irrigation works were constructed in Mesopotamia and Egypt, making it possible to support larger and larger populations in limited areas. We will return to this topic in subsequent chapters.

Finally, as recently as the nineteenth century, certain Western societies developed a new pattern, industrial agriculture, whereby machines began to be used for farming, animal husbandry, manufacturing, and other subsistence activities. As a result of the Industrial Revolution, the family farm was transformed into a highly mechanized and capital-intensive operation, and more recently is being replaced by agribusiness.

Because procurement systems are so varied, most societies do not fall tidily into one or another food procurement pattern. When we refer to foragers,

One recurrent pattern in human history is the abandonment of environments that no longer prove adaptive. (a) In ancient times, for instance, the once-thriving cliff dwellings of the Pueblo Indians in the American Southwest fell into ruin. (b) A more recent example is the desertion of Love Canal, near Niagara Falls, New York, which was built over a dumping ground for toxic wastes. As a result, community residents suffered at abnormally high rates from various physiological and genetic disorders.

([a] Myron Wood/Photo Researchers; [b] Michel Philippot/Sygma)

(a)

(b)

subsistence farmers, pastoralists, agriculturists, and industrial societies, we are merely pointing out a cultural emphasis on the use of particular food procurement methods. The specific procurement systems that people use involve varying strategies and varied degrees of reliance on the same strategy. People typically combine several methods. In most societies, for example, subsistence farming is supplemented by hunting and collecting wild foods. In others, horticulture (subsistence farming without the use of plows) is practiced alongside plow farming: The former in steep and rocky areas, the latter in flatter areas where plowing is possible. Pastoralism is generally found in conjunction with other pro-

curement strategies—in some cases with hunting and gathering, in other cases with small-scale horticulture. And, needless to say, many agriculturists raise animals not only for transportation but also as sources of protein, wool, and hides.

Adapting to Environmental Problems

The assumption that a given food procurement system is an adaptation to a certain range of environmental conditions still does not explain very much. It is certainly true that the characteristics of environmental zones of different sorts—grasslands, deserts, tropical forests, temperate forests, the Arctic, and the subarctic—place limits on the kind of life that can be sustained in them. One does not farm in the Arctic, nor does one herd animals in a tropical rain forest. Yet these broad environmental factors account for only a small portion of the variation we see in procurement systems. They do not tell us why inhabitants of similar regions—indeed, of the same region—often practice widely different procurement strategies, or why inhabitants of different regions sometimes practice remarkably similar strategies.

In order to understand how and why specific procurement systems develop, we must consider them as responses less to broad environmental characteristics than to very specific environmental problems in local areas. Some common problems faced by local populations are fluctuations over time and space in quantity, quality, and availability of resources, and the activities of other human groups in competition for those same resources.

Adapting to Available Resources

Every local environment or habitat has a limited potential for supporting any of the populations within it, both human and nonhuman. This demographic potential is called the environment's **carrying capacity**—the point at or below which a given population tends to stabilize. The most obvious limiting factors may be the availability of food or water. Others include disease, temperature, and even the regularity and predictability of critical resources. The fact that a food source is available during the year, for example, matters less than the ability of the people who rely on it to predict with accuracy *when* it is going to be available. The best way to determine carrying capacity is to observe the demographic characteristics of the population: rates of birth, death, and migration. Researchers may also estimate an environment's potential carrying capacity for a particular population by computing the minimum amount of water and of vegetable and animal matter available on a regular basis for human consumption. A long-term project in East Africa is illustrative of some of the issues involved in such research, as we see in Box 2.1, *The South Turkana Ecosystem Project*.

The carrying capacity of an area is affected not only by the total amount of food available, but also by the availability and distribution of essential dietary items such as protein, vitamins, and minerals. In other words, the nutritional quality of resources is as critical as their quantity and availability. To avoid chronic malnutrition, humans must somehow adjust to the variations in nutritional value among available foods. While some physiological adjust-

ment is evident among human populations in areas of diverse resources (as with populations occupying extremely high, arid, or cold regions), generally people solve the problem through restrictive dietary practices and in the way they prepare their foods.

A final factor affecting carrying capacity is the human ability to recognize resources. Even the determination of what plants and animals are edible varies considerably among cultures. Goosefoot and lambsquarter, two plants that we consider weeds, were important sources of both seeds and greens among many Native American groups. These and many other plants and animals that we do not now consider edible are staples (and even delicacies) in other societies. Many resources identified as usable in one culture are ignored in others.

As these examples illustrate, an environment's human carrying capacity is not a simple reflection of local resources. Also, as we will see in later chapters, carrying capacity depends on the organization of the society and on the exchange of food and tools among populations.

Adapting to Resource Fluctuation

Populations must adjust not only to the quantity and quality of resources but also to fluctuations in their availability. For example, over a five-year period an area may produce an average of 100 kilograms (about 221 pounds) of corn per year, but if production drops to 50 kilograms (about 110 pounds) one year, the people must adjust or risk starvation.

The Shoshone Indians, who lived in North America's Great Basin before the coming of the Europeans, provide a good historical example of adjustment to fluctuations in resources. Because of extreme variation in rainfall in this region, the Shoshone were never able to predict with any certainty where or how much plant and animal food would be available from one year to the next. The Shoshone adapted to these environmental uncertainties by relying on a wide variety of resources and pursuing a highly mobile way of life, changing their location and residence patterns according to the kind and quantity of resources available. During most of the year a Shoshone family traveled alone or with one or two related families, gathering roots and seeds and hunting small animals. Periodically, however, when rabbits or antelope became unusually plentiful, several families might band together temporarily for a collective hunt. And when isolated families heard reports that a resource such as pine nuts seemed promising in a particular locality, they would plan to arrive together in time for the harvest and would separate again after the resources had been collected (Steward, 1953).

Box 2.1
The South Turkana Ecosystem Project

THE SOUTH TURKANA ECOSYStem Project is a collaborative effort of scientists from universities in Kenya and the United States, with research interests as diverse as human genetics, demography, rangeland management, plant ecology, nutrition, and ethnology. About half of the scientists are anthropologists, many affiliated with the State University of New York at Binghamton. The lands of the Turkana in northwestern Kenya are subject to extremes of temperature; daytime highs average 87 to 100°F (35–37°C) and highly erratic rainfall that varies from 5.8 to 19.5 inches (150–500 millimeters) a year. This low and variable rainfall, combined with intense solar radiation flux, results in a short growing season; farming is limited. Most of the Turkana (a population of 150,000 to 200,000 distributed among a number of tribes and subtribes) exploit this region by nomadic move-

ments of their polygynous family settlements and the five species of livestock that they herd: camels, zebu cattle, goats, sheep, and donkeys. Home settlements will move, on the average, one or more times each month (Little, 1988, p. 697). The Turkana live almost entirely on the products of their animals, and starvation is a constant specter. As part of the project, one study conducted by rangeland ecology specialists and ethnographers (Coughenour et al., 1985) addressed a key issue in the study of pastoral adaptations to extremely arid lands: How do these people maintain enough animals to sustain themselves without degrading their habitat? Using detailed measurements of energy expenditures, the researchers were able to map plant-animal-human food pathways. They not only studied animal requirements, but also measured ground cover and the diets of a

sample of nomadic households. They found that the Turkana derived 92 percent of their food energy from animal products (meat, milk, and blood) and from maize meal, sugar, and other foods that they acquired by bartering animal products. Though their animals produce less milk and meat than American and Australian breeds, they are more resistant to disease, heat, and drought-related stress.

The Turkana can maintain an adequate diet and keep a critical reserve to face unexpected losses without degrading their rangelands because of two factors: The number of animals they can keep is limited by the availability of water holes, and they manage a mix of five species, each with its unique productive qualities. When milk from the cow fails, they turn to their camels; when meat is needed, they can kill small animals such as sheep or goats. Cattle that do not produce

---

People who live by cultivating crops or raising animals generally have a more stable food supply than those who depend on wild resources alone. But these groups are also affected by seasonal and yearly fluctuations and must adjust to them. Since population is more concentrated in these groups than among hunter-gatherers, the effects of food shortages may be even more devastating to them. The Ariaal of western Kenya (Chapter 5) depend on agricultural produce for the bulk of their caloric intake. However, droughts and fluctuations in rainfall can result in crop failure, in which case the Ariaal can fall back on their cattle and goat herds for their food supply. Thus their cattle may be seen as a means of storing energy as much as a means of producing it.

Another example involves an ancient American people that farmed in an extremely unpredictable climate. The Anasazi Pueblo Indians relied on a diverse set of agricultural strategies in order to minimize risk of crop failure in an area of high aridity. One strategy used in the fourteenth and fifteenth centuries was "pebble mulching;" that is, deliber-

ately adding small pebbles to the soil of their gardens. This served to conserve soil moisture, reduce erosion, and to extend the growing season (Lightfoot, 1993, p. 116).

Consumers in our society rarely experience sudden short-term fluctuations in resources, since we depend on the products of a huge area serviced by an efficient transportation system. A wide variety of fruits, vegetables, grains, meats, and dairy products are available to us throughout the year. This steadiness of supply is due to our technology: Producers have means of storing and transporting food so as to cover shortages, and our technology enables us to minimize some fluctuations in resources (although often at considerable cost).

When a rancher's pasturelands go dry, the rancher feeds his cattle by hauling forage and water to them with tractors and trucks rather than by moving the animals. Similarly, a farmer can bring water to his crops through irrigation, control insects with chemical sprays, and spread fertilizer to add nutrients to the soil of a depleted field. The farmer

milk provide blood, which is nutritionally rich. The livestock is often scrawny by European standards, but if the rains bring a bumper crop of vegetation, the animals put on weight rapidly and their fertility rate goes up.

Another study sheds light on the role of blood as human food in such a system (Dyson-Hudson & Dyson-Hudson, 1982). Turkana cows yield only one-tenth the milk of well-fed American Holsteins, but their blood is a more efficient source of energy than their meat (which involves much waste and of course requires the slaughter of the animals). Twenty-one pints (9.9 liters) of blood are taken from each thousand-pound steer every four to six months; lesser amounts are taken from breeding stock and smaller animals. The use of blood in the Turkana diet greatly enhances the herd's productivity, particularly because it supplements the diet during the season when cows are not producing milk.

Among the people themselves, Paul Leslie and Peggy Fry (1989) found extreme seasonality in births, with more than half occurring between March and June. The rate of conception, then, is highest during the early dry season (July through September), when the food supply has been at its peak for some time. The Turkana claim not to time their children's births (as some African populations do) and attribute the seasonality of births to the separation of spouses during the pastoral cycle, high temperatures that inhibit coitus, and other factors. Whatever the reason, the human population closely tracks environmental fluctuations.

In yet another study, three researchers (Little, Galvin, & Leslie, 1988) examined the population's health in an effort to determine the effects of their high-fat diet based as it is on milk, blood, and meat. Blood pressure is lower among all age groups than in a comparable American population, cardiovascular disease is rare, and general nutritional status is good, though the eye infections common to the area are prevalent. One of the researchers, Kathleen Galvin (1988), used project data to explore variation in Turkana nutritional status from season to season and according to food availability. She found that the nutritional status of a population at risk may be evaluated by means of dietary, ecological, and anthropometric measures of body fat and robustness: mid-arm circumference and skin-fold thickness. She cautions against reliance on any one measure, particularly when little body fat is normally present in the population. Her findings, like those of the other participants in the project, have a significance far beyond the Turkana ecosystem.

These plus other completed and ongoing studies of the Turkana Ecosystem Project not only contribute to a much fuller understanding of the Turkana people and their ecosystems, but they also have a wider significance for pastoral, ecological, and medical research.

can even grow crops in the dead of winter by constructing hothouses. But these techniques have costs that are passed on to the consumer. Modern agriculture depends on machine technology and is thus subsidized by the large-scale use of fossil fuel in the form of gasoline and diesel oil.

Despite the apparent advantages of modern agricultural techniques, we should not make the mistake of assuming that industrialized societies are somehow better at minimizing uncertainty in food production than technologically simpler ones. Perhaps the greatest paradox of recent human adaptation is that responses aimed at stabilizing and increasing food production are in many cases having the opposite effect. That is, they are creating a new and more serious threat to the stability of the procurement system. In order to diminish the threat of drought or irregular rainfall, for example, a community may increase its dependence on irrigation agriculture, only to discover that the increased irrigation has elevated the salt content of the soil to the point where it can no longer support crops.

Thus, while people in technologically advanced societies may accomplish impressive feats of environmental engineering, they must still remain sensitive to the environment in which they live. Ultimately the success of a group's adaptation to its resources depends not only on its ingenuity in manipulating its ecological system, but also on its care in maintaining that system. As a consequence, the internal distribution of resources among people through social interaction is as important as are the resources on which they depend.

Political Ecology

The type and distribution of basic resources are only two aspects of an environment. Human populations make up another and no less basic aspect. Every society must adjust to the presence and activities of neighboring peoples just as it must adjust to variations in local resources. The study of this adaptive process is important enough to constitute an entire subfield of human ecology: **Political ecology**—the study of how people compete to gain access to, maintain control of, and utilize natural resources.

There are many ways in which politics determine how humans interact with their environments, and also many environmental factors that affect the political process. Many anthropologists consider most human ecological studies to really be analyses of political ecology, since the main determinants for how resources are accessed and distributed are political. This might also be called the "political economy" approach, since it considers the ways in which politics and economics intersect (Peet & Watts, 1994). Politics obviously reward some more than others. Among the Turkmen of Northern Iran, for example, wealthy and influential men occasionally hire teams of large tractors and set them to plowing arid and only partially arable public lands that the rest of the community uses for grazing. They then seed the new fields and, if they are lucky with the rains, make a handsome profit on the resultant wheat crops (that are guarded by their hired help); the soils, however, quickly erode and the common pastures are lost to both farming and grazing.

Access to Resources: Cooperation and Competition

Local populations and the individuals within them by necessity cultivate and maintain multiple political and social ties with each other that allow them to cope with uncertainties of all sorts. Until very recently in the West, and still in many parts of the world, local populations depend on local food resources. At the same time, as we have noted, the potential for agriculture or other forms of food procurement is highly variable, with sharp contrasts between highly productive and marginal areas. Even within regions, members of particular societies are often differentiated in terms of access to critical resources and their place in the system of production. There is inevitably a great deal of exchange of food items, labor, and other services both within communities and among them—virtually no local population is completely self-sufficient. Pastoral farmers and herding households exchange continually. The pastoral Yörük (see Chapter 5) sell their animal products in markets, the Pygmies of the Ituri Forest in Zaire trade forest products for grain with their Bantu farming neighbors, and so forth. In the settlement of the arid reaches of the Little Colorado River, as we saw with Abruzzi's study of Mormon

colonization (1996), the political ties of each community to the central church hierarchy were critical to survival; local communities were supported by the church during lean or disastrous years.

The nature of resources affects political behavior. Competition for resources will arise only where those resources (such as fields or irrigation works) have a high intrinsic value and are in a clearly bounded area. In Swat, Pakistan, as we will see in the following case study, culturally different neighboring populations make it difficult for landowners to expand into areas that are not already owned by Pathan households; the fields over which they contend are highly productive and worth defending. Hunters and gatherers, on the contrary, generally occupy lands where resources are not concentrated; thus, land ownership or control is not a major source of competition.

Environmental uncertainty is another factor encouraging individuals and groups to maintain a multiplicity of political associations. Most communities periodically face conditions of drought, crop and animal epidemics, disease, and the like that necessitate seeking help from others—even from those with whom relations may be strained or hostile. For example, observers of social life in the Middle East have been struck by the great amount of time and energy individuals spend socializing and politicking. Whether it be the ubiquitous teahouses of rural Turkey, Iraq, and Iran; the village guesthouses of Syria; or the urban coffee shops of Egypt, clusters of men and women meet (usually separately) on an almost daily basis to reaffirm existing ties, to forge new ones, and to keep an eye on the activities of others. Farming and pastoralism in these regions are carried out in an environment that demands close attention to ever-shifting political winds in addition to changing market conditions.

One result of this variability and interdependence is that we frequently find prosperous communities abutting poorer ones; households and groups are simultaneously faced with the need to compete and to cooperate. Peasants and pastoralists may fight for the same well; upstream villagers may fight with downstream neighbors over water rights; communities, neighbors, and even relatives may find themselves in competition even as they rely on each other for help and the exchange of goods. Individuals try to maintain as wide a range of contacts as possible and are continually prepared to shift alliances as interests dictate. Since the most important predator or competitor any local population might face is its neighbors, politics are an integral part of the environmental setting.

"Scramble Competition" among the Pathans of Pakistan

The Pathans of Swat, Pakistan, have important leaders who achieve their positions by competitive economic, military, and social activities carried out over a long period of time (Barth, 1959; Boone, 1992). Here population densities are high, positions of authority are formalized, and power is centralized in these positions. There are many reasons why this is so, although the lines of causality are not entirely clear. For example, with the development of irrigation agriculture, some communities and some regions emerge as especially favored, grow rapidly, and expand at the expense of others. Certainly, the extension of political control, via warfare or alliances, entails the development of mechanisms for enforcing order over a large area. Like the Turkmen khans, whose power is based on their economic wealth, the large landowners among the Pathans also assume leadership roles. However, unlike the khans, who acquired their lands from the state, the Pathan landowners compete for power and authority, each vying to increase his wealth at the expense of competitors. In what James Boone calls "scramble competition," would-be leaders "scramble" for clients—tenants and warriors who will remain loyal and perhaps aid in extending their leader's power and reputation (Boone, 1992, p. 326). First, the landowner builds his economic resources by encroaching on the land of his neighbors, farming it, and staking claim to the property. If he is successful, this strategy leads to increased wealth, which is used to attract more followers to work his land and defend his holdings. Essential to the success of this enterprise are the great feasts and other forms of display and hospitality he sponsors and which, in turn, contribute to his reputation as a powerful leader.

But there are limits to the ability of any one leader to completely dominate the valley. What often emerges is a balance of power, since each leader runs the risk that his followers might defect if a competitor offers better terms. In a sense, there are two scrambles going on: One for followers among large landowners and the second, among followers or tenants to secure the most hospitality and best rewards for their labor and support (Boone, 1992, p. 326). Even though this competition is carried out largely (but not entirely) in the social arena, it results in certain men acquiring great influence over others. Such a person has the ability to give away food in time of need, mobilize public opinion, and generally shape public policy. They can also mobilize armed retainers when needed. But since there are always rivals waiting for their own opportunity for advancement, the leaders have to be careful not to alienate their followers. ▶

Politics and Access to Resources

In order to secure resources, a group must have some assurance of continued access to an area where those resources are located. People define and regulate access to productive resources in a variety of ways depending on the nature of the resources and the means available to control and use them.

Most agricultural and industrial societies maintain clear-cut rules that define rights to productive land and other resources. Among most hunting-and-gathering societies, an individual's rights to use resources are relatively unrestricted. Hunters and gatherers such as the Eskimo and the Dobe !Kung must be able to move according to the seasonal availability of resources; otherwise, they might starve when normal fluctuations in climate deplete the local water supply or alter the distribution of wild animals or plants. The more uncertain or mobile the food supply, the greater the need for flexible boundaries and collective rights of access. The extent to which people define and defend a territory also depends on the gains versus the costs of maintaining exclusive rights. A group that stakes out and defends territory retains the resource supply in that territory. But to guard a territory requires time and energy that might be spent in other activities. It also involves risk; one can be killed defending a boundary. Finally, reliance on a restricted area for resources may be disadvantageous, as it would be for many hunter-gatherers. To the degree that costs outweigh the gains, territoriality will be relaxed. To the degree that the gains outweigh the costs, territoriality will be strictly observed. Thus, while hunters and gatherers have territories to which groups lay primary claim and stake out possession of strategic resources such as wells or rich stands of vegetable foods, they do not necessarily defend the boundaries as vigorously as farmers defend their fields (Dyson-Hudson & Smith, 1978). Generally, permission is readily granted to outsiders to visit wells or traverse territories.

The gains/cost formula is well illustrated by the pastoral Pokot of East Africa, a population closely resembling the Ariaal (Chapter 5). The Pokot's sorghum fields are critical to their survival and they are relatively easy to defend, for they are small and located near the people's houses. The fields are carefully guarded against both intruding animals and human thieves. The pastureland on which the Pokot graze their cattle is almost impossible to defend, and it would be unwise to try to defend it. It covers too large an area, and the water resources and the quality of grass vary seasonally in any one area. A well-defended patch of brown grass with dry water holes would benefit no one. The Pokot therefore exercise far less control over grazing land than over fields and farmland.

Maintaining control over a territory, whether loosely or strictly, is only the first step in regulating access to resources. Every society has principles that govern who may use which resources and under what circumstances. One important principle observed in our own society is that of private ownership of property, or freehold. Americans regard land, water, minerals, machinery, and all types of productive resources as things that someone can own. Owners, whether individuals or corporations, decide who has access to their resources and when. They may exploit them in any way they wish; they may also rent or sell them. Of course, even capitalist economies recognize that the concept of private property has limits. Systems that provide essential resources, such as transportation and electricity, are often considered public utilities and are heavily regulated, sometimes even owned outright by the government. Zoning laws further define actual use of private property. And social constraints may restrict the way one disposes of it. Few urban neighborhoods in the United States allow one to keep chickens in the back yard, although not too long ago this practice was widespread. At the same time, effective ownership may depend on active use: In many European and American cities, squatters have taken over buildings that the owners have left unoccupied. In many less-developed countries, entire sections of major cities are given over to illegal shantytowns formed by rural settlers who simply erect rough dwellings on vacant land, without municipal approval or title to the land. In Turkey, for example, such settlements are called *gecekondu*, or "built in the night." Taking advantage of a customary law that prohibits the destruction of one's domicile, poor people rapidly put up a house and dare the authorities to evict them. In many nonindustrial societies, groups rather than individuals control the land and other productive resources, along with the equipment necessary for production. The individual gains rights to these resources only by virtue of affiliation with a group. We can see this form of corporate ownership best by looking at the way such groups control land.

Gender, Politics, and Property

The interests of men and women often conflict when it comes to property; the resolution of divergent claims and interests is inherent in the political process. In most of Europe, until relatively recently, the rights of women to own and inherit property (especially land) was limited. This reflected political structures in which most formal political power was vested in males. This is not surprising, since all of Europe was once governed under Roman law in which male heads of households were legally recognized as owners of, and as being responsible for, all household possessions, including wives, adult but unmarried daughters, children, slaves, and other chattel. In the last century, this has changed greatly but men and women still participate differently in the economy and with respect to control of resources. The move toward greater equality in property rights seems closely linked to the increased involvement of women in wage labor, thereby gaining greater control over household resources. This is not always without conflict. Henry Rutz (1992) has found that in Fiji, a country that has developed wage labor opportunities for women only recently, as women began earning money from wage labor, their fathers or husbands would attempt to appropriate it. This in turn lead to elaborate negotiations about how much women should contribute to household or community activities and how much they could spend themselves. In Canada, a recent study has shown that within twenty years, 1966 to 1986, the number of dual-income households has doubled to 62 percent (Cheal, 1993, p. 199). At the same time, the number of households reporting joint bank accounts and joint ownership of real estate rose approximately 70 percent (p. 201). Still, over 20 percent of family homes are held in the husband's name; only 5 percent in the wife's.

The following case study from Kenya, illustrates something of the ongoing conflict over property rights in a society where cattle are major economic and prestige items.

CASE STUDY

Whose Cows are They, Anyway?

Regina Smith Oboler was carrying out ethnographic fieldwork among the Nandi of western Kenya (1996). She happened to attend a church wedding and was intrigued to find that the clergyman's sermon focused on the appropriate marital roles of husband and wife. In particular, he harangued against married women who claim to own cattle; once married, all property belonged to the family, and the cows to the husband. This remark was met by nervous laughter; most in the audience knew the ambiguity that surrounded Nandi cattle ownership.

Many Nandi women do claim to own particular cows, but, in general, Nandi people, when asked "who owns cows?" will say that men do. With regards to particular animals, a man may well claim to "own" a cow that his wife also claims. Part of the problem is linguistic. The term "own" has many connotations among the Nandi; several people can have rights in the same animal at the same time. In fact, Oboler suggests that the concept of ownership is misplaced in speaking of indigenous African property systems; there is no single individual who has the kind of absolute rights that the English use of the term implies (p. 269). Usually the right of any individual to control cattle is constrained by rights in the same animal held by other individuals (p. 269). Almost everyone agrees that ". . . husbands and fathers do not have the right to use family cattle in ways that are not to the benefit of wives and children" (p. 266). A woman is given rights in cattle when she marries and, since the household is usually polygynous, she expects that her children will ultimately inherit the herd she builds up. Some cattle are also given directly to women as gifts or as part of their bridewealth; such cattle can be used only by the bride or by her full brothers. Some cattle are acquired by men through purchase with cash earned in wage labor; even so, they are expected to use it to benefit equally the houses of each of their wives.

Currently, there is a new element of ambiguity: People are selling traditional East African cattle and replacing them with high milk-producing European dairy cows. These cattle are usually regarded as if men had bought them with wages, even though often they had to sell inherited or bridewealth cattle to purchase them. This seems to threaten the rights of women. Thus the sermon that Dr. Oboler heard can be seen ". . . as an attempt to put the force of religion behind a new norm, one favorable to the husband's position" (p. 270). ◗

Ownership versus Use Landholding Systems. In traditional societies that do not recognize individual ownership of land, the kin group or the community at large either is the landholder, or at least has a great deal to say about who uses what resources. Individuals or households may have the right to use these resources for limited periods, but they do not own them—they can neither buy nor sell the land they farm. Such kin group or community landholding rights are often termed "corporate" rights. Thus, while people in most industrial countries acquire land and the resources on it through inheritance, purchase, or rental, people in most nonstate societies gain their right to land as a birthright or through marriage to a member of a landowning group. As a member of a band, for example, a Dobe Ju/'hoansi (!Kung) man or woman automatically has the right to hunt and collect wild foods within the area used by that band. The !Kung say it does not matter who owns the land itself, since one cannot eat the ground. Rather, each band collectively holds the right to exploit specific water resources and patches of wild plant foods (Marshall, 1965).

With few exceptions, pastoral peoples follow the same rule. Grazing lands are generally treated as a communal asset, open to all members of the tribe—or at least to all members of the large and cooperating kin groups that typically migrate and settle together. Horticulturists, on the other hand, are generally concerned with allocating rights to use specific plots, for they invest a great deal of time and labor in these plots. Like hunter-gatherers and pastoralists, they acquire rights to land by virtue of group membership, but in order to retain the right to a particular plot, one must actively use it. Among the Tiv of Nigeria, for example, the head of the household is allowed to cultivate any unused piece of land within a territory belonging to his lineage. He may lay claim to as much land as his household can handle. So long as the household actively works these fields and keeps them clear, the members are entitled to their exclusive use. When fields revert to fallow, however, rights lapse and the land becomes part of the public domain, to be claimed by other families in the lineage. Nevertheless, a Tiv man always retains the right to some land—if not to one particular field, then to another—simply because he is a member of a certain kin group (Bohannan, 1960). In other horticultural societies, rights of use may be acquired simply through residence in the village or through the performance of some social obligation, but again the land must be cultivated if those rights are to remain in force. As with hunter-gatherers and pastoralists, collective as opposed to private ownership of land may be critical to a horticultural group's way of making a living.

Private Ownership and Commercial Farming. In areas that were ruled by European colonial powers, European systems of private ownership usually replaced traditional land-use systems. As a result, the economic system became more impersonal and

Box 2.2

Money Makes Us Relatives: Women's Labor and Ideals of Social Relations

DURING TWO YEARS OF FIELD-work (1986–1988), Jenny White studied a number of families who had migrated from rural areas of Turkey to live in poor, working-class neighborhoods of Istanbul and who are now engaged in small-scale production.[1] Women play a central role in producing knitted, stitched, and embroidered clothing and decorative items either at home or on a piecework basis in family atelier workshops. Many of the goods produced in this fashion are exported to Europe, the Middle East, and the United States, where they are sold at prices astronomically higher than the cost of their production. They are also sold either directly or through middlemen to tourists, as well as directly to friends and neighbors.

Both the women who work at home or take in piecework and the organizers of their labor (generally men) regard this work as part of the women's traditional domestic activities rather than productive labor. "For the working-class women of Istanbul, labor, along with honor and childbearing, is a central defining theme of their lives" (p. 7). Since the women insist that this labor is not work, they do not keep track of the time they spend on it—a piece of work is taken up and put down throughout the day by different adult women and unmarried girls, becoming integrated into their other activities. "Both piecework and the family atelier are particularly suited to the organization of women's labor... since the women are able to reconcile earning additional income with traditional role constraints that discourage [them] from leaving the home, making contact with strangers, and taking over the male role of provider" (p. 109).

In a recent survey, it was found that 64 percent of women spent between four and seven hours a day doing paid work, mostly piecework knitting. One of the women White visited, Sengül, a Koran teacher, owns a knitting machine and produces clothing to sell to friends and neighbors. But when White pressed her as to why she was doing this knitting, she became uncomfortable and insisted that she did not do a lot of it, taking orders only from friends and working only in spare moments between housework, taking care of the children, and entertaining relatives and neighbors. She did not see herself as "belonging to a category of people who do regular work, sell to strangers, and rely on the money earned in this way" (p. 113), although clearly her income from this labor contributed significantly to the family budget. When asked how many sweaters

---

less tied to a larger system of social relationships. Sometimes already-existing discrepancies between the property rights of men and women were amplified. Very often, even in horticultural and pastoral societies, property rights differ by gender; even the egalitarian Dobe !Kung recognize different rights to possession for men and women. When the colonial powers imposed the concept of private property as a means of controlling productive resources, they usually allocated ownership to men rather than to all individuals (Etienne & Leacock, 1988). Among the Buganda of Central Africa, for example, chiefs traditionally allotted portions of their estates to tenant farmers. These grants could be revoked at any time. Once the British took control of this region, they passed a law enabling tenants to do as they liked with their land grants, even pass them on to their heirs without the chief's permission. The aim was to protect tenant farmers from exploitation—and, in the process, to bring them more thoroughly under colonial control through land registration and sys-

tematic taxation. As a result, in Uganda land is now individually owned.

By different routes the movement toward private land rights has taken place in many other societies. Private ownership allows a certain freedom for individuals to make a living by using their land for their own exclusive benefit. This freedom, however, significantly alters an individual's ties to the group, along with the psychological and social advantages it once afforded. Under a system of corporate rights, since ownership is collective, the individual has a sense of place—a knowledge of belonging, in perpetuity, to this group and this piece of land. Under private ownership, land is transferable and it may well belong to someone other than those who work on it. Individuals who must sell their labor because they do not own the land they farm may come to be commodities themselves, with few economic rights in, and limited benefit from, what is being produced.

Not infrequently, rural people rise up in open rebellion or revolution in order to assert their

she made in a month, she replied, "Last month ... I had guests from the village so I couldn't do very many. About fifteen I guess ..."(p. 114). Since she had previously estimated that it takes her two days to make a sweater, this meant she worked every day, a fact about which she seemed embarrassed.

In most working-class neighborhoods there are also ateliers run by families that give out piecework to women in the neighborhood. This arrangement allows the women to work at home and thus to see their labor as part of their roles as women, family members, and neighbors. Women doing piecework will generally do so in the company of other women, thus making the work part of other social activities that bring them together. Hatice and her husband, Osman, run an atelier in the squatter district of Yenikent, specializing in clothes made from scraps of fine leather sewn together by crocheted panels. They have three daughters, who help out in the atelier, and one seven-year-old son. The family members prepare the leather and yarn and then gives them to neighborhood women with instructions for assembly. Osman keeps a book that lists what each woman takes and what she brings back.

These women are generally from the neighborhood, although some are from nearby neighborhoods. Murat, a neighbor who runs his own atelier, says, "They are stranger women but they are [the ones who have been made kin through money]" (p. 119). Osman and Hatice do not differentiate between donated labor, such as that of Güllü, their eldest daughter's best friend, who punches holes in the leather and takes the outfits home to assemble them, without pay, and the paid labor of the neighborhood women. "In their view, the women are kin (*akraba*) by virtue of their participation in the exchange of labor for money, providing of course that this is done ... as collective reciprocal assistance with no expectation of return" (p. 120). Just as this relationship, while clearly a commercial transaction, is euphemized as a kin relationship, so Güllü's donated work is explained in kinship terms; she is Emine's "sister." Kin relations are based on "participation in a web of reciprocal obligations and indebtedness," so in this situation money becomes "a thing or a service ... which can be freely given, just as labor is freely given. ... Labor, whether paid or unpaid, is seen as part of the obligations for mutual assistance that is required for group membership" (pp. 120–121).

The idea that women's labor, either at home or in the ateliers, is not "work" allows women to contribute financially to their families while remaining within their traditionally perceived roles in the family and neighborhood. It also is one of the major factors keeping production costs low and profits high for distributors, middlemen, merchants, and exporters.

SOURCE: Material for this box is taken from White, J. B. (1994). *Money Makes Us Relatives: Women's Labor in Urban Turkey,* Austin: University of Texas Press.

---

perceived rights to land or better conditions. The Chinese Revolution, the Mexican Revolution, and the Cuban Revolution were essentially agrarian movements, although led by urban educated intellectuals. At the present, there is a similar peasant rebellion underway in Chiapas, Mexico.

Of course, private ownership is not the only European model to have been transferred or adopted elsewhere. Various forms of collective farming, essentially products of European socialist or utopian philosophy, are still operating in Russia, South America, Asia, and Africa, as we will see in the case study on collective farming in China in Chapter 6. One common denominator of these systems is that they are usually imposed on peasant farmers by outsiders, so that in some respects they contain the most oppressive aspects of absentee landlordism: The people who farm have a limited say in the actual management of their work and must sell their crops at prices set by impersonal agencies.

CASE STUDY

Where the Dove Calls

There is little that is of greater importance to farmers than access to land and water. What follows is a description of the complex ways in which land can be held in even a small community and the logic that underlies what seems to be a strange combination of private and public or communal resources. Cucurpe, whose name, according to the Opata Indians, means "where the dove calls," is a farming community in northwestern Mexico studied by Thomas Sheridan. He writes:

To those of us who have grown up in the modern cities of Mexico or the United States, a place like Cucurpe seems idyllic, offering us a vision of a distant agrarian past. But if we go beyond that vision, we see that life in Cucurpe is predicated on struggle, not pastoral harmony: Struggle to raise crops when the rains won't come or when floods wash away the topsoil; struggle to keep cattle from turning into emaciated ghosts; struggle to prevent neighbors from diverting your irrigation water or fencing your pasture or stealing your land. [1988, p. xv]

The modern community of Cucurpe is, as it has been since the arrival of the Spanish, caught up in conflict between **corporate ownership** and private land tenure. It is one of the more than 22,000 corporate farming communities in Mexico, where 70 percent of Mexico's farm population live (Sheridan, 1988, p. 198). "Corporate" here means that some village resources are legally owned by the community as a whole; in this case, about half the land and most water rights. This conflict over access to land is complicated: It involves fending off the private ranchers, who are ever-ready to intrude on the grazing lands of Cucurpe. The conflict is also internal: Between those who have land and communal rights, those with some land and no communal rights, and those without land at all, but who seek it.

Even though the community is described as corporate, this does not means that there is economic equality or even that all have equal access to resources. Communal lands are interspersed with private holdings, the owners of which also can claim rights to corporate lands. Wealth distinctions are extreme. People view these distinctions of wealth in terms of three groupings. *Los ricos,* the rich, produce entirely for the market (not for domestic consumption), employ labor, use mechanized technology such as pumps and tractors, and own considerable land and cattle. The wealthiest ten households own over half of all private land in the community and have little interest in preserving any communal rights; generally, they would prefer to privatize all resources. *La gente ordenada* or the middle class, about 60 percent of the households, are generally self-sufficient peasant farmers utilizing both some private land (*milpa*) and running cattle on the commons, or corporate lands. They work their own fields and do not employ labor. Their interests in the corporate resources are very strong, as they rely on free grazing for their cattle and free water for their fields. *Los pobres* or the poor, about 18 percent of the families, own no more than five or six cattle, little or no land, and must work for others to make ends meet. Many of *los pobres* feel that they should be given community-owned land to develop and farm and thus find themselves in competition with the others who view these claims as threatening to their own interests. However extreme these differences may appear, within the community care

is taken to minimize them socially. The wealthy do not flaunt their wealth, and all take pains to avoid conspicuous consumption within Cucurpe itself.

This is an extremely arid region where water is a critical resource. There are three major forms of land use, largely distinguished by the availability of water. *Milpa* are fields created laboriously by clearing stones and brush, leveling them by hand, and then bringing in water via canals from one of the drainage systems. They are usually privately owned or treated as though they were private, even if technically the title is with the community. *Temporales* are fields carved out of the margins of water courses. They are not irrigated, but absorb sufficient runoff water in good years to raise squash and vegetables; they are also treated as though they were private. *Agostadero,* or grazing land, is communal and members can use it at will if they are not restrained by some community decision. These three forms of land use allow people to pursue a diversity of strategies, depending on whether they emphasize raising cattle for market, cash crops, subsistence crops, or some mix of these and wage labor.

For those who would specialize in ranching, something to which most aspire, a privately owned spread of less than 1,000 hectares would be an unreliable economic base. Any family without outside sources of income (some have jobs on ranches or remittances from relatives in America) will require access to at least two of the three major zones of land use; no one can make a living by committing to only one. Here lies the root of both conflict and cooperation. Politics are heated and unrelenting, reflecting the inequitable division of resources. Ranchers cut fences and are confronted by armed youths from the village; delegations of the poor petition for land; others complain about inequitable use of pastures; those with *milpas* come together to resist the claims of those without. But usually these conflicts are played out in nonviolent ways: In the courts, in town meetings, and through ever-changing coalitions.

As this scenario suggests, the community is not an expression of peasant communal solidarity (Sheridan, 1988, p. 189). Households plot, compete, and only sometimes cooperate. Sheridan's analysis indicates a predictable order underlying the ever-present disputing and alliance-making—what he terms the political ecology of land use. *Agostadero,* or rangeland, is a resource that individuals cannot own and defend alone unless they happen to be extremely wealthy. Members of the community can best get access to this land by working together in defending their rights, keeping outsiders off, and convincing the government of their rights. The land itself is not very valuable in small aggregates, but when taken as a whole it is worth maintaining as a corporate or common grazing area. Thus, while the rich try to use their influence to gain control of common grazing land, or even to steal it, most of the others in the community will respond cooperatively to defend it even where it is necessary to suppress old antagonisms. Another resource held corporately is surface water: While rich families can drill wells and run pumps, most must use surface water diverted to the fields by canals and dams. This cannot be done by families acting alone; they must cooperate or not gain access. Here the middle class of peasantry gets little support from either the rich or the poor: Both, one way or another, would like to get access to *milpas* and *temporales*. All small land-owning families assist in building and maintaining these canals, and each has a right to a specific amount of water for the household's *milpa*. They guard this right jealously and pass their fields onto their sons and daughters, even though technically some of the land is really corporate property. Families invest great effort in building their fields and planting them, and resist any attempt by the landless to have them redistrib-

uted. For middle-class peasants, the *milpa* is the key to survival; even though they make more money from cattle, they can rely on the *milpa* for food.

Thus, the ranchers and the wealthy continually spar with those who defend the corporate rights of the community; those with fields contend with those without, while those without strive to get the community to grant them land on which to farm. Both the landless and the small holders unite (or partially unite) to defend the grazing areas from the rich, but even in this there are bitter divisions: Some of the farmers own many cattle, while others own only a few. Everyone knows that the grazing is being damaged by overstocking, but since it is common land there is little regulation. Thus the owners of only a few cattle feel that they are victimized by those who own many. Still, "Cucurpe is not a battle ground between collectivism and free enterprise. On the contrary, most Cucurpeños want to be as independent as possible—to run their own cattle, farm their own fields" (Sheridan, 1988, p. 146). Most peasant villages, upon close examination, are likely to show similar sentiments and similar divisions. ◗

Summary

EVOLUTIONARY ECOLOGY IS A THEORETICAL ORIentation that emphasizes the adaptive significance of culture and behavior, from procurement systems to kinship systems to political and religious life. There are two aspects to this orientation: evolutionary theory and ecology (the study of the interplay between organisms and their environment). Anthropologists are concerned with the ways in which individuals and groups adapt to their ecological environments. In its simplest sense, adaptation refers to the ways organisms make adjustments that facilitate their survival (and hence reproductive success), which determines their genetic contributions to future generations. The success or failure of adaptive responses can only be measured over the long term, and the evolutionary consequences of any observed behavior are unpredictable. We, like many other species, adapt by learning new ways of doing things. No adaptation or response can be seen as a perfect solution; each carries with it certain costs and hazards. Also, any adaptation is opportunistic in that it makes use of whatever is already at hand. Variation, whether biological or behavioral, is the key to the process of adaptation. The recognition of variability draws attention to the process of selection among choices, the process of decision making. To understand the nature of human decision making or problem solving, we have to consider the environment in which it takes place. Environments are dynamic. One ecologist, Lawrence Slobodkin (1968), has argued that four patterns of change underlie the dynamics of all environments: changes in the novelty, frequency, magnitude, and duration of environmental events of all sorts. The organism with the best chance of success is not necessarily the one most perfectly adapted to its environment, but rather the one that maintains its ability to respond to the environment in a wide variety of ways—to be flexible. A multitude of strategies for coping with different environmental problems are practiced in any human population. Nevertheless, behavior is usually fairly predictable and conventional.

People guide their decisions according to expectations about consequences. To predict the course of future behavior or the way a population may respond to some novel event, anthropologists have to work with certain assumptions about human decisions or choices. Larger patterns or processes are simply the expressions of myriad individual acts and beliefs. Assumptions of rationality and individual self-interest are obviously too simple and too narrow to account for the entire range of cultural behavior. Despite their limitations, however, such assumptions are useful in that they allow us to form expectations of behavior with which actual behavior can be compared.

Anthropologists may use the concept of an ecosystem—the flow of energy and nutrients among the numerous species of plants and animals in a particular setting—to describe how human populations influence and are influenced by their surroundings. For an animal species, commitment to its niche (its adaptive strategy in the larger scheme) is relatively binding; the human species is distinctive in its capacity to alter its adaptive strategy and accommodate itself to many niches. However, humans are still subject to the rules established by the flow of matter and energy. We depend, as do all living things, on other species and must adjust our numbers and activities to our environment and available resources. An ecosystem may be in equilibrium—all of its components in balance—or it may not be, and thus be changing. All ecosystems are limited in their capacity for change; it is often human activities that place the greatest strain on natural ecosystems. Each local environment also has a limited potential for supporting any of the life forms in it. The point at or below which a population tends to stabilize is called its carrying capacity.

Specific human food procurement systems develop in response to both general environmental characteristics and environmental variables in the local area. These variables include the quantity and quality of available resources, fluctuations in the availability of resources, and the number of other groups competing for the same resources. A population's long-term success in adjusting to its resources may depend on its ability to maintain its ecological system; in this respect, simple societies can be as successful as technologically advanced societies. A vast array of adaptive strategies are employed throughout the world, but within that wide range are certain common patterns. Among food procurement strategies, for example, there are five basic patterns: foraging or hunting and gathering, subsistence agriculture, pastoralism, intensive agriculture, and industrial agriculture.

The type and distribution of basic resources are only one aspect of an environment. Human populations make up another and no less basic aspect. Every society must adjust to the presence and activities of neighboring peoples, just as surely as it must adjust to variations in local resources. The study of this adaptive process is important enough to constitute an entire approach in human ecology. This approach, called political ecology, is the study of how people struggle to gain access to, maintain control of, and utilize natural resources in the face of competing interests. The nature of resources also affects political behavior. Competition for resources will arise only where those resources (such as fields or irrigation works) have a high intrinsic value and are in a clearly bounded area. In Swat, Pakistan, we saw that culturally different neighboring populations make it difficult for landowners to expand into areas that are not already owned by Pathan households; the fields over which they contend are highly productive and worth defending. Hunters and gatherers, on the contrary, generally occupy lands where resources are not concentrated; thus, land ownership or control is not a major source of competition. Most agricultural and industrial societies maintain clear-cut rules that define rights to productive land and other resources. Among most hunting-and-gathering societies, an individual's rights to use resources are relatively unrestricted.

The interest of men and women often conflict when it comes to property; the resolution of divergent claims and interests is inherent in the political process. In most of Europe, until relatively recently, the rights of women to own and inherit property, especially land, was limited. This reflected political structures in which most formal political power was vested in males. In the last century, this has changed greatly but men and women still participate differently in the economy and with respect to control of resources. The move toward greater equality in property rights seems closely linked to the increased involvement of women in wage labor and greater control over household resources.

In societies that do not recognize individual ownership of land, the kin group or the community at large either is the landholder, or at least has a great deal to say about who uses what resources. Individuals or households may have the right to use these resources for limited periods, but they do not own them—they can neither buy nor sell the land they farm. Such kin group or community landholding rights are often termed "corporate" rights. Thus, while people in the most industrial countries acquire land and the resources on it through inheritance, purchase, or rental, people in most nonstate societies gain their right to land as a birthright or through marriage to a member of a landowning group.

Key Terms

carrying capacity	human ecology
corporate ownership	industrial agriculture
ecosystem	intensive agriculture
food procurement systems	pastoralism
foraging	political ecology
horticulture, or subsistence agriculture	resilience
	stability

Suggested Readings

Abruzzi, W. S. (1993). *Dam that river! Ecology and Mormon settlement in the Little Colorado River Basin.* Lanham, MD: University Press of America. See pp. 68–69. A rich account, using ecological models, of Mormon settlement in the nineteenth century.

Bates, D. G., & Lees, S. H. (Eds.). (1996). *Case studies in human ecology.* New York: Plenum. A collection of case studies illustrating many aspects of human-environmental relations, organized around broadly defined procurement strategies.

Boyd, R. & Richerson, P. J. (1985). *Culture and the evolutionary process.* Chicago: University of Chicago Press.

Discusses the ways psychological, sociological, and cultural factors combine to change societies. The authors also develop models to analyze how biology and culture interact under the influence of evolutionary processes to produce the diversity we see in human cultures.

Campbell, B. (1994). *Human ecology: The story of our place in nature from prehistory to the present.* Hawthorne, NY: Aldine. This book is intended as a supplementary text for social science courses dealing with our current ecological crisis. It uses the study of human prehistory as a means to understand our present evolutionary and ecological situation.

Cultural Survival, Inc. (1994). *State of the peoples: A global human rights report on societies in danger.* Boston: Beacon Press. A selection of papers by both cultural anthropologists and others that describe the urgent threats facing distinctive societies around the world as they adapt to a rapidly changing world.

Moran, E. F. (1982). *Human adaptability.* Boulder, CO: Westview Press. A review of principles of adaptation as well as an introduction to ecological concepts and methodology. Although somewhat dated, this book is the best general review of the topic for anthropologists. The volume is particularly useful for its case study approach to human adaptation in different environmental contexts.

Smith, E. A. & Winterhalder, B. (Eds.). (1992). *Evolutionary ecology and human behavior.* New York: Aldine. An excellent discussion of the general principles of evolutionary ecology, together with very interesting illustrative case studies.

Stringer, C. & McKie, R. (1997). *African exodus: The origin of modern humanity.* New York: Henry Holt. A fine defense of the "out of Africa" model, which is generally the accepted one.

Tattersal, I. (1995). *The fossil trail: How we know what we think we know about human evolution.* Oxford: Oxford University Press. An up-to-date account of hominid evolution, including a careful analysis of competing models.

Wrangham, R. & Peterson, D. (1996). *Demonic males: Apes and the origins of human violence.* New York & Boston: Houghton Mifflin. A thoughtful review of what is known of ape social behavior and its possible significance for understanding human aggression.

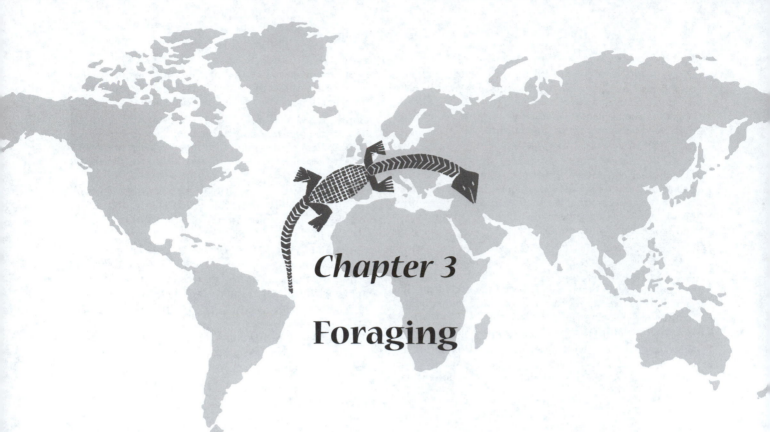

Chapter 3

Foraging

Humans and their immediate hominid ancestors have lived on the earth for more than four million years, and for more than 99 percent of that time they grew no food. They lived by hunting animals and gathering the plants that grew wild in their habitats. This adaptation is usually called foraging or hunting and gathering. This complex form of subsistence requires careful scheduling for collecting many (often hundreds) species of plants and hunting game; detailed environmental knowledge; and sophistication in storing, processing, and preparing food items. Further, in many instances it involves active management of resources by such techniques as water diversion, building weirs or dams constructed out of branches, and selective burning of grasslands or forests (see Gottesfeld, 1994).

Between 30,000 and 40,000 years ago anatomically modern humans appear in the archaeological record in sites across Europe, Asia, and Africa, and, soon thereafter, in North and South America. While there are many theories as to how modern Homo sapiens ultimately replaced the closely related species of Neanderthals, all seem to agree that it occurred because of major cultural breakthroughs in subsistence technology critical to foraging (Jolly &

White, 1995; Tattersal, 1995). The modern hominids, as evidenced from their camps, kill sites (where game was killed or butchered), and from remains of stone tools, developed a hitherto unknown sophistication in hunting and gathering involving the cooperation of many individuals, probably from different groups or bands. They made specialized tools consisting of different parts (such as spear throwers); bladed instruments using wood, antlers, and ivory; they created sturdier housing and clothing; and they produced art—as shown so strikingly in the cave paintings of France and Spain. At this time, we also find the first evidence for long-distance trade as a means of providing tool-making materials to groups whose environments did not supply them. This could have also facilitated the development of a collective body of knowledge among hundreds of local groups over wide areas. At the same time, there is striking evidence for cultural diversity: In Africa, for example, there were at least eight different traditions of tool making among early humans.

Today, foraging as a primary subsistence strategy is relatively rare and becoming rarer, not just because local people are quick to adopt new technologies but also because the lands available to sustain people in this endeavor are being encroached upon by outsiders. A review of the approximately 860 historically known hunter-gatherer societies tabulated in the Ethnographic Atlas found that only 179 survived into recent times (Ember, 1978, p. 440). Of those 179, far fewer remain today and none are unaffected by close relations with the products of industrialism and market economies. In fact, existing foragers are threatened on every continent where they still attempt to follow their traditional adaptation, as we see in Box 3.1, *Death of a People: Logging in the Penan Homeland.*

Anthropologists, in describing any society in which they are not actually working at the time they are writing, often employ the convention known as the **ethnographic present.** The term indicates that the information being presented applies to the time when the data were collected; it doesn't necessarily describe the way the people in question may be living at the time the report is read. All of the peoples we discuss should be understood with this fact in mind, for lifestyles and technologies can change radically from one year to the next.

In this chapter we will look at two examples of foraging or hunting-and-gathering groups. The first are the Dobe Ju/'hoansi or !Kung (also sometimes called the Basarwa), who lived, when the first studies were carried out, by gathering nuts, vegetables, and fruits and by hunting wild animals on a semiarid plain in southwestern Africa. In their case, the term "foraging" is certainly appropriate; while they made economic use of hundreds of species, the bulk of their diet was supplied by plants. The second case is a composite portrait of the people whom outsiders usually refer to as the Inuit or "Eskimo;" that is, the indigenous populations of the circumpolar regions of arctic Alaska and northeastern Canada. Many of these peoples still support themselves primarily by hunting and fishing (using modern technology to do so), but also increasingly by performing wage labor in the oil fields.

In certain respects, the lives of these modern hunter-gatherers, until quite recently at least,

---

Box 3.1

Death of a People: Logging in the Penan Homeland

AT THE BEGINNING OF THE CENTURY, Wade Davis writes, over 100,000 nomadic hunter-gathers roamed the forests of Sarawak, Malaysia, on Borneo, the world's third largest island; now only 7,600 remain: the Penan people (Davis, 1993, p. 24). Eighty percent of Borneo is covered by a dense equatorial rain forest—one of the oldest living terrestrial ecosystems, and central to the life of the Penan. In many respects, the Penan resemble the Mbuti pygmies of Zaire in that they depend on the forest for food and they revere it as an intricate living thing. "Identifying psychologically and cosmologically with the rain forest and depending upon it for diet and technology, the Penan are skilled naturalists, with sophisticated interpretations of biological relationships" (p. 25). A partial list of their plant lore shows that they recognize over one hundred fruit trees, fifty medicinal plants, and eighteen sources of poison or toxins (used in hunting and fishing). Unfortunately, their way of life is threatened.

Throughout their territory, the sounds of chain saws and logging tractors pierce the air as logging concessions, granted by the government of Sarawak, fell trees in the Penan's rainforest home. The assault is not new; between 1963 and 1985, 30 percent of the forests of Sarawak were logged, while another 60 percent have been given in concessions. Where do these ancient trees end up? For the most part, they are shipped to Japan, where they are transformed into cement molds, disposable containers, and shipping flats. Granting concessions has, in effect, created a class of instant millionaires among members of the Sarawak State Assembly (pp. 26–27). In 1987, the Penan and their neighbors, the Dyaks, responded by organizing resistance. They held meetings, rallies, and ultimately placed barricades on logging roads, bringing operations to a temporary halt. Despite international protests, the government retaliated and made arrests. In 1988, the blockades went up again, as they did in 1990. Even though a state task force recommended that the Dyak-Penan region be respected as biosphere reserve, this has not been acted upon. Ultimately the fate of the Penan will rest with world opinion; the prognosis is not good.

probably paralleled the lives of early prehistoric humans. This is one of the reasons they are of such great interest to anthropologists and also are the source of some controversy (Wilmsen, 1989a, 1989b; Lee, 1993; Burch & Ellanna, 1994). The study of recent or contemporary foragers may help us to understand why and how some aspects of human culture developed as they did, but it is important to bear in mind that the hunter-gatherers of today are not "throwbacks" or "living fossils." As Wilmsen and others have stressed, every modern population has a long and varied history regardless of whether written records exist, and cannot be seen as direct evidence of how earlier populations might have lived (1989). On the contrary, they are twentieth-century people with twentieth-century problems. As Eder (1996) has pointed out in the case of the Batak in the Philippines, hunter-gatherers are quick to incorporate new technologies into their subsistence systems. They deal with governments that have jurisdiction over them and with neighbors whose cultures may be quite different from their own. All hunter-gatherers have been drawn into exchanges with other groups: Doing occasional wage labor for nearby agriculturists and pastoralists, buying from and selling to traders from industrialized societies, and even at times receiving welfare from their governments.

Modern foragers are people for whom some version of this ancient subsistence strategy is still effective in their particular environments. The fact that most hunter-gatherers throughout history lived in areas far more hospitable than those they inhabit today implies that food sources were more abundant and reliable, nutrition better, and population densities higher than we see today among foragers. As we examine some of the methods of food procurement used by hunter-gatherers, their systems of kinship, residence patterns, and other cultural traits, we will see that these behaviors constitute solutions to the problems of making a living in their particular habitats.

The Organization of Energy

Hunters and gatherers subsist primarily on wild plants and animals. Unlike agriculture, the hunting-and-gathering economy does not involve direct or intensive intervention to regulate the growth and reproduction of the life forms on which people depend. Thus the diet of hunter-gatherers is more strictly determined by habitat than that of other groups. In fact, abundant wild resources are available in any American city, but not in quantities sufficient to sustain a population of any great size.

As local environments vary, so do the dietary staples of their inhabitants. Peoples who live in areas where plant life is more abundant or reliable than game depend primarily on vegetable foods—nuts, fruits, and the like. Such is the case, for example, with the Dobe dwellers of the Kalahari. The Eskimo, by contrast, rely much more heavily on meat and fish, for plant life is scarce in the Arctic. Whatever its emphasis, however, the diet of hunter-gatherers tends to be highly diversified, since it must be responsive to seasonal and annual fluctuations in resources. Scott Cane, writing about the foragers of the Central Desert region of Australia, describes several hundred species ranging from tiny plants and insects to large animals that the people incorporate into their seasonal diets, as well as the elaborate efforts made to secure adequate water and nourishment during the dry months (1987).

This is not to say that foragers do not manage their resource bases. In both North and South America, indigenous foragers use fire to burn forest cover on a regular basis in order to promote the growth of vegetation supporting favored game animals (Lewis & Ferguson, 1988) or favored root tubers or berries (Gottesfeld, 1994). Coincidentally, this periodic burning may be instrumental in promoting the long-term health of the forest as well, since it prevents the buildup of undergrowth that can cause dangerous fires or harbor disease.

Most, if not all, foraging peoples engage in varying degrees of exchange with other societies. The Mbuti Pygmies of Zaire, although often described as self-sufficient hunters, sell antelope and other game to visiting traders and buy the agricultural products and manufactured foods of their Bantu and Sudanic neighbors (Milton, 1985). It is extremely doubtful that they could have survived otherwise (Hart & Hart, 1986). The Dobe people also trade with and work for the Bantu farmers (Wilmsen, 1989a, 1989b). The Eskimo hunt not only for their subsistence needs, but also to enable them to trade for the numerous products of industrial society on which they have come to depend—snowmobiles, kerosene, rifles, canned goods, even televisions and motor vehicles (see, for example, Feit, 1994, pp. 421–440).

One of the reasons anthropologists find hunter-gatherers especially fascinating is that these people show us how humans can live on a low-energy budget. A **low-energy budget** is an adaptive strategy by which a minimum of energy is used to extract sufficient resources from the environment for survival. All humans, of course, have the same basic nutritional requirements and constraints, modified only slightly by body stature and environmental factors such as altitude or climate, for example. What does

Table 3.1 Edible Seeds Found in Australia's Central Desert

Scientific Name	Aboriginal Name	Habitat	Relative Importance
Acacia acradenia	Wilbud	Sandplains	Minor
Acacia adsurgens	Nganamarra	Sandplains	Moderate
Acacia ancistrocarpa	Wadayurru	Sandplains	Moderate
Acacia aneura	Mandja	Flood, Laterite plains	Moderate
Acacia coriacea	Gunandru	Deep sandplains	Major
Acacia holosericea	Gilgidi	Adjacent water	Major
Acacia ligulata	Wadarrga	Sandplains	Moderate
Acacia monticola	Birrbin	Sandplains	Moderate
Acacia stipuligera	Djibrin	Deep sand, dune flanks	Major
Acacia tenuissima	Minyinggurra	Sandplains	Moderate
Acacia tumida	Ngadurrdi	Sandplains	Moderate
Brachiaria miliiformis	Balgurrba	Adjacent water	Minor
Bulbostylis barbata	Lyillyil	Adjacent water	Minor
Capparis loranthifolia	Yidaringgi	Flood plains	Minor
Chenopodium inflatum	Garndubungba	Clayey sand	Minor
Chenopodium rhodin- ostachyum	Galbarri	Clayey sand	Major
Cyperus iria	Yanmid	Adjacent water	Moderate
Dactyloctenium radulans	Burrandjarri	Adjacent water	Moderate
Daspalidium rarium	Yulumburru	Rocky ground	Minor
Diplachine fusca	Miarr Miarr	Floodplains	Minor
Echinochloa colunum	Dudjurnba	Adjacent water	Moderate
Eragrostis eriopoda	Wangganyu	Sandplains, near water	Moderate
Eragrostis laniflora	Burrindjurru	Deep sand	Minor
Eragrostis tenellula	Marradjirralba	Various	Moderate
Eucalyptus camaldulensis	Yabulin	Creeks	Minor
Eucalyptus microtheca	Dindjil	Adjacent water	Moderate
Eucalyptus odontocarpa	Warilyu	Deep sand	Moderate
Eucalyptus pachyphylla	Djibuburru	Deep sand	Moderate
Fimbristylis oxystachya	Lugarra	Sandplains	Major
Hedyotis pterospora	Yurrundju yurrundju	Sandplains	Minor
Panicum australiense	Yidagadji	Sandplains	Major
Panicum cymbiforme	Gumbulyu	Deep sand	Major
Panicum decompositum	Willinggiri	Flood plains	Minor
Portulaca filifolia	Bulyulari	Sandy ground	Moderate
Portulaca oleracea	Wayali	Sandy ground	Moderate
Scirpus dissachanthus	Gunamarradju	Adjacent water	Moderate
Sida sp. A (unnamed)	Dadji dadju	Sand dunes	Minor
Stylobasium spathulatum	Nirdu	Sandplains	Major
Tecticornia verrucosa	Mangil	Claypans	Minor
Triodia basedowii	Nyanmi	Sandplains	Minor
Triodia longiceps	Lanu lanu	Rocky ground	Minor
Triodia pungens	Djinal	Sandplains	Minor

vary is the amount of energy we expend, directly or indirectly, in support of a particular population. We humans are distinctively adept at extracting energy from the environment, but we also expend great amounts of energy in doing so. A single sack of potatoes, for example, represents a considerable investment of energy: In manufacturing the fertilizers and pesticides that were used on the potatoes; on powering the machines that planted, fertilized, sprayed, and harvested the crop; in packing and transporting the harvest; and so on. In comparison with other animals, humans—especially in industrialized societies—live on a high-energy budget. Foragers are the dramatic exception to this rule.

In general, the primary source of energy that hunter-gatherers expend in food procurement is that contained in their own muscles. While they may invest energy in building shelters, traps, and even boats or weirs, relatively little effort is directed into the construction of a complicated infrastructure of food procurement—cleared fields, irrigation systems, or fuel-burning machines. As a result, hunter-gatherers spend much less energy to support a single unit of population than do other peoples. And since they generally support themselves rather well in terms of nutrition, leisure time, and general physical well-being, their system must be regarded as remarkably efficient.

They are efficient, too, in preserving their resource bases. Because of their low expenditure of energy and because they tend to exploit a wide variety of foods, hunter-gatherers place relatively limited demands on any one of their resources. At the same time, their way of life seems to limit their population growth; their numbers tend to remain proportionate to those of the animal and plant species on which they depend. The combined result of this adaptive strategy—low-energy needs, a wide resource base, controlled population—is that foragers interfere relatively little with other components of their ecosystems. Because humans are the most versatile predators in their habitats, they do affect the populations of the species on which they feed. However, their ecosystems appear to be in relative equilibrium and their resource bases may remain unthreatened, at least in comparison with those of other economic systems. This "conservationist" approach is largely inadvertent and easily altered by new technologies that have been introduced during periods of rapid population growth.

One such rapid expansion of population accompanied the development of agriculture in most parts of the world. With this development, many foragers became pastoralists or horticulturists, relying on domesticated plants and animals for their subsistence.

Later, as new agricultural techniques (such as irrigation and plowing with livestock) were introduced, horticulturists turned to intensive farming, which led to further growth in human populations. While the populations in some socities have stabilized, most are still experiencing population growth as new technologies are introduced. The resultant demand for ever more food encourages people to increase their efforts to produce reliable harvests.

Thus people come to reshape their environments—digging canals, planting crops, eliminating insects—and in the process they are locked into a struggle to maintain themselves at the expense of the equilibrium of the ecosystem. Of course, hunter-gatherers are also quite capable of over-exploiting their resources. The Miskito Indians of Nicaragua came close to wiping out the local turtle population. Though turtles are their primary source of protein, they were lured by cash payments from turtle-packing companies to hunt the sea animals to the verge of extinction. Fortunately, the nine-year war with the Sandinistas interrupted the commercial fishing operations and the sea turtle population has recovered. Now the Miskito are actively trying to gain rights to their sea territories so they can again use traditional means to manage this resource. No longer partners in the commercial fishing operation, Miskito communities are now fighting to preserve their valuable resource (Nietschmann, 1995). Likewise, when the native North Americans suddenly found themselves in contact with a European market for beaver skins in the eighteenth century, they hunted nearly to extinction an animal on which they had depended for centuries. In both cases, we see essentially the same process: Once people who have been exploiting a resource for a limited market (themselves) are tied in to an unlimited market, the attraction of short-term gains often leads to the depletion of the resource.

As these examples suggest, those hunting-and-gathering peoples who have preserved their resource bases have not necessarily done so because they embraced a conservationist ethic, although some may do so (Gottesfeld, 1995). Nor can it be safely claimed that they deliberately limit their population in order to adjust it to their resources. It appears, rather, that several interrelated factors have operated to maintain these peoples in balance with their resources. These factors include limitations imposed by their storage technology, the absence of a wider market for the food produced, the lack of fossil fuels, and other environmental conditions that constrain population growth. As we examine the Dobe !Kung (Ju/'hoansi) and the Eskimo (Inuit), we will see how people in two societies make a living and how various cultural practices contribute to their adaptation to harsh environments.

Social Organization

No one type of social organization inevitably issues from any food-procurement strategy, including foraging. The way foragers organize themselves politically and socially varies widely. However, since the environments of most recent and contemporary foragers tend to be the less-desirable habitats with relatively sparse and highly variable resources, the groups occupying these environments share certain broadly defined attributes of social organization.

Foragers typically live in small groups; camps of closely related families. The size of the camps, and of the society as a whole, is limited by the local supply of natural resources. Unlike agricultural societies, hunter-gatherers cannot easily increase food production to accommodate an increase in population. Their population levels reflect the availability of food during the worst season of the year, since for the most part they lack the technology for bulk food storage. When food (or even water) cannot be stored, the season in which the least food is available limits population, no matter how abundant food may be in other seasons. And since their lands today are marginal, their population densities are generally low. This, of course, was not true for many earlier populations where abundant and predictable food sources permitted large, settled concentrations of population such as on the northwest coast of North America.

A critical factor in the adaptation of modern foragers is the rule of **reciprocity**—that is, the systematic sharing of food and other goods. Food procurement is generally viewed as a family or household enterprise, and the tasks that it involves may be divided along sexual lines. While early studies identified men as hunters and women as gatherers, recent research has revealed that this division of labor is not universal. For example, among the Ache of Paraguay, men do considerable gathering along with the women (Hill et al., 1984), while in the Philippines, Agta women do a significant amount of hunting (Estioko-Griffin & Griffin, 1981). Regardless of this variation in gender roles, the individuals who do the hunting and gathering generally share their food with the entire local group. Rarely does anyone go hungry if others have adequate food, and no one has to work all day every day. Likewise, tools, ornaments, and other material possessions pass from hand to hand in an endless round of gift giving and gift taking so that inequalities of wealth are minimal.

Some members of a hunting-gathering band will have more influence than others and men tend to have more influence than women, but it is rare for anyone to have institutionalized power—that is, an office authorizing one person to make decisions for others. Decision-making power is spread fairly broadly among all the families in the group. Those who disagree are likely to simply move away.

Systems of social control in foraging groups also tend to be informal. Order is maintained on a day-to-day, consensual basis rather than through adherence to codified laws enforced by an administrative hierarchy. Codes of conduct and their enforcement are integral parts of the group's traditions, myths, and religious ideology. Both the definition of crime and the appropriate punishment reflect the consensus within the group at any given time. Some Eskimo, for example, had "dueling songs" to resolve all disputes except those involving murder (Hoebel, 1954). The two disputants, with their families serving as choruses, perform songs to express their side of the story and to vent their anger, and the winner is chosen by the applause of those attending the song duel. No decision is made as to who is right or wrong in terms of a body of law existing apart from public opinion. The most important thing is that the parties feel that the complaint has been raised and laid to rest; they then can resume normal social relations.

In extreme cases, individuals who repeatedly violate rules and social expectations in foraging societies may be ostracized by the group. But most commonly, the dispute is between two parties and if it cannot be resolved, the disputants and their families simply move apart.

This type of social organization, characterized by great fluidity, flexibility, and equality, is by no means inherent in the hunting-and-gathering way of life. When food resources are regularly available in relative abundance, foraging can support a highly structured cultural system accompanied by high population density. We know from archaeological evidence in the Old and New Worlds that some foraging societies of the past (much like fishing communities today) had large year-round settlements numbering several hundred members, with considerable inequality of status and wealth (Price, 1981; Hayden, 1994). Indeed, various groups of Native American hunter-gatherers lived in permanent villages, had chiefs and hierarchies of other officials, and observed rankings of wealth and power—all predicated on a complex division of labor that involved castes and slavery. They traded with other groups, conducted warfare, incorporated captives into their labor force, and so forth. In such complex foraging

Box 3.2

Adapting to Others:
The Batak Foragers of the Philippines

IT HAS BEEN GENERALLY ASSUMED that as hunting and gathering societies take up farming, they are almost immediately incorporated into the wider society and that they make a sharp transition from mobility to a sedentary lifestyle. In other words, as hunters and gatherers become more integrated with (and often dependent upon) the wider social system, it is assumed that they settle down.

James Eder, who conducted research among the Batak of the Philippines, a tropical forest foraging people, extends this line of reasoning. He postulates that the nature and direction of the changes a hunter-gatherer society undergoes as it becomes increasingly connected to the wider society are to some extent determined by its own cultural characteristics (Eder, 1988). Using historical accounts, interviews with the oldest Batak, and comparative observations of other hunter-gatherer societies, he has examined how Batak hunting and gathering practices have altered over the past hundred years as they incorporated other practices into their subsistence system. He also found that the Batak are becoming more, not less, mobile as they become more integrated in the wider society.

The Batak inhabit the mountains of central Palawan Island and are distributed in eight groups, each associated with a particular river valley. The number of households in each group range from three to twenty-four, and the groups are located between 3 and 10 km upstream from coastal Filipino villages. Like other contemporary hunter-gatherer societies, the Batak no longer rely exclusively on hunting and gathering for subsistence, although foraging still provides them with about half their basic needs. They are still able to provide for their subsistence exclusively by hunting and gathering for extended periods of time, even a year or more, as they did during World War II and during an unsuccessful government attempt to relocate them in 1970 (Eder, 1988, p. 38). Nevertheless, trade, horticulture, and wage labor are also part of their current economy. In fact, trade and horticulture are probably not at all new to the Batak, but wage labor emerged more recently, with the arrival of the first lowland settlers during the latter half of the nineteenth century. As the Batak became more involved with the settlers, their desire for lowland foods and manufactured goods increased and patron-client relationships rapidly evolved, tying individual Batak to individual settlers. An even more recent development has come in the form of foreign tourists, who have discovered the Batak, and now provide them with a minor source of income as guides.

Another change wrought by the arrival of settlers was in the Batak settlement pattern. When root crops were still the mainstay of Batak horticulture, periodic visits to swidden fields (partially cleared areas in the forest) were part of a pattern of year-around residence in temporary forest camps. However, today the Batak plant their swidden fields exclusively with upland rice, and during the agricultural season it is from their field houses that they make periodic foraging trips to the forest.

A further change in settlement pattern dates from the early twentieth century, when government officials encouraged the Batak to come down out of the mountains and settle permanently on the coast. In 1930, five of these coastal settlements were declared to be reservations exclusively for Batak use. The legal disposition of the land was never clear, and in any event the settlements were too small to provide the Batak with adequate subsistence. Thus, although the Batak did build houses on the reservations, they never occupied them full-time. In fact, by the 1950s the reservations were overrun with non-Batak settlers and the Batak, in a pattern of movement that still continues, began relocating their settlement sites further up their respective river valleys, leaving themselves relatively isolated but conveniently situated for access both to the lowland areas and the forests (Eder, 1988, p. 40).

Eder uses seven criteria against which to measure changes in Batak hunting and gathering practices: seasonality, encampment duration (mobility), encampment size, resource utilization, division of labor, hunting technology and length of workday.

Seasonality. Eder's data showed that forest camps were used more frequently during the first six months of the year (when the weather is dry and not suitable for agricultural pursuits) than the latter six months (which are mainly rainy and swidden-oriented). Since the Batak do most of their hunting and gathering from forest camps, his data suggest a marked seasonality in contemporary foraging. Although he concedes that this may always have been the case, his own view is that it is a more recent development: The tropical monsoon forest in which the Batak live has a distinct dry season that would promote growth of edible plants; in addition, the Batak themselves maintain that they once lived off the land and state that in any season at least a few of the eight species of wild tubers they utilize are available (1988, p. 44).

Encampment Duration. According to Eder's informants, in the past forest camps would be occupied for periods of up to three to four weeks. Today, the occupation periods are considerably shorter, usually a matter of two to seven days. The reason for this is that individuals now must balance the demands of hunting and gathering against those of cultivation and participation in the market economy. Occupation periods are now shorter, and forest camps are left, not for other camps, but to return to swiddens and settlement houses. Although the encampment duration is short, the Batak spend 40 percent of their time in camps of one sort or another—indicating that they now have a greater rate of residential mobility (Eder, 1988, p. 45). However, the shorter duration of encampments makes travel to and from camps more costly in terms of energy—energy expended over several days rather than weeks. The Batak also do not make their camps as far away from the settlements and from one another as they did in the past, and thus resources are more quickly depleted in regularly visited areas. The energy costs of round-trip travel to camps are further increased because today the Batak bring along a lot more baggage: Pots and pans, flashlights, radios, and so on (1988, p. 53).

Encampment Size. Eder found that it was rare today for more than seven households to camp together, whereas in the past thirty to forty households would commonly join forces. In part this is due to demographic changes—there are simply fewer Batak today. However, more significantly, Eder traces the change to the same scheduling conflicts that affect encampment duration. Each household has a different swidden location, the timing of their agricultural cycle differs, each has a different set of ties to lowlanders. "Not everyone, in effect, can get away to the forest at the same time" (1988, p. 46).

Resource Utilization. Eder offers two explanations of why the Batak today utilize a much narrower range of plant and animal resources than in the past. First, wild resources are seasonally available and cannot be utilized if their availability coincides with the planting or harvesting season. Second, not only are the Batak aware that the lowlanders consider them "primitive" because of the forest foods they use, they also regularly obtain many lowland foods (sugar, coffee, etc.), which may have changed their preferences for traditional foods (1988, p. 48).

Division of Labor. Eder found that there have been subtle changes in the division of labor as a consequence of certain foraging activities being discontinued, the depletion of game, and the fact that from August to October the women harvest the rice fields while only the men occupy forest camps. This latter development has had the consequence that today, over the period of a year, husbands sleep separately nearly 10 percent of the time—a new phenomenon among the Batak (1988, p. 49).

Hunting Technology. Traditionally, the Batak hunted with blowguns. However, the use of blowguns ceased after World War II and now the chief weapons are spears, used in conjunction with hunting dogs, bows and arrows, and homemade guns.

Length of Work Day. Although he has no time allocation data from the past with which to compare his own observations, Eder concludes that contemporary Batak work longer hours. He bases his conclusions on the fact that at least some foraging now is for trade as well as subsistence and that the women are now involved in making articles for use in agriculture, such as harvesting baskets and rice-drying mats.

Eder concludes from his study that despite the fact that the overall returns of hunting and gathering for the Batak today ought to be higher than in the past—fewer Batak forage in the same location, and they stay for shorter periods of time—they are, in fact, lower. Because the Batak are now engaging in a range of economic activities, none will be as remunerative as they would be if pursued full-time. Not only has Batak hunting and gathering ceased to be as successful as it once was, Batak horticulture, because it is pursued only part-time, also does not create the returns that, for instance, the lowlanders' farms do. On the other hand, they are sucessfully maintaining themselves and have been quick to incorporate new technologies into their subsistence system.

In the light of recent findings, including Eder's, it is necessary to reexamine many anthropological theories regarding the relationship of hunting and gathering societies to the wider social systems into which they are becoming integrated. One should not assume that change is a simple process whereby traditional hunter-gathers are absorbed or quickly overwhelmed by contact with farming populations. Also, one need not assume that increased participation in agriculture is inevitably associated with increased sedentism and decreased mobility. People are resourceful and innovative; hunters and gathers no less than others.

Kwakiutl dancer and leader Charlie George of Blunder Harbour, B.C. in 1950. Coastal waters rich in marine life supported a large population of village-dwelling hunter gatherers before the arrival of European settlers.

(William Heick)

societies, competition among individual and groups was intense and, as Hayden suggests, very closely related to the fact that certain resources were abundant, concentrated, and capable of being stored or transformed into political power and prestige. In short, they very much resembled advanced agricultural societies.

Settlement Patterns and Mobility

A major concern of anthropologists who study human-environmental interaction is the manner in which people distribute themselves over the landscape. What is the nature of the settlements they occupy? How frequently, if at all, do they move? How are such decisions affected by the variability of resources from place to place and from time to time? Forager groups today tend to be nomadic. Their seasonal migrations on their home ranges are adjusted to the availability of resources in different places at different times. Once again, the limits of storage and transport technology are important. Most foragers deal with variability in resources by moving people to the food rather than by moving food to the people.

Often the camps of related families form larger groupings, called **bands**, within a territory. The members of a band may come together at one or another of these camps for ceremonies, or the band may simply be an aggregation of people who regularly intermarry. The bands are strikingly flexible in their composition, expanding and contracting in response to fluctuations in resources. When certain resources are scattered, the members of the bands also scatter. Later, when game converges in one area or when large permanent water holes offer the only available water, camping groups come together again to exploit these resources jointly. Social habits also play a part in the flexibility of the bands. Groups are continually reforming as families visit or entertain their kin, move away from bands with which they do not get along, or move into bands that are short on people or long on resources and fellowship. Generally, foragers exhibit a territorial system of land use; that is, they identify a particular tract of resources as belonging to a particular local group with outsiders having limited access (Gottesfeld, 1994). The main source of variability in this is the degree to which usage is exclusive and the willingness of the putative owners to defend their territory by force.

While most contemporary foragers make use of mobility to track seasonal food sources, more sedentary patterns can be found. The Kwakiutl of the American northwest coast, the Chumash of Southern California, the Ainu of Japan, and the Andaman Islanders of India are foraging groups whose members lived in large, sedentary villages. In such cases, the key factor seems to be the availability of large quantities of stable and storable resources. Especially important are environments containing great quantities of fish and shellfish, which are often fairly concentrated, predictable, and abundant. Also, as we see in Box 3.2, *Adapting to Others: The Batak Foragers of the Philippines*, one should not be too quick to generalize about the relationship of sedentism to foraging or farming.

Resilience, Stability, and Change

Of all the adaptive patterns, that of foragers interfered the least with the resilience of their ecosystems. While interaction and exchange occur, ties of dependency between families (and especially between groups) are minimal. These people adjust to the environment by making use of any local resource that is abundant. At the opposite extreme are societies such as our own, that use a vast array of chemical and mechanical strategies to control the environment irrespective of changing conditions.

The viability of the hunter-gatherer strategy is based on the limited degree to which environmental problems are transmitted from one group to another. Some groups succeed; some fail. Yet this is the food procurement strategy that humans employed as they became the dominant species on earth. It is interesting to note one circumstance in which this form of adaptation came into direct competition with a technologically more advanced system of procurement. As we will see in greater detail in Chapter 7, the Vikings of Norway settled Greenland in the tenth century and maintained colonies whose economy was based on farming, seal hunting, and fishing. They did not, however, adopt the patterns of hunting used by the indigenous Eskimo, whom they feared and despised. The Viking practices were not well-adapted to the environment in Greenland and the settlers were unable to secure food in sufficient abundance to support themselves. Eventually, the colonies died out, leaving Greenland once again the exclusive domain of the Eskimo (Pringle, 1997; McGovern et al., 1988, 1996).

The superiority of the indigenous hunter-gatherer adaptations to the European technology introduced into Greenland is not an isolated instance. In 1846, Sir John Franklin and his entire expedition

(two ships, 200 men) starved to death in the heart of Netsilik Eskimo territory, presumably because they could or would not use Eskimo food-procurement techniques (Cyriax, 1939). The Burke and Wills expedition of 1861 attempted to cross Australia from south to north and return; all but one explorer starved to death as they refused to forage and or accept assistance from the Aborigines until it was too late (Moorehead, 1963).

Let us now examine two foraging populations that illustrate the points we have been stressing. Keep in mind, though, the warning regarding the rapid changes that such peoples everywhere are undergoing. The two societies we will explore are those of the Dobe Ju/'hoansi, or !Kung, of southwest Africa and the Inuit (or, as they are still commonly referred to, the Eskimo) of Alaska and northeast Canada.

The Dobe Ju/'hoansi

The Ju/'hoansi are one of five culturally related groups of southern african who are known collectively as the San. The San are something of a historical mystery.[1] An educated guess is that they once occupied most of southern Africa but were eventually displaced by successive waves of Bantu and European invaders. Those who were not killed or absorbed into the invaders' populations were gradually forced back into the arid wastes of the Kalahari Desert and its surrounding areas in Botswana, Namibia, and Angola. Most of the estimated 50,000 San who still live in and around the Kalahari are slowly being absorbed by the surrounding agricultural, industrial, and pastoral communities although they still maintain their distinct cultural identity.

The several hundred Ju/'hoansi San who live in the Dobe area, on the northern edge of the Kalahari, are an exception. Although the Dobe Ju/'hoansi have been in contact with Bantu and Europeans since the 1920s, share water holes with Bantu pastoralists, and sometimes work for them, the majority (over 70 percent) were almost self-sufficient hunters and gatherers at the time they were first

---

[1] Until recently, they were known as Bushmen, a name given to them by the Dutch who settled in South Africa in the seventeenth century. Africanists, however, now prefer the term San, which means "original settlers" in the Cape Hottentot dialect. The population described here was often referred to as the !Kung; Richard Lee, who has worked with them since 1962, advocates referring to them as they prefer to call themselves—which is the Dobe Ju/'hoansi (pronounced "doebay zhutwasi"). To confuse matters further, the preferred usage of the Botswana government is Basarwa.

Figure 3–1. *!Kung territory*

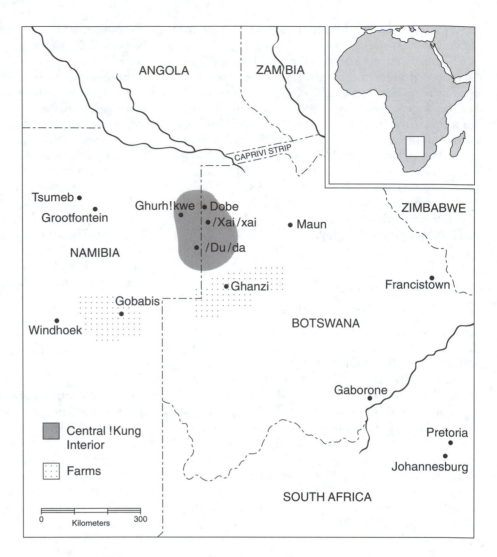

studied by contemporary anthropologists. Since their way of life has changed dramatically, our description will begin with how they once lived and conclude with their present situation. In the mid-1960s, when Richard B. Lee lived with them, they had no interest in agriculture, herd animals, or firearms. They neither paid taxes to nor received services (except for smallpox vaccinations) from the government of Botswana. They traded with neighboring Bantu pastoralists but worked for them only occasionally. Thus, although the Dobe Ju/'hoansi are not isolated, until recently they were largely independent—mainly because they occupy territory that no one else wants.

Until 1992 they were in the middle of an international power struggle among white-ruled South Africa, Angola, and Namibia, a newly independent state. As a consequence, the Ju/'hoansi's traditional freedom of movement was severely curtailed beginning in the early 1970s. Parts of their territory are still divided by a massive chain-link fence. Many

Ju/'hoansi were employed by the South African army as scouts, and all, willingly or not, are involved in the processes that are transforming this once remote land. Their situation is changing rapidly, and in all likelihood the life we describe will soon be transformed beyond recognition. As Richard Lee has remarked, those working with the Ju/'hoansi in the 1980s and 1990s find it hard to visualize the society that he found and described in 1965, and thus came to conclude that he had misinterpreted what he had witnessed (1993). We will refer to both early and recent accounts, beginning with an account of their way of life when Lee first encountered them.

Climate and Resources

The Dobe area is an inhospitable environment for humans, a fact that has protected the Ju/'hoansi from invasion and assimilation, if not from contact. Dobe is a transition zone between the Kalahari Desert to the south and the lusher regions, inhabited mainly by agriculturists and pastoralists, to the north. It consists of semiarid savanna with a scattering of trees and grasslands and very few permanent water holes. The temperature ranges from below freezing on winter nights to 37°C (100°F) in the shade during the summer. Even more variable than the temperature is the rainfall. For six months of the year, the area is completely dry; during the other six months, there are heavy rains. Furthermore, rainfall varies considerably from year to year. In 1967–1968, for example, rainfall in the area was 250 percent greater than it had been in 1963–1964 (Yellen & Lee, 1976). Such variation in rainfall, along with the sandiness of the soil, makes agriculture impossible. Nor is the area an ideal hunting ground; because the vegetation is scattered, it cannot support large migratory herds.

Nevertheless, the Ju/'hoansi manage a livelihood in this habitat, in part because they exploit such a wide variety of resources.[2] Despite the extremes of climate, Dobe supports about 500 species of plants and animals. Of these resources, the Dobe Ju/'hoansi use about 150 plants and about 100 animals and they eat approximately 100 species of plants and 50 animals (Yellen & Lee, 1976). They gather wild nuts (chiefly from mongongo trees), berries, melons, and other fruits; dig for roots and tubers; collect honey in season; and hunt everything from warthogs, kudu, and leopard tortoise (three favorites) to springhare, guinea fowl, and rock pythons. The larger animals, such as the antelope and kudu, are shot down with poisoned arrows. The Ju/'hoansi hunt the smaller animals with dogs or trap them in ingenious snares. Very young animals, inept at running, are sometimes simply chased and snatched up. Although the Dobe Ju/'hoansi definitely prefer some of these foods to others, their versatility in using a wide range of resources ensures that they are seldom without something to eat.

Most of their other needs are also easily supplied by the resources of the area. Their huts are constructed of branches and grass found throughout the area. Ostrich eggshells, also readily available, make ideal water containers. A wooden digging stick, whittled in an hour, lasts several months. A bow, arrows, and a quiver, which take several days to make, last years. The people's few luxuries—ostrich eggshell necklaces, thumb pianos, intricately carved pipes, and children's toys—are likewise made from materials readily at hand. Indeed, there is only one important resource that the Dobe Ju/'hoansi traditionally obtain through exchange with other groups: Iron for making tools. But even in this case they exercise a certain independence: They collect scraps of metal from the Botswana Veterinary Station fences to make arrowheads.

Limited in their needs and resourceful in filling them, the Dobe Ju/'hoansi have little difficulty obtaining food and raw materials. The scarcity of water is the major problem, and it is this factor that in large part makes the Dobe Ju/'hoansi a nomadic people.

Settlement Patterns

As rainfall determines the availability of water in the Kalahari, it also determines the people's settlement patterns. During the dry season, from June through September, the Ju/'hoansi congregate in relatively large camps of about twenty to forty people around the large permanent water holes, the only available sources of water (Yellen & Lee, 1976). In this period, the people rely primarily on roots and tubers found within a day's walk (about a six-mile radius) of their camps. The cool, clear weather makes for good tracking and hunting, and small groups of women periodically hike to the mongongo forests to collect nuts. By August, however, many of the preferred local foods have been eaten up and rising temperatures make hunting and long gathering treks hard and uncomfortable. At this time, the Ju/'hoansi turn to less desirable foods—gums and the larger, bitter-tasting roots and melons that they passed up a month or two earlier.

But this period of austerity does not last long. In October the rains begin, filling the hollow trees and the standing pools in the upcountry with fresh water and transforming the parched landscape into a lush green, thick with new plant and animal life. This is the season of plenty. The Ju/'hoansi now separate into groups of perhaps two or four families and scatter over the land to take advantage of the new crop of fruits, melons, berries, and leafy greens and the new generations of birds and animals that follow the rains. For seven to eight months the small groups move from camp to camp, staying an average of about three days in each spot and returning periodically to the permanent water hole. This pattern continues through April, when the pools of water begin to dry up. In May the wandering upcountry groups return to the permanent water hole to set up new camps, and the cycle begins again (Yellen & Lee, 1976).

[2] In the mid-1960s their population was 466—379 permanent residents and 87 seasonal visitors (Lee, 1968, p. 30). In this discussion we will rely heavily on the preliminary work of Richard B. Lee and Irven Devore, along with the more recent writings of the rest of their Harvard team, many of which are collected in *Kalahari Hunter-Gatherers* (1976), edited by Lee and Devore. We also use Lee's monograph, "The Dobe Ju/'hoansi" (1993) and Wilmsen's 1989a book.

The !Kung are extremely mobile. They construct huts in two or three hours and can abandon them in minutes.

(M. Shostak/Anthrophoto)

The Dobe Ju/'hoansi, then, are an extremely mobile people. Accordingly, their goods are the kind that can be moved easily or left behind. Even houses fall into this category. When a group sets up camp, in a matter of two or three hours each woman constructs a small hut (perhaps 1.5 meters—about 5 feet—in both height and diameter) for her own nuclear family. The huts are arranged in a circle around an open space where the camp activity takes place. Very little goes on in the huts. Indeed, it is unusual to find anyone inside a hut, except perhaps a person who is taking a nap or seeking shelter from a storm (Draper, 1976). A hut serves simply as a storehouse and as a marker, a sign of a family's residence in the camp. When the camp is broken up, the huts, representing little investment of time, energy, or material, are abandoned. Each member of the Ju/'hoansi tribe can pack all of his or her possessions into a pair of leather carrying sacks and be ready to move in a few minutes (Lee, 1993, p. 43).

Social Practices and Group Composition

The Dobe Ju/'hoansi are very gregarious people; they spend about a third of their time visiting other camps and another third entertaining guests. (The size of the camp Lee studied on his first trip varied from twenty-three to forty persons in a single month.) This tradition of conviviality, along with fluctuations in the availability of resources, keeps the Ju/'hoansi on the move. The two factors should not be thought of as independent. In fact, the habit of visiting is probably an adaptation to the necessity of adjusting the populations of camps to local resources. It also facilitates exchanges of information about game and other matters of concern to the dispersed local groups. Both Lorna Marshall (1961, 1965) and Richard Lee (1993) describe the constant babble of voices at night in Ju/'hoansi camps, when residents and visitors exchange notes on rainfall and water holes, ripening vegetables and fruits, and animal tracks in what amounts to a debriefing.

Ju/'hoansi social customs provide not only for short-term visits but also for much lengthier stays. When a couple marries, for example, the husband moves to the wife's camp for an indefinite period of **bride service**—payment for his bride in the form of labor—and he may well bring his parents or a sibling with him. Usually he stays with his wife's people until the birth of their third child (about ten years). At that point he may return to the group into which he was born (perhaps taking some of his wife's kin along), or stay where he is, or move to a camp where one of his brothers is doing bride service or where his wife's siblings have settled. Bride service may also have evolved as a way for parents to keep their brides, who can be as young as nine or ten, at home for a longer period of time (Lee, 1993, p. 66). Since people are marrying later today, this service is also changing.

Such shifts are not limited to bride-service graduates. Any Ju/'hoansi family may leave their group and move into another group where they have kin. Kinship is interpreted very broadly. The Ju/'hoansi recognize ties among all individuals who share the same name, and address all of that person's relatives by kinship terms. Because the number of names used among the Ju/'hoansi is limited, a person is quite likely to find a name-mate in camps where he or she has no relatives and be welcomed there too. Thus the Ju/'hoansi have considerable freedom of choice with regard to residence. Lee (1968) estimates that every year about a third of the population makes a shift in group affiliation.

These changes in group composition, like the rounds of brief visits, help the Ju/'hoansi to tailor the populations of their camps to local resources. At the same time, the flexibility of the group helps to prevent quarrels from turning into serious fights, which are carefully avoided. The Ju/'hoansi are keenly aware that they all possess poisoned arrows and that fights have been known to end in killing. To avoid such an outcome, families that cannot get along together simply separate—one or both of them moving to another group.

Reciprocity

The Ju/'hoansi have a saying, "Only lions eat alone." One of the characteristics that distinguish human beings from other animals, they are saying, is sharing and exchange. Though all humans share periodically, the Ju/'hoansi system of distributing goods is characterized by continuous giving and receiving of gifts. Reciprocity, or *hxaro*, is the basis of their economy and much of their social life as well (Lee, 1993). *Hxaro* is practiced daily as adults hunt and gather over a wide area. Working individually or in pairs, they find a variety of foods that they share with the entire camp.

It is easy to over-romanticize the altruism of this system. The appropriate distribution of food is a common cause of quarreling among the Ju/'hoansi. The way the day's take is divided depends on a variety of factors. In some cases, as when someone has brought in a large animal, the distribution is rather formalized. The owner (the person who owns the fatal arrow, whether or not he actually killed the animal) divides the meat into portions according to the size of the hunting party. The recipients then cut up their shares and distribute them among their relatives and friends, who in turn give pieces to their relatives, and so forth, until everyone has eaten.

The size and distribution of shares of meat are matters of individual discretion, but the Ju/'hoansi take care to meet their families' needs and to repay past generosity. Smaller animals and vegetables are distributed more informally. A family may invite someone standing nearby to sit at their fire, send children to neighbors with gifts of raw or cooked vegetables, or take fatty bits of meat and nuts with them on a visit. Thus each family's dinner is a combination of the food its members collected and the food they are given. The exchange of food constitutes an effective system that permits each family to store up good will and obligation against times of need.

The various artifacts used or enjoyed in daily life circulate in a similar manner. When a person receives an arrow or a dance rattle as a gift, he keeps it for a few months then passes it on to someone else with the expectation of receiving a gift of more or less equal value in the future. As with food, the giver expects no immediate return, nor is there any systematic way to calculate the relative worth of gifts or to guarantee that the other person will reciprocate in kind. The Ju/'hoansi consider bargaining and direct exchange undignified, and although they trade with the Bantu, they never trade among themselves. Food sharing and gift giving are based on norms of reciprocity that are understood and accepted by all Ju/'hoansi; as they put it, "we do not trade with things, we trade with people" (Lee, 1993, p. 104).

Quality of Life

We have briefly described the Dobe Ju/'hoansi's way of life. Before Lee and his colleagues began their study of these people, it was widely assumed that the Dobe Ju/'hoansi (indeed, all foragers) waged a constant struggle for survival, battling hunger and poor nutrition from day to day. After all, the Ju/'hoansi live in an area where game is scarce, their weapons are unsophisticated, and they have no way of storing their food. On the surface, they seem to lead a precarious, hand-to-mouth existence. Yet as Lee established through his painstaking research in the 1960s, the appearance bears little relation to the reality. In comparison with some other groups, the Dobe Ju/'hoansi lead secure and easy lives (Lee & Devore, 1968; Lee, 1969, 1993).

Diet and Nutrition

From July 6 through August 2, 1964, Lee kept a diary of subsistence activities at an average dry-season camp. (Remember that this is a period of relative scarcity.) Each day he recorded the number of people in camp, the number that went out to hunt or gather, and the hours each spent acquiring food. He weighed all the animals the hunters brought back to camp during this period and all the bags of nuts and other foods that the women acquired in the course of each day's foraging. He even counted the number of mongongo nuts the Ju/'hoansi cracked and consumed in an hour. By dividing the population of the camp in a given week into the total amount of meat and vegetable foods acquired and then into the total number of hours devoted to their preparation, Lee was able to calculate the Ju/'hoansi work week and daily consumption of food. The results were surprising.

Lee found that the vegetable foods the women gather account for the bulk of the Ju/'hoansi diet by weight; the meat that the men bring in amounts to only 20 to 25 percent. Meat, then, is a delicacy for the Ju/'hoansi, not a staple. The reason is obvious: A man who spends four hours hunting may kill one animal (this is the average), whereas a woman who goes out to gather vegetable foods always finds something for her family to eat, even if it is not an especially choice item. Lee estimates that gathering is 2.4 times as productive as hunting in the Dobe area. One man-hour of hunting brings in approximately 800 calories; one woman-hour of gathering, approximately 2,000 calories. Thus the success of the hunt is not the critical variable in survival as it was once thought to be. It is vegetable foods, not meats, that form the basis of the Ju/'hoansi diet—and it is the women, not the men, who are the chief breadwinners in Ju/'hoansi society.

Drought-resistant mongongo nuts are the Ju/'hoansi staple, making up 50 percent of the vegetable diet. The average daily consumption (about 300 nuts) provides an individual with 1,260 calories and 56 grams of protein—the equivalent of 2.5 pounds of rice or 9 ounces of lean meat. In addition, everyone in the camp Lee studied ate an average of about 9 ounces of meat per day. Together mongongo nuts and meat gave each person 2,140 calories and 92.1 grams of protein per day—well over the U.S. recommended daily allowance (1,975 calories and 60 grams of protein) for small, active people such as the Ju/'hoansi.

Not only do the Ju/'hoansi eat well, they do so with little effort. By counting the numbers of hours each person devoted to acquiring food during the twenty-eight-day period, Lee discovered that by Western standards the Ju/'hoansi invest relatively little energy in the quest for food. Typically a man will spend five or six days hunting, then take a week or two off to rest, visit, and arrange the all-night dances that the Ju/'hoansi hold two or three times a week. Furthermore, it is not at all unusual for a man to decide his luck has run out temporarily and take a month's vacation. The women also have considerable leisure. In one day a woman collects enough food to feed her family for three days. Household chores take between one and three hours. Plenty of free time is left to rest, visit, and entertain. Lee calculated that the average Dobe Ju/'hoansi adult spends only six hours a day acquiring food, two and a half days a week—a total of fifteen hours a week.

Demography

The work week figures are all the more surprising when one considers Ju/'hoansi demography. It was once thought that few people in such societies lived beyond what we consider middle age. This assumption, too, has proved to be unfounded—at least for the Dobe Ju/'hoansi. Lee found that 10 percent of the Dobe residents were over sixty years old. These old people do not participate directly in food procurement. Neither do the young, who constitute another 30 percent of the population. Unlike other African foragers, Ju/'hoansi children do not actively contribute to subsistence activities; they are kept in camp or with their mothers until adolescence (Jones et al., 1994, pp. 189–215); a fact that puts a greater strain on those who actively provision the family. (Ju/'hoansi do not expect young people to work regularly until they marry, usually between ages fifteen and twenty for women, twenty and twenty-five for men.) Thus, 40 percent of the population are dependents who live on the food that the young and middle-aged adults bring in. Such a proportion of nonproducers is surprisingly high, resembling that in agricultural communities.

At first glance these figures may suggest that if the Dobe Ju/'hoansi worked harder, they could support a much larger population. This is not the case, however, for while the people as a whole could certainly spend, say, twice as many hours collecting food, the Dobe environment could not produce twice as much food for them to collect or twice as much water for them to drink.

This observation brings us to a factor that seems to be crucial to the Dobe Ju/'hoansi's way of life: The control of population growth. The well-being of any group, human or otherwise, depends in large part on the ratio of population to resources. For hunter-gatherers this ratio is especially critical, since, unlike agriculturists, they cannot increase their resources.

The Dobe Ju/'hoansi are particularly interesting in this regard, for their fertility is unusually low. On the average, Ju/'hoansi women do not become pregnant again until four years after the birth of the previous child. The Ju/'hoansi do not have a long postpartum taboo (that is, prescribed abstinence from sexual intercourse after childbirth), nor do they use chemical or mechanical birth control devices. The women of Dobe attribute their low fertility to "the stinginess of their god, who loves children and tries to keep them all to himself in heaven" (Howell, 1976, p. 147). Prolonged breast feeding is probably a factor. Because they have no soft foods on which to wean infants, Ju/'hoansi mothers nurse their babies for at least three years, until the child is able to digest the tough foods of the Ju/'hoansi diet (Draper, 1976). Breast feeding is not a guaranteed birth control technique, but it does inhibit ovulation to some degree. Nancy Howell has suggested that gonorrhea, probably introduced through contact with Bantu and Europeans, may have reduced the fertility of some Ju/'hoansi women. Of course, infant mortality, including occasional infanticide, is also a factor in the wide spacing of Ju/'hoansi siblings. Twenty percent of infants die in their first year (Howell, 1976).

This factor of controlled population, along with other factors that we have discussed (high mobility, flexibility of group membership, reciprocity, and a low energy budget) allows the Ju/'hoansi to strike a balance with their environment. This is not to suggest that the foraging life does not have its own hazards and limitations. Climatic and other disturbances can cause hunger, even starvation. By keeping their numbers and their energy needs low and by operating on the principle of flow—flow of groups over the land, flow of people between groups, flow of resources among people—they are able to fit their needs to what their habitat has to offer from day to day. As a result, they live a relatively easy life; they eat well, work only in their middle years, and have time to rest and play. They are also well-prepared for hardship. In times of shortage, Bantu pastoralists fare worse than the Ju/'hoansi, and Bantu women turn to foraging with the Ju/'hoansi to feed their families. Though the Dobe Ju/'hoansi may not qualify as "the original affluent society," as Marshall Sahlins has termed the early hunter-gatherers, their adaptive pattern is still remarkable in that it yields them such a stable and comfortable existence within such an austere habitat.

Traditional diet in the Dobe area relied heavily on nuts, roots, and grass seeds gathered by women.
(M. Shostak/Anthrophoto)

The People of the Dobe Today

In 1963, three-quarters of the Dobe area people had been relying on hunting and gathering and there was a virtual absence of institutions associated with the state and a market economy: Stores, schools, clinics, feeding stations, drilled wells, or air strips. In 1967, the first trading post opened near the region (although the Ju/'hoansi had no money) and also a fence was erected that cut them off from their nearest neighbors, the Nyae Nyae. Since foraging was greatly restricted by the fence and since the government offered assistance in starting cattle herds, many began to build semipermanent mud-walled houses near cattle kraals (enclosures). Many, too, became dependent on government feeding programs, a problem made worse by the game laws of the 1980s that limited their rights to hunt. Even the shape of the village changed, reflecting a changed social order (Lee, 1993, p. 156). Instead of houses drawn up in a circle, the new ones are all in a line and focused on their private property, the herds. While formerly their diets had made them a population with remarkably low levels of serum cholesterol and a general absence of heart disease, this has changed (pp. 156–157). Their present diet is dominated by refined carbohydrates, together with heavy tobacco and alcohol consumption. Many men were induced to sign up with the South African Army during its long war in Angola, dramatically increasing the cash in circulation. The film, *N!ai: The Story of a !Kung Woman*, documents the militarization and alcohol-induced brawling that characterizes some settlements.

Namibian independence from South Africa in 1990 has brought its own changes, some good and some bad. On the negative side, the people of the Kalahari have become relatively poor and are a weakly represented minority in their own lands.

Positively, the new government is recognizing their rights to control their own traditional lands and to restrict outsiders from setting up commercial ranches at will, although elements of this have yet to be worked out (Lee, 1993, pp. 164–165).

Not all has changed; when Richard Lee and others returned, they found familiar faces and people caring for each other and sharing in the manner they recalled from the 1960s. Moreover, the people have retained their dignity and cultural self-identity. Lee attributes this to what he calls their "communal mode of production" and egalitarian spirit (1993, p. 174). This has enabled them to persist in the face of integration into the contemporary market economy. People still take care of one another and, while eager to accumulate consumer goods, they take care to do so within limits. Care for the elders and the infirm is seen as natural—their entitlement—and not a burden. There are lessons for us here, he concludes.

The Inuit or Eskimo

Until quite recently the Eskimo peoples[3] who lived on the vast, treeless plains (or tundra) and along the changing coastlines of the Arctic were isolated from the rest of the world by their formidable environment. Like the Dobe Ju/'hoansi, they occupied land that no one else wanted and so for centuries they remained self-sufficient hunters and gatherers, relatively uninfluenced by the agricultural and industrial societies that grew up to the south of them in the more fertile regions of the North American continent. The Inuit Eskimo language family, dialects of which are spoken by the dispersed people we will be describing, is distributed over a vast area, from Northwest Alaska and Canada to the coasts of eastern Greenland and Labrador. For this reason we shall refer to them as Inuit (Burch, 1994).

Since the beginning of this century the isolation of the Inuit has slowly broken down. Money has become an important factor in their relationship with their environment. While most Inuit groups are fully settled today, some are still hunter-gatherers and in some ways resemble the Dobe Ju/'hoansi. At the same time, because of cultural changes resulting from their buying and selling in the world market

and because of their residence in the United States and Canada—not to mention their unique habitat—they provide an interesting contrast to the Ju/'hoansi.

The Arctic Ecosystem

If the Dobe seems an inhospitable environment, the Arctic circumpolar region of North America seems almost uninhabitable. Throughout much of the region, from October through July, the waters are locked in ice while the land lies frozen and almost bare of plant and animal life. During this period (the local population's fall, winter, and spring), the Arctic animals, with the exception of seals and walruses, either migrate south or hibernate. By midwinter the ice is six to seven feet thick. Temperatures during the eighteen-hour Arctic nights may drop from a mean of −16°C (−30°F) to −27°C (−50°F). Forty-mile-an-hour winds with gusts up to seventy miles an hour are common. In the Hudson Strait area, forty-five-foot tides build walls of broken ice along the coast, making navigation extremely hazardous.

In most years, the freeze continues into late July. Then this land on top of the world enjoys a brief summer. Temperatures rise above freezing, and daylight lasts as long as twenty-two hours. Lichens, mosses, shrubs, and tufted grasses sprout on the tundra, attracting a variety of wildlife: Herds of caribou, musk oxen, polar bears, foxes, rabbits, and migratory birds. Seals and walruses bask in the sun; whales may appear; large schools of salmon run downriver to the sea in July or thereabouts, returning to inland lakes in August. But this Arctic summer lasts a short six to twelve weeks. The sea begins to ice over in late September, and the long freeze begins once again.

Foraging in this environment is quite different from living off wild foods in the Dobe area. Except for the summer berries, there are no vegetables, edible roots, or fruits in the Arctic; the long, dark winters, incessant winds, poor soil, and short growing season discourage plant life. The Inuit's subsistence strategy is centered on animal life—on hunting, fishing, and, to a lesser extent, trapping and gathering of duck eggs, clams, and the like. And whereas the availability of water largely determines the migrations of the Dobe Ju/'hoansi, it is the availability of animals and fish that structures the Inuit's patterns of movement.

The Seasonal Migrations

Like the Dobe Ju/'hoansi, most circumpolar populations are to some degree nomadic people, changing the sizes and locations of their camps as their

[3] Our discussion will be based primarily on Asem Balikci's now-classic study (1970, 1989) of the Netsilik Eskimo of northeastern Canada and Ernest Burch's study of the Inupiat in northwestern Canada (1970, 1994) with reference also to William B. Kemp's study (1971) among the Baffin Island Eskimo and a recent summary and synthesis by William Sturtevant and David Damas (1984). Keep in mind that the various groups we describe are widely separated and that among the Eskimo there are many variations in language, custom, and ways of making a living.

resources change with the seasons. The pattern of these migrations is essentially the same as with the Ju/'hoansi: Dispersal in small groups in the season of plenty, concentration in large groups in the time of scarcity. Again employing the ethnographic present, we will examine the pattern of livelihood and social life of one population, the Netsilik Eskimo, and then turn our attention westward to their distant relatives in Alaska.

In the summer, when food is abundant, the Hudson Bay Netsilik Eskimo traditionally form small groups of twenty to thirty people consisting of one or more extended families, and move inland to take advantage of fish runs and caribou migrations. Each August, for example, the Netsilik carry their belongings up the waterways to the stone weirs (circular dams) they have built to trap schools of salmon. Some of the fish are eaten raw, on the spot; the rest are dried and stored for the winter.

Toward the end of the month the group packs up once again and moves farther inland to await the coming of the caribou. Depending on the terrain, the Netsilik may construct knife-lined pits in the caribou's paths (which are well-known to the Inuit) or stalk them with guns, much as in earlier days when they hunted with bows and arrows. Another common technique is to stampede the animals into a trap. Howling in imitation of wolves, a few men drive the herd into a narrow valley where hunters lie concealed, or into a river where the hunters wait in kayaks. Caribou provide not only meat but also another crucial resource, skins for clothing. In 1970, Balikci estimated that a family of four needs about thirty skins to see them through each winter. In October and November the Netsilik live primarily on food stored during the caribou hunts, supplemented by occasional fresh fish and musk ox. The most important activity in this period is making winter clothing, a job that is performed by the women.

In December, the scattered Netsilik come together once again in their winter camps along the bays and straits, where fifty, sixty, or as many as one hundred people join forces to hunt the major cold-season resource—seals. Although some seals migrate south for the winter, others remain in the Arctic, digging breathing holes up through the sea ice. (Seals need air every fifteen to twenty minutes and dig several holes.) Hunting seals in midwinter involves hours of silent, motionless waiting at the breathing holes, harpoon in hand. For much of the winter, seals plus an occasional fox are the only sources of fresh food.

In May or June, when the ice begins to melt, the Netsilik move to tents on solid ground. Hunting seals is easier and more productive in these months,

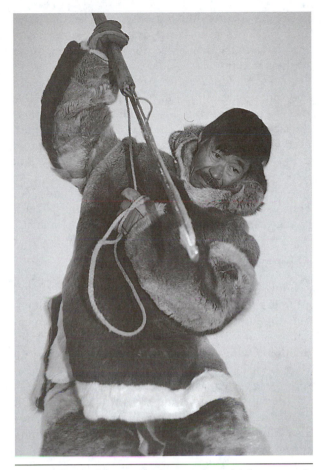

Most Eskimos have turned to modern, high-powered rifles, but they complain that these weapons have destroyed the mutual trust between animals and humans.
(Gordon Wittsie/Peter Arnold Inc.)

for the animals often come out of the water. By July the ice starts to crack and seal hunting becomes dangerous, so the Netsilik camps divide once again into smaller groups for their annual inland treks (Balikci, 1989, chap. 2).

The Inuit's seasonal round is similar to that of the Dobe Ju/'hoansi, but there are important differences between the patterns of the two groups. For one thing, the Inuit, unlike the Ju/'hoansi, can store food. When fish are running and game is abundant, they collect as much as they can and smoke or store the surplus in stone or ice caches. However, the cold also requires the Inuit to work on a higher energy budget than the Ju/'hoansi. In such a climate, simply to stay alive (to say nothing of hunting) requires a relatively high-calorie diet. Furthermore, the Inuit have to invest a good deal of energy in the task of protecting their bodies from the cold: Building shelters (traditionally igloos in the winter and skin tents in the summer), making clothing (multilayered garments, boots, and mittens), and heating their shelters (with seal-oil lamps or kerosene stoves). And they have to feed their sled dogs, a vital component of their traditional nomadic way of life.

These activities require not only considerable energy but an accumulation of material goods. While the Ju/'hoansi travel light, the Inuit, with their dogsleds and snowmobiles, motorboats, tools, rifles, clothing, lamps, and stockpiles of food, have a good deal to carry around. Furthermore, their tents and igloos, unlike the Ju/'hoansi's disposable huts, take time to build and cannot be lightly abandoned. Hence, even during the summer season, the Inuit change camps much less often than the Ju/'hoansi.

Demography

From what we can gather from early explorers' and ethnographers' accounts, this way of life did not enable the Inuit to support sizable numbers of dependents, or at least not in bad years. Old and sick individuals who could not keep up with the group were occasionally left behind to manage for themselves—in other words, to die (Balikci, 1970). Furthermore, the unequal sex ratio in some Inuit groups at the turn of the century suggests that they also limited the number of the dependent young through female infanticide (see Freeman, 1971; Balikci, 1970, 1989).

In some cases, population controls were probably quite deliberate attempts at family planning. The threat of hunger is a recurring theme in Inuit conversation, even in communities where the evidence indicates that hunting accidents have caused many more deaths over the years than hunger (Kemp, 1971)—and one way to stave off hunger is to limit the number of nonproducers to ensure that at least some children survive. The archaeological record does contain evidence of some large and formal villages that were exceptions to this pattern, but they appear to have been short-lived.

The ratio of population to food resources may become a more realistic worry in the near future, for Inuit populations are rapidly increasing. With improved health care supplied by the United States and Canadian governments, the mortality rate has declined steadily in recent years. At the same time, their fertility rate has increased. In the Inuit community of Wainwright, Alaska, for example, the average woman gives birth to nine or ten live children in the course of her reproductive years. The average Dobe Ju/'hoansi woman, on the other hand, has five. As a result, the population of this group is growing at a rate of 3 percent a year (Milan, 1970), six times

the 0.5 percent rate of the Dobe Ju/'hoansi. Other groups are expanding at similar rates, putting a strain on their ecosystems.

Social Relationships

The Inuit, like most other hunter-gatherers, have extensive networks of kin, but the most important social unit is the extended family. This is considered to be the "real family." Jean Briggs notes in her study of the Uktu in Hudson Bay (neighbors of the Netsilik), "Whenever possible, it is with their 'real family' that the people live, work, travel, and share whatever they have. Moreover, it is only with their 'real family' that they appear to feel completely comfortable and safe" (1970, p. 39). These extended families are organized into larger kin groups that generally camp and work together. Like the Dobe Ju/'hoansi, however, Inuit families have considerable latitude in choosing the people with whom they will camp. It is common for everyone in an Inuit society to be considered kin to everyone else—if not by blood, then by marriage, adoption, or shared names (a practice that we have already seen among the Ju/'hoansi). These extensive ties allow families to shift about on short-term and long-term visits and thus enable the Inuit to adjust the makeup of their groups according to the availability of resources and personal preference, especially in the scattered inland camps during the summer and fall.

In their personal relationships, the Inuit place great value on restraint. Demonstrations of emotion are frowned upon. Briggs (1970) noted that Uktu husbands and wives and their older children never kiss, embrace, or even touch one another in front of anyone else. Even more unwelcome is a show of negative feelings, especially anger. To these Inuit, the ideal personality traits are shyness, patience, generosity, and an even temper.

It is no surprise that many local populations traditionally had no formal group leadership. Though a man with a reputation for wisdom or expertise in hunting may come to have some influence in decision making, anyone who tries unabashedly to impose his will on others is regarded with deep suspicion. Likewise, the Inuit have no formal code for dealing with people who violate social norms. Stingy or bad-tempered individuals are not directly criticized or punished; rather, the others will try to soothe or tease them out of their folly. If this strategy does not work, the offender is simply avoided. The worst punishment that Inuit societies can inflict is ostracism, a very serious threat in harsh Arctic conditions.

The Impact of Modernization

After Balikci's investigation, William Kemp (1971) made a careful study of energy use in one of the last all-Inuit communities on Baffin Island, to the north of Netsilik territory. The value of his observations lie in his documentation of the effects of new technology on energy use. These were changes that have transformed all Inuit communities, including the Pella Bay community studied by Balikci.

The village Kemp studied consisted of four households whose total population varied from twenty-six to twenty-nine over the period of the study. Three of the families lived in wood-frame tents covered with skins and old mailbags that the people had sewn together and insulated with a layer of dry shrubs. These tents were heated by traditional seal-oil lamps. The fourth family lived in a prefabricated wood house supplied by the government and heated by a kerosene stove.

This house was not the village's only sign of industrial technology. Among them, the villagers owned two snowmobiles, a large motorized whaling boat, and a twenty-two-foot freight canoe with an outboard motor, along with several large sledges and thirty-four sled dogs. In 1971 hunting was still the most important subsistence activity, but they were also hunting with rifles as well as harpoons. The younger men spent only part of their time hunting; they also mined soapstone and carved it into statuettes for export, and some of the young men left the village periodically to work for wages at government construction sites. In one year, village members earned $3,500 from carvings, $1,360 from animal skins, $1,225 in wages, and $670 in government subsidies.

Energy Flow among the Baffin Islanders. Kemp's 1971 analysis of energy flow in this small community was similar to Lee's study of the Dobe Ju/'hoansi's subsistence practices and standard of living. But Kemp had to take into account the use of fuel as well as muscle power, the hours spent working for wages as well as foraging, and the acquisition of store-bought as well as wild foods. To calculate the energy flow, he reduced both the number of hours individuals spent at various activities and the various foods they acquired and consumed to the common denominator of kilocalories (thousands of calories). This procedure enabled him to analyze in considerable detail the sources of energy, the routes along which it flowed, and the uses to which it was put.

Kemp calculated that over the fifty-four weeks during which he kept records of village activities, the

An Inuit woman shopping in a supermarket in Baffin Island, Canada. Even though all now purchase most of their food from shops, hunting remains culturally and nutritionally important.

(Kevin Fleming/Woodfin Camp & Associates)

Inuit expended some 12.8 million kilocalories of human energy in hunting, mining, and carving; working for wages; taking care of household chores; traveling; and visiting. In addition, they used 885 gallons of gasoline, 615 gallons of kerosene, and 10,900 rounds of ammunition. During the same period they acquired 12.8 million kilocalories in wild food for human consumption (plus 7.5 million kilocalories in food for the dogs) and 7.5 million kilocalories in store-bought food. Thus important sources of energy lie outside the local economy, and indeed the Inuit are as dependent on industry and fossil fuels as is the rest of North America's population. They may spend more time and energy in hunting, but such activities as wage labor and soapstone carving force them to depend on critical inputs of imported energy.

When observed, the Inuit ate well. Game—primarily seal but also whale, caribou, and other animals—remains their dietary staple, accounting for 85 percent of their food. In Pella Bay, the villagers have given up seal hunting and rely mostly on caribou, which has a better taste, and does not involve traveling far from the settlement. The Baffin Island villagers rarely bought canned meat and vegetables, though they did purchase sugar, powdered milk, quantities of flour and lard for bannock (a pan-baked bread), and small amounts of such delicacies as peanut butter and honey. Kemp estimates that this combination of wild and store-bought food provides each adult with 3,000 calories a day. The Inuit's calorie intake, then, is about 50 percent higher than that of the Dobe Ju/'hoansi. Their protein intake,

The contemporary Inuit settlement of Igaluit, Baffin Island, Canada. Recent changes in Canadian law that gives native peoples control over their resources has transformed Inuit society in recent years.

(Bryan & Cherry Alexander)

accounting for 44 percent of their calories, is also quite high—a reflection of their heavy dependence on game. Of their remaining foodstuffs, 33 percent are in the form of carbohydrates and 23 percent in fat. Such a diet fortifies them for the exertions of Arctic life. Kemp noted, however, that when the men of one household abandoned hunting for a month to work for wages and the family ate only store-bought food, 62 percent of their diet consisted of carbohydrates and only 9 percent of protein—an unhealthy balance. Such a diet resembles that of the poor in North American cities, who rely heavily on factory-prepared snack foods.

Changes in Settlement Patterns and Hunting Techniques. The products of industrialization—motorized vehicles, high-powered weapons, store-bought foods—have affected the relationship between the Inuit and their environment throughout the circumpolar region. Almost everywhere the people have become sedentary, living in year-around villages or towns. Settling in towns has meant that Inuit children can attend schools near their homes; going to high school no longer means that a student has to move to a distant boarding school (Burch, 1994). Snowmobiles and boats enable hunters to travel to their hunting grounds in a relatively short time, so it is no longer necessary for the whole village to pack up and move. Store-bought food provides the insurance against hunger that was once provided by sea-

sonal moves to exploit a wide variety of game. However, caribou is still an important food item among the Inuit (Burch, 1994), and it is easily hunted with new high-powered rifles.

While many Inuit value the introduction of the rifles, some complain that it has destroyed the mutual trust between humans and animals (Kemp, 1971). Seals are wary of the rumbling motors and rifle reports; only young animals can be coaxed within shooting range. Also, when guns were first introduced in the late nineteenth century they led to the near-extinction of native caribou herds. Today, however, caribou have been reintroduced and are now regulated by the U.S. government (Burch, 1994).

The Inuit point out that rifles are not necessarily better than their old weapons. In the spring, for example, seals fast, losing their winter layer of fat; when melting snow reduces the salinity of the water, the animals are less buoyant. Unless an animal that has been killed by a rifle is immediately secured with a harpoon, it will sink—a fact that renders long-range weapons useless. Kemp notes that in one thirty-hour session of continuous hunting, the Inuit killed thirteen seals but retrieved only five.

Kemp observed that, in the fall, the hunt yielded enough food to last through the winter, so the villagers were able to spend more time visiting than hunting in February, March, and April. Although they might have used this time to collect extra skins for trading (and perhaps dangerously reduce the seal

Box 3.3

Claiming the Land

IN ALASKA, THERE HAS BEEN A profound transformation in the economies and ways of life of indigenous peoples in the course of the Cold War and in the aftermath of oil exploration. During the long period of rivalry with the former U.S.S.R, the U.S. government considered Inupiat territory on the Beaufort Sea to be a front-line area. While building bases offered a certain amount of employment, traditional patterns of hunting and fishing were disrupted by the appropriation of 4,500 acres (as an air base) and all of Barter Island—causing forced relocations (Chance, 1990, p. 141). Later, following several years of planning in which the Inupiat were not invited to participate, the Atomic Energy Commission, with the support of the Alaskan state government, announced a plan to detonate one or more atomic weapons in Inupiat territory in order to create an artificial harbor (Chance, 1990, pp. 140–143). This occasioned such local outrage that people organized in opposition, thus for the first time creating a united Inupiat political organization devoted to securing their aboriginal land rights—a movement that came to cooperate with other Native American political action committees (Chance, 1990, pp. 140–143). Soon they were able to defeat the proposed harbor project and, more importantly, set in motion a political mechanism—the Alaska Federation of Natives—for dealing with nonindigenous forces—namely, the state and federal bureaucracies, oil companies, and business interests. This organization was soon to become a significant political voice.

After years of litigation, Inupiat and other Alaskan populations have received substantial allocations of land as well as a percentage of oil and gas royalties. While welcome to many, it is, for others scant compensation for what they have lost—their autonomy. Oil wealth has transformed life; the village of Katovik where Norman Chance had lived in 1958 now has modern housing, a new school with an indoor pool, government offices, and shops (1990, pp. 200–201). While subsistence and nutrition are still based on fishing and hunting, the Inupiat use three-wheelers and snowmobiles to check their nets and take game. While the older generation retain the old skills, the younger, educated members of the community do not have the self-reliance of their parents. They are, however, being educated in modern facilities, they travel widely, and they are finding employment in the larger U.S. economy. This, in turn, has given them a new perspective on their personal needs—one that is much like that shared throughout the American population. The dilemma facing the Inupiat—indeed, all of us—is how these new needs can be satisfied in the face of unequal distribution of wealth and without even greater environmental risks being taken (Chance, 1990, p. 218).

population in the process), they chose to travel instead. Whether this choice was based on conservationist concerns is debatable. The people may have been conscious of the need to preserve the supply of wild game. They may also have decided that the returns on hunting were simply less than those gained from the time spent on craft production, wage labor, or even than the rewards of visiting friends and relatives. Practices that limit hunting—visiting days, the soapstone industry, even the custom of observing Sundays as a day of leisure—help the Inuit maintain a balance between their needs and their resources.

Adaptation is not simply a matter of the direct interplay between technology and the environment. Rifles and snowmobiles do not inevitably spell ecological disaster, for social customs intervene between technology and the uses to which it is put. The need to earn money through carving takes young men away from the hunt. And the same snowmobiles that enable them to kill more sea mammals give them the option to forgo hunting and visit distant kin when they have enough to eat.

Surviving in the Modern World. The Inuit ethic of sharing is evident in the way the Pella Bay Inuit adapted to the introduction of the mission store. As the Inuit became more and more integrated into the wider market economy, the original store was replaced by a cooperative store, owned and managed by the Inuit to serve the community. This proved to be a successful operation, not only addressing the needs of those who wanted to buy and sell goods, but also providing an interface between the community and the government, negotiating for government contracts and the like. The co-op became "the principal economic integrator of the community and the mediating agency between the community, the government and the Euro-Canadian economic system in all matters of commerce and economic enterprise" (Balicki, 1989, p. 253).

While modernization has transformed the lives of the Inuit, they have managed to retain elements of their traditional culture. Despite the physical distance that now exists between members of a kin group, they maintain ties through telephones and CB radios. In the Inupiat territory, in northwestern Alaska, where 74 percent of the population is Inuit, the Inuit language remains in use and is taught in schools, and traditional food is still preferred by most. In Box 3.3, *Claiming the Land*, we see how the Inuit continue to change and how they have begun to fight for the rights to their land.

In September, 1988, the Canadian government passed legislation giving the Inuit and other native peoples of the Canadian northern territories formal title to their extensive and potentially resource-laden lands. The economic and social future of the Inuit appears to be far brighter than that of other contemporary hunters and gatherers.

Summary

THE FORAGING ADAPTIVE PATTERN, WHICH HAS been dominant for much of human existence, is illustrated in this chapter by the Dobe Ju/'hoansi of the Kalahari Desert and the Inuit of northeastern Canada.

Foraging peoples traditionally have been self-sufficient but they are becoming less so as they become less isolated from the dominant societies around them. Unlike societies that cultivate their food resources, hunter-gatherers eat what nature provides and diversify their diet to accommodate fluctuations in resources. Survival necessitates an adaptive pattern that balances resources, the group's technology, and its social organization.

Foragers typically live in small, flexible groups that can scatter when natural resources become scarce and converge when resources again become plentiful. Some hunter-gatherers move regularly from campsite to campsite as resources become available in various locations; others occupy a permanent settlement from which they move to temporary camps to exploit seasonally available resources. Their kinship system creates ties over large areas, so that people can move in and out of groups as resources fluctuate. Reciprocity—the sharing of food and other goods—also allows hunter-gatherers to adapt to fluctuations in resources. Their systems of decision making and social control tend to be informal.

One reason for the success of hunter-gatherers is their low energy budget. They invest relatively little energy in the quest for food resources and obtain substantial returns. Their traditional adaptive strategy of low energy needs, a wide resource base, and a controlled population results in minimum interference with their ecosystem. Hunter-gatherers risk wiping out their resources when they attempt to exploit them for an unlimited world market.

The Ju/'hoansi San occupy the Dobe area on the northern edge of the Kalahari Desert. They are able to satisfy their needs and live comfortably in this inhospitable region by exploiting a wide variety of resources. Seasonal migrations are necessary because of fluctuations in the availability of water. The nomadic Ju/'hoansi possess only goods that can be moved easily or left behind. Social practices contribute to the mobility of the Ju/'hoansi and the flexibility of their groups. The Ju/'hoansi enjoy visiting kin in other camps, and bride service can take families to other groups for indefinite periods. Flexibility in group composition helps tailor population size to local resources and also helps to reduce friction among group members.

Although meat (hunted by men) is a prized resource, vegetables and fruits (gathered chiefly by women) are the staples of the Ju/'hoansi diet. The quality of the Ju/'hoansi's life is apparently quite high; their diet is nutritionally sound and procured with relatively little expenditure of energy, and they enjoy a great deal of leisure time. A low birth rate is crucial to the Ju/'hoansi adaptive pattern.

The Inuit have traditionally depended on a seasonal quest for animals to provide food, clothing, tools, and fuel. Contact with the world market, however, has eroded the isolation and self-sufficiency of the Inuit.

The Arctic environment dictates the adaptive patterns of the Netsilik of northeastern Canada and the Baffin Island Inuit. These people change the sizes and locations of their camps as their resources change with the seasons. In the summer they disperse to take advantage of abundant food, and in the winter they come together to hunt seals. Unlike the Ju/'hoansi, they are able to store food for the long winters but their climate forces them to adopt a higher energy budget than that of the Ju/'hoansi and to accumulate material goods (such as heavy clothing, snowmobiles, lamps, and rifles) that reduce their mobility. In the past the Inuit have kept their population level in harmony with their food resources, but now their population is rapidly increasing, with a resultant strain on their ecosystem.

Extensive kinship ties allow the Inuit, like the Ju/'hoansi, to move easily in and out of groups, but the most important social unit is the extended family. The Inuit frown on shows of emotion or of negative feelings. They have no formalized leadership or code of social control.

A study of the Baffin Island Inuit revealed that their intake of energy is high and their output low. They hunt seal, caribou, and other animals, and catch fish in weirs (circular dams) they have built of stone. Their natural resources are supplemented by store-bought food, particularly the ingredients to make bannock (unleavened bread baked in a shallow pan) and such items as snowmobiles and kerosene stoves.

Industrialization is changing the life of all Inuit. Seasonal migrations are no longer necessary, as they can quickly travel to their hunting grounds by snowmobile, and store-bought food provides insurance against hunger. The introduction of high-powered weapons almost led to the destruction of the Inuit's traditional resource base, but the U.S. government intervened and the caribou herds have returned. Today most Inuit live in villages with most of the amenities of contemporary North American life. Still, they retain their languages, social identities, and many traditional food preferences.

The Inupiat of Alaska illustrate some of the problems contemporary U.S. native peoples face as well as how they have organized to take at least some political control over their own destinies.

Key Terms

bands

bride service

ethnographic present

low-energy budget

reciprocity

Suggested Readings

Bailey, R. C. (1991). The behavioral ecology of Efe Pygmy men in the Ituri forest, Zaire. *UMMA Anthropological Papers*, 86. Ann Arbor: Museum of Anthropology, University of Michigan. A detailed volume of Efe foraging activity with a focus on time allocation and hunting returns, using a socioecological approach.

Biccheiri, M. G. (Ed.). (1988). *Hunters and gatherers today: A socioeconomic study of eleven such cultures in the twentieth century.* Prospect Heights, IL: Waveland Press. Historical reconstructions and ethnographies provide a general perspective on the adaptations of hunters and gatherers.

Burbank, V. K. (1994). *Fighting women: Anger & aggression in aboriginal Australia.* Berkeley: University of California Press. Contemporary and controversial, this book focuses on the aggressive behavior of Aboriginal women in Australia and offers an interesting perpective on domestic violence.

Burch, Ernest S. Jr. & Ellanna, Linda J. (Eds.). (1994). *Key issues in hunter-gatherer research.* Oxford: Berg. A collection of recent articles based on research among contemporary hunter-gatherers, with an introduction and concluding sections dealing with the general state of such research and its prospects.

Chance, N. A. (1990). *The Inupiat and arctic Alaska: An ethnography of development.* Fort Worth: Holt, Rinehart & Winston. A detailed account of how one population has coped with a changing political environment and sucessfully gained control of much of their traditional lands.

Howell, N. (1979). *Demography of the Dobe Ju/'hoansi.* New York: Academic Press. A thorough analysis of two years of demographic fieldwork with the Dobe Ju/'hoansi that uses stable population theory for its perspective on the functioning of this group.

Lee, R. B. (1993). *The Dobe Ju/'hoansi.* Fort Worth: Harcourt Brace College Publishers. A broadly oriented case study on the hunter-gatherer way of life of the Ju/'hoansi of the Kalahari Desert, exploring topics such as subsistence techniques, kinship, religion, and environment.

Peterson, N. & Matsuyama, T. (Eds.). (1991). Cash commoditization and changing foragers. *Senri Ethnological Studies 30.* Tadeo Umesao, gen. ed. Osaka: National Museum of Ethnology. A collection of eleven essays that address the effects of cash and commoditization processes on recent foraging societies on four continents.

Schrire, C. (Ed.). (1984). *Past and present in hunter-gatherer studies.* Orlando, FL: Academic Press. This collection of papers attempts to understand both the past behavior and current ways of life of hunter-gatherers by focusing on the history of their interactions with other peoples.

Siskind, J. (1973). *To hunt in the morning.* New York: Oxford University Press. An intimate account of fieldwork among the Sharanahua Indians of the Amazon jungle. It is especially interesting for its emphasis on the way modernization is affecting this population.

Sturtevant, W. C. (Ed.). (1984). *Handbook of North American Indians*, vol. 5, Arctic. Washington, D.C.: Smithsonian Institution. Part of an encyclopedic summary of the information available about the prehistory, history, and cultures of the aboriginal peoples of North America in archaeological and ethnographic accounts. The organization of these volumes is by geographical area. Volume 5 deals with the special problems of the regions and populations that together form the Arctic habitat zone.

Turnbull, C. (1961). *The forest people.* New York: Simon & Schuster. An intimate view of the Mbuti Pygmies of equatorial Africa that explores the relationships of the people to the forest and to their horticultural neighbors.

Wilmsen, E. N. (Ed.). (1989). *We are here: Politics of aboriginal land tenure.* Berkeley: University of California Press. An anthropological investigation that explores the issues of aboriginal relations to land and territory.

Winterhalder, B. & Smith, E. A. (Eds.). (1981). *Hunter-gatherer foraging strategies.* Chicago: University of Chicago Press. A collection of ethnographic and archaeological analyses that apply optimal foraging theory.

Chapter 4

Subsistence Agriculture

In Zimbabwe, a man and his sons burn trees and brush to open a circular field on which they will plant millet; in Brazil, a woman pushes seed yams into the soil of her irregularly shaped garden; in Peru, a family works together to place stones to form a terrace that they will plow in order to plant corn. These mundane, everyday acts, taken cumulatively, sustain many of the earth's some 5.5 billion people. This chapter will look at societies that practice agriculture relying primarily on localized inputs: Human labor, locally made tools, and, if used at all, animals for traction (plowing, pumping, and transport). Such forms of agriculture are often termed *subsistence agriculture*; production, even if traded, sold, or bartered, is primarily aimed at household provisioning rather than investment.

Food production, however simple or complex in terms of technology, is the very foundation of contemporary human existence. Foraging, as we have seen, involves the collection of naturally occurring food resources in a given habitat with relatively little intervention or management. Agriculture involves the domestication and management of edible species that characteristically cannot survive or reproduce without human assistance. We have no direct evidence that people who lived in prehistoric times consciously or unconsciously tried to influence the reproductive cycles of the species on which they depended, but since they were intelligent, experiments certainly occurred. Over the ages, however, as people and animals and plants interacted, selective pressures changed the reproductive success of the animals and plants favored by humans.

These changes need not have resulted from a conscious manipulation of a species by the people who used it. Such changes could have come about as inadvertent by-products of the way people were altering their environment—being selective in the killing of members of a particular population, for example, or harvesting grain in such a way as to change the genetic makeup of seeds by selectively retaining some and discarding others. Such selective pressures eventually led to *domestication*, the process by which people began trying to control the reproductive rates of animals and plants by ordering the environment to favor their survival—protecting them from pests, predators, and competitors, for instance, and supplying them with water and nutrients. Ultimately these efforts led to agriculture, one of the most significant achievements of the human species.

The development of agriculture irrevocably affected the course of human cultural history. The full impact of these changes can be seen in the societies that practice intensive agriculture (discussed in Chapter 6), the most productive and technologically sophisticated form of food production. But the contrast from the hunting-and-gathering adaptation can be seen clearly even in societies that practice a modest and comparatively simple form of agriculture: Horticulture.

Horticulture, meaning "garden cultivation," is almost always accompanied by some reliance on hunting, fishing, and collecting wild plants. However, unlike hunter-gatherers, horticulturists depend primarily on domesticated foods, especially plants; and unlike intensive or industrialized agriculturists, they raise these plants in small plots using relatively simple methods and tools. Agricultural techniques, along with other forms of behavior, vary widely from group to group. Yet the shared procurement strategy—production of food crops primarily for personal consumption—creates certain broad similarities in settlement patterns, social organization, and interactions among groups. First, we will examine how the strategy developed and its general features. Then we will focus on two specific groups of farmers: The Yanomamö of Venezuela and Brazil, who live in a tropical rain forest; and the Himalayan Tamang of Nepal, who have adapted to a high-mountain habitat by means of plow agriculture combined with animal husbandry. Although these cases represent very different technologies, they share the fact that human labor is the main input, they can produce themselves all or most of the tools they need for farming, and their households are highly self-sufficient.

The Horticultural Adaptation

Development

By approximately 12,000 years ago a number of local populations in the upland areas of Mesopotamia in the Middle East had started to grow crops, and by 10,000 years ago most of the people of the Middle East had come to rely very heavily on wild cereals: Wheat and barley (Fagan, 1992, p. 290ff). This development was closely paralleled in Asia and Africa as well. By about 9,000 years ago, there were signs that people had begun to plant and harvest crops and to domesticate various animal species. This shift in adaptive pattern is of great interest to anthropologists and because it ultimately set in motion greater changes in social life and technology than had occurred over the preceding millennia.

While the earliest evidence of cultivation and herding appears in the Middle East, where wheat and barley were the first staple crops, horticulture also appeared early in China and Southeast Asia. Surprisingly, millet, not rice, was the primary crop in early Chinese cultivation. The origin of rice, one of the world's most important crops, is still poorly understood. While our knowledge of the domestication process in Africa is incomplete, there is evidence for the cultivation of sorghum, millet, and a variety of other plants that dates back some 4,000 years. In Mesoamerica and South America, cultivation appeared thousands of years later than in the Old World. Corn, beans, and squash were the important crops cultivated in higher-altitude areas; manioc was grown in coastal zones.

Some archaeologists have suggested that agricultural experiments began when humans noticed plants growing from seeds in their garbage dumps. There is evidence that hunter-gatherers were well aware of the relationship between plants and seeds, and it is possible that horticulture began with tending useful herbs. The interesting question is why hunter-gatherers would give up a stable existence for one that requires substantially more work.

However one judges the record, it is clear that people came to exercise more control over their environment. Ultimately, they chose more productive resources, stored seeds, selected from among the seeds those most likely to generate productive plants, and altered the conditions under which the plants were growing by removing weeds and supplying additional water.

Despite many regional differences, the common thread underlying the development and spread of agriculture is that it accomplished population growth or, at least, pressure on resources, and the instability that accompanied it. The most common early strategy for solving the problem of food procurement was to move to a new location, but as population levels became high in relation to available resources this alternative became less possible and more settled patterns of existence resulted. This new pattern of sedentism probably upset the balance between human groups and the resources on which they depended. When mortality, fertility limitations, or migration were not sufficient to keep a population within acceptable limits, some groups began to manipulate the natural availability of resources (by planting, etc.). This strategy made it possible to sustain a larger number of people without depleting their resources. As these groups grew and spread, other groups imitated their practices. Because they could increase the carrying capacity of their environment in ways in which hunter-gatherers could not, horticulturists became more predominant.

It is important to emphasize that the initial expansion of horticulture did not occur because it was a universally superior adaptation to hunting and gathering. People often had to work harder. Analyses of skeletal material from the time periods suggest that overall health decreased and disease and malnutrition increased. But the increased productivity and reliability of the food supply provided the basis for further population growth, a cycle that has continued to the present. Both depend on the elaboration of methods of cultivation.

Energy Use and the Ecosystem

The objective of any form of agriculture is to increase the amount of predictable or reliable energy that a given unit of land can yield for human use. Although horticulturists usually extract far fewer food calories or other products per acre than do plow farmers (let alone modern, intensive farmers), they also expend less labor than intensive agriculturists. They use neither their land nor their labor to the fullest. Simply producing enough to feed the family takes much less work than people are capable of doing, so that many of the able-bodied (such as adolescents) may not have to work at all while those who do work may do so intermittently and spend more time hunting or in other activities. That is not to say that horticulturists are lazy. They may simply have more options as to how to use their time. A comparison of four populations in the Brazilian Amazon finds that while all hunt to acquire needed protein, those who live in the best horticultural areas hunt the most. Meat is a desired luxury and the men can afford the time to seek it (Werner et al., 1979, pp. 303–315). Horticulturists have time left over after the minimum required subsistence tasks to devote to elaborate food preparation, ceremonies, and luxury items beyond their basic needs.

In general, the lower the energy demands a human group makes on its environment, the less the group alters that environment. Clifford Geertz, in an early and very influential discussion of the subject, has argued that swidden farmers in the tropical lowlands do not so much alter their ecosystem as create "a canny imitation" of it (1969, p. 6). Their ecosystem contains a remarkable diversity of living things packed in a small area; that is, the ecosystem is generalized rather than specialized. Although

tropical soil is often thin, it can support this dense variety because the nutrients are rapidly recycled rather than being locked up in deep soil. The dense canopy of trees prevents this layer of rich organic soil from being washed away by rain or baked hard by the sun.

The plots of the swidden farmers copy these qualities of the tropical forest. Unlike the specialized fields of most intensive agriculturists—all rice or all tomatoes—the swidden plot contains a jumble of crops, from roots and tubers to fruit trees and palms, flourishing primarily in a bed of ash. Like the trees of the uncultivated forest, the domesticated trees of the swidden plot form a cover that filters sun and rain, thus protecting the soil from erosion or parching and at the same time reducing the encroachment of undergrowth. And within a few years this plot reverts back to forest.

Horticulture differs from intensive agriculture in several ways. First is the relatively simple technology associated with this type of farming. Only small and often scattered plots of land are cultivated at one time, and they are usually worked without the help of plows or animal traction, to say nothing of machines. The only tools used are simple hand tools: Knives, axes, digging sticks, and hoes. In other words, horticulturists, like hunter-gatherers, still rely mainly on the energy stored in their own muscles in order to procure their food.

Second, in comparison with intensive agriculture, horticulture provides a relatively low yield per acre of land; for this reason, it is frequently categorized as **extensive agriculture**. For every unit of energy produced, horticultural methods require much more land than intensive agricultural techniques. The amount of energy horticulturists extract from the land is enough to sustain them, but they generally do not produce large food surpluses for the purpose of trade. While trade is often of concern to horticulturists, usually it is for the acquisition of items produced by another population. Exceptions occur when horticulturists are in close contact with hunter-gatherer groups, from whom they may acquire animal products. The Mbuti Pygmies of northeastern Zaire, for example, are a hunting people that supply their Bantu-speaking horticultural neighbors with meat and honey from the forest (Peacock, 1984, p. 15).

Third, in general, horticulture allows for household self-sufficiency. Each group, and in most cases each household, is capable of producing most of the food it needs. Most important production decisions are made at the household level. Horticulturists need not depend on other groups for food because they cultivate a wide variety of crops with an exceedingly modest technology. This orientation toward self-sufficiency is one of the reasons that the production of horticultural societies remains low.

Horticultural Cultivation Methods

Most contemporary horticulturists occupy marginal territories: Either tropical regions, where soil is thin; or arid regions, where the water supply is a constant problem. In this respect, they resemble hunter-gatherers. They often have been excluded by competing groups from better-favored lands where intensive agriculture is possible. In such circumstances, they cope with the challenge of agriculture in several ways. They may concentrate on crops that make few demands on the soil. They may plant next to rivers or in areas that flood in the rainy season. They may plant in several locations so that if one field fails, another may still feed them, or they may shift their fields regularly to avoid depleting the soil. Many horticulturists use several of these techniques. The last, however, which in its present form is called **slash-and-burn agriculture**, or **swidden agriculture**, is the most common.

Slash-and-Burn Agriculture. Slash-and-burn agriculture is a method of farming in which fields are cleared, the trees and brush are burned so that the soil is fertilized by the ash, and the fields are then planted. Each field is used for perhaps two or three years, then it is left to regenerate for about ten years while the farmer moves on to other fields. Swidden agriculture was practiced in Europe until the beginning of the Christian era and in North America until about the seventeenth century. (Indeed, it has been suggested that one reason for the success of the European colonists in North America was that they imitated the slash-and-burn techniques of the Native Americans.)

Unfortunately, all too often traditional horticultural plots are being consolidated into open-field farms and ranches in environments unsuited to such enterprises. The Amazon rain forest is being burned and bulldozed at an ever-increasing rate to make way for ranches and open-field farms (Posey, 1984, pp. 95–96), whereas horticulturists such as the Yanomamö (whom we will meet shortly) have managed to exploit the rain forests without harming the environment. With more intensive land use in the same areas, the thin soil rapidly erodes.

The slash-and-burn technique demands a fine sensitivity to the environment. Swidden farmers must know exactly when to move their fields and when to replant a fallow field. They must also make rather precise calculations as to when to burn—on a day when there is enough wind to fan the fire but not enough to spread it to the rest of the forest. Horticulturists in general (swidden and otherwise) know an enormous amount about their environment, including minute details about different kinds of soil, about the demands of different kinds of plants, and about the topography and microclimate of their habitats. This knowledge is the secret of their survival.

Polyculture. The mix of crops, or **polyculture**, can vary considerably among swidden cultivators even in the same general region, as studies in the Amazon have shown (Flowers et al., 1982, pp. 203–217). Earlier studies have emphasized the diversity of crops and the apparent helter-skelter aspect of horticulture—a complex mix of plants and trees that is as ecologically diversified as the forest itself. Recent work shows that very often the people rely on one or two main crops but intersperse them with useful trees; the planting is not done in a random or unplanned fashion, but is carefully patterned so that as the garden ages different crops become available in turn (see Flowers et al., 1982; Beckerman, 1983; Boster, 1983). Thus even the return to fallow is carefully regulated, each stage providing some product to the cultivators.

All agricultural systems, at least temporarily, simplify specific portions of their natural ecosystems. It is also claimed that fertility is sustained by the complementary characteristics of different plants: The nutrient enriching tendencies of some balancing the nutrient robbing tendencies of others.

Social Organization

Horticultural or extensive farming societies, however varied, tend to share a number of very general characteristics when compared with low-energy budget foragers. One is **sedentism**, the practice of establishing a permanent, year-round settlement. Whereas hunter-gatherers invest time and energy in moving from place to place to find food, farmers invest their energy in increasing food production in one place—their fields.

Population density is also generally higher. In a group that is not on the move constantly, infants, old people, and sick people have a better chance of surviving. The fertility rate may go up, for when men are no longer called away to the hunt, they spend more time with their wives (Binford, 1968). Similarly, storage, which equalizes the distribution

Box 4.1

Learning about Monoculture from the Mountain Ok

POLYCULTURE (THE PLANTING OF more than one crop in a field) has long been considered the key to ecological stability and sustainable, reliable yields in traditional horticulture. Monoculture, as practiced in intensive systems of agriculture, has often been linked to major disasters such as the Sahelian famines of the 1980s. Unfortunately, monoculture is usually the easiest way to increase yields—something that is desperately needed in many countries. For years, many researchers have argued that polyculture is more "natural" than monoculture, in that the mix of different species in a field parallels the diversity of the forest and thus the mix provides a great resistance to diseases that might threaten a single species. The issue is an important one, as securing a reliable, locally-produced food supply is the only thing that can stand between survival and starvation for many millions of people living in tropical areas.

A number of researchers are now suggesting that the issue is not simply the contrast between monoculture and polyculture. From research on one population, we learn that it is possible to intensify horticultural systems through a form of monoculture without sacrificing reliability. In a study of the Mountain Ok of central New Guinea, George Morren and David Hyndman found that a sustainable and low-risk *Colocasia* taro monoculture has persisted there until the present day (1987). Taro is a starchy edible root crop common in the Pacific. They argue that these taro monocultures exhibit many ecological and systemic properties commonly attributed to polycultures.

The Mountain Ok, numbering 28,000 and speaking eight closely related languages, inhabit an extensive region (20,000 km² or 12,500 mi²) of central New Guinea, which can be roughly divided into highland, mid-altitude, and lowland. Although they exhibit considerable sociocultural variability, which is partly a reflection of environmental diversity, Morren and Hyndman found a common cultural pattern throughout the area that gave it a clear identity.

The Mountain Ok appear to have access to the same range of agricultural technology regardless of region. They practice forms of slash-and-burn agriculture, show a cultural preference for *Colocasia* taro, practice extensive swine production, use minimal tillage, have short croppings and long fallows.

However, Morren and Hyndman found that local swidden gardens are clearly differentiated according to crop composition. For the high-altitude dwellers, the sweet

---

of resources through the year, is easier in a permanent settlement. Sedentary groups, then, tend to have higher population densities than nomadic or semi-nomadic groups.

Both these conditions—sedentism and increasing population density—tend to result in a more complex society. Agriculture is a group effort, involving considerable cooperation in clearing fields, planting, harvesting, and storage of crops. The crops and fields have to be protected from predators, including the threat of theft by others. At the same time, since agriculturalists invest time and energy in the land, organization is required to regulate access to the land and to resolve disputes that inevitably accompany life in a large residential grouping. Finally, a group that contains many people, interacting on a permanent basis, needs to order the relationships of the group members: To determine who owes loyalty to whom, who can marry whom, who must give in to whom in a quarrel, and so forth. Hunter-gather-

ers have fewer such problems. They can work individually, they own the land collectively, and when disputes arise, they can simply pack up their belongings and move. The horticultural life presents more social challenges that must be met through a more complex social structure. Horticulturists, for example, frequently consider land to be the property of the group. However, individual households have exclusive access to the crops they produce on a given plot. Though farmers, too, may move when disputes break out, once they have invested in a plot, it is harder to do so.

Relations Within the Community. The basic unit of a society heavily dependent on farming is the household, a small group of people closely related by marriage and kinship who work together to produce food, share in its consumption, and cooperate on a day-to-day basis. Thus it is a unit of production and consumption analogous in many ways to a small

potato is the staple and they keep taro gardens separate from sweet potato gardens. On the other hand, the mid-altitude peoples plant only taro gardens, and these monocultures are, the researchers find, highly flexible and low-risk.

The Mountain Ok of the mid-altitude range are able to practice a conservative form of swidden cultivation because generally population densities are low and land is extensive. Their use of flat or gently sloping land reduces the risk of erosion; they clear secondary rather than primary forest (and can thus take advantage of greater soil fertility); and they make small gardens with large forest margins between gardens, so that the fields are better shielded from pests and successional fallows are enhanced. Rather than totally clearing a field, they stunt the trees by scorching or ringing and often plant in undisturbed forest litter (which also improves fallows). By not completing clearing until the crop is established, they ensure that young plants are protected, moisture is retained, and

erosion avoided. They harvest only once a year, saving vital nutrients for trees; and, by leaving the gardens a minimum of twelve years fallow, they allow for the restoration of essential nutrients.

All agricultural systems, at least temporarily, simplify specific portions of their natural ecosystems (p. 306). Recently, the view that disturbances (agricultural or otherwise) play an important role in sustaining and even increasing diversity of natural species in tropical forests has begun to supplant the older view that monoculture is a major departure from natural complexity. Tropical forests are a patchwork of areas, varying in size, in which single species predominate. From this perspective, a swidden field is simply a large patch.

Polyculture is advocated because the use of many different varieties of plants is seen as minimizing the risk of pests and disease. However, these same effects can be achieved in monocultures by interplanting different varieties of the same species. Morren and Hyndman note that the Mountain Ok do indeed plant a very large number

of different varieties of the staple taro crop—some groups recognize over 100 different cultivars—and new varieties are constantly being introduced through diffusion or by discovery and trial (p. 308).

As Morren and Hyndman illustrate in their study of the Mountain Ok, using the three criteria of ecosystem simplification, biological variability, and vulnerability of the food supply, the taro monocultures they describe exhibit all the advantages often regarded as characterizing polyculture. Nonetheless, they warn that monoculture should not be regarded as an exclusive category. Rather, specific cases must be placed in the broader context of the surrounding ecosystem. It is possible to practice monoculture and reap its productive rewards while not sacrificing flexibility if there is access to other food sources at the same time, fields are widely spaced and retain forest borders to shield plants from pests, and many variants of the same species are interplanted to decrease the risk of disease.

family firm in our society. These family-based households, as we have mentioned, are relatively self-sufficient since their gardens or fields allow them to produce almost everything they need. Nevertheless, they cannot afford to be completely independent of one another, for agriculture creates vulnerability. Once a family has invested its energy in a plot of land, crop failure or a raid by another group can wipe out its livelihood in one stroke. Therefore, as insurance, households must make alliances and integrate themselves into a larger social unit: the community. They achieve integration primarily through kinship ties and participation in community-wide religious or political groupings. In some respects, collective land ownership by kin groups or small, closely knit communities is reinforced in the horticultural communities of the tropical lowlands by the practice of having long fallow periods. These long periods during which families cease to cultivate their plots to allow the forest to regenerate do not encourage individuals to assert exclusive control over any given plot. Also, in most circumstances, the fact of collective ownership limits incentives for long-term investments in the agricultural infrastructure such as constructing terraces or systems to control the flow of water.

Kinship is often (though not invariably) the basis for recognition of individual rights to the use of land. Kinship is almost always the basis of extensive gift exchanges that establish reciprocal ties and obligations throughout the community. By regularly sharing surplus produce among friends and kin, horticultural families ensure that they will not be stranded if they fall on hard times. Indeed, it might be said that gift exchange is the horticulturist's way of storing food or ensuring future assistance, just as among hunter-gatherers.

After kinship, the second integrating force is political organization. While differences in wealth are usually slight or nonexistent in most horticultural groups, there are differences in power. Farming communities tend to have better-defined leadership roles than do hunter-gatherers, although the authority of the leaders varies from group to group. As we shall see, the headman in a Yanomamö village is simply a man with influence; he has no formal office and no right to coerce others. Whatever the allotment of power, the headman serves to integrate the horticultural community by helping families to settle their quarrels, arrange their marriages, and so forth; and by leading them in feasts, religious rituals, and raids.

Relations Between Communities. As social organization within communities becomes more structured, so do relations between communities—whether friendly (as in the case of exchange) or hostile (as in the case of conflict). Both of the groups we will be describing engage in some trade. The Yanomamö acquire metal tools from neighbors, government officials, and missionaries. Their involvement in trade is expanding each year as they are increasingly drawn into the national economies of Venezuela and Brazil. Historically, the Tamang of Nepal traded salt and some food crops to obtain a narrow range of items they could not produce themselves; today, they are far more closely integrated into the Nepalese market economy—in large part due to improved transportation that links them to the capital (Fricke, 1994).

Yet self-sufficiency is still the rule among extensive agricultural communities, and much of their intergroup exchange is a form of gift giving rather than impersonal commercial trade. A Yanomamö man gives a man in another village a dog; some months later, the second man gives the first a bow. Neither party necessarily depends on what the other gives: Both can acquire dogs in their own villages and make their own bows. What they do need is each other's support, either in warfare or in obtaining a wife. Thus just as gifts passed within groups serve to foster good will, so gifts passed between groups help to create and cement alliances; exchange is as much a social as an economic transaction. Arranging marriages with other groups is the ultimate expression of solidarity among the Yanomamö and many other tribal agriculturists.

In sum, social organization among farmers is decidedly different from that of most hunter-gatherers. Hunter-gatherers form small, relatively amorphous groups whose resources and members flow back and forth in such a way as to blur boundaries between subunits. The nuclear family remains intact, but it is not a distinct economic unit; the economic unit is the band as a whole. A farming society, by contrast, is a complex structure made up of well-defined and largely self-sufficient households within relatively stable and self-sufficient communities. These communities in turn are likely to have relatively formalized relationships with one another, often mediated by a system of kinship-based groups, each with its own territory and insignia.

The Yanomamö

Napoleon Chagnon, who has worked periodically among the Yanomamö for twenty-five years (for a cumulative period of field research adding up to more than sixty months), believes them to be one of the largest unacculturated tribes in South America, numbering about 20,000 members (1992, 1997). When Chagnon arrived among the Yanomamö people in 1964, missionaries had already established posts in two villages, but many of the Yanomamö knew of the outside world only indirectly from the metal axes and pots they obtained through trade. Today interaction with outsiders in missionary settlements and through work for ranchers and government agents has brought the Yanomamö into far greater contact with the external world. There are now few Yanomamö who have never seen a non-Yanomamö. Thus this case study is first presented in the ethnographic present (as the Yanomamö appeared when anthropologists first began to work with them) and updated to show them today.[1]

Farming in the Jungle

The Yanomamö live in villages of 40 to 250 inhabitants (the average is 70 to 80), widely scattered through the dense tropical jungle in southern Venezuela and northern Brazil. For the most part, the land is low and flat, with occasional rolling hills and mountain ridges. It is crossed by sluggish, muddy rivers that become rushing torrents in the rainy season. Palms and hardwoods create a dense canopy over a tangle of vines and shrubs. The rain pours down two or three times a day, increasing in intensity between May and August. The humidity rarely drops below 80 percent, intensifying what to us would be uncomfortable year-round temperatures of 26° to 32°C (80° to 96°F).

This habitat provides the Yanomamö with a variety of wild foods. They collect palm fruits, nuts, and seed pods in season; devour honey when they can find it; snack on grubs, a variety of caterpillars, and roasted spiders. They fish by a rather ingenious

---

[1] The material on the Yanomamö, unless otherwise noted, is from Chagnon's updated book, *Yanomamö, the last days of Eden,* San Diego, CA: Harcourt Brace Jovanovich, 1992, and 5th ed. (1997).

Figure 4–1. *Yanomamö territory.*

method known among many nonindustrialized groups: They dam a stream, pour a drug in the water, wait for the stunned fish to float to the surface, and then scoop them into baskets. They hunt monkeys, wild turkeys, wild pigs, armadillos, anteaters, and other species with bows and poisoned arrows. A survey of their hunting practices and game brought into the villages indicates that their intake of protein is approximately 75 grams per person per day, well above the 30 to 50 grams necessary to support an adult (Chagnon & Hames, 1979).

Wild foods alone are not abundant enough to support the Yanomamö at their present population level. Fruits and tubers are seasonal. Animals are small, many are nocturnal, and most live singly, so that they are difficult to hunt (Good, 1995, pp. 59–60). Chagnon notes that although on one occasion he and a group of Yanomamö hunters killed enough game to feed an entire village for one day, on another occasion five days of searching did not yield enough meat to feed even the hunters (1992). Moreover, the Yanomamö's technology does not allow them to exploit the rivers as they might. Their bark canoes are too awkward to navigate upstream, and so fragile that they are generally abandoned after one trip downstream.

Even though they hunt from necessity since they do not raise animals, they tend to engage in hunting much more than is required from a nutritional perspective; they go on hunting treks because they enjoy doing so (Good, 1995, pp. 59–63). Even though it is the men who actually hunt, it is not unusual for the entire community to set off on a month-long trek to the coolest portion of the untouched forest. Also, meat is the only item that is shared village-wide and is therefore of great social importance; sharing creates important bonds among families, and not to share can be disruptive of normal relations (Good, 1995, p. 61).

Thus the Yanomamö depend mostly on their gardens, which provide 85 percent of their caloric intake. The most important crops are plantains and bananas (which together make up 52 percent of their diet in calories); manioc, a root crop used to make flour for cassava bread; sweet potatoes, taro, and maguey; and peach palm trees. Less important crops are maize, avocados, squash, cashews, and papayas. The Yanomamö also cultivate cane for arrow shafts; cotton for hammocks, belts, and cords; hallucinogenic drugs; and a variety of "magical" plants. One of these plants (cultivated by men) makes women sexually receptive, another (cultivated by

A Yanomamö man uses a hoe to cultivate his garden plot in a clearing in the Brazilian jungle.
(Robert Harding Picture Library)

women) calms male tempers, and others cause miscarriages and similar calamities in enemy villages. Finally, every Yanomamö garden has a sizable crop of tobacco, which is highly prized and is chewed by men, women, and children.

Like other Indians of the South American jungles, the Yanomamö practice slash-and-burn agriculture. To clear land for a garden, they first cut away the undergrowth and small trees with steel axes obtained from missionaries and through trade (or from anthropologists). They let the cut vegetation dry in the sun, then burn it off on a day when the wind is right. This task done, they set about felling the large trees, which they leave in the fields to mark boundaries between individual family plots and to chop for firewood when the need arises. The most difficult part of planting a new garden is carrying cuttings from plantain trees in the old garden to the new site. This is an arduous job, for a single cutting can weigh up to 10 pounds (4.5 kg). Planting other crops involves little more than making a hole with a digging stick and depositing seeds or small cuttings. Gardens are individually owned while they are being tended, and each man plants a variety of crops on his land.

Newly established gardens produce in spaced cycles. Thus, at the beginning there are alternating periods of scarcity and plenty. Then, after two or three years, the gardens mature, and overlapping plant cycles produce a constant supply of food (Chagnon, 1997).

The Yanomamö do most of the heavy work of clearing the land during the rainy season, when swamps and swollen rivers make it impossible to engage in visiting, feasting, or fighting with other villages. Once established, a garden takes only a few hours a day to maintain. Men, women, and children leave for their plots at dawn and return to the village around 10:30 A.M. (if the men have decided not to hunt that day). The women also gather firewood and supervise the children playing nearby. No one works during the midday heat. Sometimes a man will return to the garden around 4:00 P.M. and work until sundown. Most men, however, spend the afternoon in the village, resting or taking drugs, while the women go out to collect more firewood and haul water.

Cleared land in a tropical forest will not support crops indefinitely. Once a garden has been cultivated continuously for two or three years, the farmer gradually begins to shift it. Every year he abandons more land at one end of the plot and clears more land at the other end, transplanting crops to the new addition. The garden "moves" in this way for about eight years, after which time the weeding problem becomes insurmountable and the soil unproductive. The plot is then abandoned and an entirely new site is cleared. Left fallow, the old plot recovers its natural forest covering in about ten years. It should be noted that the Yanomamö are somewhat unusual in their swiddening. Most horticulturists use their plots for longer periods and carefully supervise the long fallow period, going back regularly to harvest wild fruits and other resources as they appear (Denevan et al., 1984, p. 346).

Village Life

The Yanomamö live near their gardens in circular villages they call *shabono*. Each man builds a shelter of poles and vines for himself, his wife or wives, and their children. These homes are arranged around a central courtyard, and the spaces between them are thatched to form a continuous roof with an open space over the courtyard. The shabono, then, is roughly doughnut-shaped. For safety, most Yanomamö groups also construct a high pole fence around the shabono, with a single opening that can be barricaded at night.

What authority there is in the village rests in the person of the **headman**, an individual who has proved his superiority in combat, diplomacy, hunting, or some other skill. Headmen have no official right to order others around; they lead only to the extent that people respect or fear them. Kaobawä, the headman of the village in which Chagnon lived in 1964–1965, is probably typical. Kaobawä had demonstrated his fierceness in numerous raids and quarrels. He also enjoyed a large natural following: Five adult brothers and several brothers-in-law, who were under obligation to him for the sisters he had given them in marriage. Having established his superiority, he simply led by example. People came to him of their own accord for advice, which he dispensed with an air of quiet authority.

Most members of a village are related to one another, either by blood or by marriage. Kinship among the Yanomamö is reckoned by **patrilineal descent**; that is, it is traced through the male line. Both men and women belong to their father's lineage. Typically, a village consists of two patrilineages whose members have intermarried over several generations. Within a single lineage, all males of the same generation call one another "brother," and all females call one another "sister." For a man, however, the really important ties are not with his "brothers" but with the men of the lineage from which he can acquire a wife. Wives cannot be chosen according to fancy. Yanomamö marriage rules specify that a man must choose a woman from a lineage other than his own. In practice, his choice is narrowed to a small group of women in the village's one (or two) other lineages.

Neither the composition nor the location of a Yanomamö village is permanent. Villages move every few years. Sometimes the group relocates for the purpose of acquiring fresh lands, but as a rule there is plenty of land to cultivate in the immediate vicinity for villages are widely separated. As with many other horticulturists, a growing shortage of firewood is an important reason for movement. However, the Yanomamö also move because hostilities make it impossible for them to stay where they are. Sometimes internal feuds divide a village into two factions, which then go their separate ways. More commonly, a village moves because warfare with other villages has escalated to such a degree that the only way to survive is to flee. Kaobawä's group, for example, had made sixteen major moves in seventy-five years. One move was motivated by the need for fresh land, one by a desire to acquire steel tools from a group of foreigners newly arrived downstream, and the remaining fourteen by either bloodshed within the group or warfare with neighboring villages (Chagnon, 1983, pp. 174–177).

Warfare and Violence

Violence, in fact, is a salient feature of Yanomamö social life; internal hostilities are exceeded only by external hostilities. Intervillage duels, raids, ambushes, and kidnappings are almost daily fare. Why is there so much conflict? According to Chagnon, the reason that is given by the Yanomamö is women (Chagnon, 1997; Horgan, 1988, pp. 17–18). Other observers have alternative interpretations. Some feel that while the Yanomamö may explain their actions in terms of conflict over women, there are other, underlying causes. Brian Ferguson views Yanomamö conflict, internal as well intergroup, as arising out of the impact of external forces, notably the governments of Venezuela and Brazil, which have altered tribal territories and destabilized social relations among populations far from centers of power (1995a, l995b). We will consider these interpretations as well as Chagnon's.

Unbalanced Sex Ratio. The only forms of family planning the Yanomamö practice are a long **postpartum taboo**—a woman may not have sexual intercourse while she is pregnant or while she is nursing a child—and infanticide. If, despite the taboo, a woman does become pregnant while she is still nursing her last child—a practice that itself decreases the likelihood of pregnancy—she will kill the new baby rather than deprive the older child of milk. A woman is also likely to kill her first baby if it is a girl, for her husband of course wants a son, and displeased Yanomamö husbands can be brutal, even murderous. The practice of selective female infanticide creates a sexual imbalance among the Yanomamö. The boys of a given village invariably outnumber the girls, sometimes by as much as 30 percent (Chagnon, 1992). The fact that older, more powerful men usually take second and third wives makes the shortage of women a particular problem for the younger men. Chagnon has reported that men who have been successful in raiding and who are known to have killed enemies are far more likely than other men to have two or more wives, further exacerbating the situation (Horgan, 1988, pp. 17–18).

The unbalanced sex ratio increases conflicts within and between villages. Competition for the limited number of women eligible as brides under the marriage rules turns biological and classificatory brothers into potential enemies. Suppose there are ten young men in a lineage, only seven young women eligible for them to marry, and older men take two of these girls as brides. The men grow up knowing that only five of them will be able to marry within the village. Somehow they must outshine or disgrace the competition, and this necessity tends to undermine whatever solidarity might develop among them as brothers. (A young Yanomamö may seek a bride in another village, but most are

Horticultural societies are not entirely peaceable. In fact, violence is a salient feature of Yanomamö social life. These Yanomamö are preparing to depart on a raid.

(Napoleon Chagnon/Anthrophoto)

reluctant to do so because they would have to undertake years of bride service.)

In addition, the shortage of women increases the temptation to commit adultery—a temptation to which married men succumb as readily as bachelors, especially during the four years or so when their wives are taboo. If a man succeeds in seducing another man's wife and is caught, the husband will retaliate with all the ferocity he can muster. Club fights over women are the major cause of villages splitting up. After they split, hostility between the two groups tends to continue on its own momentum, each group taking turns avenging wrongs inflicted by the other group.

Warfare between totally separate villages follows the same pattern. Fights over women may precipitate the conflict, or one village may suspect that its crops are being pilfered by a neighboring village. If a child falls sick, the illness will be blamed on sorcery emanating from another village. (The Yanomamö may invoke evil demons to steal the souls of children in enemy villages.) Whatever the original causes, contests over women are usually part of the ensuing hostilities. Typically a raiding party will kill one or two men and abduct any women they can lay their hands on. This raid precipitates a counterraid to avenge the murders and recapture the women. The retaliatory raid in turn triggers another, and so on.

Eventually the members of one village will be put to flight. Abandoning their gardens and homes, they take refuge in another village until they can plant new gardens. This arrangement, while necessary for the group's survival, further exacerbates the woman-shortage problem, for the hosts are almost certain to take advantage of their guests' weakened position to demand temporary or permanent access to their women.

Thus the Yanomamö, according to Chagnon's accounts, are locked into a vicious cycle. The more the men fight over women, the more eager they are to have sons who will help in the fighting, the more female infants they kill, the fewer women there are, and the more they fight. Moreover, the men encourage their sons to be suspicious, hot-tempered, and quick to take violent action against the slightest offense. Teasing fathers often provoke small sons to hit them and then reward the boys with laughter and approving comments on how fierce they are becoming. By raising their sons in this way, the Yanomamö perpetuate hostilities in the effort to defend against them.

Environmental Factors.

Chagnon's explanation for Yanomamö warfare is not without its critics. Most observers agree with his data indicating a high frequency of fighting and high mortality associated with it, and most agree that warfare of the sort reported is (or was) widespread among Amazonian groups. But Marvin Harris and others have argued that the importance of women has been overstressed and that environmental factors are directly or indirectly implicated. Harris (1974, pp. 276–279) and Daniel Gross (1975) state that underlying the frequency of warfare is a shortage of game and other sources of protein. Although the Yanomamö grow more than enough produce to fill their stomachs and have miles of virgin forest to clear for new gardens, the foods they cultivate do not provide large amounts of protein. To meet these protein requirements, they must hunt and fish. Harris suggests that at some point the Yanomamö began to intensify their agricultural activities and that their population level rose accordingly. As the population grew, they killed increasingly larger numbers of wild animals, thus depleting their game resources. Today, Harris argues, there is not enough protein to go around and what the Yanomamö are fighting over, albeit unwittingly, is hunting territory.

Gross traces not only warfare but also several other aspects of Yanomamö culture to the scarcity of protein. Above all, the settlement pattern—the establishment of small, widely-dispersed villages separated from other villages by a no-man's-land and abandoned every few years—is, according to Gross, a strategy for preventing the overexploitation of game in any one area. Likewise, infanticide and a long postpartum taboo lower the protein demand by keeping the population in check. The hypothesis that Yanomamö warfare—the most striking aspect of this tribe's culture—may be an adaptation to protein limitations is intriguing, but so far it has not been substantiated by any reports of protein deficiency among the Yanomamö. One study has found some signs of infant malnutrition but also evidence that children who survive childhood mature into healthy adults (Holmes, 1985). Although warfare may indeed serve to preserve hunting territories, it does not appear that this is the immediate or conscious objective of the combatants (Chagnon & Hames, 1979; Chagnon, 1992). Such different observations, while difficult to resolve, provide new and innovative directions for research.

Political Alliances.

In this hostile social environment, the Yanomamö devote considerable time and resources to cultivating alliances with neighbors. Overtures begin cautiously, with parties of visitors bearing gifts. The gifts are not free, however; the takers are obliged to reciprocate at some point in the future with gifts of equal or greater value. If visiting goes well, specialization in craft production may begin: One village may rather suddenly abandon the making of pots and the other the manufacture of arrow points, so that they become dependent on each other. These contrived shortages express growing trust; all Yanomamö have the resources and skills to make everything they require.

After a period of trading, one group takes the next step toward alliance by holding a feast for the other group. They harvest and cook great quantities of food, amass goods for exchange, and prepare elaborate costumes and dances. Because giving or attending a feast implies a higher level of commitment, the occasion must be handled with caution and diplomacy. The dances and songs are essentially displays of strength. Each side tries to impress the other with the fact that it does not really need allies and probably never will.

Almost invariably, disputes break out and the toughest men of the two villages challenge one another to contests of physical strength: Chest-pounding duels, in which two antagonists take turns socking each other squarely on the chest; and side-slapping duels, in which the contestants take turns hitting each other on the flanks. The object is to stay in the game until your opponent withdraws or is knocked unconscious. If tempers get hot, these fights can escalate into club fights, full-scale brawls in which the men of each village beat one another over the head with eight-foot poles.

An occasional club fight leads to full-scale violence, destroying the alliance altogether. Usually, however, these carefully graded levels of hostility allow the Yanomamö to vent their ever-present aggression, display their fierceness, and still finish the feast on a friendly note. If all goes well, the fighting ends in a draw and gifts are exchanged. The guests depart peacefully, the hosts can expect to be invited to a return feast, and each group assumes it can count on the other for refuge and food in times of trouble.

The final step is an exchange of brides between the two groups. This step is not taken unless the villages are convinced of each other's good intentions or unless one is so weak it has no choice. Villages that exchange women usually can expect support in their raids and skirmishes with other Yanomamö. But even alliances based on marriage ties are tenuous; no village honors a commitment when it sees some advantage in breaking it.

In sum, the Yanomamö are great fighters and poor allies. Consequently, their social world is one of chronic suspicion and hostility. The human costs are high. Warfare accounts for at least 30 percent of all male deaths; approximately two-thirds of people aged forty or older have lost at least one close biological relative, a parent, sibling, or child (Chagnon, 1992, p. 239). This figure seems startling, but it is comparable to those of New Guinea tribes and of Native American societies that feuded regularly.

The problem, as Brian Ferguson points out, is not so much whether or not the Yanomamö fight, but whether this is a long-established feature of their way of life (1995b). No one, including, of course, Chagnon, argues that the Yanomamö are the "living embodiment of a violent evolutionary heritage" (Ferguson, l995a, p. 62). But the interpretation of their level of conflict depends on the extent to which this is caused by forces outside their immediate habitat, which is the view argued by Ferguson (1995a and 1995b). While it is obvious, as we shall see shortly, that the Yanomamö are greatly affected by contemporary developments in Venezuela and Brazil, what is not so plain is how deeply they have been affected by outside events over the last 300 years.

Outside influences began when the colonists arrived in the early seventeenth century and began raiding for slaves; the ensuing conflicts wiped out a number of societies in the Yanomamö region and destabilized others. Most important, apart from direct contact, was the competition among groups that developed as trade goods were introduced. This competition often was played out in warfare (Ferguson, 1995a). Rather than a pristine example of tribal warfare, Ferguson suggests, "The Yanomamö case shows the extraordinary reach and transforming effects a centrally governed society or state (here the states of Venezuela and Brazil) may have, extending way beyond its last outpost" (1995a, p. 63).

Future Prospects for the Yanomamö

The Yanomamö at the end of the twentieth century are in a much more precarious position than at any time in their history. Generally, anthropologists de-scribe what happens when two cultures impinge on each other as **acculturation**, which leads to changes in both cultures. In particular, the politically or technologically dominant society exerts the greatest impact. This process is transforming all the Indian tribes of the Amazon rain forest, and resembles what was experienced by native populations throughout North and South America in the early days of European colonization. They have been abruptly brought into contact with a technologically advanced and alien cultural system. However, the case of the Yanomamö is so extreme that Chagnon refers to it as "catastrophic change" (1992, p. 243).

When Napoleon Chagnon arrived in 1964, the villages closest to European settlements had seen only a handful of whites and those of the interior none at all. Trade goods had been reaching them, passed on through intermediate groups, but no extended contact had occurred between the Yanomamö and the outside world. Since the period of first contact, roads have been built to provide access to the Amazon region. With the completion of the first road, change has occurred rapidly and often against a backdrop of misery and misfortune.

The arrival of the roads brought an immediate adaptive response. The Indians nearest the road ranged themselves alongside it to beg and barter for shorts, shirts, food—doubtless it seemed like an easier way to make a living than their traditional horticulture and hunting. Some went to work on farms and sawmills; for twenty or thirty days' work, they received a little money (not more than $2 or $3) and some cigarettes and used clothes. They tried to emulate the ways of the Brazilians (*civilizados*) and not to appear to be *indios bravos* (wild Indians).

The "roadside" Yanomamö came to differ from the unacculturated villagers of the interior. They adopted Brazilian haircuts, took up smoking cigarettes, bought canned foods and candy, and added lots of salt to their food. In fact, their traditional diet was superior to that of the average Brazilian farmer; with contact, their diet declined in terms of calories earned per unit of labor expended. But because they wanted to appear like the Brazilians and to interact more with them, they adopted as many Brazilian practices as they could. Not only did they adopt such utilitarian items as aluminum pots and pans, steel axes, shotguns, and other tools that facilitated subsistence activities, they also came to depend on large numbers of consumer items that tied them ever more closely to their Brazilian suppliers. As John Saffirio and Raymond Hammer write (1983), it is doubtful that they would have embraced this alien culture so wholeheartedly if they had understood that in so doing they were losing their po-

Box 4.2

Are the Yanomamö Safe?

ANTHROPOLOGIST LINDA RABBEN argues that while Brazil has taken a big step by demarcating Yanomamö territory, it is unclear how the boundaries of their reserve will be protected and by whom (1993). As recently as 1991, the governor of Amazonas threatened to send state police with machine guns to shoot agents attempting to demarcate indigenous territory in his state; in 1993 the federal government admitted that 11,000 prospectors had reentered Yanomamö territory and it appears unable or unwilling to expel them. Still, demarcation seems to be the only possibility for preserving indigenous peoples and their resources. Other Brazilian populations such as the Kayapo are lobbying to have their lands effectively protected, enlisting foreign assistance where possible. Prince Charles of Great Britain and the rock star Sting have lobbied for them, and in 1993 the perimeter of their lands was physically marked using funds raised largely by such foreign help.

But marking boundaries alone cannot protect indigenous peoples. Many in Brazil cannot understand why groups such as the Yanomamö should be protected while millions of small farmers have no land and 100 million city dwellers live in dire poverty (Rabben, 1993, p. 14). Thus, the pressures on their territories are increasing, not decreasing. Many local politicians see foreign efforts to help native peoples as threats to sovereignty and economic development. The situation is further complicated by dispute and controversy among those who would assist them. Chagnon, who has spent his entire career with the Yanomamö, has been accused of overstressing their warfare and aggressive male behavior—thereby indirectly encouraging outsiders to view them negatively. Recently, Jacques Lizot went so far as to suggest that depictions of Yanomamö warfare actually incite intruding gold miners to massacre them (Lizot, 1994). Chagnon, who has been an advocate of Yanomamö rights throughout his career, responds by pointing out that Brazilian gold miners are unlikely to have read any of his scientific publications, and furthermore, they are hostile to all indigenous groups who stand between them and gold (Chagnon, 1995, pp. 187–189). Chagnon has been attacked also in letters sent by Lizot and Salesian church officials to academic leaders accusing him of promoting "racist" theories—a notion that is not sup-ported by a reading of his numerous publications (see Wolf, 1994). Salesian missions operate among the Yanomamö ostensibly to help them as well as to convert them, but according to Chagnon and others, the shotguns given to converts are used against their neighbors and thus add to Yanomamö mortality rates. While it is entirely appropriate to disagree with a scholar's findings and interpretations, it is unfortunate where it interferes with the advocacy that endangered populations such as the Yanomamö so badly need.

While demarcation is a necessary step, Rabben argues, indigenous groups need the active support of public opinion to obtain control over their resources. This has to occur at local, regional, national, and international levels. There also has to be international monitoring. At the moment, miners are largely undeterred by federal police and the government has been able to do little to prevent malaria and other contact diseases from causing high mortality of indigenous populations. Unfortunately, we must conclude that the Yanomamö are not yet safe.

litical autonomy and entering Brazilian society at the very bottom of the social and economic hierarchy.

Along with contact have come diseases to which the Yanomamö have no immunity. They have been decimated repeatedly by epidemics; one disastrous influenza epidemic in 1973 killed a quarter of the population in the villages sampled (Chagnon & Melancon, 1983, p. 59). These scourges have had a severe impact on the traditional social organization; ritual specialists have died before passing on their knowledge and skills, kin groups have been broken up and forcibly resettled, and leaders have succumbed to these new diseases.

While the Yanomamö's territory has been exploited for 20 years by lumbermen cutting down their rainforest, the most serious assault came in 1985 with the discovery of gold in the Amazon. This discovery, which coincided with the completion of the Perimetral Norte highway that cut through the heart of the Yanomamö territory, precipitated a gold rush into the Amazon. Since 1985, over 50,000 miners have invaded Yanomamö territory (Gorman, 1994). Once again, epidemics took an almost instant toll: Villages studied soon after the road was constructed had lost between 30 and 51 percent of their populations (Chagnon, 1992). The mining operations have further ravaged the fragile environment, damming rivers and polluting water. Even though the land rights of the Yanomamö were protected in the Brazilian constitution, the government made no effort to enforce those rights.

However, the plight of the Yanomamö did not receive international attention until four Indian men were killed when they wandered into an illegal mining village. Ironically, the public outcry that resulted was not in response to the killing, but in response to action taken by then-President Sarney. He ordered all journalists, missionaries, anthropologists, medical workers, and international workers out of the territory and embarked on a plan to reduce the Yanomamö territory from 37,000 square miles to 12,000. This announcement led to a four-year battle for the preservation of the Yanomamö land rights fought by international rights organizations as well as Brazil's own Indian protection agency. Finally, in November, 1991, the new president, Collor, authorized the official demarcation of 36,000 square miles of Yanomamö territory, providing $2.7 million to physically and legally implement this demarcation. Soon after, a demarcation order was also issued for the Kayapo (Rabben, 1993).

Despite these gains, the future of the Yanomamö is still in question. Miners continue to operate illegally in their territory, and there are reports of continuing violent confrontations between the Indians and the miners. In 1993, Chagnon was part of a team that investigated a massacre of Yanomamö women and children. According to Chagnon, this was in retaliation for earlier killings of miners by the Yanomamö. Apparently, some Yanomamö men had shot two Brazilian miners after they had killed five Yanomamö men near an illegal mining site (Chagnon, 1993).

As we can see in Box 4.2, *Are the Yanomamö Safe?* (page 81), the authorization for the demarcation of indigenous territories does not necessarily guarantee the preservation of the Yanomamö.

Subsistence Plow Farming

The subsistence plow farming techniques used by the Tamang of Nepal (discussed in the following section) are technologically different from what we have described as horticulture. However, the broad outlines of the domestic economy are similar: Egalitarian, independent households as primary units of production and consumption. Depending on the nature of the terrain, fields are usually small and irregularly shaped and inputs are generally limited to what the household can supply itself: Labor for planting, weeding, and harvesting, animal traction, natural fertilizers, and sometimes water. Generally speaking, such farming using animals involves a significantly shorter fallow period than does most swiddening. At most, fields are left fallow for a single year.

A higher annual production per acre means that the land can support larger communities. However, as with the horticulturists, production is organized to fulfill the subsistence needs of the household rather than to produce a marketable surplus that could, in turn, be reinvested. The main differences have to do with the utilization of livestock, the exploitation of a number of distinct microenvironments within the region, and relations with the outside world. None of these differences, it should be stressed, is absolute.

The fact that households make significant use of large domesticated animals for food and traction creates an increased demand for household labor to manage them, so the households of such farmers tend to be large. The family must also have access to land for grazing and housing its cattle, oxen, or other domestic animals. This usually means that they are simultaneously exploiting a number of distinct ecological zones: Fields specific to whatever crops may be planted, orchards for arboreal produce, grazing areas, and places in which fodder is collected for the months when animals cannot be pastured. This gives the household both additional sources of food and a means of storing surplus production—on the hoof.

While most horticulturists today are integrated into market economies in some manner, it is safe to say that all plow farmers are. Not only are they participants in the market system, their production sustains a larger political system in which they are dependent players. They are the "peasantry." Despite the fact that they operate within a larger market economy, they can also be viewed as subsistence farmers because they produce primarily for family subsistence rather than for profits to be reinvested (Wolf, 1966). Much of their produce may be sold, but the profits accrue to middlemen and urban elites, not to the peasants. For them, farming is a way of life and a means of sustaining a household within a community.

It is, then, much more than simply a strategy for making money. Such farmers, often materially poor, closely identify with their villages and way of life. The term "peasant" subsumes a great diversity in standards of living, even within one country. The common element is a farming household whose efforts are directed to maintenance and subsistence—not reinvestment of capital for profits. In most cases,

Using animal traction for plowing and cultivating vastly increases the productive capacity of farmers.

(Betty Press/Woodfin Camp & Associates)

peasant families are dominated by holders of power outside the local community. In tsarist Russia before 1889, for instance, a peasant household was bound to a landed estate; to leave without permission was to risk death or imprisonment. The peasants of Western Europe acquired full civil liberties only in the nineteenth century, and often their standard of living, however simple, set them apart from the poor people of the cities. Still, their form of farming permitted little accumulation of capital or material wealth.

In Latin America, India, and the Middle East, many peasants gain access to land through some form of sharecropping; that is, they work land owned by others in exchange for a share of the yield. Sharecropping is one means of getting land to farm; there are others. The way people control the lands they farm is a major determinant of the degree of political freedom they enjoy, and usually of their material well-being.

Farmers who control their own land and tools, such as the Yanomamö and the Tamang, decide for themselves how hard they will work and dispose of their produce as they choose. Usually, peasants do not have this freedom. Their access to land, equipment, and capital—even the allocation of their own labor—is regulated by people more powerful than they. Even the local agriculturists who own their own land, elect their own leaders, and control their own labor are heavily dependent on an administrative and commercial network. In one way or another, the middlemen who link the farm with distant markets, the rulers, governors, and tax collectors—even the merchants in faraway cities or on local estates—determine how and what the peasants produce and what they earn for these products (Wolf, 1966).

The Tamang

In June, 1981, Thomas Fricke, armed with a Fulbright grant, an ability to speak Nepali, and a set of questionnaires, arrived in the Himalayan village of Timling after a week's walk through Tamang country.[2] While fully aware of the larger nation of

[2] The following discussion, unless otherwise noted, is based on Thomas Fricke's *Himalayan households: Tamang demography and domestic processes*, originally published in 1986, but significantly revised in 1994.

which they were a part, few men in Timling (and even fewer women) had been to the capital of the nation, Kathmandu. Although they were relatively poor and isolated, the people of Timling were warmly receptive to Fricke's presence. He quickly settled into the top floor of a rented house, made it known that people were welcome to drop in for tea and a cigarette, and, more importantly, established an informal clinic from which he dispensed aspirin and treated minor wounds. Soon people came to take his presence for granted and he could turn to his main objectives: The study of population dynamics and the domestic economy in a small farming community.

Within weeks of his arrival, he began making a careful map of the village, giving each house a number for use later to ensure that his data did not exclude the poorer ones. Soon thereafter, he began the arduous task of visiting each of the 132 households and collecting detailed data on marriages, kinship, age and gender of all members, as well as economic data. In the final stages of research, again using his list of households, he selected some thirty households as a special sample in which more detailed questioning would occur. Even though much of his research, like that of Chagnon among the Yanomamö, was highly structured and quantitative, the personal was never far removed:

> The anthropologist, crouching near a peasant's cooking fire and sharing corn beer, lives in a world of imposing immediacy. In a village of a hundred or so households, those events that are swallowed up by the grand scale of an urban or national context take on an enlarged, often passionate significance. One night there is laughter and joking with a father-to-be about the paternity of his child. Another day there is the intrusion of sudden death when a hunter loses his footing on a rain-soaked trail. The anthropologist observes, or hears about, these happenings as they occur and gives them a kind of permanency by writing them down. [p. 7]

The Tamang people, including the inhabitants of Timling, are a widely-dispersed population of Tibetan origin living in Nepal. Their numerous villages stretch in a broad arc north and eastward from Kathmandu, the national capital. Those who live near the capital are more integrated into Nepal's national life and culture than are those to the east and north, such the people of Timling. The Temang practice a form of Buddhism that closely resembles that of their more famous neighbors, the Sherpa, who are well-known internationally as mountaineers and guides. The village of Timling is only fifty miles from Kathmandu, but to reach it the traveler has to take a five-hour bus ride, followed by a four- or five-day trek, depending on the season. Until the eighteenth century, the region of Timling was a small, independent chiefdom; one among many. Even though now, administratively, it holds a marginal and dependent status within the kingdom, it is somewhat misleading to characterize Timling as a typical peasant society. Unlike many peasants, the people maintain control over their own lands and variation in wealth among households is not great.

The Tamang as a whole are organized into patrilineal clans or lineages called *rui*. As is the case with the Yanomamö, the Tamang practice exogamy; that is, marriage must be outside the clan. In some parts of the country, the clans of the Tamang are ranked hierarchically so that wealth, social standing, and political influence is distributed unequally. This is not true in Timling, whose people are, writes Fricke "an extraordinarily egalitarian group, with no institutionalized basis for distinguishing among the status of clans" (p. 32).

The Village

The 132 households are laid out in four neighborhoods, or *tol*, each associated with a dominant clan (although others will be present as well) and each with its open-air meeting place. Sons build their homes on land they inherit from their fathers; thus, they may add to the size of a neighborhood. Most houses are of two-story construction and built with stone and timber, with wood or slate roofs. In one neighborhood, the homes of clan members display large stone phalluses under the eaves that are supposed to ward off ghosts and other malevolent beings. The upper stories are used primarily for storage, with the family living quarters downstairs where the symbolically important cooking hearth is located. The hearth is emblematic of the household as an independent unit. The fire from the open hearth fills the houses with smoke, but the overall effect is a warm, dry haven in the colder months or during the monsoon rains.

Timling is, by any standard, a fairly dangerous and dirty place. During the monsoon rains, the central paths of the village turn into running streams. Since these paths are also the repository of human waste, the drinking water frequently becomes contaminated during monsoons. On the often treacherous trails, the risk of accidents is high given the slippery rocks and sheer drops of hundreds of feet. On the positive side, the village is too high to be afflicted with malaria-bearing mosquitos, and leeches, fleas, and lice are limited seasonally by the winter cold and summer dry seasons (p. 114).

Religious practices incorporate both Buddhist beliefs and shamanistic practices. The two sorts of religious specialists reflect this mix; about half are *lamas* trained in the Buddhist tradition and capable of conducting elaborate rituals on a calendar that is coordinated with the agricultural cycle, and the others are *bompos* (**shamans**) who appease forest deities that bring illness to villagers and their herds. A shaman is an individual who has unique skills in curing, divination, or witchcraft, usually involving the ability to communicate with the world of spirits. Parents regularly bring in *bompos* to heal their sick children with all-night rituals involving spirit possession and the sacrifice of chickens and goats. The *lamas* carry out death rituals or funerals, cleanse the village periodically by casting out evil spirits (a task that involves the entire community working together for three days), and annually bless the fields.

Political organization is focused on the clans and neighborhoods. Technically, the village is part of a national system of administration; in practice, most decisions of communal interest are made within the clans via meetings and a council of elders. Disputes are resolved locally, usually by informal sanctions and fines, and violent conflict is rare (unlike the Yanomamö).

Field, Forest, and Pasture

Timling's agro-pastoral economy is directed toward the subsistence needs of its people and, until recently, has been largely (but never entirely) self-sufficient. Until 1956 they traded locally mined salt with Tibet; today, they trade for small amounts of grain and manufactured commodities in a market town some four days' walk to the south—part of a gradual but steady shift to a cash economy. As with any population, we have to think of their present adaptation as part of a long historical process that is ongoing. In previous periods, the ancestors of the present population had exploited the lowlands, using classic horticultural techniques. Gradually, as a result of pressure on resources and declining lowland forest area suited to swiddening, they increased their reliance on animal husbandry. Today, plow farming is the principal strategy of food production, supplemented by pastoralism or animal husbandry.

The main characteristic of mountainous regions is that relatively short distances involve great changes in altitude, thus offering a wide variety of ecological zones for potential exploitation. Timling's territory contains three large, vertical zones based on how people use the altitude-related climate differences: Cultivated areas, forests, and pasture lands. The best cultivable land is the lowest (of that to

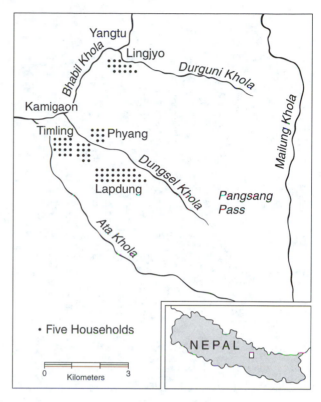

Figure 4–2. *Timling and its daughter villages.*

which they have access), from 5,300 to about 6,000 feet. This lies below the critical snowline (the village itself is frozen hard through much of the winter), and is intercropped with millet and maize. Somewhat higher fields, from 6,000 to 7,000 feet are planted in maize, potatoes, millet, and barley in an alternating cycle. The poorest arable land, up to 8,500 feet, is used for potatoes and wheat in a three-year cycle, including a one-year fallow period. All in all, the 132 households farm approximately 418 acres (or .65 acre per person). This modest amount of land, when combined with animal production, supplies enough food to sustain a household. The typical breakdown of crops in terms of land is 26 percent planted in maize, 16 percent in millet, 15 percent in wheat, 29 percent in barley, and 15 percent in potatoes (p. 68).

Communal grazing is available to some degree in all three zones, but most grazing land lies in the high pastures above 12,000 feet. The seven square miles are grazed by herds of sheep and goats, including some from other villages, from May until mid-September (p. 65). In order to save labor, all of the village's sheep and goats (about five or six per household) are combined into three herds. In addition to sheep and goats, most families maintain cattle or oxen for plowing, and, in a few cases,

A Tamang man and his cow. The man is wearing typical highland clothing except for his shirt, which was purchased at a bazaar five days' walk from Timling.
(Courtesy of Tom Fricke, The University of Michigan)

water buffalo for milk. Over half of what a family has invested in animals (in the sense of capital) is devoted to cattle, which are used primarily for traction; sheep and goats are used for food and wool. Most families produce their own sturdy clothing from wool—essential in this harsh environment.

Work in Timling is a matter of survival. Each household can be thought of as an independent economic unit defined by the need to provide food for the hearth (p. 73). All households are involved in agricultural, pastoral, and maintenance efforts in a cycle determined by the requirements of the different crops and animals. The principal sources of food are the crops, even though men regard herding, which they do almost exclusively, as preferable to the arduous tasks of plowing, seeding, weeding, harvesting—and even guarding the plots from monkeys and bears that would forage on them. In all, it appears that the people of Timling have to work almost twice as hard during the year as do the Yanomamö; even household maintenance requires great effort. The mountain environment requires substantial structures for housing. To build a house,

the Tamang must go to the forest, cut logs, float them downstream, and then laboriously drag them up the hillside and fashion them into boards. The Tamang must also work hard to gather firewood, since a single family will burn about 154 person-loads of firewood each year. Water has to be fetched. The family makes its own tools, storage baskets, and clothing. In this cold environment, each person requires two outfittings of heavy clothes. In all, a typical home requires 185 ten-hour person-days per year of hard work just to perform general maintenance, even though cooking itself is a fairly simple procedure. Daily meals usually consist simply of flour and water cooked as a thick gruel, perhaps accompanied by boiled nettles or potatoes. Meat is eaten only occasionally, when sacrificed in rituals or when an animal falls to its death, as they sometimes do on the steep trails.

The Domestic Cycle

Given the nature of agriculture and private ownership of fields and cattle, the **domestic cycle**, or how households are formed and organized and how they develop is very important. If one simply looks at Timling's households at a point in time, as Thomas Fricke did in his initial study, almost 70 percent were nuclear in composition—that is, a married couple and their unmarried children.[3] But, as he notes, this is misleading, as each family unit is transformed over time. Children are born, grow up and marry, and deaths occur. The rule is that daughters, when they marry, leave their natal home and move to their husband's, where they reside with his parents, single siblings, and possibly married brothers. This is called, by anthropologists, **patrilocal residence**. A more mature household will often contain at least two married couples of two generations and their children—referred to as an **extended family household**. Even though most households go through this phase in their development, only a few (about 5 percent) are extended at any given time. The reason is that soon after the oldest son marries, the next son begins thinking along similar lines. Once the second son does marry, the eldest son, his wife, and children are likely to move out to build their own house, set up their own hearth, and tend their own plots—thus beginning their own domestic cycle within a new nuclear household.

---

[3] The people of Timling accept polygyny but it is now rare. The most common cases occur when men from the village move to India to work, often establishing second marriages there.

A son inherits his share of lands and animals at this point, usually prior to his father's death. The rule is for the youngest son to marry and continue to live in his parents' house until their deaths, when he will inherit the remaining property. This mother/father/youngest son unit is termed a *stem family*; about 25 percent of Timling's households were of this sort. The composition of the household is of vital importance to its members' quality of life; the sudden death of a young adult can dramatically affect the ability of the family to adequately provision itself. Generally, mature households have a more favorable ratio of workers to consumers, which reduces the effort devoted to sustaining daily consumption and which may allow for the purchase of additional land or the opening of new fields—all of which can be used to support new households when married sons leave.

Sexuality and Marriage. Marriage is a vital transition event, far surpassing such earlier celebrations as those marking the maturation of the child: A girl's first menses, and a boy's *chewar* (first hair cutting). Marriage marks the move to adulthood and ties households together in a web of mutually supportive relationships. Marriages can be arranged by parents or simply entered into by a couple choosing to live together without ritual or money changing hands. When money or wealth is exchanged, it is given by the husband's family and relatives to the girl's father and then passed on to the bride as a form of inheritance. She will have no further claim on her parents' property. Sexual activity begins at puberty and is not viewed with disapproval. Unmarried couples find their ways into the forest and young girls bring their lovers home at night, although trying to keep their amorous activities secret in a crowded communal room is a virtual impossibility.

Clearly, attitudes in Timling toward sex, and especially female sexuality, are drastically different from those of the Yanomamö, where men regularly fight over women and adultery is considered a serious offense. In Timling, if an unmarried woman has a child she simply names the father. If he is a single man he may or may not marry her, and if he is already married he is asked to help support the child. A male child will inherit from his father even if his father and mother never marry and he is reared in his mother's household. In any event, by age twenty most women are married and either beginning their own households or residing patrilocally as part of their husband's natal household. Children of unwed parents are not stigmatized. The main concern is to establish paternity for reasons of clan membership and inheritance. Clan membership is socially crucial, since one is the member of one's father's clan and to marry within the clan is forbidden. The people of Timling do not practice any form of contraception; on the contrary, they promote fertility. While the birthrate is not among the world's highest, probably for reasons of health and because of spousal separation when men go to work abroad, a woman can typically expect to have five or six children. For the time being, at least, children are seen as a source of future household wealth and security, not as dependents who must be supported and among whom land must be divided.

Prospects for Timling's Future

When Thomas Fricke concluded his first fieldwork, he was mildly pessimistic regarding Timling's future. Judging from the experience of other Himalayan communities, he feared that as they continued to be drawn into Nepal's national economy and as the population continued to grow, standards of living would decline and an increasingly uneven distribution of wealth would ensue. Children would no longer be a source of family security but simply mouths to feed from a declining resource base. The villagers themselves were optimistic, thinking that the then-approaching road that would link them to markets would enable them to sell fruit and find better employment. In his most recent visits, Fricke found both views to be true. The village has changed greatly; in some ways for the better, and in other respects not. Now there is an active government-run school and children are receiving a formal education; a clinic has opened and health and hygiene have improved. By 1992, most of the villagers had converted, at least nominally, to Christianity; the effects of this transition on traditional attitudes and values are yet to be seen. Now many people are living and working outside the village; some have second homes in the capital. Younger men are finding employment as trekkers—working with parties of tourists who come to hike in the spectacular mountains. The economy has become monetarized at the expense of the previous era's system of reciprocity, and some villagers have clearly improved their standards of living. Others, particularly older people, feel that they are being neglected in their old age as their sons and daughters go abroad to work or settle elsewhere where resources are more abundant. Just as with the Yanomamö, willingly or not, they are becoming active players in an increasingly interconnected world with perhaps the first harbinger of change being the sudden visit by an anthropologist.

Summary

FARMING SOCIETIES DEPEND ON DOMESTICATED foods, especially plants; that is, people try to control the reproduction rates of their food resources by ordering the environment in such a way as to favor their survival. Human labor and simple tools are the primary means of working the land, and extensive farmers do not produce consistently large surpluses for others' consumption. Their subsistence economies make both the group and the individual household largely self-sufficient and independent. Yet trade with neighboring groups is an important feature of their survival strategy and is integrated with their agricultural activities, as are some hunting and gathering activities.

Since contemporary horticultural societies generally occupy marginal territories and do not use major technological aids, they have developed a variety of techniques to exploit their environment. The most common technique is slash-and-burn (or swidden) agriculture. Trees and undergrowth are cut and burned to form a layer of fertilizing ash. Several varieties of plants are cultivated for several years, then the area is left to lie fallow and new land is cleared. The success of swidden agriculture, and of horticulture in general, depends on an intimate knowledge of the environment.

Subsistence farmers can support more people per unit of land area than can hunters and gatherers, but in comparison with other agriculturists they operate on a low energy budget. They do not have to use their resources or labor to the fullest in order to subsist.

Among the social conditions that normally accompany a dependence on agriculture are increased sedentism—the practice of establishing a permanent, year-round settlement—and increased population density. These conditions tend to increase social complexity and interdependence.

The household is the basic unit in horticultural societies; the integration of families into a community is achieved primarily through kinship ties and political organization. Kinship networks are often the basis for both recognition of individual rights to the use of land and extensive gift exchange throughout the community.

Relations with other communities may be peaceable or warlike, or somewhere in between. Trade, alliances, and intermarriage foster peaceful relations; while competition for resources, raids, and exploitation provide excuses for war.

The two farming societies discussed in this chapter are the Yanomamö of Venezuela and Brazil and the Tamang of Nepal. As the two peoples inhabit different environments, their adaptations have taken very different forms.

The Yanomamö hunt and gather, in addition to practicing swidden agriculture in their dense tropical jungle. Authority in their villages rests with the headman, who leads by example rather than by institutionalized power. Kinship is reckoned by patrilineal descent (through the male line), and a typical village consists of two lineages that have intermarried. Strict marriage rules specify that a man choose a wife outside his lineage.

Villages normally move every few years, mostly because of internal feuds or warfare with other villages. The Yanomamö social world is one of chronic suspicion and hostility. Political alliances are cautiously negotiated by the exchange of gifts, followed by trading, feasting, and exchange of brides, but even alliances based on marriage ties are tenuous.

Some anthropologists attribute the hostile social environment to a shortage of sources of protein. Marvin Harris believes that Yanomamö warfare is concerned—unwittingly—with hunting territory, and Daniel Gross holds that the settlement pattern—widely dispersed mobile villages—is a strategy for preventing the overexploitation of game in any one area. Yet Napoleon Chagnon, who has studied the Yanomamö longer and more intensively than anyone else, finds no evidence of protein deficiency among them. Chagnon attributes their bellicosity to intense competition for women, caused by their practice of female infanticide and the custom of powerful men to take more than one wife.

The peaceful village of Timling could not be in stronger contrast to the Yanomamö way of life. They have a relatively relaxed attitude toward sex, prize peaceful relations with others, and engage in no warfare. Their mountain environment is in sharp contrast as well; they exploit a variety of vertical climate zones, some of which they plow and plant in wheat, corn, potatoes, and millet; others of which they use for animal production and foraging for firewood and building supplies. Whereas the Yanomamö, until very recently, were relatively cut off from people living in state- or urban-based political systems, the people of Timling, however independent, have long been in close contact with Tibet and Nepal—as well India and Bhutan, where men have long gone to work. Their religion, while containing unique elements, is part of a much larger, literate tradition of Buddhism. Both the Yanomamö and the people of Timling face uncertain futures—the Yanomamö because their lands are being encroached upon by farmers and miners and because of alien diseases introduced by foreigners. The people of Timling do not face such direct threats to their survival, but are at risk of losing their independence and self-sufficiency as they are drawn into a national culture and its market economy.

Key Terms

acculturation	patrilocal residence
domestication	polyculture
domestic cycle	postpartum taboo
extended family	sedentism
household	shaman
extensive agriculture	slash-and-burn (swidden)
headman	agriculture
horticulture	subsistence agriculture
patrilineal descent	

Suggested Readings

Chagnon, N. A. (1997). *Yanomamö: The last days of Eden*. San Diego: Harcourt Brace Jovanovich, Inc. A distinguished albeit controversial anthropologist reviews his work among the Yanomamö, answering those who have criticized his analyses in the past while stressing the problems the Yanomamö face today.

Damas, D. (1994). *Bountiful island: A study of land tenure on a Micronesian atoll*. Ontario: Wilfrid Laurier University Press. This book examines the land tenure system in an atoll society and its relationship to population densities and land ownership.

Grinker, R. R. (1994). *Houses in the rainforest: Ethnicity and inequality among farmers and foragers in central Africa*. Berkeley: University of California Press. A groundbreaking ethnographic study of a farmer-forager society in Northeast Zaire and its complex social relations.

Lepowsky, M. (1994). *Fruit of the motherland: Gender in an egalitarian society*. New York: Columbia University Press. An ethnography of the Vanatinai of New Guinea that contradicts the ideology of universal male dominance by exploring gender roles, ideology, and power.

Reed, R. (1997). *Forest protectors: Indigenous models for international development*. Boston: Allyn & Bacon. This is an excellent account of the indigenous knowledge and historical experiences of the Guarani, a population occupying a subtropical region across parts of Paraguay and Brazil.

Sahlins, M. (1968). *Tribesmen*. Englewood Cliffs, NJ: Prentice-Hall. A now-classic discussion of the economic arrangements, social structure, and ideologies of tribal societies, most of which are horticulturists.

Werner, D. (1984). *Amazon journey: An anthropologist's year among Brazil's Mekranoti Indians*. New York: Simon & Schuster. An informal and sympathetic portrayal of modern anthropological field data collection and analysis among horticulturists in the rapidly changing Amazon.

Whiteley, P. M. (1988). *Deliberate acts: Changing Hopi culture through the Oraibi Split*. Tucson: University of Arizona Press. A detailed portrait of the history and social organization of a Hopi village that focuses on social change over a hundred-year period.

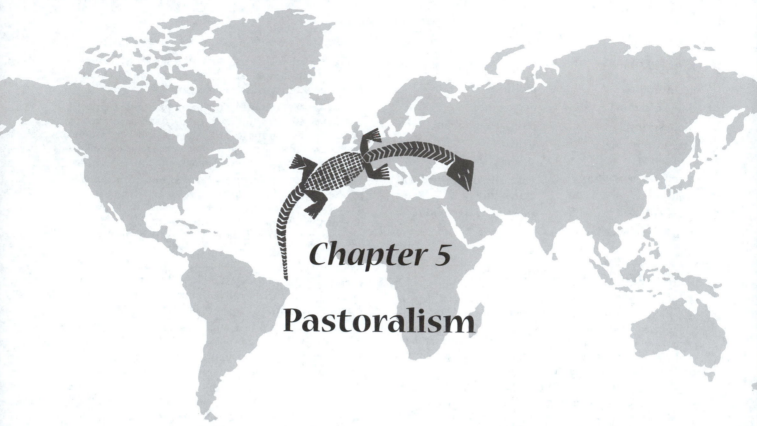

Chapter 5

Pastoralism

Pastoralism, as we saw with the Tamang, is *animal husbandry*—the breeding, care, and use of herd animals such as sheep, goats, camels, cattle, horses, llamas, reindeer, and yaks. When animal husbandry is pursued as a primary adaptation, it is a highly specialized strategy of land use that in certain respects resembles hunting and gathering. In terms of productivity, however, it is more comparable to intensive farming. Like most hunter-gatherer groups, pastoralists use lands whose vegetation they only minimally manage: They graze their animals on wild grasses, shrubs, and sometimes fallow crop lands. Like agricultural populations, pastoralists invest time and energy in the management of productive resources—their livestock.

Most pastoralists are nomadic, moving their herds from pasture to pasture on a seasonal schedule within a well-defined territory. The degree of mobility varies from group to group, and even from year to year within a group, depending on such environmental factors as rainfall, vegetation, and the availability of water holes. Economic and political constraints also affect the pattern of nomads' movements. Pastoralists must deal with the demands of other groups—even governments—in order to gain access to pastures and to the markets where they can exchange animals and animal products for clothing, tools, weapons, and food.

The extent of *specialized pastoralism*, the adaptive strategy of primary reliance on animal husbandry, varies with environmental and market conditions. Few groups rely exclusively on their herds for day-to-day subsistence. To do so would entail heavy risks in two respects. In order to keep their animals alive, pastoralists have to adjust to the vagaries of the environment: Cold, lack of water, lack of pasturage, and so forth. At the same time, they must coexist with other groups with whom they may be in competition. Given these complications, it is no surprise that when the environment permits, pastoralists tend to pursue a more generalized subsistence strategy, raising at least some crops along with their animals (Barfield, 1993; Berleant-Schiller & Shanklin, 1983).

In fact, most pastoralists, no matter how specialized, subsist more on grains than on animal products. The camel-herding Bedouin of Arabia greatly prize their independence but are now, and always have been, linked by numerous economic and social ties to the larger, sedentary society. Even before the coming of trucks, camps in

Arabia were regularly visited by merchants laden with wares to trade for camels. The merchants would set up shop in distinctive white tents (in contrast to the black tents of the nomads) and it was a breach of the codes regulating warfare to rob or harm these visitors, so important were they to the well-being of the pastoral community. Today, of course, most Bedouin households have trucks or jeeps and can drive to the nearest town to shop.

Before we take a close look at two pastoral societies, let us see how pastoralism developed and what its social consequences are for groups that pursue it.

The Pastoral Adaptation

Development

The archaeological record indicates that mixed farming based on a combination of domesticated plants and animals preceded specialized pastoralism (Redman, 1978). Mixed farming was a multifaceted strategy that provided a hedge against droughts, crop failures, diseases, and other natural calamities. For farmers, livestock not only provided valuable material (skins for clothing and shelter) and food products, but the animals themselves were a means of storing food against future use—a freezer on the hoof. At the same time, if the animals died, the crops were there. Diversification provided both the alternatives and the reserves necessary to survive fluctuations in the food supply. Such diversification is still common in many parts of Africa, Europe, and the Middle East, particularly in mountain villages.

Despite the many advantages of diversification, changes in agricultural practices, especially the development of canal irrigation and intensive agriculture, created the preconditions for specialized pastoralism. Increased productivity based on canal irrigation made possible population growth and the expansion of settlements, with a consequent increase in land devoted to intensive farming and a decrease in land available for animals. It also stimulated interregional trade. Grazing areas were pushed farther from the settlement region into territory where forage was not so lush. To get adequate food and water for their herds, animal owners had to expend more labor and travel greater and greater distances. Furthermore, the animals were more vulnerable to predators and especially to raiders. Thus, care of the animals began to drain energies away from agriculture. At the same time, agriculture became more time-consuming, for farmers now had to clear, tend, and repair the canals in addition to working the fields. The increased demands of each of these strategies may well have led to a divergence, with certain households specializing in increasingly intensive agriculture and others concentrating on animal husbandry or pastoralism.

In some cases, plow farmers may have attempted to move into intensive agriculture but failed in their attempts to utilize canal irrigation. Extensive irrigation may cause the **water table** (that is, the level of water under the earth) to drop, so that wells and canals run dry. Or the water may so increase the salinity of the soil that crops begin to fail. Canals also fail in areas of inadequate stream flow. Other agriculturists who had always struggled to raise crops in marginal areas had incentives to concentrate their attention on animal husbandry. Eventually the differences in strategies between the farming and herding groups led to spatial and cultural differentiation as well, creating distinct groups of pastoralists and agriculturists.

Pastoralism, then, may have developed hand in hand with intensive agriculture. Whatever the reasons for its development, pastoralism is a strategy predicated on agricultural surplus and on regular interaction between herders and farmers. Pastoralism may be an alternative to agriculture, but it is almost never independent of it.

The Organization of Energy

Like horticulture, pastoralism is more productive than hunting and gathering. Hunters do not try to increase the numbers of animals or use the products of living animals. They may, as we have noted, hunt in a conservative fashion in an effort not to eliminate their prey altogether, but they do not practice animal management. Pastoralists do invest labor in breeding and caring for their animals, and so increase their reproduction and survival rates. Tim Ingold notes that apart from reindeer herders, pastoralists are usually concerned with the production of milk, hair, blood, or wool, and with traction—using animals as vehicles or sources of work energy (1980, p. 87). Meat production is almost incidental with one or two notable exceptions. By investing human labor in the production of milk rather than meat, the herder gains a greater net return: The animal need not be killed to be useful. In fact, successful herders can generally increase their holdings at a faster rate than farmers, for as the animals reproduce, the offspring can be incorporated into their herds. Of course, this advantage is partially offset by the precarious nature of herding in most areas: Animals are susceptible to disease, drought, and theft, any of which can reduce a rich household to poverty overnight.

Full-time pastoralism may be less efficient than farming in areas where cultivation is possible. People can produce approximately ten times as much food, measured in calories yielded per acre of land, by raising grains instead of livestock. But in areas where agriculture is risky or impossible, pastoralism is a useful strategy for converting forage—sources of energy that humans cannot use directly—into milk, blood, and meat. These foods are stored in the form of animals until the people need them either to eat or to trade for agricultural foods, clothing, and other items they cannot otherwise obtain. Furthermore, the fact that animals can move themselves permits herders to move the production system to the resources.

By using a strategy of simultaneously exploiting more than one environment, pastoralists have found a relatively efficient way of extracting energy from an environment not suited to agriculture. For example, the herds of most East African pastoralists are mixed, and include not only zebu (oxen distinguished by a hump, much like a camel's) but also large numbers of goats, sometimes sheep, donkeys, and, in very dry areas, camels. The importance of the mixed herd lies in the fact that each species has its own feeding preferences so that not one but several environments are exploited. However, since pastoralism produces much less food energy per acre of land than agriculture, specialized pastoralists necessarily have low population densities.

Nomadic Movement

In nonindustrial societies, **sedentary pastoralism,** or animal husbandry that does not involve mobility (ranching, say, or dairy farming) is relatively rare. The practice more generally followed is **nomadic pastoralism**, the adaptive strategy of moving the herds that are one's livelihood from pasture to pasture as the seasons and circumstances require. Land that is rich enough to support a herd indefinitely in one location will yield far more output if it is given over primarily to crops. By taking advantage of the mobility of herd animals and their own ability to group and regroup, however, pastoralists can adapt to marginal areas by moving as conditions dictate. Mobility is the key that unlocks widely dispersed resources and allows a population to gain a living from an environment that could not sustain a settled community.

While the main reason for pastoralist migrations is to secure adequate grazing on a year-round basis, this is not the only reason. William Irons (1975) has pointed out that the Turkmen pastoralists of northern Iran move to maintain their political and cultural

independence, as well as to seek grazing lands. In the past, they also frequently raided non-Turkmen sedentary populations and caravans. If they were pursued by a more powerful force, they could simply disperse with their animals into inaccessible areas. Though they were "pacified" by the Iranian government in the early twentieth century, they have managed until recently to retain considerable control over their own affairs. They did so by using the one skill they had developed far beyond the abilities of other populations—moving.

Today, even within the boundaries of contemporary state bureaucratic systems, mobility often allows nomadic pastoralists to maintain greater political autonomy than settled communities enjoy. With continuing political uncertainty in Iran, both nomadic and settled Turkmen are reasserting their claim to a separate identity, and the nomadic groups are apparently the more successful in their efforts. In other countries, nomads may be able to avoid onerous civic duties such as military conscription and taxation.

The economic strategies of individual households within a given population of pastoralists often vary considerably. Such variations are sketched very clearly in the ever-changing composition of the camp group and in individual decisions on migration. Some groups among the Turkmen of Iran, for example, may move frequently one year and be largely sedentary the next. Regular patterns often underlie this variability. In Turkey, Yörük households with many animals may move early in the spring to pastures in the mountains, braving cold weather to get to the first grasses. Others with smaller flocks may feel they cannot afford the risk of losing even a few animals to the cold, and so move later in the season. In general, though, the variability of movement patterns is due to the variation in types of herds, quality of grazing lands, climate, and availability of water. An area of rich pasture land and mild climate does not require as many moves as one dominated by poorer-quality pastures (Barfield, 1993).

There are two basic systems of nomadic movement, despite much variation. One pattern, plains or **horizontal migration**, is characterized by regular movement over a large area in search of forage, a necessary strategy where no particular area is capable of sustaining a herd for a long period of time. The Bedouin of the Arabian Peninsula exemplify this form of nomadism; members of Bedouin tribal groups are dispersed over hundreds of square miles as they make use of the scant vegetation of an extremely arid region. Although they gather in larger encampments around seasonal water holes, the density of population is strikingly low. This pattern has

Camels have declining economic importance in Arabia, but are still vitally important livestock in East Africa and the Sahel, where water is a scarce resource. Here Ethiopian herders water their herds.
(Woodfin Camp & Associates)

been widespread throughout the cattle- and goat-keeping portions of Africa, the deserts and steppes of Central Asia and the Middle East, and, in later times, the plains of North and South America.

The second pattern is that of seasonal movement of livestock between upland and lowland pastures, or **transhumance**. This form of nomadism has been found throughout the mountainous zones of the Middle East, parts of Eastern Europe, Switzerland, Central Asia, and, in later times, North and South America. Transhumant nomads often camp together for extended periods of time in two major grazing areas: Summer pastures in the mountains and winter pastures in the valleys. During the migrations between seasonal encampments the roads and trails are crowded with people and animals on the move.

Despite the fact that most pastoral populations adopt a nomadic lifestyle, we often see individual families giving up herding altogether for other pursuits. This is what families in the Middle East tend to do when they have accumulated enough wealth to invest in a more secure form of capital, such as land or a shop, or when their herds have become so small that they can no longer support the household. In many regions, settlement, followed by a return to herding, is a regular process (Salzman, 1980). On the other hand, agricultural households may shift to herding if they consider it advantageous to do so. Thus most of the people described as pastoralists have strong cultural ties in sedentary communities and usually have relatives there as well. The Bedouin of the Negev in Israel, for example, have been largely forced to settle for political reasons but still keep as many animals as they can manage.

However we may think of nomadic pastoralists, we should not fall into the trap of perceiving them as inflexibly committed to a single way of life. Nomadism is a strategy, a means of making specialized animal husbandry work. A group can be more or less nomadic depending on conditions. People can organize themselves into sizable groups and stay together for extended periods when they gain advantages from that strategy, but they will work separately when that approach is more productive. Although we often speak of "group cohesiveness," "corporateness," and "economic stratification" as characteristics of a society, we should not lose sight of their ultimate origins in individual behavioral motivation. What we see as patterns of social organization are the outcomes of the strategies individuals adopt as they cope with their problems and evaluate their opportunities.

Social Organization

There is no single form of social organization that is peculiar to nomadic pastoralists; such adaptations occur in varied environmental, political, and cultural contexts. The social life of Lapp reindeer herders may closely resemble that of neighboring Finnish communities. The Bedouin of Arabia may be culturally similar to tribal villagers in Iraq. Still, most researchers who have studied or worked with nomadic pastoral societies see certain aspects of social organization related either to the necessity (or capacity) for mobility or to the requirements of the animals they tend.

Virtually all nomadic pastoralists are organized in tribes, sociopolitical communities whose members are bound by ties of kinship—most commonly by presumed descent from one or more common ancestors. Such groupings can easily encompass

Box 5.1
China's Cowboys of Inner Mongolia

WE CAN OFTEN LEARN A GREAT deal about social organization by looking at how people cope with change. One instance is described in a recent study by Burton Pasternak and Janet Salaff of Han Chinese living in Inner Mongolia and following a pastoral mode of production (1993). Their work shows how ecology and technology create diversity in China, despite strong pressures from the state and cultural institutions for uniformity. Working with Chinese colleagues, Pasternak and Salaff studied four communities over a number of years. The Han are Chinese immigrant farmers who, beginning in the late 1940s, left traditional riceland farming, crossed the Great Wall, and began farming and herding in the grasslands of Mongolia.[1] They came seeking a better life but found a setting where the indigenous people were hostile, the climate precarious, and the land difficult. Only those who were prepared to alter their behavior were to succeed on China's famed—and feared— northwestern frontier. We will look primarily at those who chose pastoralism as their new economy.

The Han people, whether they speak Mandarin or some other dialect, have a common history and culture; in short, a style of life that the researchers call the "Chinese Way." The Chinese Way, in addition to representing common values and beliefs about family and identity, also represented a particular division of labor, organization of households, and gender roles. However successful the Han have been over the centuries in adapting to China proper, primarily through intensive farming techniques allowing them to squeeze ever more food out of severely limited land, the Great Wall always seemed to mark the limits of where the Han could live in the Chinese Way—it marked the end of civilization for them.

Inner Mongolia is a natural laboratory in which to study how ecology shapes social organization. The seasons are extreme, with very cold winters and cool and short summers. Most of the region was stripped of forest cover in the nineteenth century and now erosion threatens farmlands and pastures alike. In 1990, the population was 80 percent Han, with the indigenous Mongolians a distinct and often resentful minority in one of China's poorest regions. Fieldwork was difficult for the anthropologists, who found a fine brown dust in everything they ate; water was either so scarce as to make bathing impossible or so plentiful as to turn the dirt road to a sea of mud. Even privacy was a serious problem; there were no latrines on unobstructed plains often lacking even rocks or trees.

While some Han adapted to the new region through farming, other Han populations adopted pastoralism—a strategy unfamiliar to them. In this, they came to resemble their Mongol neighbors in important ways while still maintaining their Han identity and language. Mongols and Han herders remain separate subcommunities and rarely intermarry. When Han first took up herding, they focused mainly on dairying, as they were more famil-

---

many thousands of individuals through the expedient of recognizing subgroups defined by degree of kinship: Clans, lineages, or even large family clusters. Such groupings do not depend on a definition of community that rests mainly on residence in a territory or locality; a member of one's tribe is a relative.

A member of the cattle-keeping Nuer tribe in Sudan, described by E. E. Evans-Pritchard (1940), is a Nuer wherever he or she may happen to be. Every Nuer is also a member by birthright of one of a series of "segments" or genealogical parts of the tribe, each having a distinctive name, not unlike a family name in our own society. Each segment of the Nuer tribal system is supposed to assist the others largely in accordance with the closeness of the presumed relationship between them. This segmentary lineage system, widespread in Africa and the Middle East, provides a highly flexible means of adapting group size to the resources at hand. Groups come together or split up along lines of kinship. Though not all or even most tribal societies are pastoralists, most nomadic pastoralists are organized in tribes of one sort or another.

Camp Groups and Household Organization. Individuals and households in herding societies frequently change their patterns of movement and the groups with which they camp. They move in response to changing economic and political conditions and also to new social circumstances. Individual households camp with people with whom they enjoy good relations, and such people are most often kin. There appear to be strong constraints on the number of households that can readily coordinate their activities in an egalitarian society that lacks

iar with cattle from their past experience as settled villagers. This meant that they could remain largely sedentary, with their cattle kept near their homes. They supplemented this activity with fishing and cutting and selling hay. Neither strategy was used much by the traditional Mongols, who ranged far afield with herds of sheep and other animals. In time the Han began to shift to sheepherding, even though it required much more male labor and meant either moving their dwelling or having the men absent for long periods. Sheep have to be moved regularly and require close supervision and guarding, as the pastures are distant from the main settlements. The Han began to experiment with sheep because, despite the costs and risks, the payoff in wool, meat, and milk production was greater than with cattle alone. With time, they came to emulate the Mongols in other respects; some adopted Mongol traditions and became yurt-dwellers in distant pastures, making tent-like homes out of felt covering a framework of wood and wicker, consuming mutton and beef instead of pork, using strong alcoholic beverages, and drinking strong tea mixed with milk.

The Han shepherds have become the new nomads, or what Pasternak and Salaff call China's new cowboys. But it is the requirements of sheep herding, not cultural assimilation, that have encouraged similarities with Mongol social organization and ways of life. This is reflected in the division of labor, age at first marriage, fertility, and family age/size composition. Sheep herding requires high levels of continual labor for supervision and herd management, and animals are kept on distant and regularly changing pasture sites. Since the minimum size of a herd that can be profitably managed is nearly 200 animals, this represents a major capital investment, as well as one that is highly vulnerable to disease and predation.

While women and children may help out in managing the animals, the pastoralists feel that only grown men can adequately care for the flocks in distant and sometimes dangerous pastures. As a result, there is a sharper division of labor by sex: Han women usually stay home tending to the family's cattle and gardens, while men work hard in the pastures, where, in addition to shepherding, they cut hay and bring drinking water home in heav-

ily laden carts requiring great physical strength to manage. In short (and unlike other nomadic populations elsewhere), the labor of women and children is apparently of relatively less importance.

The Mongols, likewise, place a high value on male labor and regard women's work as a distinct sphere of activity that men do not enter. Since male labor is more remunerative, young girls are more apt than boys to be able to go to school; but unlike farmers (since female labor was less in demand), the sons of pastoral households married at a later age and lived more often in smaller, neolocal domestic units. Han pastoralists average nearly 4.5 people per household as opposed to farmers who average 5.0. Farmers usually try to keep a large household together after one or more sons marry; the pastoralists (like the Mongols) usually start new, independent households. Farmers, too, have higher fertility than herders; reflecting, the researchers argue, the higher value placed on child labor.

[1] This box is based on the work of Pasternak and Salaff (1993) and Pasternak's summary of this in *Portraits of Culture*, 1994, Ember, M., Ember, C., & Levinson, D. Englewood Cliffs, NJ: Prentice Hall.

strong leadership roles. Two observers have noted considerable uniformity in the average size of nomadic camps or migratory groups—usually in the range of 100 to 300 persons (Tapper, 1979, p. 81; Johnson, 1983, p. 176).

When Gregory Johnson examined a large number of nomadic societies whose people lived together by choice rather than by coercion, he found that a camp group comprised on average six households or clusters of very closely related households, such as father-son groupings (1983, p. 183). If conflict were to occur in the camp group, often the easiest solution was for the antagonists simply to move apart. In many respects the shifting composition of nomadic camping-and-herding groups resembles the camps of nomadic hunter-gatherers. People use mobility to minimize conflict and to associate with those they find congenial.

In most pastoral societies it is possible to speak of the **co-resident household**, a grouping whose members often dwell in tents as a basic economic unit and coordinate their herding and other productive activities. In a society in which groups move frequently and the composition of larger groupings changes regularly, the household takes on added social significance—particularly, Ingold contends (1980, pp. 188–189), when market relations engender competition. The household, like the camping group of which it is a part, must respond to changing economic circumstances—sometimes by an increase in size, sometimes by dispersal into smaller households. One study in China's remote northwest frontier, profiled in Box 5.1, *China's Cowboys of Inner Mongolia*, gives us an insight into the ways in which pastoral production can shape household organization.

Hierarchical Tribal Organization. While pastoralists' camp groups may resemble the fluid camps of hunter-gatherers, most such societies have a more complex sociopolitical organization that unites the constituent households and camping groups in tribes. Some nomadic tribes, such as the Bedouin of Arabia and the Mongols of Central Asia, have strong leaders. Undoubtedly, the existence of such roles reflects the fact that these peoples were in close contact, even regular conflict, with agricultural communities and lived within the boundaries of nation-states. The Qashqa'i of Iran, for example, have an elaborate hierarchy of leaders, each part of a fairly well-defined chain of command (Beck, 1986, 1991).

A hierarchical tribal organization often has highly specified membership criteria (as by patrilineal or matrilineal descent) and is composed of well-defined subgroups. Such an organization allows for more than just communication across great distances. It is a means of coordinating large-scale migrations, gaining access to grazing land, holding and defending territory, and even on occasion gaining control over sedentary farming populations.

A study by Arun Agrawal of nomadic shepherds, the Raikas of Western India, show how this works. The Raikas are the largest group of nomadic pastoralists in India, migrating from settlements in Rajistan and Gujarat with flocks of sheep for more than two-thirds of the year. Generally shepherds move to a new camp location almost every day; there are several hundred thousand shepherds on the move. Their mobile camps—*dang*—have as many as eighteen herds (or up to 7,000 animals) and over one hundred men, women, and children. "Daily movements of fifty to one hundred human beings and their animals demand critical collective decisions" (Agrawal, 1993, p. 263). They achieve this by delegating decision making to three groups in each tent.

The first is the *nambardar*, who is the senior leader because of his wide experience, wealth, and contacts with leaders of other camps. He spends his time scouting possible routes and visiting other camps. The second leader, the *kamdar*, makes decisions while the *nambardar* is out of camp and participates in the council of five elders, made up of men representing a broad spectrum of Raikas' interests. The third level of decision making is the *mukhiya*, a man who is the leader of the individual herders in the camp and who intimately knows the needs and characteristics of the herds. The leaders are chosen on the basis of experience, age, wealth, and kin relationships. The *nambardar* makes most decisions about migration, marketing, camp-wide shearing, and camp-wide management; he is the best informed about the possible routes and camp sites. The *kam-*

dar serves to manage internal relations in the camp during the *nambardar's* frequent absences and to coordinate with the council of elders—thus maintaining a check on the *nambardar's* authority. Finally, decisions having to do with herding, labor, and when to bring the animals home rest with the *mukhiya*, who best knows flock management (Agrawal, 1993, p. 270).

Wealth, Inequality, and Status

In many traditional pastoral societies, livestock constitutes the sole form of economic wealth. Rights to animals are held by individual households and are passed down from father to son. Because some may inherit more than others or may have more success in managing their herds, the number and quality of the herds vary from household to household. However, everyone is subject to loss of livestock through disease, theft, drought, or just bad luck—a wealthy household may be reduced to poverty in one season. Thus, in many pastoral societies where there is no market for livestock, periods of wealth and poverty are temporary and tend not to create permanent disparities in economic status.

However, it is probably safe to say that distinctions of wealth are more evident among pastoral populations than among the horticulturists we discussed in Chapter 4. Among the Komanchi sheep herders of Iran, for example, Daniel Bradburd (1990) found not only great disparities of wealth among households, but also systematic exploitation of poorer households by wealthy ones. Such disparities are reflected in marriage arrangements and in many other areas of social life; the poorer households have a limited opportunity to improve their lot (Bradburd, 1990). This case may be extreme, but economic differentiation among households is common. Among the Ariaal of Kenya, to be discussed shortly, drought tends to kill off a larger percentage of the wealthy herders' animals since they are not cared for as carefully as the animals of small stockowners (Fratkin & Roth, 1994, 1996). But since the rich have more animals, particularly drought-resistant camels, they survive periods of drought with far less risk of being impoverished and forced to settle permanently in one location.

The Social and Symbolic Value of Livestock. In addition to the fact that livestock are central to the pastoral economy, they also have considerable social and symbolic value. For example, some Bedouin tribes keep small herds of pure white camels; others maintain special racing camels. Today, as most camels are being replaced by trucks, their continuing value resides in their significance as a cultural symbol marking their identification with the past and with familial honor (Barfield, 1993, p. 89).

Among the horse-riding pastoralists of Central Asia, horses are prized far beyond their utilitarian value. In fact, sheep and goats have much more value in subsistence terms. However, while horses were never the primary focus of these people, they endowed their riders with the speed to facilitate communication and cooperation and the mobility and power to triumph in battles. Thus they symbolize military and political power.

In East Africa, cattle have a paramount and pervasive symbolic value. Melville Herskovits (1924) long ago identified this focus on cattle as the "East African **cattle complex:**" A socioeconomic system in which cattle represent social, not economic, wealth. They were exchanged as part of marriage ceremonies, ritually slaughtered at other ceremonial events, given as gifts, and prized for their beauty. According to Herskovitz, the possession of large herds was such an important status symbol that cattle were neither traded nor used as a regular source of food. This symbolic explanation was used to account for an excessive number of cattle in a culture that did little trading.

However, further research has revealed that, while cattle are clearly central to the social life of these herders, they also have an economic function. First, the cows' main contribution to the subsistence economy is milk, which is the primary pastoral product. Since the cattle that can survive in the harsh environment of East Africa aren't very productive, large herds are necessary to satisfy subsistence needs. Also, although eating beef except on ritual occasions was forbidden, these ritual sacrifices occurred often enough to suggest that beef was a significant source of food. Keeping great numbers of cattle was also part of a subsistence strategy that divided and dispersed herds over a wide area as a kind of insurance against loss of all one's cattle in one place to raiders from a neighboring group or to disease.

We shall consider two groups of pastoralists, each with a distinctive adaptive pattern. The first group, the Ariaal of northern Kenya in East Africa, are among the African tribes for whom cattle are economically and culturally important. Yet they also keep camels as well as sheep and goats—whose products they consume or trade for grain, tea, and sugar. Even though they are pastoralists, they eat meat only occasionally. Milk, blood, and a porridge made of sorghum and other grains form the basis of a diet won from a harsh and unpredictable environment.

The second group, the Yörük of Turkey, raise their herds for the purpose of exchange with other

A Yomut Turkmen elder on his prized horse. Horses were formerly an important key to Turkmen military prowess, as well as a source of prestige.
(Daniel Bates)

groups. Traditionally the Yörük cultivated no crops, preferring to use the income from their stock to buy grain and other foodstuffs from the agriculturists of their region. Nor did they have permanent settlements; they moved regularly and on a tight schedule in order to get adequate pasturage. Economic factors have caused them to change their pattern somewhat in recent years, however, and the majority now live in towns and villages.

The Ariaal of Northern Kenya

In 1974, Elliot Fratkin stopped his unreliable motorcycle in the dusty market town of Marsabit, unable to continue to Ethiopia, where he had planned to carry out fieldwork among pastoralists. The border was closed because of a coup against Haile Selassie (Fratkin, 1991, p. 4).[1] Sitting dejectedly in a bar and considering the problem of what to do next, he was approached by a young man who invited him out to a settlement ten kilometers to the south to see a dance. He accepted, and thus he began a study of the Ariaal that has continued until today. The dance

---

[1] The following account of the Ariaal is based on Elliot Fratkin's 1991 book, *Surviving drought and development: Ariaal pastoralists of Northern Kenya,* unless otherwise noted.

Elliot Fratkin with his field assistants Patrick Sunewan and Larian Aliayaro. Fratkin, in keeping with the general ethnographic approach to fieldwork, has spent many months living with the people about whom he reports.

(Elliot Fratkin)

that he witnessed was not a tourist show; over 300 warriors were in the middle of a ritual lasting several days that was held to minimize the disharmony caused by the recent killing of one of their leaders (1991, p. 5). He remained two years; he returned in 1985 for more work and again in 1990, 1992, and 1994. Thus, Fratkin has been able to see how Ariaal society has changed: How they have coped with the many intrusions into their earlier way of life, and, in particular, how the development projects that were meant to assist them actually worked out. Well-intentioned efforts at relieving famine and drought often have had unintended, negative consequences.

The Ariaal probably number some 7,000 persons living in Kenya's most arid and least densely populated district; other pastoral populations nearby include the closely related Samburu (70,000) and the Rendille (15,000), and the more distantly related Maasai (350,000) who live to the south.

The Origins of the Ariaal

While ethnic identities often seem fixed and timeless, it is important to keep in mind that social identity is always being transformed with the passage of time: New formations arise and others disappear. The Ariaal are a good example of this process. Today, they strongly stress their unique identity and the ways in which they differ from their neighbors. Still, there is good evidence that this identity has its historical origins in groups of refugees from the Samburu, Rendille, and possibly Maasai groups who came together as a result of intertribal warfare and drought. Over the years they coalesced as a distinctive population with its own approach to pastoralism. The last quarter of the nineteenth century was a turbu-

lent era for pastoralists in Kenya. Not only was there a prolonged period of drought, but a number of epidemics devastated many herds. It was in this context that warfare broke out as pastoralists raided each other's herds, particularly among Maasai groups. Impoverished groups of Samburu, whose herds were ravished by rinderpest, fled to Rendille territory where they formed mixed Samburu/Rendille communities subsisting on camels and sheep and goats.

They were, by necessity, confined to fringe areas that neither the main elements of the Samburu nor the Rendille exploited. However, as is often the case with the impoverished or socially marginal groups, they soon came to prosper by adopting practices from each neighboring population and developing their own distinctive pastoral strategy. They made careful use of a wide range of resources—raising camels as well as cattle and small stock, strategically deploying labor, and maintained close relations with their more populous neighbors. The Ariaal speak Samburu (a Nilotic language related to Maasai) and most are also fluent in Rendille (an Afro-Asiatic language related to Somali); they intermarry with both; and they share some religious and social customs with each (but in their own unique mix).

The Ariaal Adaptation

What really distinguishes the Ariaal, apart from their own assertions of identity, is their approach to animal husbandry. They have adapted to the plains and slopes around Mt. Marsabit and the Ndoto Mountains—an ecologically marginal region that they successfully exploit by using a highly diversified system of husbandry based on large inputs of household labor (Fratkin, 1991, p. 16). Unlike the Sam-

Figure 5–1. *Territory of the Ariaal, Samburu, Rendille, and Pokot.*

buru (whose economy is based on raising cattle and small stock) and the Rendille (who raise camels and small stock), the Ariaal utilize all three types of animals, thus using a broader spectrum of resources and affording greater economic security.

The complexity of the terrain and the variety of resource potentials it offers provide the key to their subsistence strategy. The Ariaal live in a semi-desert environment with low and variable rainfall, and marked seasonality; they "... use their domesticated animals to convert patchy and seasonal vegetative resources into a constant supply of food in the form of milk, meat, blood, and a surplus with which to trade for grains, tea, and sugar" (p. 39). Water is clearly the factor that determines much of the Ariaal's herding activity and patterns of movement. The Ariaal have almost 10,000 square kilometers in which to herd, but this region is among the most arid in Kenya. The highlands receive an average of less than 500mm (20 inches) of rainfall per year and the lowlands average 250 mm. The rainfall is erratic and irregular, so that one cannot predict its occurrence or intensity (p. 39). However, most rainfall occurs in two seasons: the "long rains" between March and May, and the "short rains" in October and November. The periods between the two rainy seasons are called, very appropriately, the "long hunger" and the "short hunger" (p. 39).

During the wet season, provided the rains come as hoped, the Ariaal can utilize surface water in temporary flood plains, in pools, and in transient rivers. During the dry seasons, they must rely on hand-dug wells around the base of the mountains as well as a limited number of mechanized wells (pp. 39–42). They cannot, however, live or camp too near the water sources or their herds will destroy the vegetation.

The key to survival is herd diversity and mobility. Herd diversity allows a family to use different pastures and insures against loss due to epidemics (p. 37); mobility is an effective adaptation to their arid environment, where rapid deterioration of vegetation for grazing requires regular herd movement. Moreover, vegetation is only rich in nutrients during the limited growing season.

Diversity in Livestock. Ariaal herds generally consist of cattle, camels, and small stock such as sheep and goats. Cattle, which are grass-eaters and require water every two days, need to be kept in the highlands. Desert-adapted camels can go for days without water and eat leaves and shrub stems that do well when grasses are in decline. Sheep and goats do well in the desert, but must be kept near water sources to meet their need for water every two days. Because of these different requirements, the animals are divided into **domestic herds**, which are kept near the settlements, and **camp herds**, which are taken great distances in search of grazing and water. The domestic herd usually contains stock that produces milk (cattle and camels), a few male camels and donkeys for transport, and some sheep and goats for meat and trade. The camp herd will contain the balance of the non-milking animals.

In this harsh environment, a high rate of livestock mortality is a constant problem. In some years, the Ariaal may lose half their animals. The Ariaal have adapted, as have many East African pastoralists, by keeping a large number of diverse livestock. This is in contrast to many herders in better-endowed regions, who generally prefer to concentrate on few species and to maintain their number at a lower level so that each animal is well fed. The Ariaal prefer female animals due to their reproductive and milk-producing capabilities. After a drought, females can replenish the diminished herd. Females also can supply the Ariaal with milk, which constitutes about 70 percent of the diet in the wet season. The balance of their diet is supplied by meat, purchased grains, and occasionally blood tapped from living animals.

Camels are the primary milk producers, particularly during the dry months when they continue to produce (unlike cattle, sheep, or goats). Unfortunately, they are very slow to reproduce and up to one-third of their offspring may die. Like many East African herders, the Ariaal keep the East African breed of zebu cattle, which have a back hump to enable the animal to store calories in the form of fat. They cannot survive in the lowlands, and their milk production (in this very arid environment) is half that of camels. Still, they reproduce at least twice as fast as camels. One important function of cattle is to serve as exchange goods, particularly for wives, and as ritual sacrifices at weddings, etc. Cattle also are a major source of cash when sold to purchase store-bought maize meal—ground corn meal, which is a crucial food item when milk is scarce.

The value of small stock cannot be underestimated in the household economy; some households have as many as 300 goats and sheep. Poor households tend to have proportionately more small stock. Camels and cattle, which are considered prestige items, are slow to reproduce and are expensive to buy. The Ariaal tend to prefer goats to sheep, since they do better in the intense heat, but both animals reproduce rapidly and are easily sold or traded if the family needs cash. They are also a ready source of meat.

Seasonal Movements. Ariaal herding camps, in their search for graze and browse, disperse over a large area, particularly in the dry months of the year (October through February or March). In the driest months, the household breaks up into two quite different units. In one, the **domestic settlement**, the younger cattle, along with a few camels and goats and sheep, are maintained by older married men, women, and adolescent children of both sexes. Since the domestic herds have to be given water every two or three days, these settlements are often near trading centers and permanent sources of water.

The second unit, the **stock camp**, keeps the mature nonlactating cattle, camels, and some small stock far out on the plains or up in the Ndeto Mountains. The stock camp is staffed by young unmarried men, members of the warrior age grade (discussed on pages 101–102), and older boys, who are faced with the dangerous and exhausting task of tending the camp herd. The herd must be continually moved over long distances during the day and guarded at night against human and other predators. The stock camp's livestock may be drawn from as few as one or two households or as many as a dozen or so if a number of households lack sufficient labor to tend their own.

The cattle in the dry-season stock camps are mature animals strong enough to withstand the rigors of being herded to distant grazing areas and to require watering only every three days or so. Camels are usually herded separately in the desert plains. The fact that camels and goats browse on leaves and branches not only widens the resource base to include shrub land, but very likely also keeps the thornbush from spreading at the expense of grass. In many of the drier parts of East Africa, thorn shrubs and trees of the genus Acacia are dominant over the grasses; by keeping the acacias in check, the browsing activities of goats help make possible the grazing activities of cattle (Conant, 1982).

The consumption of blood drawn from living cattle and other livestock is common in East Africa. Among the Ariaal, blood is regularly taken from all livestock. Men and older boys are responsible for bleeding cattle by shooting a blocked arrow into the jugular vein; the blood is then caught in containers. In the settlement camps, blood is usually mixed with milk, since women are not supposed to drink pure blood; the pure blood is consumed largely by the warriors in the stock camps, where there is little milk. Up to four liters may be drawn from a mature camel or oxen every three to four weeks.

The remote camps place the herders at some risk from raids by neighboring groups, who, much like the Ariaal themselves, are always searching for grazing and water resources in a region where both are diminishing. The neighbors of the Ariaal who might be in competition include the Turkana and the Boran. The Samburu and the Rendille are traditional allies, and their frequent sharing of water and grass resources is facilitated by gift-giving and marriage exchanges. It is when the dry season is prolonged that the risk of conflict or the weakening of established ties is greatest.

The Household: Organization and Status

The economy and social life is rooted in the household. Fratkin puts it this way: "An Ariaal household can be defined as the smallest domestic group with its own livestock and which makes decisions over allocation of labor and livestock capital. Daily life and social interaction are focused on the household and the settlement in which it is located" (1991, p. 57). The settlement consists of independent households who, whether temporarily or not, live together; usually, the settlements are composed of patrilineally related men and their families.

Households are typically headed by a married male stock owner and include his wife or co-wives, children, and occasionally a dependent mother-in-law or married daughter who has not yet joined her husband's village. Each married woman is responsible for building and maintaining her own house; consequently, an individual household may consist of three or four houses including two co-wives, a widowed mother, or a poor affine (in-law) and their children. While household maintenance takes some time, most settlement life revolves around animal care. Just as in the distant herding camps, animal care in the community involves a great deal of cooperation in watering and grazing the animals.

From one season to the next, each household can drastically alter its herding strategy and change herding partners. A large household (one with several wives and married sons) may split up into smaller units, which then scatter over thousands of square miles of rangeland. Ties of kinship are obvi- ously more difficult to maintain and manipulate among pastoralists than they are in the more densely populated and far more stable farming areas. In such circumstances, people tend to establish extra-descent group ties through the device of **age grades**. An age grade consists of people of the same sex and approximately the same age who share a set of duties and privileges.

Just as with the Tamang of Tingling there is a great deal of variation among households due to the domestic cycle. Among the Ariaal this is amplified by variability in inherited wealth, with some men gaining larger herds than they can manage with their labor while others may not have enough to support themselves and be forced to work for other households in order to buy animals and build up their own herds.

The Age Grades and Age Sets

The Ariaal age-grade and age-set systems, like those of many other East African peoples, are highly complex institutions with multiple functions. These systems are widespread throughout East Africa and are particularly prominent among such pastoral groups as the Ariaal, Rendille, Samburu, Turkana, and Pokot. Among the Ariaal, the age grades serve primarily to organize labor and structure politics. Men pass through different age grades as members of named cohorts or **age sets** that are formed every fourteen years.

Males are divided into boys, warriors, and elders; females into young girls, adolescent girls, and circumcised (by clitoridectomy) married women. Each age grade has its distinct insignia and rules about what it can and cannot wear, what foods it may consume, and with whom it may associate. Each grade is also associated with particular rights, duties, and obligations. Age grades determine the formal political structure and the system is based on the primacy of elder males over younger males and men over women. Elders are the heads of households and function as the leaders of the tribe.

The warriors are responsible for herding, and spend approximately fourteen years as herdsmen caring for animals in the stock camps. They grow their hair into long red-dyed plaits and may not eat food that has been even seen by women. When young men between the ages of eleven and twelve are initiated into the warrior grade together, they will mark this by being circumcised as a group and given a group name that they will use for life, and which will, even subsequent to the death of the last member, be used to identify historical periods.

Adolescent girls are responsible for tending the small stock near the settlements, and are forbidden

Ariaal woman milking her goat. As with many East African people, small animals are predominately the concern of women.

(Elliot Fratkin)

to associate with any married men—even their own fathers. When they move into the "married woman" stage, they become dependent members of their husband's household and lineage. Adolescent boys and married elders may milk camels, but women and warriors may not. These and many other ritual prohibitions, rights, and duties sort society into specific work groups.

The Ariaal rise through the age grades with a specific cohort of their contemporaries that is separately named and that stays together for life. Progression through the age grades is automatic, and it is assumed that each member of an age grade will be able to perform the age-appropriate role. The age grades through which age sets pass are effective ways to organize labor. Age sets also provide the basis for exchanges and alliances that cut across the boundaries of patrilineal clans and lineages. Men, for example, form close friendships with age set mates and exchange gifts of cattle and small stock; they may even take up residence in a settlement belonging to another clan by using the age set connection.

Gender Roles and Power

Clearly, social and economic roles are allocated according to gender as well as age among the Ariaal. The division of labor starts very early and lasts until death. By age two or three, girls and boys are encouraged to participate in symbolic activities that quickly become gender-specific tasks. Girls play at such chores as gathering sticks for fuel, carrying water, milking, and gathering food. Boys play at tending livestock, hunting, making spears and bows and arrows, and being warriors. By the time they reach age four or five, their play has become work. The small amount of water children can carry and the help they can give in managing livestock soon become measurable contributions to a household's energy budget. The children soon add the care of younger children to their tasks. While women are responsible for their own infants, almost all child care is in the hands of slightly older children and of some elderly men and women.

Ariaal women and girls commonly milk all of the domestic cattle, sheep, and goats. Women supervise or carry out gathering the firewood, the grass for thatching, and the thornbush needed to build and repair houses and fences. They haul water to the homestead, while men dig the step wells. Among the Ariaal, the men, exclusively, tend camels, as well as all animals sent to distant pastures. This is not always the case in pastoral societies, as we see in Box 5.2, *Being a Shepherdess in the Negev*. Men are also responsible for butchering livestock. While the Ariaal cut the throats of goats, cattle are often killed with spears in the context of a ritual.

Women play critical roles in economic life; indeed, their labor and reproduction is essential to the household's well-being and the social standing of its male head. This is reflected in both the idealization and practice of polygyny. More than half the households contain co-wives. At marriage, a woman's father is given a customary "bride-wealth" payment of eight cattle. Shortly thereafter she joins her husband, who is of another lineage and thus another settlement. If her husband dies, she will still live with her husband's lineage, and may well bear children fathered by his younger brother (this is called levirate fatherhood). It is very hard for a woman to return to her natal settlement should she wish to divorce or move after a husband's death; her family would have to return the cattle they had received.

Ariaal women are virtually powerless in the formal political arena. They may not participate in public discussion, where decisions affecting the group are usually taken consensually by elder males. They also have very little economic power. While her husband will "give" her a herd of milking stock to tend, she may not sell or dispose of them. She does control the house itself, since she builds and repairs it. All animals are male-owned; all food, in principle at least, is controlled by her father or husband. She will not inherit either from her father or husband. All livestock passes to the male children. Thus the

Box 5.2

Being a Shepherdess in the Negev

BEDOUIN ANTHROPOLOGIST AREF Abu-Rabia describes contemporary Bedouin pastoralism in great detail (1994). The Bedouin of the Negev today pasture their flocks of sheep in the general vicinity of their homes, although in the past they were much more mobile. Generally herding is seen as the work of men and boys, but because so many of them are employed in construction work, even young girls are involved in shepherding. In fact, women have come to feel that girls are better at caring for the sheep than are men or boys; after all, in her traditional role a girl already was milking the ewes and devoted to the flock (p. 62). Women are the first to rise in the morning and the last to go to bed; girls are taught to take advantage of being with the flocks to collect firewood, to spin wool and goat hair, and to embroider. Since two or more girls watch the herd together, this is an opportunity to practice the art of trilling—a distinctive form of singing for which Bedouin women are well known. "The bond of the Bedouin woman to the flock is expressed in the following song:

'Oh, happy am I, the shepherdess, giving utterance to my freedom. My destiny and that of the flock are bound together.'" [1994, p. 62]

But there is a difference in male herding and the activities of young girls. Because of strict codes of family honor, young women cannot risk being in the company of unrelated males. As a consequence, they have to watch the flocks in the vicinity of the house, where they can be watched in turn by their relatives. Usually younger women go into the fields in pairs, and, while the flock is in the pasture, they sit on top of a hill so that they can be seen from a distance. This watch is maintained because female seclusion is basic to their sense of family honor—a belief shared by both sexes. "Men and women constantly discuss the subject, and so heighten awareness of the women's honour" (Abu-Rabia, 1994, p. 60). While restricting the activities of women, the notion of family honor does not hinder their productive roles in the domestic economy. They are central to it.

---

work a young man does for his elders is eventually paid for in the form of gifts or inheritances. Women, on the other hand, receive no compensation for their labor.

Can the Ariaal Survive Development?

Until quite recently, the Ariaal lived in a situation of benign neglect as far as the outside world was concerned. Ariaal pastoralism traditionally was dependent on the local ecosystem, constrained by the availability of water and the range of environments that could be exploited by mixed herds of goats, cattle, and camels. They had close relationships with the Rendille and Samburu, with whom they intermarried, traded, and sometimes competed. Until Kenya attained independence from Great Britain in 1967 the Ariaal were fairly self-sufficient, trading with neighbors when necessary. Responses to external events were relatively rare. But since independence, such external factors as government-provided health and education services, famine relief, and the construction of wells and roads have forced basic changes in their way of life, especially among those living near administrative centers and missions.

Many missions have opened schools with the explicit aim of separating children from their traditional religious beliefs (and hence their native culture). Missions and national and international agencies have all intervened in ways that threaten the delicate balancing act that has so long enabled the Ariaal to survive drought and epidemics.

Since the Kenyan government opened the region to foreign missionaries in the 1970s, dozens of Christian mission stations have been opened. The government and the missionaries, despite very different ideologies, share the view that pastoralism is a primitive, backward way of life and that people should be settled in towns (Fratkin, 1991, p. 77). While the missionaries wish to make converts, the government's policy is based on the notion that pastoralism is incompatible with a modern society and maintaining tight control over its citizens. Whatever the goals, moving pastoralists to towns is problematic in an arid region that cannot support an agricultural subsistence pattern.

One means by which the pastoralists are brought into larger settlements is through food subsidies or handouts. This is a practice used to gain converts in many parts of the world by many different religions. The insidious aspect of this approach is that people quickly incorporate the cheap or free food into their domestic economy, soon becoming dependent and losing their traditional self-sufficiency. As a result, many Ariaal families are camping near mission stations. Often households split, with one wife and her children living near town and the second wife staying with the husband in the traditional settlement.

Paradoxically, a further problem involves efforts to promote conservation. Many people automatically blame nomadic pastoralists for overgrazing and the spread of desertification. In fact, the Ariaal system of production prior to the settlement of communities near the missions and administrative centers was entirely conservationist in effect. Animals were moved regularly to follow the major peaks in vegetative production; they were not kept on declining pastures or browses, as to do so would be counterproductive. However, the handouts and restrictions on land use have led to overgrazing of land near mission and government-created towns.

Elliot Fratkin, while pessimistic about the future of the Ariaal people's traditional economy, does see hope in their natural resilience and ability to respond to changing circumstances. He has some practical suggestions which, if adopted, could improve their chances as Kenya continues to develop a modern infrastructure.

1. Development planners need to appreciate the sophistication of adaptive systems, which, like those of the Ariaal, have developed over long periods of time.
2. Planners should concentrate on assisting animal production through veterinary services and pest control, rather than trying to curtail production to reduce herd size.
3. Grazing restrictions should be lifted, since they interfere with herd dispersal, the ecologically and economically sound practice of grazing many herds over a wide area.
4. The market economy would be enhanced by improvements in transportation, auction facilities, and information, and by deregulating animal prices.

Lugi Lengesen, Elliot Fratkin's close friend among the Ariaal, sums up his prospects for the future. "This is not good land to grow corn or raise gardens. That is something people in the south know how to do very well. But we Ariaal know how to grow our cattle and camels, we know this land because it is our farm. Give us veterinary medicines for our animals, medicine for our infants, schools to educate our children in livestock and health, and markets and transportation to sell our animals. Then places like Korr can become beautiful."

The Yörük of Turkey

The Yörük are transhumant sheepherders who move their flocks back and forth between two grazing zones in southeastern Turkey. In winter, they camp on low plains on what is geographically an extension of the Syrian steppe. In spring, when the weather warms, they move the herds inland some 100 kilometers (62 miles) to craggy, mountainous summer pasturelands. Traditionally, the Yörük kept camels to transport their belongings during migrations; their economy was based on the sale of sheep and sheep products (Bates, 1973). Today the nomadic Yörük use trucks and tractor-drawn wagons to move their flocks and possessions. The Yörük's sheep, unlike the Ariaal's stock, serve almost exclusively as the capital basis for market production. Although the nomadic Yörük do eat some of their animal products—milk, butter, cheese, and yogurt—for the most part these products, along with wool and male lambs, are sold. And with the money they receive the Yörük buy their necessities—chiefly the agricultural products that constitute most of their diet.

This, then, is not a subsistence economy. The Yörük are completely dependent on a market economy not only to sell their animal products and buy their food but also to rent the lands on which they graze their sheep. They actively use the market system to increase their holdings in livestock, to accumulate cash to buy consumer goods, and even to acquire land or urban houses. As a result, even relatively small fluctuations in market prices can bankrupt a household—or make it rich.

When wealth and poverty were relatively temporary conditions, and when each household expected to increase its herds over time, the society was relatively egalitarian. By and large, no one family or elite group held substantial economic or political power over others. This is the situation among many herding peoples, since the volatility of animal capital works against the long-term perpetuation of rule by a special class within their society. Today, the situation among the Yörük is changing. Poverty is no longer a temporary condition among herders, and the group of well-to-do merchant families who have emerged in recent years may well constitute a distinctly privileged group.

The Market Economy

The market economy is part of the Yörük way of life. All transactions are made on the basis of established market values, even when goods and services are bartered. If a Yörük family trades wool for tobacco, for example, the exchange is made according

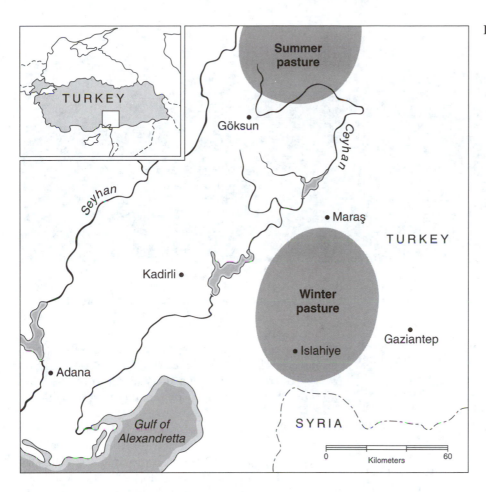

Figure 5–2. *Yörük territory.*

to the relative market value of each item. Supply and demand within a particular area can alter the values, of course, but such variations only restructure market prices to fit local conditions. The vast majority of transactions, however, involve cash or promissory notes. Often a herd owner will contract to supply animals or milk at a future date, accepting an advance payment in cash. Fluctuations in the market prices of animal products, of the foods the Yörük buy, and of the land they rent become significant problems to which they must continually respond.

While the Yörük are dependent on the market, they are just as dependent on other groups: The condition of the crops grown by those other groups, their needs, and the value they place on their own and the Yörük's goods. For the Yörük, the presence of other groups constitutes an all-important environmental variable that shapes their economic decisions at every turn.

Probably the most significant feature of such interactions is the Yörük's reliance on other groups for pastureland. Unlike the Ariaal, for example, the Yörük do not own or even have traditional claims to the pastures they use; they must rent them. In some cases they also have to pay for access to lands along the migration route, although not when they move

the animals by truck. Thus, although the outer limit of their migration schedule is established largely by climate and topography, political and social factors help determine the actual schedule. When Yörük herd owners want to move their animals, they must take into account the wishes of the people who own the land that the animals must cross. This land is predominantly agricultural. The pastoralists would prefer to keep the animals longer in the lowland plains, but herd movement too late in the season would cause extensive crop damage. They would prefer to return to the plains earlier in the fall, if they did not have to wait for the harvest.

As one might expect, disputes often develop between pastoralists and agriculturalists over crop damages. In recent years, the Turkish government has intervened to regulate the herd migrations and to see that all claims for crop damage are satisfied. Without governmental regulation, some agricultural lands would probably have to be abandoned because damage would be too frequent and too costly. This was a common problem in the past. Each annual migration, then, is a complex strategy determined by the availability of grass, planting or harvest schedules, and the restrictions set by the government.

In spring, the Yörük move their animals and camps to high-mountain pastures. Today this move is usually made by trucks carrying both sheep and herders.

(Daniel Bates)

Social Organization

As with the Ariaal, the composition of Yörük camp groups changes regularly. As many as twenty households or as few as two may camp together; larger clusters generally gather in the summer pasture areas. Although in some pastoral societies (such as the Ariaal) the labor of herding is pooled among members of a camp group, the Yörük household is, in effect, a self-contained producing unit: It relies almost exclusively on its own labor. The rental of pasturelands is an important function of the larger camp group. Though the families that make up the camp do not generally pool their labor, they do pool money to rent their grazing lands jointly.

The composition of a camp group depends on several factors, but not on the same kind of rigid rules that govern Ariaal camp groups. Kinship is one such factor. The Yörük place great emphasis on patrilineage, and often families that camp together are patrilineally related. Some households, however, camp with people more closely related to the wife than to the husband. Sometimes this arrangement simply reflects the woman's wish to be with her sisters or brothers for a season or two. Or it may be a way for the family to secure better grazing than they could get by cooperating with the husband's patrilineal relatives. In other cases, family quarrels may be the determining factor. Thus, while kinship to some degree determines the camp membership, sentiment and economic strategy keep such communities flexible.

Adapting to a Changing Economy

In recent years the Yörük have had to face a variety of new situations. One major problem is inflation, which has affected the entire country. Although rental fees for pastures have gone up rapidly, so have the prices of animal products. This development has

resulted in a significant transformation of Yörük society. Generally speaking, small animal husbandry has enabled them to cope with a changing economy better than most other groups. At the same time, new developments in mechanized transport and in the opening of new markets in the oil-rich Arab world have created new possibilities for some Yörük.

New Strategies. The Yörük today actually practice three adaptive strategies: nomadic pastoralism, sedentary agriculture, and trade or shopkeeping in town. The nomads have developed a very specialized adaptation, engaging in animal husbandry and trading in animals and animal products. At the same time, entire villages of settled Yörük now engage in agriculture, shopkeeping, and commerce. The ability of the Yörük to adapt to their changing environment is evident by looking at some of their activities. Some, for example, operate mobile dairies and follow the herders, buying their milk and converting it to cheese for urban markets. During the Iran-Iraq war in the 1980s, those that owned trucks transported goods to the war-torn countries. Today, some Yörük have become brokers, buying large numbers of animals and shipping them to distant markets in Arab lands where meat is in great demand. Very frequently entrepreneurs engage in several of these activities simultaneously, sometimes coordinating their ventures in town and only sometimes camping in tents.

One point must be stressed. Yörük society, like most others, is changing rapidly, and the challenge to the ethnographer is to describe a way of life without implying that what is observed is a timeless pattern. Daniel Bates first went to southeastern Turkey in 1968, but few of his initial economic observations still hold today. Culturally, too, the Yörük are changing. In 1968, patterns of male-female interactions, recreation, and socializing were very different. Now even pastoral households have access to television

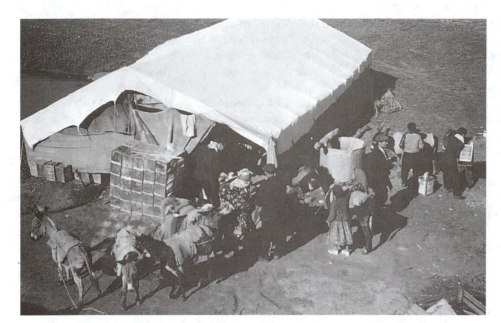

In the late 1960s entrepreneurs established mobile dairies that follow the herds, collecting milk and processing it into cheese for urban markets.
(Daniel Bates)

sets, refrigerators, and other modern appliances. They usually keep them in village or town dwellings, where they spend part of each year and where children of school age live while attending school.

While the nomadic herders and the new class of businessmen and farmers are economically distinct, they differ little in cultural identity and there is no antipathy between them. After all, they are all Yörük. Some of the strategies are actually complementary: the town-based businessmen often depend on the herders for their trade, while the herders depend on the small businessmen for the credit they need in order to go on herding in a volatile market economy. The different strategies are also interrelated in that families move from one to another as circumstances warrant. Many people who were settled in a town when Bates revisited the area in 1978 were once again living in tents in 1983. While they had liked town life, they decided they could make more money raising livestock than selling shoes. Today, wealth or access to capital determines whether a household herds or settles down to other endeavors.

In 1978, and later in 1983, Bates found that the herders who were using trucks to transport their animals between pastures no longer migrated as a group. Herding had become a form of ranching, where the "ranch" consists of many pastures used sequentially, as sheep are trucked among them. The contemporary Yörük household stays behind in a town or village, leaving herding to the menfolk or hired shepherds. In fact, by 1983 some herders were making so much money from animal export that they could afford to rent wheat fields and turn them into pastures, and thus could spend most of the year in one place.

Far fewer families were being supported by pastoralism in 1983, and those few were the better-off members of the society. The majority of households that had been nomadic in 1968–1970 had settled in villages and towns as laborers and tenant farmers, unable to continue making their living in the traditional way because of the rising costs of pasture and feed. Some were living precariously; those who had invested what they had in a shop or some other business had prospered.

The adaptation of the Yörük, then, is a matter not simply of accommodating to the physical environment but of finding a niche in a larger social system. To understand even their pastoral economy, we must take into account who owns what. Likewise, it is impossible to discuss the specialization of nomadic pastoralism among the Yörük without reference to other specializations within the larger society on which the Yörük depend for trade. Thus, the effective environment of the Yörük has a political and social dimension as well as a physical and biological one.

Increasing Stratification. Wealth is no longer spread evenly among the Yörük. The new economic system has transformed a generally egalitarian society to one that is decidedly stratified. The poorer herders, those with just enough animals to make herding viable, are often in debt and seldom have the ready cash they need to rent pastureland, pay for winter grains, or, more recently, hire truck transport. To pay debts accumulated during the winter, they are forced to shear their sheep at the beginning of spring. But early shearing leaves them at a disadvantage in the migration to high pastures: They must wait longer before leaving, as shorn sheep are vulnerable to disease in snow and extreme cold. When they finally do leave, they may travel over lands already grazed by sheep belonging to wealthier herd owners who could afford to forgo an early shearing. The poor grazing leaves the last flocks tired and hungry by the time they reach summer pasture. The sheep of the poorer herd owners are more likely to die during migration than those of the wealthier ones. The affluent herders not only have healthier sheep, but they are also able to transport animals to choice but distant grazing areas.

Even after selling their spring wool, many Yörük herders do not usually have the cash necessary to rent summer pasture. Needing an additional source of income or credit, many supplement their income by selling milk to the mobile dairy tents that follow the flocks. Many of these dairies are owned by the wealthier herders, who have established dairies and have bought stores and land in an attempt to diversify. Just as there is a limit below which a flock is not economically viable, there is an upper limit as well. Huge numbers of animals require a large deployment of labor, so the wealthy can only increase their wealth through diversification once their herds reach an optimal size.

The dairies are rather sizable enterprises with a ready supply of capital that enables them not only to buy the herders' milk but to purchase it in advance. Such milk futures are purchased at a relatively low price, but they give the poorer herders the money they need for pasture rental. Once the dairymen have the milk, they process it into cheese and sell it for a substantial profit in urban markets. Thus, the dairies allow the herders to fend off bankruptcy at the same time that they yield high profits to the dairymen.

It is easy to see that such a system encourages **economic stratification**, the creation of increasingly fixed classes of rich and poor. In the past, the Yörük had no such permanent economic groups. As long as the people remained herders, they could expect to go from rags to riches and back again several times in the course of their lives, because animals are such a volatile form of capital. But once the temporarily wealthy began to invest their wealth in more fixed forms of capital such as farms, shops, and dairies, their wealth ceased to be temporary, and indeed, it began to increase. The increase in wealth enabled them to settle down. The traditional way of life—nomadic, egalitarian—is slowly giving way to a more complex, stratified pattern with a variety of strategies feeding into one another and reinforcing economic differences.

Future Prospects

In many respects the Yörük are prospering in the rapidly developing domestic economy of modern Turkey, since animal production is a profitable endeavor. Few families still live in the traditional tent—at least not throughout the year. They now live in town, and the children are attending schools. However, many of the young among the Yörük are abandoning the pastoral lifestyle and moving to Ankara, the capital, or to Istanbul, which is now swollen to over 12 million people. Some have migrated, legally or not, to Europe or the United States in order to secure a better future.

The reasons why the Yörük would leave a region in which their main subsistence strategy seems to be working very well are quite simple. With over two-thirds of the population below the age of twenty, the local economy cannot absorb all of them into the work force. Education and access to information about the rest of the world gives rise to demands for a standard of living and consumer items that cannot be met through local wage employment. Finally, pastoralism is now a highly specialized and capitalized mode of production, and is engaged in by fewer and fewer households, each managing larger and larger herds.

Summary

PASTORALISTS ENGAGE IN ANIMAL HUSBANDRY: THE breeding, care, and use of herd animals such as sheep, goats, camels, cattle, horses, reindeer, or yaks. Most pastoralists in nonindustrial societies are nomadic. Both the mobility of pastoralists and the degree to which they rely on animal husbandry varies with environmental, social, and economic conditions. Few pastoralist groups rely exclusively on their herds; they tend to pursue a more generalized subsistence strategy.

Nomads follow two basic patterns: horizontal migration, characterized by regular movement over a large area in search of fodder; and transhumance, or seasonal movement between upland and lowland pastures.

Specialized pastoralism, or exclusive reliance on animal husbandry, may have developed from a farming/herding pattern. Changes in agricultural practices, such as the use of canal irrigation, may have pushed grazing lands farther from settlements. The consequent increased demands of both herding and agriculture may have led some families to specialize in agriculture and others to choose herding exclusively. The divergence of strategies may have been encouraged by the failure of irrigation for some groups. Extensive irrigation may cause the water table (the level of water under the earth) to fall, or it may increase the salinity of the soil until crops no longer thrive.

While pastoralism is a relatively efficient means of extracting energy from a harsh environment, it produces less energy per acre of land than agriculture, and population densities are correspondingly low. Pastoralism is an alternative to agriculture, but it is almost never independent of it. If pastoralists don't raise vegetable foods, they acquire them through trade.

In nonindustrial societies, sedentary pastoralism, or animal husbandry that does not involve mobility, is generally rare. The usual pattern is nomadic pastoralism—the practice of moving one's herds from pasture to pasture as the seasons and circumstances require. The main reason that pastoralists migrate is to secure adequate grazing land in a marginal environment. However, migration may also be a means to maintain political autonomy or even to control settled groups. The composition of local groupings in pastoral societies often shifts as nomadic camping units move, break apart, and come together with other units.

Virtually all pastoral populations are organized in tribes, communities of people who claim kinship, usually by descent from one or more common ancestors. Tribal organization provides for positions of leadership and allows for coordination of social and economic activities.

The basic economic unit is the household. Households may move frequently one year and be largely sedentary the next. One household may herd alone, while others may temporarily combine forces. Families may shift between agriculture and herding, or they may give up herding for other pursuits such as shopkeeping.

The Ariaal of Kenya maintain a subsistence economy through a balanced and diversified strategy of keeping cattle, camels, and small stock (sheep and goats). The Ariaal display many aspects of the East African cattle complex, a socioeconomic system in which cattle represent social status as well as wealth. The cattle play a significant symbolic role in social ties, obligations, and rituals. The traditional bridewealth is eight head of cattle given to the father of the bride-to-be.

The basic unit of social organization is the household. A household consists of one or more houses belonging to the wife or wives of the male head of household. Households are located in settlements usually belonging to one patrilineal clan, a large group whose common descent is traced through the paternal line. The Ariaal marry out of their natal clans and, to some extent, intermarry with the neighboring Rendille and Samburu. The groom's family gives bridewealth to the bride's family to compensate them for the loss of their daughter's services. The labor of women and girls is crucial to the functioning of households. Men tend the camels, as well as manage the family's livestock on distant grazing and browse lands.

The Ariaal are organized in age grades, each grade consisting of people of approximately the same age and sex, who share a set of duties, prohibitions, symbols, and privileges. Most important, age grades structure the organization of labor. Young men of the warrior grade, for example, will spend approximately fourteen years as herdsmen caring for the animals in the stock camps, which are distant from the households' main settlement residence. After completing their duties, the same named set of men will all become elders.

While the Ariaal have survived drought and famine because of their ability to simultaneously exploit a number of species of livestock and different microenvironments in their 10,000 sq. km. range, they may not be able to withstand development. Northern Kenya has seen a great deal of missionary and governmental activity aimed at settling the pastoralists and, for rather different reasons, changing the Ariaal way of life. What is happening to the pastoralists (as with other such populations in East Africa) is that they are becoming dependent on food subsidies and handouts; their traditional grazing areas are restricted and their herds are limited in size.

The Yörük of southeastern Turkey traditionally have been nomadic pastoralists who move their sheep between summer and winter pastures. The Yörük are dependent on a market economy to sell their animal products, buy their food, and rent the lands on which they graze their sheep. The activities of the Yörük are shaped not only by climate and topography, but also by political and social factors; the strategy of their migrations is determined by the availability of grass, village planting or harvest schedules, and the restrictions on migration set by the government.

Yörük social organization is flexible. The composition of a camp group may be determined by kinship, sentiment, or economic strategy. Each family within the camp group is a self-sufficient producing unit, although the camp group does rent pastureland jointly.

In recent years the nature of animal husbandry has changed. The rents charged for pastureland have risen, but new opportunities have also opened up. Now many Yörük avail themselves of truck transport and sell animals in Arab countries. As a result, they now practice diverse and complementary strategies: Sedentary agriculture, trade, brokerage, and shopkeeping, as well as pastoralism. Until recently, wealth determined whether a household herded or settled down. The rich herders tended to diversify into trading or farming, while the poor struggled to keep their herds. While some of the poorest herders of earlier years have become rich in today's market, this economic system has created increasingly fixed classes of rich and poor for the first time in Yörük society.

Key Terms

age grade	economic stratification
age set	horizontal migration
animal husbandry	nomadic pastoralism
camp herds	sedentary pastoralism
cattle complex	specialized pastoralism
co-resident household	stock camp
domestic herds	transhumance
domestic settlement	water table

Suggested Readings

Abu-Lughod, L. (1988). *Veiled sentiments: Honor and poetry in a Bedouin society.* Berkeley and Los Angeles: University of California Press. A person-centered ethnography of a community of Bedouins in the western desert of Egypt that focuses on the oral lyric poetry that is used by women and young men in this once nomadic but still pastoral society.

Beck, L. (1992). *Nomad: A year In the life of a Qashqa'i tribesman in Iran.* New Haven, CT: Yale University Press. This political ethnography of elites is a historical and anthropological account of the Turkic-speaking Qashqa'i. The Qashqa'i are a predominantly pastoral nomadic people, but they have highly developed sociopolitical institutions, including a ruling elite that has participated in national and international politics.

Black-Michaud, J. (1986). *Sheep and land: The economics of power in a tribal society.* Cambridge: Cambridge University Press. An examination of the Luristan region of western Iran and the ways in which different populations relate to each other through exchanges between sedentary agricultural and nomadic pastoral populations.

Bradburd, D. (1990). *Ambiguous relations.* Washington D.C. and London: Smithsonian Institution Press. This ethnography of the Komanchi, nomadic pastoralists of south-central Iran, views their society within the larger spheres of the nation-state, the Islamic world, and the global economy.

Ekvall, R. B. (1968). *Fields on the hoof: The nexus of Tibetan nomadic pastoralism.* Prospect Heights, IL: Waveland Press. A clearly written case study of pastoralism in a region that is poorly understood ethnographically.

Fratkin, E. (1991). *Surviving drought and development: Ariaal pastoralists of Northern Kenya.* Boulder, CO: Westview Press. Focusing on drought and famine, this ethnography gives us a lucid narrative of the Ariaal and their ability to persist in being pastoralists despite environmental and political pressures to settle.

Galaty, J. G. & Bonte, P. (Eds.). (1991). *Herders, warriors and traders: Pastoralism in Africa.* Boulder, CO: Westview Press. A collection of articles on pastoralism in East and West Africa.

Goldstein, M. C. & Beall, C. M. (1994). *World of Mongolia's nomads.* Berkeley: University of California Press. This study looks at a community of Mongolian herders and their adaptation to a market economy since the Soviet bloc breakup.

Janzen, J. (1986). *Nomads in the sultanate of Oman: Tradition and development in Dhofar.* Boulder, CO: Westview Press. A comprehensive and insightful analysis of the traditional living conditions and economic circumstances of the nomadic-peasant population of Dhofar and the rapid changes to which they have been subjected.

Khazanov, A. M. (1984). *Nomads and the outside world.* Cambridge: Cambridge University Press. A good discussion of the many ways in which nomadic pastoralists are integrated into states and empires. The author is a specialist in Central Asia, but deals with pastoralism in general.

Meir, A. (1997). *As nomadism ends: The Israeli Bedouin of the Negev.* Boulder, CO: Westview Press. An account of the social, spatial, and ecological changes faced by the Bedouin of the Negev.

Pelto, P. J. (1973). *The snowmobile revolution: Technology and social change in the Arctic.* Menlo Park, CA: Benjamin. A study of how the Skolt Lapps of Finland incorporated the snowmobile into their traditional economy, which was focused on reindeer herding.

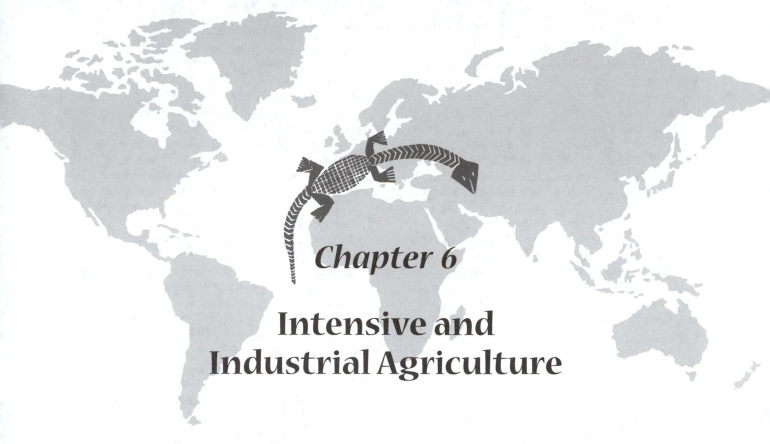

Chapter 6

Intensive and Industrial Agriculture

If one were to observe the heartland of the Middle East from an earth-orbiting satellite, most striking would be the sharp contrast between the great expanses of desert and the lush green of cultivated areas. One can stand with one foot in a wheat field and the other in the desert. The Middle East, where agriculture began some 10,000 years ago, is the home of some 200 million people, most of them supported by the crops produced on less than 10 percent of the land by a land-use strategy referred to here as intensive agriculture. Agricultural production is vastly increased through such technological innovations as irrigation, chemical and organic fertilizers, mechanization, and fossil fuel powered equipment.

The impact of intensive land use is evident in Egypt. For example, in 1995, 98 percent of Egypt's population was concentrated on less than 4 percent of its territory; an average of 1,200 to 1,400 people occupied every square kilometer of arable land. Today Egypt has to import large quantities of foodstuffs from other regions of the world. The irony is that both great productivity and accelerating social and economic hardship all too often march hand in hand.

In Roman times, Egypt was a major source of grain for the Mediterranean world; an ancient historian, Ibn Batuta, said, "when famine strikes Egypt (whose lands have been irrigated longer than those of any other area), the world itself cannot feed her people."

Similar patterns of recurring famine and rural hardship are found in other regions where civilizations arose with the development of intensive farming. China, for example, where 1.2 billion people are supported by the production from 11 percent of its land area, has a long history of chronic famine and mass starvation—particularly among the people who themselves produce the food that sustains the country. The present government apparently has reduced the possibility of famine in the near future, but even with increased production and improved food distribution, the threat of hunger is real. As China's population continues to grow, the country has not only more people to feed but less land with which to do it. Urban centers are spreading and the fertility of the soil is diminishing: land is being lost at a faster rate than it can be reclaimed (Smil, 1984, 1994). China has lost about one-third of its crop lands in the last 40 years; per capita farmland availability was reduced by 10 percent in the 1990s and a further 15 percent will be lost by the year 2035 (Smil, 1994, p. 8). Even as the country strains to produce ever more food, the very fact of intensification has caused worsening erosion and soil degradation (Tyler, 1994, p. 8).

India and Bangladesh experience similar pressure on their land; Indonesia, once the most productive region of southeast Asia, is seeing its people's well-being decline. To arrest such a decline, governments often encourage even greater efforts in agriculture, including the destruction of tropical rain forests, to support people forced out of other areas. In Africa south of the Sahara, where population-driven land-use intensification (along with long periods of drought) have often led to devastating environmental problems such as spreading desertification, the spectre of mass starvation looms (Stevens, 1994, p. 10). Nevertheless, within each of these areas we find numerous striking instances of human resourcefulness in the face of environmental problems. This chapter deals with the rise of intensive agriculture and its social corollaries: urbanism, social stratification, and the emergence of a class of peasant farmers. We also discuss the emergence and consequences of industrial farming, which now sustains most of the world's 5.7 billion people (Cowell, 1994, p. 10).

The Development of Intensive Agriculture

The interrelated processes of agricultural intensification and ever-rising requirements for food in combination with declining resources are seen throughout the world. Anthropologists and scientists in other fields have long been concerned with the origins of intensive farming and early civilization, with the social and economic structure of rural society, and with the strategies that have enabled diverse populations to adapt to environmental and other problems. In Chapter 2 we said that intensification involved increasing the yields from labor or land; this implies that there are at least two routes to intensification, and actually many more, due to the complex ways in which land and labor are interrelated. Usually, the perspective of most American or European economists is to concentrate on the former: agricultural history is usually described in terms of progress in labor-saving technology—the plow, seed drills, cultivators, threshers, and the like—because the economies of the Western World experienced labor shortages over much of their his-

tories (Boserup, 1981, p. 99; Bray, 1994, p. 3). This, of course, not only may increase food production by allowing the same labor force to cultivate more land, but also may free up labor for other endeavors. Thus Australia, Canada, and the United States produce massive amounts of food with a relatively small rural labor force.

But production can also be intensified by increasing the productivity of land without reducing the labor requirements; that is, expanding production using an existing labor force or even a larger one (Bray, 1994). This can be important, for example, where there are few alternative sources for employment, as is often the case in densely populated developing countries. Irrigation and the introduction of new crop strains are well-known examples of this form of intensification. Water control may allow for multiple harvests of a particular crop; new plant strains may also increase productivity without new capital inputs needed to reduce labor requirements. At least one anthropologist, Francesca Bray, argues that from this perspective traditional Asian rice-based farming using high labor inputs is not a case of "arrested development" when compared to Western agriculture, but is a solution to the problem of sustaining large populations with adequate nutrition (1994). We will return to intensification and its consequences later.

One of the most ancient (and still important) ways land productivity can be increased is through water management. So diverse are the ways in which moisture can be controlled, it is somewhat misleading to refer to them all as "irrigation." Simply adding pebbles to fields, as did the ancient Pueblo dwellers of North America, can enhance the field's ability to retain moisture (Lightfoot, 1994). In this sense, irrigation, or at least "moisture control," is as early as agriculture itself. Archaeological evidence in the Middle East indicates that simple systems of water control predate the rise of large agrarian states with their concomitantly dense populations. Populations near rivers or marshes would simply capture or divert annual flood waters or runoff from rains. Irrigation refers to actually transporting the water to the field and then managing its direct application and subsequent drainage (drainage is important in order to maintain a salt-free soil base).

The earliest known large-scale system of irrigation in Egypt appears with the emergence of one government throughout that land in 5100 B.C. (Fagan, 1992, p. 352). We know that even fairly complicated irrigation systems can be managed by local farmers, although the potential for interfamilial or intercommunity conflict is substantial. People who share a common water resource may have very different interests in its use. As a consequence, we see a widespread pattern of large-scale irrigation systems coming to be run by special managers, with a corresponding lessening of control by households or even by local communities. Centralized decision making facilitates mobilizing large work forces, allocating water, conflict resolution, and storage of surpluses.

In the emerging prehistoric states of Mesopotamia, this managerial role was first assumed by religious leaders and only later by secular rulers (Fagan, 1992). It is interesting to note that the earliest large-scale irrigation systems in the southwest United States were managed by the Mormon Church (Abruzzi, 1993), as we described in Chapter 2. To make water control feasible, it required the centralized control of a committed bureaucracy willing to use resources to sustain building and rebuilding dams and canals beyond the ability of local communities.

The main impetus for irrigation, in most places, is simply the need to have water available in areas where rainfall is unpredictable—not necessarily a wish to increase the average yield of a unit of land. But with the advent of irrigation, slight differences in the productivity of different pieces of land became greatly magnified. Those fields that lent themselves to irrigation—fields that were close to the water source or that drained well—produced far more than those less suited to irrigation.

Other routes to intensification include learning to breed strains of grains or other crops that mature more rapidly and bear more edible products. Rice, for example, was transformed into a substantially more productive grain staple through selective breeding by farmers in ancient China (Bray, 1994). Animal traction used to plow and cultivate fields developed very early in the Middle East and Far East (but not in the New World); a pair of oxen, it is calculated, produces over ten times the horsepower of a human being, and, when relative costs are considered, is half as expensive as human power when used in tilling a field (Giampietro, Bukkins, & Pimentel, 1993, p. 230). Crop rotation and fertilizers, too, are means of intensifying yields. Arboriculture, as practiced in the Pacific, can be the basis for intensive production, as early travelers found when they first encountered the densely populated islands of Polynesia (Kirch, 1994). Here, carefully tended breadfruit trees provided a high yield in a form that could be stored in large, underground stone-lined pits.

Where and when there was agricultural intensification, human societies tended to increase in numbers and in social and technological complexity. When farming produced more food than the farmers themselves could eat, segments of the population came to specialize in crafts such as the making of tools and pots, which they then traded for food they had not produced themselves. The division of labor within society thus became more complex, with even spatially distant groups becoming mutually dependent.

Simple horticultural societies, such as the Yanomamö of Chapter 4, have remained politically autonomous until now and can be studied as distinct societies with distinct cultures. Intensive farming communities, on the other hand, are closely interdependent and must be studied as part of a larger agrarian society. Given the fact that much of their organization is tied to distant cities and national administrative offices, they cannot be understood outside the context of the larger political and economic system of which they are a part. Thus, as intensive agriculture developed, the land fed not only the farming households and the craft workers but other emerging classes of nonproducers: religious leaders, politicians, administrators. Increasingly the economic demands of urban populations and the political power of their elites came to exercise a profound influence on the life of rural peoples, although the country folk often sought means to avoid the power of the state. Town and country came to be part of an integrated system, though the results of increased productivity were not shared equally by all sectors of the economy. As agrarian societies evolved into large-scale states, as in the ancient Middle East, some communities inevitably prospered and grew; those far from the major markets, religious institutions, and other developments of the urban centers languished. In Mesoamerica, for example, regional or "core" centers such as the Valley of Oaxaca, developed great urban complexes while peripheral zones, linked to the centers by trade or tribute, were relatively underdeveloped (Feinman & Nichols, 1992). Such regional differentiation may be the basis for significant social and cultural variability within a society, and is reflected in the subsequent development of industrialized societies.

The first cities in the Middle East (and, until recently, many African, European, and Asian cities) were little more than administrative and trading centers, established to serve the surrounding countryside that provided them with food. The priests, military leaders, and artisans who were not serving the governing elite were serving the farmers. Only after about the fifteenth century (with a few exceptions) do we see a change: the rise of cities not as agricultural trade centers and administrative centers but as manufacturing centers. The production of goods in great volume went hand in hand with the spread of trade and invention. Improved armaments and navigational equipment on sailing ships gave Europeans access to all the world's seas. European cities grew, fueled at first by the power of water, wind, and human and animal muscle, and later by fossil fuel.

The Organization of Energy

Howard Odum (1971, 1992) was one of the first ecologists to observe that the structure and function of animal, plant, and human social systems are understood at least to some extent by the way they acquire, channel, and expend the energy necessary for their maintenance. Anthropologist Leslie White was one of the first to recognize the importance of the role of energy in cultural evolution. What is often called the Industrial Age, White (1949) has called the Fuel Age.

Societies vary greatly in their energy budgets and in how energy is organized. Mechanized use of nonhuman energy sources—fossil fuel or hydroelectric power, for example—distinguish the technologically advanced societies. In the United States, about 230,000 kilocalories of energy are expended per capita; in Burundi, Central Africa, 24,000 are expended (Giampietro et al., 1993, p. 239). Moreover, in the United States only 10 percent of the country's "total time" (the population × 24 × 365) is allocated

to work. In Burundi, 25 percent of the nation's total time is needed; in short, they work twice as hard to extract a fraction of the usable energy that the U.S. worker does (p. 239). Where human labor constitutes the main power supply there is little spare energy to devote to anything other than maintaining current infrastructure, reproduction, and food procurement. Thus, intensification, which we have defined earlier as the process of increasing yields through an increase in energy expenditure, is best achieved when that increase is accomplished with nonhuman energy sources. As we can see from Box 6.1, *Human Labor as Energy*, human labor is extremely costly; exclusive reliance on it impedes development.

In the final analysis, it is energy that distinguishes intensive agriculture—both energy invested in crop production and energy extracted from the land. The exact point at which horticulture becomes intensive farming is not always clear, but one can recognize the consequences of the shift even without employing economic criteria. Rarely can large numbers of people maintain themselves in stable year-around communities without intensive food production, and nowhere do we see urban centers without a hinterland containing highly productive farms. The vast energy surpluses that flow from the countryside to the city result from the investment of energy in

Chinese farmers are masters at the science of intensive agriculture, combining skilled labor, water control, and fertilizers to reap rich harvests.
(Reuters News)

Box 6.1
Human Labor as Energy

ECONOMISTS DEFINE HUMAN labor productivity as the monetary value of what is produced (dollar value added per hour of work) by a unit of human labor. This definition, however, does not work well in thinking of labor in nonmonetarized societies or in developing societies with a significant subsistence economy. Also, it is hard to compare a monetarized economy with a partially monetarized one. Energy is an alternative measure of productivity, one that offers new insights into the changing role of human labor in relation to technological development. Giampietro, Bukkens, and Pimentel (1993) have created a sophisticated model based on this principle, which is described in a simplified manner below.

Assessing the productivity of labor requires two measurements: what has been achieved energetically, and what energy has been expended to gain it. A simple model illustrates this. If we compare the horsepower (HP) efficiency of human power (0.1 HP), a pair of oxen (1.2 HP), a 6-HP tractor, and a 50-HP tractor in tilling a one hectare field, applied human power is twice as effective as that of the pair of oxen and over four times as effective as the tractors (that is, effective in the amount of work performed per horsepower). However, if we calculate the gross energy requirements (metabolic and fuel inputs, shelter, construction costs or—for living components—reproductive costs, etc.), this is reversed: Human power is 3.45 times more expensive than the tractors, and twice as expensive as the oxen.

The indirect costs of human power are very high: people have to have food, clothing, and shelter whether or not they are actually working. Furthermore, it takes time and energy inputs to "produce" a worker. Eighty percent of the metabolic expenditure for a human worker is outside the workplace. A related issue is time constraints. Productivity has to consider how the power level affects the time to complete a task. While one person may be able to harvest a crop that requires 700 labor days, this is clearly not feasible; more reasonable would be seven farmers working 100 days or 100 workers working one week. Thus, human power, while very efficient in terms of the work that can be accomplished by a unit of horsepower, is both low in absolute levels and costly.

Any system can be seen as having energy *sources* and energy *converters* that generate power or useful work. In preindustrial or partially industrialized societies, energy sources are largely in standing biomass: the trees, plants, and animals available to support humans and that can be converted into useful work to support the population and its material culture, through human labor. This may be supplemented by animal traction, but even so, the available power is limited. In the United States in the 1850s, 91 percent of energy expended came from standing biomass; today only 4 percent does. The balance comes from fossil fuels, converted into useful work by machinery. Industrial societies are more limited by energy sources; nonindustrial societies by the low rate at which energy can be converted through human labor only partially amplified by animals and machinery.

The implications for development are serious. The addition of one bullock for every ten villagers in India would have have the effect of doubling the power level per capita in that country, but it would still remain more than a thousand times less than the per capita power level in the United States. Preindustrial societies respond to the energy limitation by scheduling agricultural activities to be as constant as possible throughout the year—avoiding periods of peak demand. Thus, traditional farmers often make use of a mix of crops and livestock, each with different labor demands. In industrial agriculture, this is not necessary, since labor is not the main means of converting energy—machines are.

The notion of humans living directly from the fruits of their own labor assisted by the family's horses or oxen may be appealing, but mechanical conversion of energy is vastly more productive and is required to raise standards of living. Unfortunately, rapid conversion of the standing biomass in preindustrial societies into energy would facilitate more useful work, but it would devastate the environment—as we see when forests are clear cut. This is, in fact, what is happening in many countries. In the Sahel and the Sudan, the World Bank forecasts that by 2000, in a rural population of 40 million, 19 million will run out of wood while 3.7 million will be severely short of food (in Giampietro et al., 1993, p. 252). On the other hand, should a region undergo rapid industrialization of agriculture, people will be displaced as their labor is less needed on the farm, contributing to rural-urban migration and subsequent urban poverty.

agriculture. The increase in the energy invested can come from many sources: from animals yoked to plows, from human labor spent in terracing land or digging wells, or from farm machinery powered by fossil fuels.

Investment of energy in order to gain an even greater return in energy is characteristic of intensive agriculture and is expressed in the management of fields and paddies. A crucial factor in the evolution of intensive agriculture was the advent of plow cultivation and fertilization, which allowed farmers to reduce the length of **fallow time**—the time that must be allowed between crops for the soil to rest and regenerate its organic and chemical content. The fallow period is critical to a high level of food production over the long term. When other factors—availability of water, type of soil, and the like—are equal, sustained agricultural yields vary with the length of the fallow period. The shifting agriculture practiced by the Yanomamö is a long-fallow system requiring as long as ten to twenty years of fallow time for each field.

In intensive agriculture, the fallow period can be reduced to the point where the land can undergo nearly continuous cultivation, and, in some areas, can produce multiple crops each season. This approach requires developed technology, large inputs of human labor, and an investment in other forms of energy. Fields have to be prepared (often specially laid out for irrigation); plow animals must be cared for; tractors fueled and maintained; water collected, distributed, and controlled; fertilizers or other nutrients spread on the fields, and crops carefully tended throughout the growing period. The result is a vastly increased amount of food per unit of land.

Both land and farmers work harder under intensive agriculture, and the result is a great increase in the production not only of food but of such crops as cotton and flax. It may sometimes appear that the possibilities of intensification seem almost limitless. Even with modern techniques, however, only 11 percent of the earth's land area is suited to intensive farming and the potential for intensification is limited. A point is always reached at which increased investment of labor or capital is not matched by productive gains; we will return to this point later. Further, intensification may lead to soil loss if nutrients are not maintained; erosion may accompany mechanized cultivation, and irrigation may result in waterlogged or salinized soils—this occurs when too much water is applied or where drainage is inadequate to prevent salts building up in the soil. Worldwatch reports that 60 million hectares (150 million

acres) of cropland worldwide has been damaged by salinization and waterlogging. India, which has the most irrigated land of any country, has damaged about one-third of its croplands and abandoned seven million hectares because of salinization. Paradoxically, the United States, which pioneered industrialized farming, also leads the world in soil loss due to erosion; 69 million acres are eroding at rates that diminish productivity (Cunningham & Saigo, 1995, p. 229).

Environmental Resilience, Stability, and Change

Intensive agriculture is accompanied by a massive reshaping of the landscape—a process that is ever accelerating. In swidden horticulture, the forest is partially cut or burned and allowed to grow back. Intensive agriculture entails laboriously clearing fields, building terraces, and excavating drainage ditches, ponds, and canals. These tasks completed, the work has just begun. The new agricultural environment must be maintained through constant effort. Although intensive agriculture allows humans more control over their environment, it can be as much a problem as a solution. By creating elaborate waterworks or clearing hillsides for terraces, a farming population may indeed protect its yields or even increase food production. But as agriculture becomes more complex and specialized, it becomes more vulnerable to disruption. Irrigation canals may silt up, fields may become unproductive as natural salts become concentrated in the soil, topsoil may erode—the list is long. These calamities accompany intensification as surely as the increased yields. A farmer who plants the same crop year after year to obtain the maximum yield is increasing the risk of total crop failure from soil depletion or disease.

The problem is not simply a lack of planning or a tendency of individual farmers to take this year's yield more seriously than environmental consequences a decade or a generation from now. In response to market demands or government inducements to produce more food, entire regions may be threatened by depletion or erosion of the soil or by its contamination by chemical residues. These problems arise in all major agricultural nations. Stability and continuity require investments in the infrastructure that are not immediately reflected in crop yields: soils protected from erosion, drainage maintained, crops rotated, and soils allowed to regenerate. If such investments are not made, the stability of the productive system is threatened.

So even as intensive agriculture solves some problems, it creates new ones. Irrigation has left such concentrations of minerals in the soil of California's Imperial Valley that productivity is leveling off and threatens to decline, and there is virtually no way to divert the contaminated water from the fields away from the downstream communities. Irrigation is often associated with environmental problems of this sort. Paradoxically, one response is to intensify production further by expanding the area under irrigation, building larger dams, digging deeper wells, using expensive chemicals to remove the salt, and using more water. Again, such efforts may solve the problem in the short run only to create more serious problems in the long run, such as causing the water table in the area to drop or further increasing the salinity of the soil. Consequently, cultivators have to work harder just to maintain the same level of productivity.

Intensive agriculturalists clearly do not free themselves from environmental constraints. On the contrary, they seem to labor under many more constraints than people whose technologies are less sophisticated. Intensive agriculturalists rearrange their ecosystems and must make tremendous efforts simply to support the artificial balance they have created. Intensification increases vulnerability. It opens up new possibilities for mishaps and magnifies the cost of mistakes. It widens the area and numbers of people who are affected, too, should a major problem occur. This is not to say that intensive agricultural systems inevitably fail or result in severe environmental problems. We have evidence of continuous, environmentally stable agriculture practiced in many parts of the world for thousands of years. And while the development of industrial methods is not a necessary consequence of intensive agriculture, certainly today's population levels require agro-industrial techniques.

From Intensive Agriculture to Industrialized Farming

In Europe, particularly in England, France, and Germany in the early nineteenth century, steam and internal combustion engines were harnessed to machines both for manufacturing and for transport. Just as with the rest of society, industrialism has transformed farming and farm society, but it can still be seen as a series of adaptive responses much like those we have already examined in other subsistence systems. It is a way of coping with challenges and resolving specific problems. As in all other instances of behavioral adaptation, the very act of coping creates the potential for negative as well as positive effects. The success or failure of industrial adaptations to human problems can be seen only in terms of long-range survival. What we call industrialism is a major societal commitment that has been underway for some 250 years. Not all the consequences are clearly understood even now. Further complicating the picture is the fact that industrialism is not an adaptation to a single local set of constraints or problems, and so the costs and benefits vary widely. Can we truly say that unemployed steelworkers of Ohio are benefiting from the system to the same degree as computer specialists in California's Silicon Valley? Are the unemployed young farmers of eastern Turkey, where the soils and rugged terrain limit mechanized farming, benefiting to the same extent that their western counterparts are when they use tractors and combines, or export fruit and vegetables raised in heated greenhouses? Unfortunately one of the consequences of intensive agriculture and industrial development is an increase in disparities among individuals occupying different positions within the economy. They also have a profound and ongoing effect on the world's population.

Population Growth

The industrial age ushered in a whole host of social changes. First, and perhaps most obvious, population increased rapidly. Europe's population grew from 100 to 187 million between 1650 and 1800, then leaped to 400 million in the nineteenth-century coal age—an increase of 260 percent (White, 1949, p. 384). Today the world's population is doubling every thirty-five years (Cowell, 1994, p. 10). Birth rates are significantly higher in the Third World than in industrial nations today, while death rates are declining; the result is explosive population growth. The Central American nation of El Salvador, the most densely populated country in the Western Hemisphere, has more than 670 people per square mile, or 5.6 million people packed into an area smaller than New Hampshire. The world's highest fertility rate is found in one of its poorest countries, Rwanda, with eight children per woman. India's population is growing at a rate of 18 million a year (Cowell, 1994, p. 10). In the industrialized nations, on the other hand, the rate of population growth has leveled off and even declined in some cases.

The changes that are occurring in human populations around the world are part of what

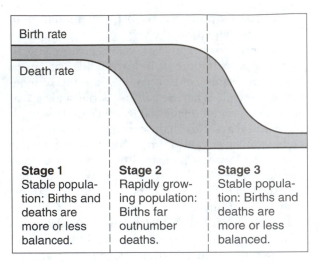

Birth rate

Death rate

Stage 1
Stable popula-
tion: Births and
deaths are
more or less
balanced.

Stage 2
Rapidly grow-
ing population:
Births far
outnumber
deaths.

Stage 3
Stable popula-
tion: Births and
deaths are
more or less
balanced.

Figure 6–1. *Demographic transition*

demographers call the great **demographic transition**: a rapid increase in a society's population with the onset of industrialization, followed by a leveling off of the growth rate (Ehrlich & Ehrlich, 1972, pp. 18–20). Until approximately 200 years ago, the world's population stayed remarkably constant. Then, with urbanism and industrialization, it started to grow rapidly and continues to grow as more and more countries become industrialized (see Figure 6–1). The point at which it will again stabilize is still distant. Every country appears to follow roughly the same trajectory as it develops: a spurt of rapid growth followed by a slowing of the rate of increase. The economically advanced nations may have zero growth rates, as the existing population simply maintains itself. The reasons for rapid explosion followed by a declining rate of population growth are exceedingly complex. The initial spurt of growth may be caused by a declining death rate attributable to improved health care in combination with high fertility.

One factor that encourages high fertility is the value of child labor. Peasants in largely rural El Salvador say that "every child is born with his bread under his arm"; not surprisingly, the birth rate in that country is over 45 per thousand of population—more than double that of the United States. More and more families come to depend on the sale of labor to meet their needs, and very often the income they derive in this way buys less food than they could produce directly. The mechanization and commercialization of agriculture precludes that option for most families. Rural people who have migrated to the cities simply do not earn enough to get by unless their children work as well. Children can

help in the fields, work in the factories, peddle or produce crafts, scavenge, and otherwise bring in needed income. Given high rates of infant and childhood mortality, the more children a couple has, the more likely some will survive to take care of them when they are too old to support themselves. In countries that have no publicly supported health or welfare programs, these are vital considerations.

The reasons for a decline in the rate of growth following economic development are equally complex. It appears that the decline in the usefulness of child labor together with a rise in the costs of education are often important factors in the decision to limit family size. Changes in the work force are important, too, as women who work outside the home find it difficult to care for many children. Burton Pasternak and Wang Ching (1985) found that Chinese women who worked in factories tended to stop breast-feeding their infants in favor of buying prepared foods for them. This change is not necessarily a positive one in terms of the health of the child, but it does free the mother to work. It also shows the impact of women's employment on decisions to limit family size.

Unfortunately, many developing countries in which fertility remains very high for a considerable time after mortality has dropped find that their population levels are so high that the standard of living cannot be raised. All that can be said for certain is that present rates of growth cannot long continue: if they did, in 700 years there would be one person for every square foot of earth! One of the important decisions taken by the 1994 United Nations Conference on Population in Cairo was to emphasize the role of education and, in particular, education for women in encouraging decisions for smaller families.

Intensification

Increasing population demands an increase in food production through intensification, and during the Industrial Revolution this process proceeded at an incredibly rapid pace. In fact, one of the first areas in which factory production made itself felt was the farm. Steel plows, threshers, combines, reapers, and mowers developed in the nineteenth century were followed by the gasoline tractor early in the twentieth.

Mechanization. Much of the energy involved in industrialism is channeled through machines rather than through animals and humans. However, **mechanization**—the replacement of human and animal

European farmers are extremely productive, although farm sizes are much smaller than in North America. Government subsidies serve to maintain the small farms in the face of competition with foreign producers.
(George Bates)

labor by mechanical devices, enabling humans to vastly increase the amount of product derived from one unit of land and labor—began long before the industrial age. Sails have been used to power ships for millennia. Mechanical devices of increasing size and complexity have been developed over the centuries for a variety of purposes: waging war, forging metals, constructing monumental buildings, grinding grain, making cloth. It is quite astonishing to note how far mechanization had proceeded even during what are sometimes called the Dark Ages. Outside of Paris in the sixteenth century, an ingenious system of hydraulic pumps drew water from the Seine for manufacturing purposes. However, it was only with the invention of the steam engine (and later the diesel and internal combustion engines) that populations were able to harness the concentrated solar energy stored in the fossil remains of organic matter (coal, oil, and gas). With these sources of energy, people throughout the world have vastly increased the scale of intensive agriculture, enabling humans to harness more energy per capita, as explained in Box 6.1, *Human Labor as Energy.*

Despite the ingenuity of these machines, it was not until the relatively recent development of sophisticated metallurgical techniques and power transmission systems that a breakthrough was achieved in the amount of power that could effectively be delivered. Such machinery has transformed our idea of work. Labor is increasingly devoted to the management and maintenance of machinery, rather than to the products the machines make. The whole field of robotics is a case in point. Specialists in programming and maintaining industrial robots are now key personnel in heavy, light, and service industries.

New sources of energy and the technology to harness them laid the groundwork for expansion of agricultural production on a scale never witnessed before. However, farmers in industrial societies often invest more energy in fertilizer and gasoline for their tractors than they harvest in calories of food energy, even with high-yield grains. Moreover, large quantities of energy are diverted to non-food-producing activities. Thus an industrial society is significantly less efficient than a nonindustrial society in the sense that it requires more energy to support a unit of population—but it is this pattern of high consumption that produces high standards of living.

Nonmechanized Approaches to Intensification. Another means of intensifying yields is by developing new crops and new strains of established ones. Francesca Bray documents how, over the centuries, Asian farmers developed new varieties of rice, increasing productivity and shortening the growing season (1994). The U.N.'s Food and Agriculture Organization (FAO) predicts that 64 countries will be unable to feed their peoples by the year 2025 (Cunningham & Saigo, 1995, p. 204). The main hope is that new crops and strains will produce ever more food, since croplands are limited.

Following World War II, research began on ways to increase yields of cereal crops, mainly rice, corn, and wheat. The results have ushered in what is called the **Green Revolution**; new strains have tripled or quadrupled yields per hectare. Without these new varieties, there would be even more widespread hunger in the world, but the so-called "miracle crops" are really "high responders" rather than high yielders (Cunningham & Saigo, 1995, p. 105). They respond more efficiently to increases in fertilizers and water, and have higher yields in optimum conditions; they often do poorly in bad years. Thus the benefits of the Green Revolution tend to accrue to the richer farmers who can afford to buy the seeds, fertilizers, and water.

Scientists in the Philippines are rapidly closing on yet a third generation "super rice" that will help to feed Asia's growing population. "The challenge now is that every day 2.5 billion people eat rice—by 2025, or just over a generation, that number will be four billion, and that means we have to produce 70 percent more rice from less land with less water and less labor" (Mydans, 1997, p. 9). The prototype of a promising strain has already been developed that will go some way to meeting that challenge; so-called "super rice" will allow farmers to increase crop yields 20 to 25 percent (Mydans, 1997, p. 9).

Fish farming, sometimes called the **Blue Revolution**, has the potential for contributing as much to human sustenance as the Green Revolution. In just the past decade, fish farming has grown immensely. Worldwide, some ninety species of finfish and shellfish are grown commercially. Over one-half the trout and salmon consumed in the United States is farmed; in many Asian countries, two-thirds of the protein needs of subsistence farmers is provided from domestic fish ponds. Shrimp farming is the most rapidly growing productive sector in South America and Southeast Asia. While fish farming has emerged as a major export industry, it is not without its environmental costs. A salmon farm typically holds 75,000 salmon; they produce organic waste equivalent to a town of 20,000 people. In South America and Southeast Asia, millions of hectares of mangrove swamps have been cleared for shrimp farming, endangering many species of wildlife (Cunningham & Saigo, 1995, p. 209).

Specialization

Some key components of the industrial era are as important for their cognitive as for their technological effects. The development of precise instruments for measuring time was critical to most sophisticated technologies and processes. At the same time, the gears that drove elaborate mechanical clocks were pivotal elements in the directing of human attention to a mechanical view of the world, which in turn became a key to the physical knowledge on which industry is based. The view of the world as a machine underlies the concept of the assembly line, which depends on quality (or, more accurately, precision). Specialization in high-volume production depends on the availability of interchangeable parts, which requires a level of precision that did not develop in a significant way until the early nineteenth century (initially in the weapons industry). Centralization is also required because industry standards must be developed to facilitate the use of interchangeable parts. Even on the assembly line, tasks are broken down into simple components. This division of labor permits the employment of unskilled labor, the worker becoming one more component in the productive process.

Workers often come to see little of themselves in their product. Their labor is used impersonally and they respond in kind. Perhaps belatedly, industrial employers are realizing that this is not necessarily the most efficient way to organize production in a high-technology society. General Motors recently built a new facility at which teams of workers have responsibility for producing entire cars. Increasing amounts of knitwear are being manufactured in New England homes, reviving a cottage industry that had almost died out by the end of the nineteenth century.

Along with the specialization of tasks, spatial specialization continues to intensify in industrial as well as postindustrial societies. Regions, cities, and even neighborhoods become associated with particular products, while agricultural districts come to depend on a limited array of crops. In fact, the bulk of the world's population is sustained by three crops: rice, wheat, and maize (corn) (Cunningham & Saigo, 1995, p. 215). This is in sharp contrast to the self-sufficiency that marked local adaptations in earlier eras where local populations relied on local and very diverse food sources. The city's workplaces or factories come to be highly specialized. Each produces only a limited range of products, but often they are of exceptionally high volume and quality.

Today we can see this specialization on a global scale. The increasing congruence of the world's cultures is a direct product of industrialization. Advanced transportation and communication systems, along with international migration, have brought peoples once isolated into contact with other societies. Above all, geographical barriers have been broken down by the economic forces of an international market system. Products are manufactured on one continent from the raw materials of another and sold on still another. The decisions made by Iowa wheat farmers affect the price of bread in India; the cost of oil in the Persian Gulf helps determine the cost of corn in the United States. In essence, the world's people are coming to live and produce under increasingly similar economic conditions.

When agriculture becomes specialized, farmers tend to view their work as a business, emphasizing cash flow and yield per unit of capital invested. Contemporary farmers in America, Europe, and the Third World concentrate on producing cash crops while buying food for themselves in the marketplace. In most countries it is the exception rather than the norm for a rural household to rely directly on what it produces for food, shelter, and clothing. As we have seen, in Turkey nomadic herders now sell their milk and wool, and use the cash to buy margarine, flour, and factory-made clothing. Agricultural specialization allows for a broader participation in a market economy. This generally provides access to a wider range of goods and services, but it also has some negative consequences. Reliance on cash crops increases the risk of failure. Moreover, this risk increases as intensified agriculture moves toward industrialism. Now many of the world's most important cash crops are not only volatile in price, but inedible. A farm family cannot eat the cotton it cannot sell.

Agriculture has become specialized in another fashion that some feel can be dangerous over the long term. As the Green Revolution has succeeded, the number of crop varieties has dramatically decreased. A few so-called "miracle varieties" have replaced several hundred types of wheat in the Middle East; the same is true of corn in the Americas. A hint of what might happen is the U.S. corn leaf blight of 1970, in which nearly all the hybrid (bioengineered, high-yield) corn was threatened (Cunningham & Saigo, 1995). The lack of genetic diversity makes crop failure on a massive scale possible.

Social relations also change with increasing specialization because households no longer operate as integrated, self-sufficient units. When agribusiness supplants traditional farming, the farm family is increasingly removed from the family network on which it once relied not only for social interaction but for labor and loans. In places of urban employment, kin groups become removed from production or redistribution: people rely less on family members than on fellow employees or associates. Social class, professional affiliation, ethnicity, and union membership take on functions of mutual responsibility and support formerly restricted to relatives. This is not to say that kinship is unimportant, but its functions change.

CASE STUDY

The Shift to Sisal in Brazil

A CLASSIC EXAMPLE OF THE DANGERS OF SPEcialization in agriculture was investigated by the anthropologist Daniel Gross and the nutritionist Barbara Underwood (1971) in the *sertao*, an arid region of northeastern Brazil. The *sertao* has always been a place of hardship and uncertainty. Historically, its people relied on cattle raising and subsistence farming. However, the years of self-sufficiency were regularly punctuated by disastrous droughts, with resultant starvation and mass exoduses from the region. In the 1950s, many subsistence farmers thought they could see an end to the cycle of uncertainty. A new drought-resistant crop, sisal, was beginning to be harvested for export. Sisal takes four years to mature and produces a tough fiber used to make twine. The extraction of the fiber from the leaves, a process known as decorting, is a long and arduous task requiring heavy machinery.

The first sisal plantations were owned by wealthy landholders. Soon smallholders came to abandon subsistence crops in the hope of sharing in the ever-rising profits from sisal. While waiting for the sisal to mature, they worked as laborers on the plantations of others. Unfortunately, by the time their own sisal had matured, the market price had fallen, leaving them with little or nothing to show for their investments. At the same time, even harvesting the sisal was costly; the smallholders had to rent decorting machines. Once planted, sisal is extremely hard to eradicate, and many formerly self-sufficient farmers were forced to remain as day laborers on the large plantations.

Another aspect of this shift to wage labor concerns nutrition. Gross and Underwood (1971) measured the calories the laborers expended while they worked on the sisal plantations and the amount of food they could buy with their wages. They found that many workers could not afford to buy enough food to meet their own needs and those of their families. Forty-five percent of the children of sisal workers were significantly undernourished.

In contrast to the hopes raised by the shift to a cash crop, the result was a poverty more severe than the small farmers had originally experienced. Moreover, their poverty was compounded by their new dependence on the people who owned the large farms and controlled the machinery. This is the reason that rural people in many countries leave the countryside, even though the city offers them little but the squalor of an urban slum. ❯

Centralization, Collectivization, and Communism

As you will see in the case of the Vikings in Chapter 7, cultural evolution generally involves centralization, as growing populations and social complexity require that central authorities coordinate diverse activities and interests. This process, which had been going on for centuries in Europe and elsewhere, continued during the Industrial Revolution as intensification and industrialism took hold around the world. One of the early signs of political centralization is the emergence of state institutions. More recently, centralization has moved beyond state boundaries, and is now evident in the formation of large regional confederations, in the U.N., and other global organizations. Economic centralization occurs as economies become closely interdependent, and a small number of institutions such as major stock, bond, and commodity markets determine the prices of items produced and consumed around the world. Centralization is also at work when key regions emerge as highly developed, economic cores, and create (or at least dominate) distant, less developed, peripheries. Within countries, centralizing tendencies can be seen in the agricultural sector.

The twentieth century has produced an extreme form of centralization, what Wolf calls the **administrative system** or **commune**, in which land is owned and managed by the state (1966). In most communist countries such as China (until 1980) and the former Soviet Union, collective and state farms were the basis of most agricultural production. Peasants on a state-owned farm work under the direction of government agricultural experts, who set production quotas and determine how labor will be allocated. Collective farmers may escape the extreme poverty and social degradation that often characterize peasant life under the other forms of land control, but as their labor and income are at the disposal of a bureaucratic ruling class, they are still peasants in the economic and political sense of the term. Variants of this arrangement are seen in the large state-run farm projects in some parts of Africa and Latin America.

Collectivization has seemed attractive to many governments for several reasons, not all of them laudatory. The main argument in favor of collectivization is that large agricultural enterprises gain from economies of scale; that is, expensive equipment can be shared, large fields tilled and irrigated efficiently, and labor pooled. In developing countries, particularly, it often seems easier to provide schools, clinics, and marketing facilities to large concentrations of people than to dispersed hamlets and villages. Another reason for collectivization is one not often openly argued: it is one means of controlling rural people and ensuring a level of agricultural production adequate to meet the objectives of the ruling elite. The following case study illustrates some of the positive and negative aspects of modern collective farms.

CASE STUDY

Feeding a Fifth of the World: From Chinese Communes to Farms

CHINA HAS RADICALLY TRANSFORMED ITS LAND tenure and rural society in this century—not just once, but several times. Following the success of the Communist Revolution in 1949, the traditional patrimonial estates were abolished and family private holdings were restricted in size, with much property being redistributed to the landless. Very rapidly this arrangement gave way to collectivization on the Soviet model, and by the early 1950s all farming was organized around collective farms or communes. At first these communes were relatively small and often consisted of closely related families, but soon the government ordered them consolidated into far larger entities, with all planning and administration carried out centrally. In 1956, for example, the government forced cooperatives to purchase over a million double-wheel, double-blade plows, even though they were virtually worthless in paddy cultivation. Authorities even dictated a specific planting density for rice, regardless of local conditions (Lardy, 1985, p. 38; Cunningham & Saigo, 1995, p. 203). By 1960 the government eliminated almost all aspects of rural entrepreneurship and private trading, closely controlled the prices of all produce, and set rigid quotas for grain production. The most consistent aspect of agricultural policy was the underpricing of rural products so as to support a large urban population.

Because central planning was unresponsive to local conditions and prices were low, production of critical food crops dropped drastically while the authorities continued to set high production quotas in an effort to feed the teeming cities. It has been estimated that between 1959 and 1961, food shortages and rural economic dislocations resulted in the deaths of 10 to 60 million Chinese, possibly the worst famine in the history of the world (Cunningham & Saigo, 1995, p. 203)! Most of these deaths occurred in the countryside, where 80 percent of China's people still live. Agriculture improved somewhat after 1961 but then stagnated until 1978, when the post-Mao government decided to return to decentralized, family-run farming. In the subsequent four years the proportion of people earning less than 100 yuan a year (the rural poverty line) fell from 30 to 3 percent—an achievement hailed around the world. China is now number one in both rice and wheat production (p. 203). Production is 50 percent higher than in the best of the commune years; China now has less than 3 percent of its population under-fed, compared to 10 percent in the United Sates (p. 203). Yet some Chinese communes had prospered during the years of collectivization, particularly those that were small, that enlisted members who trusted one another, and that offered greater rewards for shared labor than members could reap alone. When farming was returned to the private sector, many, but not all, profited (Parish, 1985). But since private farming requires less labor than the ineffi-cient communes, this has led to unemployment on a scale not seen since World War II (Kwong, 1994). ▶

Expanding Cities and Migrant Workers

The process of devaluing agricultural products and labor in relation to other commodities, along with the mechanization of agriculture, serves to push peo-ple off the land and set up population movements both within and between nations. The migration of Europeans to North America, closely paralleling the spread of industrialization through Europe, reached a peak at the beginning of the twentieth century. More than 52 million people, or a fifth of Europe's population, migrated overseas between 1840 and 1930. By and large, the immigrants were displaced from farming by mechanization, monoculture, and other changes. They came to America believing that U.S. factories offered limitless opportunities for wage labor.

Today, small-scale agriculturists displaced by large-scale industrialized agriculture are leaving the land at an alarming rate. Some settle in towns, where they work as unskilled laborers when there is work to be had. Some settle in large urban centers. Still others become migrant laborers. Northern Eu-rope is dotted with temporary settlements of Turk-ish, Greek, and Spanish laborers who travel north every year for a few months of labor in the factories or fields and then return home. Many more migrants establish long-term residence in large cities. The or-ganization of this mobile labor force varies consid-erably, as does the profitability of the arrangement for the laborers.

The Turks—nearly a million and a half of them—who labor as "guest workers" in the factories of northern Europe generally receive the same wages as native workers and are able to return to Turkey with substantial savings. But at the same time, they are the first to be fired in times of recession and they suf-fer considerable social isolation and discrimination. Migrant workers in the United States, most of them Mexicans or Central Americans, are seldom able to earn a living that is considered adequate by North American standards or to save enough to allow them to upgrade their salable skills. Throughout the year they move from harvest to harvest, staying in crowded and often squalid migrant camps. Most

Much of the hand labor on industrial farms all over the world is carried out by poorly paid migrant farm workers who follow the harvest seasons in search of employment.

(Christina Taccone/Offshoot Photo)

Box 6.2

China's Human Traffickers

"MR. ZHENG FROM WENZHOU, China, may be unlucky to have been one of the passengers on the ill-fated Golden Venture, which rammed the shore of Queens more than a year ago. He is however, the envy of his fellow inmates at the Metropolitan Detention Center in Lower Manhattan, because his wife comes to see him every day during visiting hours" (Kwong, 1994, p. 422). Mrs. Zheng had arrived illegally in the United States three years earlier, and soon came to realize that it was not what she had hoped for. Working at low wages she was under the unbearable pressure to pay off the $30,000 debt she owed her "snakehead," the smuggler who got her in. Accordingly, she advised her husband not to come, but he misinterpreted her advice to mean that she was leaving him. Placing their four-year-old daughter with his parents, he began his journey to the United States. His odyssey began when he took a bus to the Burmese border. Then he went on foot through the jungle to Thailand, where, for $17,000, he boarded the ship that took him first to Singapore, then Mauritius, and finally to Kenya. He waited there for six months before embarking on the Golden Venture with 300 other Chinese would-be immigrants.

Mrs. Zheng has been fighting for her husband's release but it is not easy. She speaks no English, works eleven hours a day as a seamstress in Manhattan, and then travels back to her apartment in Queens, which she shares with five other "snake people"—undocumented workers from Wenzhou. Even then she works several hours at night assembling garments—trying to scrape together the money she owes her snakehead.

Peter Kwong and two American journalists decided to visit the district of Wenzhou, 200 miles south of Shanghai to see for themselves why people were leaving. Their first stop was the Zheng family home, where they showed his tearful mother a video they had made of him in jail. She could not understand why an honest person was being held in jail when all he wanted was to work. When they explained that once media attention died down, Mr. Zheng would likely be released and sent back to China, his mother broke down completely and cried that if he returned, she would commit suicide. The family, like others, had borrowed huge sums at high rates of interest to pay for his journey in the expectation that he would find work; now they were borrowing more just to pay off the interest. If he returned, they would have no way to repay the money and would be at the mercy of the snakeheads.

About forty of the Golden Venture's passengers were from Wenzhou; surprisingly, most were Christians. Mrs. Peng's only daughter is languishing in a Louisiana prison; Mr. Sung, a former low-level Communist official, has four family members in jail in the United States. He said, "We are simply trying to make a better life for ourselves by going to America." He went on to state that while market reforms have improved conditions in the countryside, as evidenced by the numerous small factories that have sprung up, the benefits have not lasted. Further, since Communist officials have monopolized the most lucrative businesses, they have benefitted the most from privatization.

The country, too, is increasingly polarized, with rural people from the interior moving southward in search of work in the coastal provinces. In an unregulated labor market, factories (including foreign-owned ones such as Reebok) pay low wages and expect long hours. Wages are low because there are some 50 million people in search of work. While the reforms have brought great increases in farm production, they have also led to a chain reaction of "inflation, congestions, depressed wages, high unemployment and social disorder to cities in the infant stages of industrial development" (Kwong, 1994, p. 423). This leads people to turn to the snakeheads, however expensive and risky it may be. "In some cases the snakeheads simply make the debtors their virtual slaves. During the day, the victims work at restaurants that have been linked to organized crime. At night, after they are brought back to prisonlike dorms, they hand over all their money and are locked up until the next day" (Kwong, 1994, p. 425).

such camps are under the direction of crew leaders, who make the arrangements between the farmers and the laborers and provide the trucks to transport the laborers from place to place. Laborers are heavily dependent on their crew leader. When work is delayed, as it often is, they must borrow from him to buy their food. And often it is the leader who sells them their food—at an inflated price. Of course, migration is not limited to rural populations. The true nomads of industrial society are middle-class, white-collar workers who move from job to job or from city to city in the same job.

The rural landless have options other than settling in industrial farming communities or joining the migrant labor force. The overwhelming majority have chosen to try their luck in the cities. Since the Industrial Revolution, population movement has been a steady stream from the countryside to the city. In many nations now becoming industrialized, this stream has become a flood as unskilled rural people pour into the cities. In most countries, one or two cities become the targets for the majority of the migrants, and these cities swell beyond their capacity to provide employment or social services. In the Arabic-speaking countries of the Middle East, only 30 percent of the population was urban in 1962, but today more than half is. The population of Cairo, for example, increased from 3 million in 1947 to over 12 million in 1994. Mexico City, now the world's largest city with more than 20 million inhabitants, is experiencing massive problems: the world's worst air pollution, frequent breakdowns in public transportation and other services, and high rates of infant mortality. Like similar cities around the world, much of Mexico City's growth is due to an influx of rural dwellers. As elsewhere, these recent migrants form an extremely disadvantaged and socially distinct segment of the population, with high rates of unemployment, high rates of crime, and substandard housing. In some respects these poor city dwellers are fortunate. A U.N. study indicates that more than 12 million people around the world live in refugee camps and many more live on the brink of starvation—displaced not just by a changing global economy but by the brutal facts of war, famine, and political oppression. The FAO estimates that 15 to 20 million people (mostly children) die of malnutrition each year (Cunningham & Saigo, 1995, p. 212).

The European Community sees this migration from the land as a threat to its future ability to feed itself, not to mention maintaining its traditional rural/urban settlement patterns. Consequently countries in the European Community provide massive subsidies to farms, which allow them to continue to compete with North American agribusiness. Peter Kwong, a New York anthropologist, describes the sometime tragic human face attached to the global phenomenon of economic migration, which usually involves poor, rural dwellers who wish for a better life, in Box 6.2, *China's Human Traffickers*.

Stratification

With the development of intensive agriculture, the difference in productivity between richer and poorer lands was multiplied, creating and amplifying regional disparities. Similar processes of regional or national differentiation continued as societies industrialized, with more extensive effects. Today we can still see this stratification occurring on a global level, as regions with access to cheap energy and sources of capital, labor, and appropriate raw materials develop rapidly while adjacent areas suddenly appear underdeveloped by comparison. Within countries, the people who control land and capital can reap far greater rewards than those who have only their labor to sell, so that great social and economic disparities are apparent.

This is cruelly evident in India, which is the world's third largest producer of staple crops. Over 300 million of India's citizens are undernourished, about 40 percent of all malnourished people in the world (Cunningham & Saigo, 1995). Nevertheless, India exported 24 million metric tons of grain in 1986, primarily to feed livestock in Europe and the Near East. The wage value of labor is so low that people often cannot support themselves. This, in turn, is partially due to the fact that commodity prices for the crops and products most commonly exported from less-developed countries have been falling relative to imported manufactured goods; a ton of rice in 1950 would purchase twice what a ton of rice would in 1985.

Peasant Farmers in an Industrial Society

The application of industrial technology to farming, while undoubtedly necessary to feed the world's burgeoning population, has wrought profound changes in almost every country. One of the most profound has been the emergence of a peasant class. **Peasants** are farmers who lack control over the means of their production: the land and other resources, the capital they need to grow their crops, and the labor they contribute to the process. The state directly or indirectly shapes their lives, since the national institutions are controlled largely by the town-dwelling literate classes. Money and energy left over from their labors are regularly siphoned off in the form of land and equipment rentals and taxes. In the past they were subject in many countries to a sort of tax to be paid with their labor for the state, called **corvée**—that is, unpaid forced labor on public projects such as road construction.

When tractors and other equipment are introduced, the richer farmer is usually the one to benefit. New technology always entails risks. Large farms offer their owners the security that enables them to assume the risks entailed by the adoption of innovations, such as new high-yield seeds. As we saw in earlier chapters, rural people have responded in diverse ways but rarely have avoided being drawn into new markets and a near total dependency on distant sources of energy.

Drawing on the experiences of a number of countries, it has been commonplace to assume that the effects of industrialization on rural farming communities follow a fairly predictable course: Peasant handicraft production will be replaced by factory goods, peasants will purchase in the marketplace much of what they used to produce at home (thus becoming dependent on money), farm production will be focused on cash crops rather than on food for consumption, and wage labor will largely replace reciprocity and family-organized farming. The social consequences are usually assumed to be negative: Poor farmers are unable to compete in a fully monetarized economy and lose their lands; small farms and plots are consolidated into larger units that are run as businesses using hired laborers (usually those who have lost their own lands); and, as the scale of agriculture increases, more and more work is provided by migrant farm workers—the poorest of the poor. This, in fact, has occurred in many places, but it is not an inevitable scenario.

The loss of distinction between rural and urban households is another consequence of the transition to market dependency. This homogenizing effect is particularly evident when market dependency is coupled with industrial forms of transport and communication. Widely separated households end up eating, dressing, entertaining, and in general living very much the same way. Farm families in this country share most of the expectations and values of urbanites of the same cultural backgrounds. Even their daily diets are very similar. We can see this same process at work on a global level as cultural and ethnic distinctions fade, with resultant worldwide similarities within class lines. Robert Murphy sees "little doubt that by the year 2000 there will no longer be primitive societies" (1986, p. 16). Eskimos use jeeps and snowmobiles, and watch the same TV shows as people in Florida and Brazil. Across continents, people are drawn into one global system; styles of life reflect this convergence.

Sharecropping

Traditionally, **sharecropping** was a very exploitative farming arrangement in which workers farmed the land owned by others for a share of the yield (Wells, 1987). Sharecropping reached its peak in the United States during the Great Depression of the 1930s, when more than 25 percent of American farms were

operated on this basis. The arrangement had advantages and disadvantages. It did ensure the landless of access to farmland, even when market conditions left them so poor that they were unable to rent land for cash. At the same time, it yielded far greater profits to landowners than they could realize from rents. Sharecroppers were invariably among the poorest of the poor. These days, however, with the price of land high and rising, many family and corporate farms have returned to sharecropping of a sort: They invest in equipment rather than in more land, use it to farm land belonging to someone else, and pay the landowner in a share of the crop. These sharecroppers are among the more successful farmers in their communities.

In some cases, Miriam Wells (1987) reports, migrant workers become sharecroppers. When crops require a great deal of skill and much labor to raise, it can make sense for the landowner to give the farmworkers a share in the proceeds. California is once more a case in point. Strawberry production has shifted to sharecropping in recent years, with much of the work being done by the same Chicanos who were formerly migrant laborers. By and large, the workers have benefited from this arrangement, as they are their own bosses and share in the profits produced by their labor. Though few have yet moved from sharecropper to farm owner, many are hopeful.

Access to Land

One way to understand the factors common to the structures of contemporary farming is to determine how people gain access to land. Very often the material circumstances of peasant households and the degree of exploitation depend on the way the land is controlled, which in turn depends on the political configuration of the larger society. The private property form of landholding most prevalent today is associated with profound societal changes stemming from the rise of capitalism and industrialism in eighteenth-century Europe and the beginning of colonial empires. Land came to be viewed not as the hereditary privilege and responsibility of a local lord or ruler but as a commodity like any other—the private property of individual owners. Land became another form of capital, with rents or the sale of crops providing the return to the owner. Wherever European colonialism reached, this form of land tenure was encouraged (Wolf, 1982). When land became a commodity, it was relatively easy to encourage increased production and the settlement of Europeans in the new colonies such as those in Africa and the Americas; this system of ownership encouraged landowners to reinvest rents in their lands and to modernize their farm technology.

Peasant Responses to Oppression and Change

Although the lot of peasant cultivators varies widely, it is rarely enviable; "peasants of all times and all places are structured inferiors" (Dalton, 1972, p. 406). Wherever a peasantry exists, it represents a politically dependent and often oppressed segment of the society. Some observers say that peasants have been beaten down too long to be able to change their circumstances; generations of oppression have turned them into passive drudges, resigned to the injustices of their position and indifferent to political events outside the confines of their villages. Others argue that peasants' passivity is a rational, conservative response: Poor farmers or peasants simply cannot afford to take risks.

Anthropologists report that most peasant farmers are far from passive and are quick to seize an opportunity. We see that all over the world peasants have effected drastic changes in the way they live. In communities throughout southern Asia, for example, small tractors are used to till the paddies, entrepreneurs start up rice mills, and people almost everywhere are raising crops and animals they never raised before. Rural change is highly visible in China, where peasant farmers are now encouraged to reap the benefits of agricultural entrepreneurship. The Russian Republic is at last taking the same approach, but very slowly. One problem faced by Russia is that after several generations of collective farming, people have become accustomed to having agricultural decisions made for them and to the security of salaries rather than uncertain profits.

Not all farming families can solve their immediate economic problems by adopting new agricultural techniques. Often the prosperity of one village household depletes the resources of a less fortunate one. One very common response is to pack up and move, just as thousands of Oklahoma farmers did during the great Dust Bowl era of the 1930s. Tens of thousands of Brazilian farm families are attempting to settle in the Amazon region, and even more turn to the cities in the hope of betterment. We may deplore the social and environmental consequences of pioneer settlements in the rain forest and of the proliferation of urban slums, but we must recognize the tenacity of people who are doing their best in a world that does not always serve them well.

Peasants do periodically mobilize themselves into armed opposition. Indeed, history has witnessed a series of exceedingly bloody peasant revolts, in which centuries of accumulated resentment, masked by apparent docility, burst forth in massive waves of violence. England in the fourteenth century and Germany in the fifteenth and sixteenth centuries were shaken by peasant uprisings. In more recent times, the Algerian, Mexican, Russian, Chinese, and Cuban revolutionaries owed much of their success to peasant uprisings that furthered their aims. The irony is that today, these aging regimes are facing their own internal crises, including rural rebellions. In Algeria, Islamic fundamentalists are waging a battle rooted, in part, in the poverty-stricken countryside; in 1995, Indians in Chiapas, Mexico rose in rebellion against the government and demanded land.

As Eric Wolf (1966) points out, peasant uprisings are usually motivated by a drive not just for practical social change, but for utopian justice and equality. Such hopes may serve to unite the peasants, but not to organize them. The organization and leadership are usually provided by politically sophisticated outsiders. When a government is strong, the usual outcome of a peasant revolt is the death of many peasants and the return of the others to their fields. (An awareness of this likelihood has no doubt served to limit the number of peasant uprisings.) When, on the other hand, the government is already weakened, especially by war, then it may in fact fall if a strong leader manages to rally the peasants to his cause. This was the case in China, where Mao Zedong's revolution was furthered by the devastation of China's long war with Japan. Even when peasant revolts succeed, their success rarely brings complete equality since urban elites often replace the earlier or traditional elite. In China, as we have just seen, even the newly installed Communist government continued policies that disadvantaged people in the countryside, particularly peasants. While the system of land control is usually changed and poverty may be alleviated, a sizable class of rural producers remains in a subordinate social and political position, so there is still a peasant class.

In the remainder of this chapter we will first see how farmers in a Japanese community cope with mechanization and industrialism, and then we will turn to the United States to observe how the American family farm has changed and see the effects of the farmerless farm in the San Joaquin Valley in California.

CASE STUDY

Change in the Japanese Farming Village of Shinohata

IN 1993, BRITISH DEVELOPMENT RESEARCHER Ronald Dore returned to the tiny, remote village of Shinohata where he had lived in the 1950s and about which he had written in the 1970s (Dore, 1994). The village is situated in the mountains, twenty-five miles from the modern city of Sano, which is located in the wide, industrialized Sano Plains. Formerly it was a five-hour walk from the last train stop. Today, Shinohata is a mere eight-minute taxi ride or a couple of stops on an express electric commuter train from Sano. No longer isolated, it is as much a commuter neighborhood as a community—although many wish it to remain a community. When Dore returned to Shinohata in 1993, about the only sight he could recognize from his old photos were the mountains and the majestic white peak of the one volcano. The village, and the lives of its inhabitants, had in the course of a short generation been radically transformed. For the better, he asked himself, or . . . ?

While there are differences in wealth, these are far less apparent than prior to land reform in 1945, when many had no land at all. Now every child has access to an education and a career. As a development expert, Dore is led to speculate about what can be learned from Shinohata's experience. In Japan, the current approach to development stresses poverty-focused planning, or aiding the very poor. In reality Japan's wealth, and Shinohata's prosperity, did not come from efforts to improve the plight of the poor; they were a by-product of years of massive industrialization and individual sacrifice in which the poor contributed, predictably, the most. Is this a model for other countries? Probably not, he concludes, as people today are no longer prepared to wait to see improvements in their lives. Capital accumulation made Japan's present prosperity, but few other developing countries have the ability to defer consumption in order to achieve it.

In 1955 when Dore first settled in the community, the economy was entirely focused, as it had been for centuries, on the agricultural round: back-breaking hand preparation of the rice ponds, mulberry and silk-worm production, and tending household gardens. Ten years prior to his arrival, immediately after the war, a land reform act had redistributed much of the land in Shinohata to those who had previously worked for absentee landlords. Now most people owned two to six acres, with no one owning more than twelve. Thus the village was a community of owner-farmers who believed themselves well off, particularly the few households whose sons held salaried jobs outside the community. While new rice strains had increased yields, the labor involved was largely unchanged. The rice fields had to be prepared with a fine, perfectly level "tilth" or bed for planting made by cutting and chopping grass collected elsewhere and mixing it into the soil,

hand transplanting, constant regulation of the water level, and maintaining earthen walls around the field. At the end of the season, the farmer was left with twelve or so bales of rice.

Between rice harvests, wheat and barley and mulberry leaves were grown on the dry fields. Women of the household fed the mulberry leaves to silk worms, turning their cocoons into silk. In 1958 only 17 of the 60 households sold over $550 worth of produce on the commercial market, and about one-third of their profit went to buy fertilizers. Their tools were simple: an ox, plow, harrow, and simple cart, along with a hand-pushed rotary tiller. Most of the energy that went into farming was human, fueled by meals that consisted of large quantities of rice, soya beans, and fresh vegetables in summer, pickled ones in winter (p. 63). The first motor scooter, sold by Dore, came in 1956; one electric line served the village's needs and piped water had just arrived at individual homes.

By the 1970s, the village was electrified; every house had telephone and electricity lines along with a proliferation of appliances. Most households had motor vehicles, and the roads and sidewalks were paved. Many of the homes also had undergone two major phases of home investment. The first was to build indoor plumbing and to modernize the household's bath—a central domestic institution then, as now. The second involved remodeling the entire house with formal porches, glass windows and doors, hardwood floors, tile and formica kitchens, and often a Western-style living room with parquet flooring, plastic-wood wall panelling, sofas, and arm chairs. No longer does the visitor simply slide an entrance panel aside and shout, "excuse me"; there is a formal door on hinges, a brass nameplate, and a bell to ring. People no longer live in a microcosm where everybody is expected to know everyone else. Even the new toilets have refinements: they are called "Western-style" but they are rarely found outside of Japan. They have electrically heated seats and a little bowl built into the top of the cistern or tank in which one can wash one's hands. The family oxen disappeared in the 1960s when most of the livestock was sold off and everyone purchased multipurpose motorized tillers. In the 1970s when cheap American grain became available as feed, cattle were reintroduced. However, they never leave their feeding sheds until they are fat enough to sell. Beef prices are the highest in the world in Japan, and little or none is imported.

Even though they are now modernized, the villagers have not acquired the modern "cult of the natural," Dore writes. They have little nostalgia for the time when each house carried its night soil to cisterns for storage and later application on the fields, or for the flies and mosquitos that the women used to swat away from the food while the men ate. In 1955, the village shop was a social as well as redistributive center; people would shop and gossip. It is gone, as is the visiting vegetable seller. Everyone shops in large markets in town and stores produce in deep freezes and refrigerators. Gardening used to be largely a utilitarian endeavor, although some homes had modest decorative rock gardens with carp ponds. Now many have decorative gardens, usually reflecting how much an urban designer was paid to set it up (prices begin at $2,000).

Most of the family's food is purchased; only four households now make their own soya sauce, once a major and prized household product. Many still engage in farming of a sort, and it is profitable since Japan offers heavy subsidies for those who raise rice. The fields are now leveled and prepared mechanically; each plot is banked with expensive cement blocks, and some are even left to grow weeds under a government agricultural subsidy plan. Weeds are no longer mulched, but fertilizers are employed instead. The seedlings are planted by an ingenious machine that plucks them from a container and plants them in finger-deep, perfectly aligned holes. Threshing, too, is mechanized. Only a few elderly ladies persist in the labor-intensive business of silk worm production. Agriculture alone no longer sustains modern Shinohata standards of living. Every family has members working in industry, commerce, or for the government. Many outsiders have moved in, either as second-home dwellers or as commuters.

The road from Sano City, nowadays crowded with vehicles, winds through the plains and up into the hills that are now sites on which Tokyo residents build second homes and where vacationers stay in lodges with exotic names such as "Monte Carlo" and "Motel Arizona." The hungry can stop at a friendly *duraivin* (drive-in); shops along the road out of town have automatically opening glass doors—a feature that in most industrialized countries is restricted to major buildings.

Socially, the community has changed as well. By 1993, the days of large communal outings to shrines or resorts was over; the fire department no longer takes the day off for a fishing and drinking party. Indeed, there are few activities that bring everyone together. Politics is a consuming issue, as the village has always made skillful use of subsidies and grants provided by the government. The villagers have no longer to work together to repair the roads or to build each other's homes. Even religious activities, which used to be occasions of near-mandatory attendance (and male drinking sessions), no longer at-

Agricultural land is disappearing in most parts of the world as urban and industrial centers spread, such as this one north of Los Angeles.

(David Parker/Photo Researchers Inc.)

tract more than the die-hards. Most excuse themselves and hurry home to television. Reaching Shinohata on his last visit, Dore was confronted by the newly renovated village hall, renamed "Multi-Purpose Center."

Are the people of Shinohata really better off with lives focused on jobs, TV, and commuting schedules? One person answered Ronald Dore in 1993, ". . . you used to say none of this 'where are the snows of yesteryear' business. None of this green nostalgia for a warmer, unpolluted, nonpolluting, natural human past. All of the changes in Shinohata are for the better. That's what you used to say. But what about now? Are you still of the same mind?" ▶

Urbanized Rural Society: Farming in the United States

Over 90 percent of American farms are family operated (contrary to the perception of many), although there are far greater differences among them than there were a generation or two ago. Farms of 3,000 acres that gross more than $500,000 a year account for only 2 percent of the total, but produce 35 percent of the output; the top 5 percent account for more than half the output (Feder, 1994, p. 1). The majority of American farmers have significant off-farm income; it is the larger ones that adopt new technology, often working directly under contract with food processors such as Frito-Lay or McDonalds. The modern American farmer has to be as much a financial and marketing expert as anything else. We will examine the development of American farming with case material from California and the Midwest.

CASE STUDY

The Development of Agribusiness in Wasco, California

AMERICAN ANTHROPOLOGISTS WERE SOMEWHAT slow to recognize the importance of studying farming communities in their own society. In the early 1940s, however, Walter Goldschmidt (1978) undertook a now classic study of Wasco, California, a town of 7,000 to 8,000 people, most of them involved in various aspects of industrialized commercial agriculture. By living in the town, participating in local organizations, conducting interviews, and examining official records and historical documents, Goldschmidt was able to trace the radical transformation that the town had undergone in the previous few decades. More recently the study of rural America has become a major focus of research, and not surprisingly, much of it has been directed to California (see Chibnik, 1987).

Until the first decade of this century, the land on which Wasco's farms now sit was desert, and the main activity in the area was sheep herding. Wasco itself consisted of one store, one hotel, and a handful of saloons frequented by ranch hands and an occasional homesteader. Then in 1907 a developer persuaded the corporation that owned the entire Wasco area to sell him part of its holdings and began to advertise for homesteaders, promising to provide the necessary irrigation. The sales pitch worked (the land was bought quickly), but the irrigation system did not. In all probability, the farmers would have abandoned Wasco to the sheep if a power company had not brought in a line, enabling the settlers to install electric pumps. This was the beginning of the industrialization of Wasco.

For small farmers, as most of the original settlers were, an electric pump is a major investment. In order to recoup that investment, the farmers turned to cash crops, specializing in potatoes, cotton, sugar beets, lemons, or grapes. Both the profits and the settlement grew. In some years the payoff for commercial farming was spectacular. In 1936—a Depression year—one farmer was rumored to have made over $1 million from his potato crop.

Such booms encouraged Wasco's farmers to expand. Some of them rented land on which to grow profitable but soil-depleting crops for a year or two. (Once the soil was exhausted, the owner would revitalize it by planting alfalfa and then rent it again.) This strategy of expansion required the planter to hire large numbers of workers and to make substantial investments in tractors and other motorized equipment. Other Wasco farmers used their profits to expand in other areas. Having made a large investment, a farmer would look for ways to maintain a steady flow of produce and income. He might, for example, buy the fruits of another landowner's trees and hire his own laborers to pick them. Or better still, he might purchase more land. In this way, the average size of landholding increased from about 20 acres when the homesteaders first moved in, to about 100 acres at the time of Goldschmidt's study—a 500-percent increase in about thirty years.

In no time Wasco was attracting outside corporations—first the utility companies, then a national bank, oil companies, and chain supermarkets. These developments changed the social landscape. The representatives of the state and national government agencies and of corporations (whose loyalties lay outside Wasco) tended to become leaders within the town. Even farmers with relatively small holdings began to see themselves as entrepreneurs rather than as tillers of the soil. One informant told Goldschmidt, "There is one thing I want you to put in your book. Farming in this country is a business, it's not a way of life" (1978, p. 22).

Wasco began to attract large numbers of unskilled laborers who could find work in the town and dream of buying a place of their own one day. First Mexicans (Chicanos), then (after World War I) blacks, and in the 1930s refugees from Oklahoma, Arkansas, and other drought-stricken states poured into the town. They were markedly poorer than the Wasco farmers, who did not consider them their racial, cultural, or social equals. The social contact between the two groups was very limited. At the time of the study, the Mexicans, the blacks, and to a lesser extent the Oklahomans lived in their own separate communities with their own stores and churches. They were outsiders in every sense, and that was just what Wasco's commercial farmers needed: "a large number of laborers, unused to achieving the social values of the dominant group, and satisfied with a few of the luxuries of modern society" (1978, p. 62). In its urban orientation, its commercial production and consumption, and its economic gap between owners and laborers, Wasco might as well have been an industrial center. Above all, in its social structure—the impersonal, purely economic relationship between the landowners and the laborers—the town showed its urban-industrial face. To see how Wasco continues to change, we turn to a more recent California study. ◗

CASE STUDY

The Farmerless Farm in the San Joaquin Valley

MARK KRAMER DESCRIBES THE SUBSEQUENT phase in the transformation of California agriculture: the farmerless farm (1987, pp. 197–278). It is tomato harvest time in the San Joaquin Valley, 3:00 A.M., and 105,708,000 ripe tomatoes lie ready for picking on some 766 absolutely flat acres of irrigated cropland. Out of the darkness rumble giant tractor-drawn machines resembling moon landers—two stories high, with ladders, catwalks, and conveyors fastened all over and carrying fourteen workers each. As they lumber down the long rows, they continually ingest whole tomato plants while spewing out the rear a steady stream of stems and rejects. Fourteen workers sit facing a conveyor belt in the harvester, sorting the marketable tomatoes from the discards.

It is a giant harvest carried out almost without people; only a few years ago more than 600 workers were needed to harvest a crop that 100 manage today. There are no farmers involved in this operation: only corporation executives, managers, foremen, and laborers. The word "farmer" has virtually disappeared; in this operation, one refers to "growers" and "pickers." Managers take courses in psychology to help them determine appropriate incentives to offer tractor drivers for covering the most ground (if speed is too great, they may damage equipment; if they go too slowly, productivity falls). Managers similarly calculate pickers' productivity very precisely and regulate it by varying the speed of the conveyor belts and by minimizing the time spent turning the machines around at the ends of rows, when the workers are prone to get off for a smoke. Right now, Kramer reports one manager as saying, the industry is moving to a new-model harvester that will do the job of fourteen men with only two. The other twelve can move on to other employment if they can find it.

Tomato consumption closely reflects the changing eating habits of American society; these days, each of us eats 50.5 pounds of tomatoes every year, whereas in 1920 consumption was 18.1 pounds. This change is accounted for by the fact that far more of our food is prepared somewhere other than in the home kitchen. This development has produced a demand for prepared sauces and flavorings, such as catsup and tomato paste. The increased productivity required to meet demand has resulted in dramatic genetic changes in the tomatoes we eat.

Processors of tomatoes demanded a product that is firmer; growers needed standardization of sizes and an oblong shape to counter the tomatoes' tendency to roll off the conveyors; engineers required tomatoes with thick skins to withstand handling; and large corporate growers needed more tonnage per acre and better resistance to disease. The result is the modern American tomato: everything but flavor. "As geneticists selectively bred for these characteristics, they lost control of others. They bred for thick skins, less acidity, more uniform ripening, oblongness, leafiness, and high yield—and they could not also select for flavor" (Kramer, 1987, p. 213). Even the chemists made their contribution: a substance called ethylene (which is also produced naturally by the plants) is sprayed on fields of almost ripe tomatoes in order to induce redness. Quite like the transformation of the tomato itself, the ownership of the farms that grow them has been altered. As one might expect in view of the massive inputs of capital needed to raise the new breed of tomatoes, most are raised on corporate spreads. The one Kramer describes consisted of more than 27,000 acres and was owned by several general partners, including a major insurance corporation, an oil company, and a newspaper; and thousands of limited partners, most of them doctors and lawyers who invested in the operation for its tax benefits. There is little room under these conditions for the small farmer—or so it would seem. ◗

The Family Farm

Even in food production there are limits to the efficiency of large farms: They require middle-level managers and get less out of individual workers than do smaller, family-managed operations. Large, corporately managed farms can make large-scale mistakes. Kramer reported that one worker in California sprayed a huge area with the wrong insecticide, and some managers' heavy investment in unsuitable crops resulted in big losses. In fact, the large farm Kramer describes subsequently sold off half its holdings as unprofitable. Under some conditions, a smaller farm can be more efficient than a huge one, but it still will be highly capitalized and employ modern equipment, up-to-date accounting methods,

Mechanization of agriculture may cost far more in terms of energy invested in farm equipment and fertilizers than is yielded in food energy. Giant tractors are used throughout North America and other industrialized countries to prepare the fields and to harvest crops.

(John Colwell/Grant Heilman Collection)

and trained management. Most successful farmers in the United States are college graduates.

Many observers report a revival of the family farm in North America, but one with a new face (Gladwin & Butler, 1982; Salamon, 1992). The family-run farm now often involves a new division of labor, with the wife assuming primary responsibility for farming operations, often of a specialized nature, while the husband holds down a salaried job and helps out when he can. This is clearly the pattern in the Midwest on smaller farms, but on large spreads of over 500 acres the family manages today much as before: with its own labor and skills.

CASE STUDY

Family Farmers in the Midwest: The Immigrant Legacy

SONYA SALAMON HAS SPENT MANY YEARS studying Midwestern farming communities and families (1992). Most of her research concerns seven farming communities in Illinois where she has been carrying out research for over a decade. Land and family are her main interests, since families cannot farm without land. Yet this resource has to be acquired and passed on in order for the community (if, indeed, it is one) to have continuity. Family land,

then, is a cultural patrimony and land tenure and farm management and inheritance shape the personalities of rural communities. About half of the communities she studied were of German descent, coming from both the Protestant and Catholic regions of Germany; the other half, which she calls "Yankees," are of largely Protestant backgrounds and came to the Midwest from New England and the British Isles. One unexpected finding of her research is that far from being homogeneous after so many years, there is a definite mosaic effect in the rural American settlement pattern—and one which is changing with time.

These two groups are only part of the ethnic diversity of region; Michigan, for example, has many farmers of Polish, Dutch, and Finnish descent but the processes of community formation seem remarkably similar. In the mid-nineteenth century, with the coming of the railways, the Midwest saw development unparalleled in American history. Within fifty years, the Midwest was transformed from forests and prairies into densely settled and intensively farmed agricultural lands. Towns and villages shot up almost overnight, populated by immigrant Europeans. There were many reasons for them to emigrate, including inheritance rules in Europe that encouraged farm fragmentation and rural poverty. The newly established railroads provided easy access to the Midwest and land grant acts by Congress made it easy, if not free, for settlers to acquire land. Even the railroads offered inducements for migrants to settle. This was not, of course, altruism—just good business. With farming came the need to transport produce to markets and industrial products to the farms.

While all immigrants faced similar challenges, different ethnic groups responded to these in different ways. Those Salamon calls Yankees came from predominately English backgrounds. While unlikely to have been landowners at home, they tended to approach farming much as in the home country. Land was viewed as a commodity, which, if possible, should be worked for profit using hired help or tenant farmers. Children of owners were not so much induced to stay at home but rather to strike out and find new farmsteads for themselves. This set the basis for settlement; successful farmers set their sons up with farms in distant regions, not necessarily next door. Absentee ownership was also common, and, in general, these farmers were not known for their "stewardship of the soil"—looking instead to profit rather than sustainability. The Yankees had the advantage of being part of the linguistic and political majority and could move rather easily. The German settlers came from different regions of Germany, spoke different dialects of German, and belonged to different churches. They shared, however, a common origin in tightly knit peasant communities that they intended to replicate in their new country. Some of the newcomers were able to acquire land; some simply worked for Yankee farmers as tenants. But even as tenants, their objective was to save enough to acquire land near other German-speaking members of their local church. Initially, the Midwest was predominantly Yankee, with much land in Illinois held in huge spreads of over 10,000 acres used mostly for livestock production. As settlement progressed, the absentee owners often took advantage of rising land prices to sell out. Usually they sold to their German tenants or neighbors. Thus, with time, the German component in the settlement pattern grew until today it is the dominant one.

Salamon distinguished two divergent strategies that shaped settlement and community patterns and continue to do so. One strategy, which she terms the "yeoman" approach, is more characteristic of the German population.[1] The other is the "entrepreneur" approach more characteristic of the Yankees.

The yeoman sees land as a sacred trust and farming as a means of membership in a community. There is a relative hierarchy in the family, since whoever owns land has power and seniority in management decisions. The yeoman's goals are to own as much land as feasible without undue debt or risk, maximize kin involvement, and avoid anything that would alienate the land from the family.

In contrast the entrepreneur views land as a commodity and farming as a business. There is a weaker family hierarchy, as farming is not necessarily thought to be the logical thing for an heir to do. The entrepreneur does not always favor ownership over renting land; renting land allows the entrepreneur to expand and utilize capital better. For this reason, their farms are larger, more capital-intensive, and more in debt.

In recent decades the approaches have necessarily drawn closer together; almost all farms are heavily capitalized, few are free of debt, and all must be as skillful in marketing as in crop production. What is clear from Salamon's research is that the family is very much part of the family farm in America, perhaps even more than ever. Since farm sizes have increased so much in recent years, something of the older prairie feeling has returned to farm life. Houses are now farther apart and families rely on church and community get-togethers to see friends and neighbors. Of course, this is mediated by the use of mobile phones and CB radios, and everyone follows local and national events in the media. ◗

Summary

INTENSIVE AGRICULTURE IS DISTINGUISHED FROM horticulture by both an increased investment in energy and increased productivity per unit of land. The additional energy may come from a variety of sources, including animals yoked to plows, fossil fuels for farm machinery, fertilizers, and human muscles. Methods of intensification include irrigation canals, terracing, crop rotation, and selective breeding of crops and livestock. Through these techniques, the output of cultivated fields is increased, more fields can be cultivated, and fallow periods can be decreased or eliminated. While both the land and the farmer work harder

---

[1] By "German" is meant those with German surnames indicating German descent; they may no longer speak German, but they do identify themselves as such in national censuses.

under intensive agriculture, the result is much higher production.

Intensive agriculture substantially reshapes the environment. By constructing irrigation systems to overcome the problem of insufficient rainfall, for instance, farmers may create new, complex problems that become increasingly difficult to solve. The more people alter their ecosystems, the more labor and organizational effort are required to maintain their bases of production.

The social consequences of intensification are far-reaching. The development of irrigation is associated with the emergence of cities and territorial states, with accompanying social changes: higher population densities, economic stratification, increased trade, the appearance of craft specialists, and the development of hierarchical civil and religious organizations. The need for centralized authority to make decisions, variations in the productivity of land in the region, and a surplus of food all contributed to the rise of cities and states. Farming communities that were at one time autonomous were absorbed by the states, and the farmers (or peasants) lost control over the social and economic system and the means of production. Peasants are agriculturists (usually villagers) who do not control the land, capital, and labor on which they depend; further, they are often subject to corvée, unpaid labor to build and maintain roads and bridges. In some parts of the world peasants gain access to land by sharecropping, or working land owned by others in exchange for a share of the yield.

Corporate ownership of land and resources, which typifies horticultural land use systems, is generally giving way to private ownership. Under private ownership, land is regarded as the private property of the individual owner. In the early twentieth century, a new form of land tenure arose and became widespread. Under the administrative system, formerly prevalent in all communist countries, the state owns the land and can control much of the peasant's labor and income. The administrative form of land control has had a mixed record. Collective farming led to the near collapse of food production in China and was largely abandoned there as public policy. Some collective enterprises do prosper, particularly those that are small, that offer participants some advantage, and that produce items that farmers could not produce by their individual efforts.

Under exceptional circumstances, peasant farmers may find their situation intolerable and rise in revolt. In this century they have supported revolutions in Algeria, Mexico, Russia, China, and Cuba. Even when such uprisings are successful, the farmers often remain disadvantaged in relation to the urban population.

Industrialism is characterized by a highly developed factory system of production based on the harnessing of vastly increased amounts of energy, on specialization, and on mechanization—the replacement of human and animal labor by mechanical devices. The rise of industrial society has provoked dramatic changes in our physical and social environments. The more energy industrial societies extract, the more they require for their survival.

Industrialism has numerous social consequences. Human populations are increasing more rapidly than ever before, with consequent pressures on natural resources. Industrialization brings a demographic transition: the population increases rapidly and persistently before the growth rate finally levels off. Massive migrations both between and within nations have occurred as people have left rural communities for the cities in the hope of industrial jobs. Increasing specialization of labor and concentration of wealth have resulted in new kinds of social relations and organizations. Differentiation between classes has increased, while differentiation based on cultural and ethnic distinctions within classes has declined. The economy brought about by industrialism has transcended geographical barriers. This chapter focuses on the industrialization of agriculture, the adaptations that people have made to this phenomenon, and the impact of technology and multinational corporations.

One example of the problems inherent in industrialized agriculture is sisal cultivation in Brazil. A group of small farmers in Brazil, hoping to share in the prosperity of the large landowners, abandoned their subsistence crops to plant sisal for export. By the time their crops matured, the price of sisal had dropped and they were forced to work as laborers on the large plantations to survive. Vast numbers of such displaced farmers all over the world finally seek a better life in the cities, where they slowly adapt to an urban and industrial society.

This chapter pays special attention to two cases of intensive farming: a Japanese village, Shinohata, whose families are rapidly being absorbed into that country's growing industrial sector; and California's industrialized farming system.

In Shinohata, farmers are rapidly adopting new technology such as chemical fertilizers, motor tillers, and power sprayers. Many younger people are leaving the village to work in factories, leading to a decrease in household size. But even though farm size has increased and town and country have been integrated, some of the expected negative results have not appeared. The household remains the basic unit of production and consumption, wealth has not become concentrated, and those who do move to the city remain in close contact with their rural families. In short, industrialization has, on balance, been beneficial to most, in contrast to the uneven situation in many other countries. This is because Japan's rapidly growing economy can absorb those who do not make it on the farm.

In the experience of Wasco, California, we see the urbanization of a rural community by mechanization—the transformation of farming as a livelihood to farming for profit, the change in social reference from the local community to that of the wider world, and the breakdown in social relations from close personal ties to relatively impersonal ones. In the San Joaquin Valley, large corporations run giant farms without farmers, relying on managers and foremen to supervise crews of migrant laborers. The family farm is still the dominant form of farming in the United States, even though a commercially successful operation now involves over a thousand acres of land. In the Midwest, there is still a definite ethnic texture to the settlement pattern, with, in Illinois, families of German descent now predominant.

Key Terms

administrative system	fallow time
Blue Revolution	Green Revolution
commune	mechanization
corvée	peasants
demographic transition	sharecropping

Suggested Readings

Bentley, J. W. (1992). *Today there is no misery: The ethnography of farming in northwest Portugal*. Tucson and London: University of Arizona Press. A thorough study of the agricultural system of northwest Portugal with an optimistic view of peasant farming.

Bray, F. (1994). *The rice economies: Technology and development in Asian societies*. Berkeley: University of California Press. This book extensively describes the history and techniques of rice cultivation.

Dore, R. (1994). *Shinohata: A portrait of a Japanese village*. Berkeley: University of California Press. A lucid and detailed account of a Japanese village over the past twenty years, including methods of rice cultivation as well as what it means to live in this village.

Durrenberger, E. P. & Tannenbaum, N. (1990). Analytical perspectives on Shan agriculture and village economics. *Monograph Series, 37*. New Haven, CT: Yale University Southeast Asia Studies. This volume discusses and analyzes the economics of Shan agriculture and farmer decision making.

Freeman, J. M. (1977). *Scarcity and opportunity in an Indian village*. Menlo Park, CA: Cummings Publishing. A study of a small village in India that has experienced an ever-widening gap between the privileged high castes and the less privileged lower castes. The economic basis of this gap seems to be that the higher castes have benefited from the growth of a nearby city, while members of the lower castes have little opportunity to improve their lot through urban contacts.

Kirch, V. P. (1994). *The wet and the dry: Irrigation and agricultural intensification in Polynesia*. Chicago: University of Chicago Press. A fine-grained review of intensive agriculture in a region that is often overlooked.

Salamon, S. (1992). *Prairie patrimony: Family, farming and community in the midwest*. Chapel Hill: University of North Carolina Press. An excellent account of family farming in the Midwest.

Scott, James C. (1976). *The moral economy of the peasant*. New Haven, CT: Yale University Press. A study of peasant politics and rebellion that focuses on the critical problem of a secure subsistence as the explanation for the technical, social, and moral arrangements of these societies.

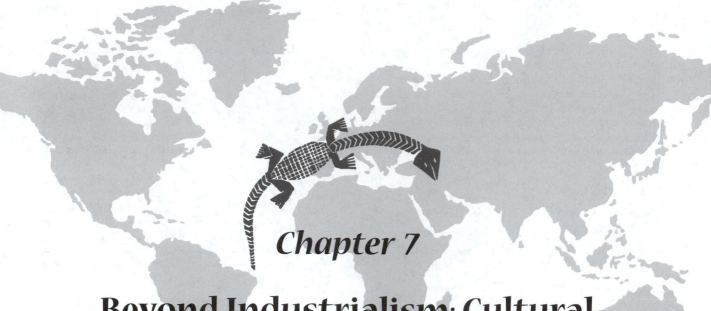

Chapter 7

Beyond Industrialism: Cultural Change and Economic Development

There is a marked tendency for human populations to maintain the status quo. People do not usually seek and accept change easily, for change always has inherent risks and uncertainty. People react to change in a variety of ways. Usually the rate of change is so slow that people are hardly aware that it is occurring. When women entered the U.S. work force in great numbers during World War II and later in the 1960s, few people observed, let alone anticipated, the social consequences. Only many years later did public policy come to recognize the changes taking place in the way we lived, married, and reared our children (see Susser, 1986). Even today little or no attempt has been made to shift public policy in ways that would cushion the social costs of this transformation that are borne by women and children (Sidel, 1986).

Observations from many sources indicate some recurring long-term processes of systemic change that cumulatively have transformed human society and that continue to do so. These patterns of general evolution—the patterns of behavior or organization that can be observed in a group or population—are the products of

short-term adaptations, and none is universal. One way to see the long-term consequences of specific adaptations is to go back in time: Archaeological data offer us an insight into the processes of long-term change. They also caution us not to predict long-term success or failure on the basis of short-term perspectives. By some criteria, bacteria may be considered to be better adapted than humans. They have remained virtually unchanged for over two billion years and thrive in an incredible range of habitats.

Adaptation and Processes of Cultural Transformation

A Case Study in Long-Term Change: The Vikings in the North Atlantic

The history of Viking exploration and settlements in the North Atlantic provides one example of an accumulation of short-term adaptations that result in an ultimately dramatic long-term change. Thomas McGovern and other archaeologists who specialize in Norse or Viking history have attempted to unravel the checkered history of Norse settlement in the North Atlantic (McGovern, 1980; McGovern et al., 1996). Numerous islands were settled between A.D. 790 and 1000, including the Shetland and Faroe islands, Iceland, and Greenland, and very likely the east coast of North America as well. The colonies had rather different histories, and the westernmost ones, Iceland and Greenland, mark the outer limits of significant Viking settlement. The once thriving settlements of Greenland (which failed by 1500) and Iceland (which suffered a significant decline in population after several centuries) offer some insights into the processes of long-term adaptation.

The Viking settlers brought with them an established food procurement system: they raised cattle and sheep, fished, and, where possible, cultivated wheat or barley. They also came equipped with a social and political hierarchy that separated the free from the slaves and encompassed quite rigid distinctions among servants, tenants, land-owners, and chiefs. By law, every free landowning farmer or household had to be associated with a particular chief. Each tenant—a family that was contracted to run a farmstead for a specified period—was bound to a landowning householder. The entire colony was run by an elite comprising chiefs and, in the later periods, the Norwegian king's appointees and church dignitaries. The early colonial period was quite successful; most of the settlers were free, and they established independent holdings on which to raise sheep and cattle wherever they found sufficient pasturage. The settlers were quick to incorporate the rich marine life into their diets. The population of Greenland's settlements grew, as did that of Iceland; the two together reached some 60,000.

With success, however, came the gradual transformation of the Viking colonies. In the beginning, each settlement was relatively autonomous and the predominant form of homestead was that of a free family working pastures and lands that they owned and on which they paid taxes. Though slaves were brought over initially, no more were imported and the labor that nonfamily members performed was provided by servants and tenants. As time passed and settlements grew, churches were erected and homesteads spread to the outer limits of pasturage in this severe environment.

Gradual social and political changes had profound effects. First, the number of tenant farmers increased in relation to freeholders as many freeholders had to sell their lands to pay the taxes levied. Thus land became much more subject to indirect management. The people who worked the land were under pressure to produce as much hay or to raise as many sheep and cattle as possible, with little thought to possible long-term effects. Evidence of overgrazing and soil erosion is abundant. Second, what were formerly petty chiefs became powerful leaders, controlling considerable land and often warring with rivals. By the mid-thirteenth century a few families had come to control most of the land. In short, land use became intensified. Socially, the society was more stratified; specialized priests, warriors, smiths, and urban craftworkers proliferated; and decision making became more centralized as power accrued to the chiefs and bishops.

In 1262–1264, Greenland and Iceland came under the direct control of the Norwegian state and most land was now controlled by church and crown. The church sent bishops to rule and encouraged the building of monumental structures quite disproportionate to the size and resources of the colonies. Taxes and tithes were collected, administered, and forwarded to the state by foreign-born appointees. The colonies were closely integrated into a growing North European economic system. But economic integration did not bring prosperity to most of the people of the colonies, and ultimately it had dire consequences. Environmental degradation through soil erosion and depletion of marine resources caused hardship. Much of the pasturage became barren rock, and by 1500 the colony on Greenland had become extinct, unable to cope with the demands of its top-heavy administration, a depleted resource base, and the harsh climate. Greenland was once more left to its North American inhabitants—the Eskimos, whose time-proven adaptations the Vikings chose to ignore or dismiss. By 1600, 94 percent of Iceland's people were reduced to tenant farming and the population declined sharply. This colony survived, but prosperity returned only in this century when Iceland reorganized itself as an independent and locally self-sufficient society (see also McGovern et al., 1996).

Processes of Long-Term Cultural Change

With this case study in mind, we can review some very general processes involved in long-term cultural change.

Intensification. The per-capita energy requirements of the simplest human cultures are very small when compared with those needed by the most complex societies. As a society increases in complexity, more and more of its energy budget must go to maintaining institutions—churches (as in our Viking example), universities, banking systems, stock markets,

This market near Nyeri, central Kenya, is open two days a week and hundreds of vendors, mostly women, come to sell produce and craft items.
(Daniel Bates)

etc. (Tainter, 1988, p. 91). A key element in the increasing complexity of the infrastructure is the **intensification** of food production. This process of intensification involves increasing the product derived from a unit of land or labor.

Most societies that rely on hunting and gathering obtain less food from a unit of land than do populations that rely on intensive agriculture. In the latter, increasing numbers of people rely on a relatively constant amount of land to produce increasing amounts of food. Again, we have seen this dynamic at work in the Viking settlements. Quite apart from land-use intensification, ever more nonfood energy is harvested and consumed on a per-capita basis.

Presently, the world's population stands at 5,500,000,000, double what it was 30 years ago and, thanks to agricultural intensification using fertilizers and new seeds, food production has roughly kept pace. Some economists feel that it will continue to do so, but at the 1994 Cairo Conference on Population and Development, this was a matter of considerable debate. However, one thing can be agreed upon: there are no reliable guides as to how long growth in food production can be sustained. Moreover, high levels of productivity entail high costs in energy use and waste removal.

Specialization.   A process parallel to intensification involved in long-term change is **specialization**, the increasingly limited range of productive activities in which a single individual is likely to be engaged. As specialization increases, the average person is engaged in a smaller and smaller percentage of the entire set of activities carried out in a society. Industrial society (or postindustrial society) is simply the latest point reached in a process that is as old as human culture. As individuals have become increasingly specialized, societies have tended to be characterized by increasing **differentiation**; that is, organization in separate units for various activities and purposes. Hunter-gatherer societies contain no more than a few dozen distinct occupations, while industrial societies may have over a million. Overspecialization, however, is a problem of some concern. How, for example, can a region whose agriculture has been devoted to one or two cash commodity crops such as coffee, cocoa, or tea, adapt to declining prices on the world market?

Centralization.   A third evolutionary process has been **centralization**, the concentration of political and economic decisions in the hands of a few individuals or institutions. This process has been related to the growth of political, economic, and social differentiation. A strong centralized power is useful, even necessary in efforts to orchestrate diverse activities and interests—not to mention efforts to defend extant resources and possibly to acquire those of neighboring populations (Lees, 1994).

The development of political centralization probably began not long after the **Neolithic Revolution**—the changeover from hunting and gathering wild food to domesticating plants and animals. With food production, populations became larger and denser and sustained themselves through increasing economic specialization. All of this required the growth of more centralized institutions to process information, manage more complex distributive and productive systems, and maintain public order in the face of conflicting interests. As a consequence, today almost all of the world's peoples live within the political structures of highly centralized states. However, as the history of the Viking settlements shows, centralization can have dire consequences when those making the decisions—levying taxes and tithes in this case—cannot perceive the long-term consequences of those decisions.

Another example is in the former Soviet Union, which is today facing an ecological disaster of almost unparalleled magnitude. The Aral Sea, in 1960 the fourth largest lake in the world, is drying up so rapidly that in 1994 it was half its original size. One scientist predicted that by the end of the century it will be nothing more than a vast briny swamp, (Micklin, 1988, pp. 1170–1173). Water that formerly fed the Aral has been diverted to complex and distant irrigation schemes, some more than 1,300 kilometers away. The water that does flow into the Aral from surrounding agricultural schemes is contaminated by chemical fertilizers and pesticides. Gone is the rich fishing industry, and communities once located on the lake's shores are being stranded as the shoreline recedes. The rapidly diminishing surface area of the lake is already resulting in hotter, drier summer temperatures and lower winter temperatures in the surrounding regions. These temperature changes and the falling water table have disrupted oasis farming in the region and contributed to the desertification of the area.

The main culprit in this case and in many others is an abstraction: a highly centralized system of planning and decision making with inadequate ability to anticipate long-term costs. Of course we know that abstractions have no influence over environmental events: the decisions are made and carried out by myriad individuals united in a bureaucratic hierarchy, each concerned with such mundane matters as career advancement, job security, and day-to-day survival. Adhering to productivity goals, limiting one's liability and responsibility for mistakes, and demonstrating bureaucratic achievement in extending the scope of one's authority are critical to the success of individuals in bureaucracies. In this context, local information and early warning signs that might signal impending environmental or social problems are easily ignored.

Stratification and Inequality. Another trend in the long-term evolution of cultures is **stratification**—the division of a society into groups that have varying degrees of access to resources and power. In complex societies, entire groups may have very little or no access to decision-making processes and little access to the resources of the larger society. As we have seen, the Viking settlements in Greenland and Iceland eventually collapsed because the tenant farmers were excluded from the decision-making process and were forced by the church and the crown to overexploit the land.

In no society do all people enjoy equal prestige or equal ability to participate in all social and economic activities. Even within the simple foraging society of the San people of Africa, some men acquire the title of "headman" and are accorded great respect. Among the Tiwi, another foraging group located in Australia, inequality, in terms of status, may affect a male's chances of marrying. Older men use

The collapse of Communism and state-dominated redistributive systems has led to informal markets springing up, such as this one in Hungary.
(Daniel Bates)

Girls are often taught at an early age to defer to their brothers and to accept roles that emphasize child care and home-focused activities. This little Yörük girl is already caring for her infant brother.
(Daniel Bates)

accumulated social credits and status to acquire a large number of wives, creating a shortage of mates for the younger men.

While inequality of this sort may entail great hardship for some members of a society, it is not the same as socioeconomic stratification, which can lead to a situation where entire segments of a population are disadvantaged in comparison with other members of the same society. This disadvantaged position, which is largely passed from generation to generation, engenders systematic constraint or exploitation by other segments of the population over a substantial period of time. In this sense, the groupings formed in stratified societies perpetuate inequality, and such inequality has little to do with the personal strengths or weaknesses of individuals.

Settlement Nucleation. In almost every part of the world, stratification and centralization have been associated with **nucleation**, the tendency of populations to cluster in settlements of increasing size and density. Cities are an exclusive characteristic of state-organized societies and arose comparatively recently in human history; at most, 7,000 years ago. Without question, the world's population is increasingly focused or dependent on cities, although we might well see shifts away from this as some productive systems and communication networks come to depend less upon concentrations of workers. Still, the overall trend is toward larger and larger urban "mega-regions," always at the expense of agricultural land. Istanbul's population in 1964 was approximately 750,000; in 1994 it was over 12 million people—far outstripping the city's ability to provide basic services such as water and sanitation. Similar instances of hypergrowth can be found in cities on every continent: Cairo, Beijing, Lagos, New Delhi, and Mexico City, to name a few.

These trends are not, of course, inevitable. New developments in technology, especially in areas related to communication and production, may alter things dramatically. Nor are these general, long-term evolutionary trends independent in a causal sense. First, important systemic relationships link them. Second, changes in each may be responses to similar environmental changes. Intensification and specialization, for example, may both serve to extract more resources from a deteriorating environment through the reorganization of work. Centralization may accomplish the same end through increased efficiency in the flow of resources or information concerning their availability. Also, we have to make a clear distinction between trends or processes that can be seen in individual populations or social systems and those that appear to extend to societies around the globe. Any particular society may as easily be in the process of decentralizing or deintensifying land use as centralizing and intensifying it. The Viking settlements are again a case in point: After several centuries of political and economic centralization, the trend was reversed rather dramatically.

Joseph Tainter, in reviewing the circumstances under which a number of complex societies collapsed, concludes that often the decline of any particular complex society or civilization can be seen as a predictable outcome of the same processes that earlier had led to its rise (1988). He examines, in considerable detail, the collapse of the Western Roman Empire, the Mayas, and the Chaco Canyon society of northwestern New Mexico. Even though each instance is unique in terms of levels of complexity achieved, environment, and details of decline, they all can be seen as illustrative of the same general principle: declining marginal returns on investment in complexity (1988, pp. 187–192). That is to say, after a point, each society was investing more in maintaining its essential institutions (temples, cities, the military, etc.) than it was able to benefit from them. Investing in complexity, like any other investment strategy, can reach a point of diminishing returns; after this point is reached, sociopolitical organizations constantly encounter problems that require increased investment simply to maintain the status quo. "Once a complex society enters the stage of declining marginal returns, collapse becomes a mathematical likelihood, requiring little more than sufficient passage of time to make probable an insurmountable calamity" (1988, p. 145).

Put in terms of our earlier discussion of stability and resilience, we can say that a complex society may reach a stage where it achieves stability at the expense of resilience. Though it is true that if we consider all societies over the course of human existence as a whole, cultural evolution has tended to proceed from the simple to the complex, it is a mistake to believe that all societies pass smoothly or uniformly in this direction. And it is also a mistake to equate increasing complexity with progress or with "improved" adaptation.

Aspects of Adaptation and Short-Term Change

There are many ways to view cultural change, and all of the social sciences are involved in the quest to understand the dynamics of societal change. But underlying the multiplicity of perspectives, most research has focused on the costs and benefits of change to the people involved; for example, which social grouping or class benefits from innovation and which pays the costs, who within a social setting is likely to introduce new techniques of production or marketing, or what are the environmental impacts of a new agricultural technique.

Innovation and Adaptation

Perhaps the best way to begin a discussion of adaptation within a social context is to examine a case in which very similar populations responded quite differently to contact with new groups. Consider the now-classic case of the Pimas and Papagos of south-

A major problem throughout the world is the increasing gulf between those with resources and those without, as seen here in Calcutta.
(Jehangir Gazdar/Woodfin Camp & Associates)

ern Arizona (Hackenberg, 1962). These two Native American groups are similar in language, in artifacts and tools, but they differ in critical ways. In the recent past the Pimas derived roughly 60 percent of their subsistence from agriculture and 40 percent from hunting and gathering. They lived in approximately a dozen permanent villages along the Gila River, where they practiced irrigation agriculture. The Papagos, on the other hand, had a semi-migratory lifestyle. They lived in "field villages" adjacent to locations used for floodwater farming, and in "well villages," hunting-and-gathering base camps located around permanent sources of water. Pima headmen had much greater authority than Papagos headmen, wealth was more unevenly distributed, and there were more formal mechanisms of intervillage interaction.

Both ethnohistoric and archaeological data suggest that the reasons these two groups, with similar habitats, cultures, and languages, developed such significant differences in subsistence strategies, settlement patterns, and social organization lie about four hundred years in the past. Until then, the area seems to have been inhabited by populations whose subsistence strategies ranged from almost total reliance on hunting and gathering to heavy reliance on irrigation agriculture supplemented by hunting and gathering. But instead of two easily distinguishable cultural traditions, the subsistence and settlement patterns ranged along a continuum, with populations varying their strategies in response to changing climatic conditions.

During the sixteenth century, the Spaniards and the Apaches came to Arizona, and both groups had an impact on the ways of life of native peoples. The Spaniards introduced winter wheat, which proved to

be a successful crop in the irrigated fields of small villages along the river. Because winter was the traditional hunting-and-gathering season, dependence on hunting and gathering decreased in these villages. But winter wheat did not prove successful in the floodwater fields of the more migratory groups, so their reliance on hunting and gathering did not decline. The Apaches, too, had a significant effect on the ways of life of the local populations. A predatory group, the Apaches frequently raided agricultural populations in the area. Consolidation and a stronger political organization centered on defense enabled people in the more sedentary villages to protect themselves. Less sedentary groups became increasingly mobile in order to avoid the invaders. Thus the joint arrival of the Spaniards and Apaches seems to have caused the Papago and Pima to develop two very distinct patterns of subsistence, settlement, and social organization.

Ecological factors seem to have played a central role in this outcome. Slight differences in subsistence strategies and economic behavior among the original populations proved to be critical in their responses to contact with the Spaniards and Apaches. The people in one set of ecological circumstances reacted by decreasing their mobility and centralizing their political organization, while those in another set of circumstances reacted by increasing their mobility and flexibility and decreasing their dependence on agriculture.

Acculturation

For some time in anthropology and other social sciences it has been somewhat unfashionable to ascribe affinity among disparate societies to the process of cultural contact or diffusion. The emphasis has been on independent invention and the unique historical record of local populations. Nevertheless, a great deal of change occurs when different cultural traditions come into contact, whether through trade, conquest, or intermarriage. The Pima and Papago case also illustrates the process of **acculturation**—cultural change that occurs in response to extended firsthand contacts between two or more previously autonomous groups. Recently scientists have discovered mummified human remains, items of clothing, and other cultural material dating back 4000 years, which link the population of the Tarim Basin, in Sinkiang Province, western China, with culturally and physically similar populations in northwestern Europe (Wilfred, 1996). Clearly, long-distance population movement and cultural contact across vast distances are not a recent phenomena. Processes of acculturation depend on various factors: the types of individuals who make contact or interact, the nature of the interaction, the specific behaviors that are modified, and the relative power and military strengths of the populations. Studies of acculturation offer anthropologists insights into the range of factors that affect the outcome of contact between societies.

Basic to the process of acculturation are the types of individuals who make contact and the kinds of contact they have. These individuals tend not to represent a broad cross-section of their societies. The native peoples of South America, for example, experienced their initial contact with Europeans when they encountered military expeditions, missionaries, and seamen—hardly a representative sample of European society. Once the indigenous states and chiefdoms were subdued, the principal aims of the newcomers were to convert the Indians to Christianity, to acquire their lands, and to make use of their labor in the newly opened mines and on the haciendas. Vast numbers of people perished. Nicaragua alone lost 92 percent of its native population in the first few generations of contact, mostly from European diseases (Newson, 1988). The great empires of the Aztecs and Incas were destroyed, indigenous religions were suppressed by force, and thousands of distinct cultures all but disappeared. The Yanomamö, the largest surviving indigenous group in Amazonia, continue to face threats to their survival. They are wracked by new diseases brought by the newcomers and their forest lands are threatened by lumbermen's chainsaws and developers' bulldozers. In Brazil, for example, some 45,000 gold prospectors and miners have illegally entered the 35,000 square mile area that is home to 9,000 Yanomamö (see Chapter 4). While the Brazilian government, under much pressure from outsiders

(Prince Charles of England has taken a stand, for example), has reluctantly taken steps to rectify the situation, the survival of the Yanomamö is still in doubt.

Adapting to Market Economies

In all societies certain individuals walk a fine line between conformance to social rules or customary practice and deviance: between doing the expected and striking new ground. Deviating from the norm, however negatively it may be viewed when certain moral codes are involved, is essential for innovation. When certain members of a society violate the rules of expected practice or dare to go beyond acceptable limits and their actions succeed in resolving some problem, they are called entrepreneurs or inventors. Probably most innovations are as much a matter of serendipity as of cold, clear calculation; people, as we noted earlier, cope with their problems opportunistically using whatever comes to hand.

The Individual and Entrepreneurial Innovation

Like all aspects of adaptation, strategies of production and exchange are never static. By experimenting with new approaches or by being forced to alter traditional ones, people inevitably discover new methods that may eventually modify their economic organization. Frederick Barth's pioneering study (1963) of fishing villages in northern Norway reveals that conditions of ambiguity can prompt acceptance of innovation. Isolated geographically and culturally, the villagers (most of whom were Lapps) occupied a marginal position in Norwegian society. Many wanted the goods that industrialization promised but lacked the means to obtain them. Fishing for export and farming for home consumption made for a precarious existence. The villagers had neither the capital nor the financial know-how to make connections with the modern world. Such conditions create a niche for the people that Barth identifies as entrepreneurs—individuals who are willing to take risks and break with traditional practices in order to make a profit. Barth suggests that in marginal communities the entrepreneur acts as an agent of change by playing the role of mediator between local communities and outside institutions. By making use of existing possibilities in ways neither local people nor state bureaucrats perceive or plan, the entrepreneur is able to bring together a relatively self-conscious group of people who see the utility of change. Under other conditions, entrepreneurs may be considered and treated as deviant or even criminal, as are drug dealers.

Acceptance of Innovation

The acceptance of innovations depends to a great extent on the fact that customary ways of acting are always subject to variation. Individuals in every society constantly make decisions, and decision making gives rise to behavioral variation. There are, nevertheless, limits to innovation. As we have noted in Chapter 2, the individual with the best chance of long-term success is not necessarily the one most perfectly adjusted to its environment at any particular point, but rather the one that maintains the ability to respond to its environment in a flexible variety of ways—that is, with a high degree of resilience. Given that we have only limited means of responding to environmental challenges and that we have limited ways of predicting how our responses to these challenges will turn out, what is the best strategy? Generally speaking, it will be the cheapest possible response—the strategy that involves the least possible loss of future adaptive ability, the minimum sacrifice of flexibility. In other words, choices among alternatives should be made to minimize uncertainty, not simply to look to large possible gains. As we noted, this seems to be the case with humans, in that people are generally conservative in their behavior and hesitant to change ways of doing things that appear to work.

In their efforts to solve some pressing economic problem, some people, even in economically centralized socialist states, manage to gain a personal advantage and ultimately effect a change in the larger economic system. Patricia Vondal (1987) describes the efforts of some small farmers in Borneo to break out of their poverty and obtain consumer goods by investing in ducks. Ducks could be sold on the regional market to satisfy an increasing need for low-cost meat in the cities. But to take advantage of this possibility, innovating farmers had to risk their land and homes to make the initial investment in the novel enterprise. Cages and other structures had to be built, bran and poultry feed either produced in quantity or purchased, market outlets secured—all of which required capital and risk. Some duck farmers failed; others reaped the rewards of the successful innovator.

Lucie Saunders and Sohair Mehenna (1986) worked together in a village in the Nile Delta, and gathered data on the economy and social life of this community spanning several generations. They found that certain families were consistently involved in risk taking through entrepreneurial innovation. At the end of the nineteenth century, when the transport system was rapidly improving and cotton was the dominant cash crop, one individual used proceeds from successful village shops to consolidate a modest estate on irrigated land. In the post-revolutionary era, land reform and new laws governing farm labor limited the profits from farming. Members of the same family, who had been innovators a generation earlier, sought out new activities. Most recently the grandsons were experimenting with the introduction of chickens. They purchased foreign stock, acquired the necessary equipment, and built hatcheries. As their profits mounted from the sale of poultry in Cairo's markets, others emulated their operations, and a new industry was founded.

Bruce Mayhew (1982) reviews a number of findings regarding the success rates for new commercial enterprises, and his findings lend support to the idea that innovation is risky business. In fact, he writes that the life expectancy of new business firms is barely ahead that of alley cats; in one American study 30 percent fail in the first year and 78 percent expire before the tenth (pp. 134–135). Just as we have seen with respect to adaptation, simply because something is attempted it cannot be counted as successful. Innovation usually means leaving the domain of known risks and venturing into uncertainty. Successful innovation may be the exception rather than the rule.

Whether or not the efforts of successful entrepreneurs reflect a conscious strategy, they can have important consequences. First, entrepreneurs most commonly engage in activities that take them over the boundary between traditional and modern economic organization. They may recognize the potential of market exchange, for example, and bring the products of new factories or imported goods into the countryside to compete with traditional handicrafts and to create new needs. Second, while an entrepreneurial effort may originate with an individual, it rarely succeeds unless others join and support the new enterprise (Barth, 1963). And finally, these entrepreneurial actions typically lead to fundamental changes in the systems of production and distribution. Farmers may begin to produce more cash crops; they—or their children—may choose to work in the factory rather than the fields. These changes in turn will begin to transform gender relations, social and family structures, and eventually the whole society.

Gender, Inequality, and Change

As we saw in Chapter 1, gender is vital to any analysis of social change. Social and economic change affects the division of labor in society and, in particular, women. As Manuel Castells sees it, gender relations—the sexual and familial relationship among men, women, and children—is, in every society, a "contested domain" (1996, p. 15). One aspect of this contest has to do with the gender structure of work and access to employment opportunities. Castells stresses the global nature of investment capital and managerial control, utilizing very recent developments in communication technology: the Internet, or Web, but also including all facets of computer-assisted information flow and exchange (1996). We will return to the broader implications of this view later, but with respect to gender in the workplace, the new industrial order has led to the feminization of wage labor globally. While this is a complex issue, one major trend has been labor market deregulation and the cheapening of wages due to the diminished power of organized labor.

Helen Safa has long studied this phenomenon in the Caribbean Basin. According to Safa, the idea of the male breadwinner is rapidly becoming a myth worldwide, and most particularly in the Caribbean (1995). In the past three decades, the size of the female workforce has more than tripled, with more women than men entering wage employment. But in many instances, this is less advantageous for women than it might seem. As Safa (1995) and Castells (1996) emphasize, labor is becoming increasingly organized outside contractual agreements between a localized management and a collective labor entity—a union, for example. It is now common for an individual worker's agreement to be with a management entity that represents a multinational company. Not uncommonly, workers are hired part-time, or on short-term contracts, with few fringe benefits such as health and retirement plans.

Women are favored recruits because they are less likely to complain about working conditions, less likely to organize, and are more willing to accept low wages for part-time opportunities to support their families (Safa, 1995, pp. 10–11). Safa has followed the processes of gender restructuring in the Dominican Republic, Puerto Rico, and Cuba. All three share a similar colonial and cultural heritage, and all three made strenuous efforts in the 1960s to break away from a sugar cane–based economy by launching export industries.

In Puerto Rico, Operation Bootstrap was part of an ambitious program to diversify the economy away from monocrop agriculture. As is often the case in efforts to industrialize, the first stage was to offer tax incentives designed to encourage the expansion of the apparel and food processing industries (Safa, 1995, p. 13). While intended to provide employment for men displaced from agricultural employment, in practice the program attracted women, for the reasons mentioned earlier. Although

manufacturing jobs increased rapidly through the 1980s, new jobs did not offset the decline in the agricultural sector. Later investment, focused on high-tech industries such as investment banking and insurance, offered white-collar opportunities to both men and women, but for the bulk of the working poor, the man's role as primary breadwinner was greatly diminished, leading to new patterns of authority and power within the household (p. 17). Since many of the new jobs taken by women were offset by jobs lost by men, net family income did not necessarily rise with female employment. Of course, since Puerto Rico is a U.S. territory, families could easily take advantage of employment opportunities on the mainland, and remittances from these migrants serve to maintain higher wage levels than would otherwise obtain (pp. 18–19).

The Dominican Republic's experience is similar in many respects, but without the same opportunities for migration to ease competition for low-paying jobs. Juana Santana, for example, works in a free trade zone and sustains her family of three children on a weekly salary of $20.00, which has to cover food, rent, child care, and transportation (Safa, 1995, p. 1). Her husband does not hold a steady job. According to Safa, this is the situation many women in the free trade zones face: low wages, poor working conditions, and partners who can provide only limited assistance (p. 1). In both Puerto Rico and the Dominican Republic, a decrease in marital stability can be attributed to male unemployment; however, the essential patriarchal nature of the household remains (p. 167).

Cuba, as one would expect, is rather different due to the social policies of the state, and centralized production. Men were guaranteed full employment (until 1990, at least), and women were strongly encouraged to enter the work force (Safa, p. 163ff). Women are further organized in various officially sanctioned groups that emphasize education as well as domestic issues such as child care and birth control. Nevertheless, women are underrepresented in managerial positions and, in general, continue to view their employment as secondary to their role as mothers. As a consequence, they are generally perceived as playing a secondary role in the workplace. While gender inequality persists in Cuba, in spite of a state ideology to the contrary, it is somewhat different from the other regions discussed. Young women are considerably more independent from male control than in earlier generations (p. 165). Marital instability also has increased in Cuba, but part of the cause may be the severe housing and food problem which puts a strain on marriages. The current economic depression, occasioned by the collapse of international Communism that deprived Cuba of its cheap oil and most of its trading partners, falls heavily on women, who have to wait in long lines to secure even basic commodities for their families (p. 166). Gender roles are profoundly affected by economic change; sometimes for the better, sometimes to the detriment of women.

Gender and Productive Labor

The success of a particular innovation may be dependent on the productive labor of women. One case illustrates some of these points. In her study of economic development based on the commercial production of arabica coffee among the Gainj of highland New Guinea, Patricia Lyons Johnson found that a household's commercial success in coffee growing was directly related to the availability of women's labor (Johnson, 1988, 1996).

CASE STUDY

The Productive Labor of Gainj Women

THE GAINJ LIVE IN THE RUGGED AND FORESTED Takwi Valley, on the northern edge of the central highlands of Papua New Guinea. Their settlements are widely dispersed and there are no large aggregations of people that could be described as villages. The Gainj remain to a large degree subsistence slash-and-burn horticulturists, growing mixed gardens of sweet potatoes, taro, yams, bananas, sugar cane, a variety of leafy greens, and some introduced plants such as corn and pumpkin. They raise a few pigs and chickens, more for their ceremonial value than for consumption. Hunting is so sporadic that it contributes little to a household's diet. Gainj men are responsible for the initial clearing and fencing of garden plots. Women are responsible for secondary clearing, burning, and planting. They also cultivate, harvest, carry, process, and cook garden produce. Since 1963, a large percentage of the men have worked as wage laborers for coastal copra (coconut) plantations, usually on two-year contracts.

Coffee was first introduced as a cash crop in 1973, and the manner of its introduction followed a pattern identified by Esther Boserup (1970, p. 53 ff.) in other parts of the developing world: regardless of the traditional division of labor in subsistence activity, cash crops and the technology that accompanies them tend to be introduced to men by men. Despite

the clear identification of women with gardening, the male agricultural extension officer provided coffee seedlings and information about their cultivation, processing, and sale only to Gainj men. The men then established a new division of labor for this new garden product: men plant the coffee trees and sell the final product; all the remaining labor—cultivation, harvesting, processing, and much of the local transportation—falls to the women. Since the Gainj accord ownership of trees and their fruit to the person who plants them, and since men plant the coffee seedlings, the profits from coffee sales go exclusively to the men. "These profits are spent on investment in all-male business cooperatives, education (almost exclusively male), air travel by men to the provincial capital, and consumer goods," despite the fact that women do most of the work (Johnson, 1988, p. 111).

Taking as the unit of study the conjugal family household (that is, a household that has a male head and at least one of his wives), Johnson compared data gathered in 1978 and again in 1983 to analyze the effects of five variables on success in coffee-growing: (1) age of male household head, (2) migration experience of male household head, (3) number of resident wives per household, (4) number of other women between the ages of twenty and sixty per household, and (5) number of dependents per household.

She discovered that migration experience had no significant effect on coffee-growing, as measured by the number of coffee gardens a household cultivated: Clearly one did not have to go out of the community to learn how to grow coffee. Age was marginally significant in that the younger male household heads, no longer able to achieve status in the traditional manner (by exhibiting prowess as a leader in warfare) tended to follow the cash-cropping path to glory and worked hard to increase their coffee crop. The number of wives per household had a significant positive effect on success in coffee production: the more wives a man had, the more gardens he could manage. But the greatest effect on coffee production was produced by women other than wives of the household head: his unmarried daughters and sisters, the wives of sons who shared the household, and widows who chose to attach themselves to the household. This finding is explained in part by the fact that few of these women have to deal with the demands of children.

Johnson analyzed the effects of the number of dependents per household in terms of "dependency ratio"; that is, the ratio of nonworking dependents to female producers (both wives and other adult women). She found that the more successful households (three or more coffee gardens) significantly decreased their dependency ratios between 1978 and 1983, while the less successful households (fewer than three coffee gardens) had increased them. The decrease in the dependency ratio is "entirely attributable to an increase in the number of producers" (1988, p. 117). Johnson points out that in all cases the producers are women other than the household head's wives.

Those households considered in 1983 to be successful in producing coffee as a cash crop were the same households that in 1978 had had more dependents and fewer adult women other than wives of the household head. Johnson postulates that it was the pressure of the high dependency ratios that had motivated their move into cash-cropping. But by 1983 these households had drastically altered their structure by adding women to lower their dependency ratios. Where did these women come from?

Fifty-four percent were young women who had not yet married. A mere 14 percent were women of marriageable age who had been brought into the household. The remaining 32 percent were widows who had joined the household. Most of the widows were close friends of the women already in the household and were related to the male head in such a way (either genealogical or classificatory) as to preclude their ever becoming his wives.

Johnson notes that both the retention of marriageable women and the admission of widows carries a cost to the household. The family that delays in arranging a marriage for a daughter forgoes, at least temporarily, the bridewealth that her marriage would bring, as well as the marriage ties that it would create. Widows more often than not bring dependent children with them; in fact, because widows with children are the least likely to remarry, they are the most likely to be available for incorporation into another household.

At the time of this study, women had not yet made serious demands on men for compensation for their labor, and any material benefits they may acquire (clothing, pots, purchased foods) do not seem to weigh heavily in widows' decisions to ally themselves with a particular household. If women do come to demand some material compensation for their labor, same-sex affective ties may become less important and the costs of such demands will have to be included in consideration of a household's economic success.

Johnson assumes that the addition of productive women enabled a household to increase its coffee production. But even if she were wrong—if, that is, it was the success of households with multiple cof-

fee gardens that led widows to join them—the conclusion that there is a dynamic relationship between the number of female hands at work and the number of coffee gardens would not be affected. Johnson warns that ethnographers should recognize not only that women's unpaid domestic work is productive, but also that in many areas of the developing world women are "crucially involved in commercial, nondomestic production, in labor that must by any standard be recognized as productive" (1988, p. 120). ▸

Facing the Twenty-First Century

While there is no sure way to predict the future, sometimes the present offers reliable clues to the shape of things to come. We know, for example, that we will rely increasingly on advanced electronics, high-speed communications, DNA-based computers, and genetically engineered food sources as we see these trends developing at present. Moreover, many products of late twentieth-century society are so much a part of our everyday lives that it is difficult to imagine living without them. Even those of us who have lived and worked in what have been called "less-developed" societies have found that few populations have not come to integrate the products of advanced technology into their ways of life. People as remote from us as the Ariaal farmers and herders of Kenya learn of national events from their portable radios and television sets. Not only are modern firearms and aluminum pots and pans part of everyday life in the Amazon basin, so are items that only a few years ago would have been called high-tech: miniature cassette players and video recorders. Lapp reindeer herders go about their business on snowmobiles equipped with mobile phones, and the camel has been long replaced in the Middle East by Japanese-made trucks.

Even without venturing beyond our own society we can see immediate costs and benefits of life in our **postindustrial society**. It has been designated "postindustrial" because its dominant technology has shifted from heavy industry (steel mills, locomotives, automobiles) to electronics and biochemistry, which make possible nearly instant global communications, space travel, and genetic engineering—not to mention the ever-present potential of nuclear catastrophe.

Among the benefits afforded by industrial and postindustrial society, we count advances in the medical sciences. The CAT scan (computer-aided tomography, a way of enhancing X-ray images of the body) was an exotic diagnostic instrument in the 1970s, available only at a few hospitals and at great expense; CAT scans are now routinely available. Computing power that twenty years ago existed only in research facilities is now lodged in automobiles and home appliances. Another benefit of industrial and postindustrial society is the enormous growth in public and private educational facilities. More than ever before, knowledge is power. Access to training is an essential component of survival in the modern world. Money, power, and social standing are all now coming to be linked as firmly to what you know as to whom you know: Young persons looking for jobs in technological fields cannot rely solely on their family and friends, the conventional support networks of the past.

But industrial society imposes equally obvious costs. Pollution from industrial sites in the Midwest of the United States ends up as acid rain in the Northeast and Canada. Controversy over nuclear waste dumps rages wherever sites are proposed. Polluted waters off our coasts have disastrous effects on marine life. The much-discussed greenhouse effect and the lowering of the ozone level in the upper atmosphere are clear and present dangers—even though no one can say with confidence just what the consequences will be. One thing seems to be certain, however: industrial pollution, together with the effects of the massive loss of rain forests in the tropics, are causing global temperatures to rise.

Another and different kind of cost is the high level of stress and anxiety that seems to be built into the special socioeconomic system associated with industrial and postindustrial systems—irregular alternations between boom and bust can have devastating psychological consequences for large segments of our urban and suburban communities.

Finally, the postindustrial world is a world on the move; from farms to cities, and from one country to the next, always searching for a way to escape the poverty that only seems to grow more pervasive throughout the world. The surge of people seeking entry into Europe and North America is tremendous. In China, a country with 900 million peasants, people are abandoning the land; over 200 new cities have sprouted up since the 1980s and people are flocking to them in order to find jobs that pay better than farming (Tyler, 1995, p. 4). Not only does this exacerbate China's loss of farm lands to urbanization, but even the diminishing farm lands are increasingly underutilized. A Chinese farmer working a one-acre plot, larger than average, explained to an American, "Look, I work on four *mou* of land year in and year

out, from dawn to dusk, but after taxes and providing for our own needs, I make $20.00 a year. You can make that much in a day. No matter how much it costs to get there, or how hard the work is, America is still better than this" (Kwong, 1994, p. 425). This simple statement expresses the motivation that underlies the decision of millions to move each year; the knowledge of better conditions elsewhere.

Beyond Industrialism

The technological and social transformation we call *industrialism* started on a small scale and was restricted to certain forms of production in a few countries, but it did not remain limited for long. In a relatively short period peoples all over the world were affected by it. Today we have moved into yet another era in the organization of production and integration of peoples. This has been termed variously the communications era, the age of the computer, and the high-tech age. The labels are not important. What is interesting from an anthropological perspective is that the processes of change appear to occur at an increasingly rapid rate.

The organization of commerce and industry is changing. The historian David Noble (1984) describes this transformation as the triumph of "numerical control" in industry. Following World War II, there was a great advance in the development of servomechanical and electronic controls capable of running complex precision tools. This development, Noble suggests, opened up the possibility of moving the effective control of manufacturing from the shop floor to the main office. The outcome is a lessening of blue-collar power in industry and further centralization of control in productive organizations. This thesis is interesting, though in some instances the same technology has broken up large industries into smaller components—another outcome of high-speed communications. Certainly it is clear that job opportunities for production-line workers are rapidly decreasing while new ones open up for people who have skills appropriate to the new technologies. The long-term significance of these changes will be profound; not only are entire segments of the populations of already-industrialized nations marginalized, but the peoples of many countries lacking an educational infrastructure will not participate fully in the economies of the future.

The "modernization" model associated with the economist Walter Rostow (1960) postulated that development was an evolutionary stage through which all countries pass; it has long since been proven wrong by experience. Today, about one

Figure 7–1. *The gross domestic product (GDP) per region and per capita in high-income and less-developed regions of the world, for 1990 and projected for 2030 shows that income distribution will remain extremely skewed in favor of the already-developed countries.*

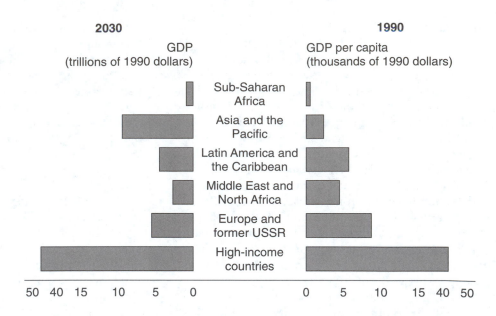

billion people live in absolute poverty; many more not far above it (Wilson, 1993, p. 27). In many countries, there are large groups of people who have not only remained impoverished, but whose living standards have declined relative to others. The people of East Pakistan, however poor they were in the 1960s, enjoyed life chances roughly comparable to the peoples of rural China, Thailand, Malaysia, and Korea. Today, the rural population of Bangladesh, as it is now known, is untouched by the prosperity that has transformed at least some of the other nations of the region. But they are not alone in the world; the peoples of the Philippines, Cambodia, Vietnam, Sudan, Central Africa, and parts of South and Central America have also seen their living conditions remain extremely low or even fall.

It is not that some populations or nations are being left out; quite the contrary, the rural and urban poor of many agrarian countries are closely integrated into the world economic and political system, but at its peripheries (see Figure 7–1). That is, they have little control over the resources to which they have access, profit little from what they sell in a market characterized by worldwide competition, and generally are without vote or voice in their own countries. This, in many respects, reflects a process of incorporation of peoples around the globe that began long before anthropology was a discipline: the expansion of European power and economic influence far beyond that continent (Wolf, 1982). Much of the present unequal distribution of the benefits of the postindustrial era, together with attendant environmental degradation as people desperately try to make a living, "is not a problem of the relationship

of people with their habitats, but of relationships *among* peoples competing for access to productive resources" (Horowitz, 1994, p. 8).

As the world's population grows, so will the competition for productive resources. The world's population doubled within the last 50 years to 5.5 billion; it is expected to double again in the next 50 years (Wilson, 1993, p. 24). Nigeria, one country whose citizens, like China's, often opt to move, has a population of over 100 million, which is expected to reach 216 million by 2010 (Wilson, 1993, p. 26). "The awful truth remains that a large part of humanity will suffer no matter what is done" (p. 27).

The Integration of the Postindustrial World

Today it is commonplace to refer to the "global economy," to the "new world order," or to the "world system." While in many ways accurate, the phenomenon of global integration or transcontinental linkages is not new. Since the mid-eighteenth century, the vast majority of tribal populations throughout the world have been in direct contact, usually to their detriment, with representatives of the industrial world. What is new is the qualitative change that occurred in such linkages in the mid-twentieth century.

In 1974, Richard J. Barnet and Ronald E. Muller wrote a book on a phenomenon closely related to the organization of production in the postindustrial era: the growth of multinational corporations. Twenty-four years later, their ideas have increased relevance. They suggest that the degree to which international corporations have taken over functions once performed by governments and succeeded where governments have failed in creating a "global organization for administering this planet" is difficult to comprehend. This is not to suggest that corporations have consciously evolved into multinationals in order to dominate the world. They simply make use of the communications and transport technology available to compete in the world marketplace. The sheer size and complexity of their operations, however, have made them a force unto themselves.

Even in 1974, the operating budgets of about five hundred giant multinational corporations exceeded those of most nation-states. In the 1980s, the operating budgets of global corporations grew at over twice the rate of the GNP of the United States and other advanced industrial nations, and this has continued through the 1990s. This fiscal expansion is based on what has been called the corporations' "global reach"—today they know no boundaries. The European Union and the 1995 North American Free Trade Agreement (NAFTA) are regional arrangements that facilitate the global organization of production, exchange, and consumption.

Through expansion and diversification, global enterprises insulate themselves from many political and market pressures. High-speed communications permit a multinational corporation to control everything from raw materials to final distribution. It may, for example, buy raw materials from a subsidiary company at less than the actual market price in order to avoid taxes, or it may sell to another foreign division at inflated prices in order to transfer income out of a country. Price-fixing cannot really be controlled under such circumstances. Further, and of greater social consequence, a giant corporation can easily shift operations to areas of low labor cost. Such a move can be catastrophic for the workers the corporation leaves behind. The very fact that a corporation operates on a global scale places it beyond the reach of national governments. Regulatory agencies lack the information and in many cases the jurisdiction to investigate global enterprises. Corporations plan centrally and act globally, and nation-states do not.

A more subtle problem, which underlies Barnet and Muller's analysis, is the instability that such global interdependence implies. India's ability to feed its people depends on modern farming, which in turn requires reliance on chemical pesticides, fertilizers, fuel, and machinery. All of these inputs are globally interconnected. Local disasters can now have immediate global repercussions, be it the 1995 Kobe earthquake in Japan, the nuclear fires of Chernobyl in the Ukraine, Arctic pollution, or acid rain in the United States and Canada. There is an obvious good side to interdependence in that global trade and communications even out some disparities—the goods of the industrial states are widely available, people can move great distances to seek out a livelihood, the effects of famine and natural disasters can be mitigated. But it also puts all of us at the mercy of events in distant places. The Kobe earthquake was followed shortly by the bankruptcy of England's oldest investment bank, Baring and Sons, with branches all over the world. The bank's traders had invested heavily in Japanese stocks, betting on anticipated short-term rises, when they were hit by a sudden decline in share prices caused by the earthquake. The 1995 collapse of the Mexican peso had immediate effects in other countries; suddenly, factories in the United States had to cut production as Mexican consumers could no longer afford to purchase foreign goods, and stock market investors around the world experienced losses due to the heavy involvement of mutual funds in the Mexican market. As the United States tried to prop up the currency of its new partner in NAFTA, the dollar itself fell to an all-time low against other major currencies (from which it soon recovered, however). Interdependence and vulnerability are two sides of the same process.

Global Communications, Global Culture, and the Emergence of "Cyberculture"

One of the key features of our interdependent world is the global communications network. Satellite communications, global television networks, fax machines, the Internet, and improved international phone service have contributed to an information revolution. The 1990 Tiananmen Square demonstrators were in communication by telephone and fax machine with people all over the world and, apart from physically removing them, there was nothing their government could do to prevent this. The organizers of the coup attempt in August 1991, which, when it failed, ended the U.S.S.R.'s existence as a state, had not anticipated how decentralized communications had become in that country. As resistance spread, anti-Communist groups all over the country were able to coordinate their actions and attract worldwide attention using computer links, faxes, and telephones.

In China and Iran, to name two countries where the authorities feel they need to control the media to retain power, millions of families now have their own satellite dishes and receive news and other programming over which the government has no control. However strongly these governments may rail against Western culture, this is what their people are getting on CNN and hundreds of other channels.

In Bulgaria during the 1980s, for example, very little direct contact with the foreign press, movies, and television was allowed. Nevertheless, dissident groups kept in close touch with the outside world via videotapes, faxes, and the telephone. Even though the countryside in some regions was dotted with radio-TV jamming towers, they were largely ineffectual against new technology. Such two-way communication was instrumental in bringing world opinion to bear on a government that had previously acted as though it were in isolation. This was an important factor in rallying individuals to oppose the government, and even members of the Communist Party realized that they could not rule without legitimacy, including world acceptability. When the Communist regime fell in 1990, the borders opened, and along with newspapers, international magazines, and serious movies, came an avalanche of pornography, cultist religious literature, and advertisements for phony investment schemes. Most would find the contents of a great deal of this newly available "information" deplorable or, as with Bevis and Butthead cartoons presently on local TV, simply without any merit.

In the 1990s, for better or for worse, Bulgaria is participating in a globally shaped media culture, as is virtually every country. The good aspects of this are obvious: Free communications are critical to maintaining Bulgaria's shaky movement toward democracy and economic recovery. The negative aspects are visible not just in the extreme cases of pornography and pyramid investment schemes, but in a diminishment of regional cultural heterogeneity. Just as world material culture is becoming more homogeneous, so is expressive culture—the arts, dress, and even social conventions.

Closely linked to new developments in computer, information, and biological technology is what some have termed **cyberculture** (Escobar, 1994, p. 211). The term comes from "cybernetics" or systems theory, and refers to the emerging importance of computer-mediated communication, including global networks such as Internet, Bitnet, and more specialized computer networks such as Peacenet and Econet. These link a vast variety of electronic bulletin boards, conference systems, and data bases, which in turn bring together millions of users. This is fundamentally different from telephonic or television communication: entire groups of individuals can interact with one another in what are called

"on-line communities" or "virtual communities" (p. 219). Groups are formed to play team games; business executives on different continents plot strategy. What makes this a form of culture is that a learned, shared code of behavior with a specialized language has emerged that does not conform to existing national and cultural frontiers. As Walker puts it, "When you are interacting with a computer you are not conversing with another person. You are exploring another world" (1990, p. 443, cited in Escobar, 1994, p. 219).

The Global Informational Society

Manuel Castells, to whom we referred earlier, characterizes the global economy as part of the "informational society" that arose in the 1980s from the restructuring of global flows of capital in conjunction with the development of computer-driven "informationalism" (1996a; 1996b, p. 145ff). This restructuring of capital flows, critical to economic growth, was a result of massive investment in the communications/information infrastructures (1996b, p. 85). This facilitated the twin developments of market deregulation and the globalization of capital (1996b, p. 85). The social consequences are, he argues, "informational," not just "information based"—as was earlier productive systems. The chemical industry, for example, has always been information- or science-based; the new socioeconomic world order is "informational" not just because particular industries are dependent on flows of information, but because the "cultural-institutional attributes of the whole social system must be included in the diffusion of and implementation of the new technological paradigm" (1996b, p. 91). In short, individuals are now immersed in a new socioeconomic culture, or cyberculture, that comprises a continually expanding variety of ways to acquire and communicate information.

According to Castells, the structure of this emergent economy is characterized by the asymmetrically interdependent organization of the world's regions. At the moment there are three major economic regions in which there are specific pivotal nodes (that is, cities or localities, such as Silicon Valley in California or New York City). These dominant regions are Western Europe, North America, and the Asian Pacific (1996b, p. 145). By asymmetrical, he means that each of these regions is integrated into networks that determine how their hinterlands are incorporated into the world economic order (1996b, p. 145). An example (not his, however) is the ancient city of Istanbul, located on the eastern edge of Europe, but closely integrated economically with Western Europe. The city is today experiencing an economic renaissance as an informational center, with over 360 multinational corporations having established major offices there since 1992. Following the collapse of the Soviet Union in 1991, the huge markets of Central Asia and the Caucasus have opened up, and these multinationals find the informational infrastructure of Istanbul far superior to the faltering communications systems of Russia. Using advanced technology, these corporations affect the flow of goods and services, as well the output of far-flung factories for a large hinterland, as well as Istanbul's traditional hinterland in Eastern Europe and the Middle East.

This informational economy is not static, however (1996b, p. 147). Currently, Asian Pacific nodes in the network are facing competition from new sites in India. What is important in considering future development is not that any particular country has a lock on the technology—none do—but that within each of these regions there are large numbers of people who are marginalized because they lack access to the technology. Moreover, outside these regions, considerable areas of the globe are becoming marginalized to an even greater extent than during the era of colonialism; they simply lack the resources that would allow them to invest in the educational and informational infrastructure needed to compete in the global marketplace.

Global communications, internationalized media products, and patterns of trade and production have led to increasing conformity in consumption and basic patterns of life. With only limited exceptions, people with similar access to resources in particular regions come to live much the same way in spite of historical differences in religion, ethnicity, and language. In an earlier era these differences would have been vividly expressed in cultural insignia; in dress, ceremony, and life style. Also, the vast majority of the world's population is directly or indirectly involved in wage labor or commercial production. This, too, tends to shape patterns of life in roughly similar ways for those involved in the same sort of production. A Turkish coal miner and an English coal miner will lead lives dominated by the tempo of the industry—in both instances, increasingly stressful as mining declines in importance. In addition to the development of broadly shared patterns of life, we see broadly shared expectations and aspirations. Increasingly, one's wants or needs are not defined by local culture or tradition, but in terms of goods and services that are part of what might be called the **global culture**: While folk medicine persists and has its place, people also expect modern treatment as well; they seek education for their children, electricity, sanitation, and consumer goods of all sorts.

The Ecological Consequences of Postindustrialism

Not only is cultural diversity yielding to a global culture, diverse habitats are also being brought into a measure of global conformity. Amazonian and Malaysian forests are converted to pastures or farms; African bush and Chinese forests are cleared for farming; farm lands in China, North America, Egypt, and elsewhere are paved over to accommodate urban expansion and industry. There are few stands of native European forest left; farmlands, highways, and planted or managed forests have replaced them. Tropical rainforests, containing about one half of the earth's species, have declined to about one half of their prehistoric area and continue to be cleared at the rate of 2 percent a year—an amount of land equal to the size of Florida (Wilson, 1993, p. 29). Thus, as technology spreads over the globe, humans increase their energy consumption with too little attention paid to the inevitable result: resource depletion.

Energy Consumption and Resource Depletion. Since World War II, per-capita energy consumption throughout the world has risen at an ever-increasing rate. However, while technology requires a higher energy consumption, it also helps to make energy sources such as low-cost fossil fuel, nuclear energy, and solar energy widely available. A recurring political issue is the need for more cheap and readily accessible energy sources. The 1990 Gulf War was fought in order to retain European and North American access to oil; energy prices in the United States are lower than almost anywhere else in the world. On every continent, we see the material effects of abundant energy harnessed to advanced technology: millions of people routinely commute long distances to work and move from country to country, homes are filled with appliances, items from around the world are available in neighborhood stores from Albania to Zambia. In the case of Albania, for example, since the collapse of communism in 1991, it is difficult to find anything but foreign products in shops; in most of Africa, this has long been the norm.

The availability of cheap energy and high rates of consumption has stimulated the mass use of numerous items that only a few years ago would be considered luxuries, if they were imagined at all. Thirty-five years ago few homes or workplaces in the United States were air-conditioned; today most are. Even the poorest individual in almost any country has access to vehicular transportation, uses facilities that run on electricity, and consumes imported goods. In short, the material culture of the world is rapidly becoming homogeneous.

The energy that pulses through human society affects where and how people live, the material goods available to them, and their relations with their physical environment. Cheap energy allows huge cities to emerge because they are sustained by foods grown in distant fields and by water from distant reservoirs. Because energy is cheap, people are consuming the world's resources at a phenomenal rate; it has been estimated, for example, that tropical forests that once covered great portions of South America and Southeast Asia will be gone by the year 2000.

Sussman et al. (1994) have studied deforestation in Madagascar and have found that rainforest probably covered 11.2 million hectares of the east coast at the time of colonization, approximately 1500–2000 years ago. By 1950, 7.5 million hectares remained, and by 1985 only 3.8 million hectares remained—50 percent less than in 1950, and only 34 percent of the original forest. They found that deforestation is directly related to population growth and the slope of the land, with the greatest amount of deforestation occurring in the more densely populated areas and on the lower slopes. Sussman et al. predict that thirty-five years from now, at current rates, only 38 percent of the forest remaining in 1985 will still exist; that is, only 12.5 percent of the original extent—a mere 1.4 million hectares, and this will be fragmented into many small parcels.

Even though a number of reserves established in the 1920s and 1930s remain relatively untouched, they appear to be protected by their remoteness and inaccessibility rather than by conservation efforts. So it is likely that as population and economic pressures increase, these areas will become vulnerable to deforestation. Conservation efforts to slow deforestation and prevent the fragmentation of areas of forest need to be concentrated at the fronts of deforestation and must involve cooperation between conservationists and local people to develop sustainable use of lands that have already been cleared. Once areas of intense deforestation have been identified by remote sensing, Sussman et al. argue that basic ethnographic research needs to be done to place this deforestation in the actual social, economic, and political context, after which scientists, in conjunction with the local people, can begin to develop alternative, sustainable land use practices. Sussman, who used satellite-based remote sensing to reveal the extent of the deforestation, believes that remote sensing can also be used to monitor the

progress of these projects and their effectiveness in slowing deforestation. Box 7.1, *Imaging Resource Depletion*, explores this imaging technology in more depth and shows how it can be used to evaluate the health of a coastal marine ecosystem in the Dominican Republic.

A giant new dam has been completed in the middle of the Brazilian rainforest. When it is in operation, it will flood more than 600 square miles of forest in order to produce electricity for the city of Manaus, on the banks of the Amazon. Manaus's population has recently swollen to over a million inhabitants—many of whom come to the Amazon to escape intolerable conditions elsewhere. Similar projects are underway throughout the Third World as governments respond to the need to feed ever-growing populations. Once such resources as the rain forests are gone, they cannot be reestablished; most of what we consume is nonrenewable.

Although development planners, economists, and politicians usually see the supply of energy as a factor limiting growth and development, and hence favor huge hydroelectric and other projects, this is short-sighted. What is more important is **sustainable energy**, energy recovery that does not damage the environment, and manageable energy. Energy experts predict that Central Africa will run out of wood—a major energy source for cooking among the very poor—before it runs out of food, although the two are closely related. Fossil fuels are a nonrenewable resource and, although inexpensive relative to long-term abundance, are being depleted. Hydroelectric projects that flood vast areas of cropland, or potential cropland, as in China and Amazonia, are also counterproductive since, as we discussed in Chapter 6, maintaining extant farms is extremely important. Finally, energy management—control over its downstream impact—is as important as simply securing it.

Pollution and Toxic Waste. Quite apart from how we will cope with the depletion of our resources there is the even more urgent problem of how we will dispose of the toxic by-products of what we have already consumed. Unfortunately, this is not usually viewed as an energy-related issue except with regard to nuclear energy. The use of any energy source has consequences, whether they are higher population levels, consumption of nonrenewable resources, habitat destruction, or environmental impacts such as global warming, water shortages, deforestation, or waste disposal. All industrialized countries are faced with the unanswered question of what to do with nuclear and other radioactive wastes. With the breakup of the Soviet Union and the economic chaos in its

In the Philippines, a family living in a slum on Manila's Smokey Mountain. The "mountain" is a garbage dump.
(Michael Macintyre/The Hutchison Library)

successor states, there is great uncertainty as to the security and safety of vast quantities of spent nuclear material. The nuclear energy program of every country was developed for political reasons far in advance of any solution to the problem of disposing of highly toxic by-products. However serious, nuclear waste is probably less critical than chemical waste in general, generated by massive deployment of cheap energy sources to build the infrastructure of the postindustrial world. There is still no easy and safe way to dispose of highly toxic chemicals such as PCBs, dioxin, etc., which are necessary ingredients in constructing our telecommunications systems, plastics industries, and so on.

Less apparent, but still very important to our future, the world's oceans are under siege. In 1995, it was found that as a result of global warming, the temperature of the Pacific Ocean off the coast of California and Mexico had increased by one degree fahrenheit over the mean recorded temperature since records were first kept. As a consequence, plankton, temperature-sensitive microorganisms, have declined approximately 40 percent. Since plankton are fundamental to the marine food chain, this is likely to be reflected very soon in declining fish catches in this once-rich fishing region.

In the Pacific and Atlantic vast amounts of human waste, toxic and nontoxic, threaten marine life as never before. The same crisis threatens the Caribbean and Mediterranean: the fishing industries of these areas are experiencing severely declining catches. In 1987, the American National Academy of Sciences reported that each year the world's fishing fleets dump 350 million pounds of plastic debris in the world's oceans. It is thought that over 30 percent of the world's fish have ingested bits of plastic that can interfere with their digestion. In 1995 much of the American North Atlantic fishing fleet stayed in port.

The problem of pollution and waste disposal is not, of course, restricted to the oceans. Over half of the solid landfill areas available to American cities in 1980 are now full. Each year the United States produces more than 20 million tons of plastics, most of which require more than five hundred years to degrade fully. Every country has petrochemical plants churning out polyethylene and other plastics. Megacities in the Third World face enormous problems; Mexico City generates 10,000 tons of waste a day, most of which is left in giant piles exposed to wind and rain. Manila has at least ten huge open dumps (Cunningham & Saigo, 1995, p. 501). Thousands of people live and work on one called "Smokey Mountain" because of its constant smoldering fires; they make a living sorting out edible and reusable items. Archaeologists of the future may find this global accumulation a treasure trove, but meanwhile the time is rapidly approaching when our wastes will overwhelm us. As illustrated in Box 7.2, *The Abuse of Environmental Rights in South Africa*, this is particularly imminent in ghettos around the world, where overcrowding and poverty exacerbate the problems of pollution and waste, seriously threatening the environmental rights of the individuals living there.

Toxic Accidents. We accept the fact that modern life demands that we continually submit to new risks; any day a major industrial accident might occur. We rely on technology that we do not understand, and we have little say in its deployment and regulation. Chronic technological disasters, as Eric Wolf has

Box 7.1

Imaging Resource Depletion

ANTHROPOLOGISTS AND HUMAN ecologists are increasingly using space-age technologies to extend their analyses of local ecologies to a regional scale. Satellites routinely collect basic data from a wide range of geographic areas. These data consist primarily of electronic records, in the form of analytical units called pixels, of the intensities of electromagnetic radiation reflected or emitted from the earth's surface. These data, over time, reflect changes in the average amount of radiation recorded, and thus can be used to identify and monitor changes in land use patterns, loss of tropical forest cover, and even ecological stress on coral reefs. The technologies involved are primarily remote sensing (RS), geographic information systems (GIS), global positioning systems (GPS), and developments in computer hardware and software associated with these systems.

While these new technologies allow for a regional view of land use not easily obtainable from ethnographic or archaeological research on the ground, many of the patterns revealed by the analysis of these data are creations of human decision making and historical events. Satellites cannot interpret what is observed nor explain changes. Consequently, all researchers emphasize the importance of understanding land use from the perspective of the people who manage the land; this is known as "people truthing." In addition, sound ethnographic information on demographic trends and land use practices is a safeguard against erroneous or exaggerated claims made on the basis of remotely sensed data; this is known as "ground truthing."

Stoffle et al. (1994) conducted a study of the coastal waters and coral reefs on the north coast of the Dominican Republic, in the area around Buen Hombre. This is a community of approximately 900 residents, living much as did the indigenous Indian people at the time Columbus first sighted the coast in the late fifteenth century. Stoffle et al. argue that were the pressures on this coastal marine ecosystem derived only from the people of Buen Hombre and similar villages along the coast, the human population could exist in sustainable balance with the ecosystem. However, this is not the case, and the future of the ecosystem is in doubt. Fishermen report lower fish catches and smaller fish sizes over the past generation; a dive shop operator from a nearby international resort hotel reports having to take tourists to new reefs because the ones close to the hotel have died during the past five years; fishermen from distant towns are beginning to fish in the area's coastal waters with illegal large nets, and the local fishermen say that the manatee have disappeared from the areas where these nets are used; and similar coral reefs to both the west and east have been characterized as "dead."

Stoffle et al., an interdisciplinary team of cultural anthropologists, remote sensing scientists, and a marine ecologist, used satellite imagery to identify changes in small areas of the coastal marine ecosystem of Buen Hombre, including the coral reef. Even though their study showed that the coastal waters and coral reefs on the north coast are still in good condition, they did find ecologically significant changes associated with changes from dark to light, indicating losses of highly productive coral, seagrass, and mangrove. By comparing the satellite imagery with marine and

argued, are revealing events because "the arrangements of society become most visible when they are challenged by crisis" (1990).

Within one month in 1989, there were four oil spills causing significant environmental damage: the Exxon *Valdez*, in Alaska; off Rhode Island; in the Delaware River; and in the Houston shipping canal. The *Valdez* spill alone dumped over 11 million gallons of crude oil into a fragile marine environment. In 1993, there was a similar very costly oil spill in the Shetland Islands, UK, which has still to be fully assessed in terms of damage. This later spill, like many others, created great uncertainty among the affected populations because of misleading and confused reports offered by the government agencies concerned (Button, 1995). These cases are not cited as an indictment of modern life, but to illustrate the problems of sustaining it; they are, in Roy Rappaport's words, part of "the anthropology of trouble" (1993).

What distinguishes these disasters from other environmental calamities such as the spread of the desert in the African Sahel or the burning of the Amazon, writes Lee Clarke, is that *organizations* have played primary roles both in causing the problems and in seeking solutions (1989, p. 2). These are tragedies over which the victims have no control and for protection must necessarily rely on organizations: state and federal governmental agencies, in-

ethnographic data, they found these changes (from 1985 to 1989) were closely related to fishing, tourism, and land use practices. They concluded that if global warming is affecting this ecosystem, its effects are still masked by the effects of these more predominant stresses. They further concluded that there are differences in the types of impacts on the ecosystem being made by the local people, who have a sense of ownership and an intergenerational commitment to its resources, and those being made by outsiders, such as urban fishermen and tourists. "Given the opportunity, local inhabitants seek to preserve the long-term productivity of the coastal environment, even at the expense of current harvest" (1994, p. 375).

While the satellite data provided a comprehensive technique for studying changes in this coastal marine ecosystem, Stoffle et al. were also able to use them to transfer information about these changes to policy makers at the village, regional, and national levels. Satellite images of the north coast reef system were shown to villagers and national government officials at two meetings in Buen Hombre, and the local fishermen were immediately able to identify familiar locations and point to named fishing spots. The images, supplemented with ethnographic and marine eco-

logical data, were instrumental in persuading government officials that measures were needed to protect the coral reef and secure the rights and interests of the local community. This is not an isolated case. Bernard Neitschmann (1995), a cultural geographer, has assisted the Miskito people of Nicaragua to map and inventory the extensive Miskito Reefs in the Caribbean in order to protect their traditional fishing grounds. A well-designed map can convey a great deal of information and can be sent to international organizations to document claims.

In fact, all over the world indigenous peoples are using maps to rename and reclaim their lands. Renaming is important because names are symbols and instruments of power, and maps are documents of possession. In Sarawak, where indigenous forest lands are under threat, simply possessing a map can get a Penan arrested (Poole, 1995, p. 1). Geomatics (satellite imagery) can be useful when it amplifies local capabilities to respond to external pressures. For example, 470 Menkragnoti Kayapo in Brazil have regained control over 4,400,000 hectares and use satellite imagery to defend and monitor this land, a small percentage of what they had earlier lost. Maps based on geomatic sources are useful to

reinforce claims, to show what has been demarcated, and to demonstrate incursions (Poole, 1995). Neitschmann puts it succinctly: "More indigenous territory can be reclaimed and defended by maps than by guns" (1995, p. 37).

The studies cited here stress the interdisciplinary nature of research utilizing satellite data, and the importance of "on the ground" research in the analysis and interpretation of the images. Francis Conant (1994) makes four predictions about the impact these space-age technologies will have:

1. Remote sensing and allied technologies will generate more fieldwork, not less, for anthropologists and others.
2. The services of anthropologists will become indispensable in the interpretation of satellite products, especially as these relate to non-Western cultural practices.
3. As a consequence of the foregoing, basic training in remote sensing and allied methodologies (in particular, GIS) will become a regular offering in undergraduate and graduate programs in anthropology.
4. These new technologies will be used increasingly in a retrospective mode to study past adaptations as well as ongoing or contemporary ecological processes (p. 406).

ternational agencies, and myriad private and public ones. These are a form of disaster for which our previous adaptations have not prepared us.

Can We Survive Progress?

In Chapter 2 we discussed "resilience," or the amount of change or impact that an ecological system might be able to sustain before becoming unrecognizably altered. Biodiversity is thought to be the key to resilience. The exponential growth of human population and technology continually erodes the resilience of our biosphere. One source of this

threat is through mass extinctions of species in every part of the world. As one noted naturalist and evolutionary biologist, E. O. Wilson, writes:

With people everywhere seeking a better quality of life, the search for resources is expanding even faster than the population. The demand is being met by an increase in scientific knowledge, which doubles every 10 to 15 years. It is accelerated further by a parallel rise in environment-devouring technology. Because Earth is finite in many resources that determine the quality of life—including arable soil, nutrients, fresh water and space for natural ecosystems—doubling of consumption at constant time intervals can bring disaster with shocking suddenness.

Box 7.2

The Abuse of Environmental Rights in South Africa

RAPID URBANIZATION COMBINED with apartheid in South Africa has brought significant health and safety hazards to millions. In the years leading to the final collapse of white political rule, the attention of the world was often transfixed by pictures of incredible urban squalor as the backdrop to scenes of violent resistance in the townships, as urban areas designated for nonwhite settlement were called. Anthropologist Ben Wisner describes and analyzes these hazards and how they may now be corrected through what he terms "two optics: environmental rights, which are human rights to healthful environment and a sustainable livelihood, and community participation" (1995).

From 1948 to 1993, urban policy in South Africa was to control nonwhite access to and residence in cities; a policy that generated constant conflict with African, Coloured, and Asian communities. This system of racial separation distorted relations with nature in a profound way (p. 3). It created overcrowding and led people to engage in dangerous and environmentally unsound practices simply to satisfy their basic needs for shelter, water, sanitation, cooking fuel, and income. Urban waterways were polluted, housing densely packed, open space rare, trees cut down, and the air polluted by the smoke of thousands of coal braziers used for cooking and heating. Personal security was bad as well; the density of houses (often rudimentary, since their owners had been forcibly relocated more than once) resulted in poorly aligned lanes with attendant injuries to pedestrians, especially children, from passing vehicles. Moreover, emergency vehicles were too large to penetrate the narrow lanes (p. 4). Unexpectedly, the collapse of apartheid in April 1994 brought new problems to the townships as a "tidal wave of immigrants from the countryside began to reappropriate urban space from which they or their parents had been removed by apartheid" (p. 5). By restricting nonwhites, some 87 percent of the population, to only 13 percent of the land, the apartheid system clearly violated the rights of millions to health and livelihood (p. 5).

Now the new government must deal with the legacy of the past policies if it is to have legitimacy. In 1993, the population of South Africa was estimated at 40 million; urban growth rates were as high as 5 percent in the late 1980s and the city-dwelling population grew from 8.5 million in 1985 to 14 million in 1993 (p. 6). Not only are these communities congested, with poor sanitation and drainage, but many were deliberately situated near areas of heavy industry where air and water pollution threaten environmental health and safety.

South Africa now suffers the consequences of apartheid, but the pattern of risk and vulnerability to hazards of urban populations in South Africa is not unique. As Wisner shows, within the past few decades there has been a world-

---

Even when a nonrenewable resource is only half used, it is still only one interval away from the end. [1993, pp. 26–27; see also 1994]

What is to be done? There is no easy solution; as Wilson notes, while scientists may have the ability and political will to control the nonliving components of the biosphere (the ozone layer and carbon cycles), they have no ability to micro-manage natural ecosystems, which are simply too complex. The only real solutions are population limits and habitat preservation—both very difficult to achieve for political reasons.

Postindustrialism is a recent development and it remains to be seen how humans will adapt to its consequences. As history has shown, an increase in energy sources creates as many problems as it solves. The impending advent of superconductors—materials that can transmit electricity with no loss to resistance—will make available even more usable energy. If we merely use this energy to support more people and to speed up consumption, the results are quite likely to be disastrous for the environment.

The problem is that change is coming so rapidly that it may outrun our ability to respond appropriately, especially with regard to natural resources. We must keep in mind that individual behavior is basic to adaptation; people generally alter their behavior to serve their self-interest as they see it. What is in the interest of elites and corporations may not be appropriate for long-range conservation of the world's resources and habitats. In earlier eras of human adaptation, people were severely constrained by their technology and by their limited access to sources of energy. By and large, people had to deal directly with the environmental consequences of

wide growth of mega-cities. "These urban regions—whether Cairo, São Paulo, Manila, Los Angeles, or Greater Johannesburg—share a number of morphological, socioeconomic, political and environmental characteristics" (p. 8). They have spread over very large areas, absorbing preexisting settlements, and have diverse economic patterns ranging from high-tech to the "parallel economies" of the homeless and street populations. Politically, mega-cities are fragmented into hundreds of jurisdictions; environmentally, they import water and energy from long distances, and they produce "mega" quantities of waste (p. 9). Polarization of wealth means that the poor tend to bear the costs of concentration. In Los Angeles, Wisner reports, the Hispanic population lives in the zone of highest air pollution, and it is their housing stock that is at greatest risk in earthquakes; in Alexandra township in Johannesburg, the population density is 688 people per hectare, while in predominantly white areas the average density is only about 40 (p. 9). Distinct hazards, ranging from the social (crime, homelessness), the geophysical (flood, fires, earthquakes, etc.), and the technological (industrial explosions, pollution) to the bio-

logical (HIV infection, rates of cancer, water-borne diseases, etc.) intersect in complex ways to produce what Wisner calls "'cascades' of secondary and tertiary hazards" (p. 10). For example, a flood in Alexandra township washed drums of toxic chemicals into residential areas. Vulnerability to these hazards is not evenly distributed by class, ethnicity, age, and gender (p. 10). "So numerous are the risks and so great the number of people exposed to them in a township like Alexandra, that South Africa has given rise to a new term: the 'situational disaster'" (p. 18).

The question facing the new South Africa is how can these environmental conditions be alleviated and disasters such as Bhopal and Love Canal (near Buffalo, New York) be avoided. Ben Wisner does not presume to have the answers, but drawing on his expertise as an anthropologist and human ecologist he suggests how to approach them.

First, local knowledge must be central to the program of reconstruction. People know of many of the hazards and are willing to take initiatives if they are consulted. Under apartheid, they were not consulted. Only local people can

closely monitor actions taken and subsequent results. While "top down" aid may be essential, if it is administered without consultation, as all too often happens when people are relocated after a disaster, their vulnerability is increased, not decreased.

Second, citizen-based, nongovernmental institutions have to be maintained and strengthened. In Alexandra, for example, church-based groups have been very active. Popular participation is vital to continued monitoring and improvement. Such participation helps to achieve a number of important goals at once: disaster prevention, disaster mitigation once a problem has occurred, and recovery.

Third, planning should be holistic, not a piecemeal response to disasters. Thus social, geophysical, and biological hazards all have to be addressed. This will involve a very large investment in urban infrastructure improvements, combined with technical assistance in reconstruction and monitoring. Environmental health will ultimately "depend on community groups sensitized to their rights and ability to call for and participate in hazard assessment . . . " (p. 22).

---

their activities. Farmers who allowed their fields to erode might face hunger. Now, many decisions that affect the environment are made by people far removed from the consequences. The manager of the factory whose sulfuric wastes contaminate a water supply distant from the head office may receive a bonus for efficiency. Perhaps we shall have to devise ways to reward those who, in the words of the ecologist René Dubos, "act locally but think globally."

Development in Ecological Perspective

About twenty years ago, a U.S. congressional mandate tied all foreign aid to a commitment to study its impacts on equity and the poor. Even though the discipline had from its beginnings been concerned with the theoretical issues of cultural and economic

change, from the 1970s onward it became engaged in the practical problems of alleviating poverty, environmental degradation, disease, malnutrition, gender inequity, and ethnic conflict.

Following Michael Horowitz (1994), who is himself a leading practitioner, some of the main contributions development anthropologists have made include:

1. Providing a critical understanding of the nature of development. This has included showing that indigenous expertise cannot be ignored, that forced resettlement of populations is costly and rarely results in improving standards of living, that "top down" planning usually only benefits those at the top, and that local communities are rarely homogeneous and should be carefully studied to determine who really benefits and who does not.

2. Showing the importance of long-term research. Typical development projects bring experts through for extremely brief periods of time; "rapid rural appraisal" say some, "rural development tourism" say others. Anthropologists at the World Bank and elsewhere have successfully argued for long-term social research in a number of regions. This has led to important recommendations, as with a project in the Middle Senegal river valley where the anthropologists demonstrated the need to augment the flood of a hydropower dam for the benefit of downstream ecosystems and smallholder productivity (Horowitz, 1994, p. 6).

3. Increased sensitivity to environmental issues and the need for an alliance between anthropologists, social scientists, and biophysical ecologists. Environmental sustainability requires a social component since both poverty and resource abuse are caused or exacerbated by similar policies seeking short-term returns on investments.

Environmental and Ecological Factors in Development. A development project may have a profound effect on the ecological system, as we have just noted. Large dams, for example, almost always have a legacy of large-scale environmental damage such as destruction of habitat, downstream pollution, increased salinity of the soil as a result of a rise in the water table, increased risk of flooding and erosion, and even, many people argue, an increase in the risk of earthquakes (Goldsmith & Hildyard, 1984). But innovations need not be so massive as a huge irrigation scheme or a giant dam to have significant effects on ecological systems. The introduction of shotguns, for example, has dramatically reduced the numbers of many game species used by the Yanomamö, not to mention the human toll (Chagnon, 1993). A new strain of rice introduced in Nepal increased yields as much as 200 percent, but because the rice grew on short, tough stalks that produced little fodder for cattle and required threshing machinery that was not available locally, the innovation was not without serious costs. The more intensive cultivation has led to loss of topsoil from erosion, and an increased dependence on firewood instead of straw for fuel has resulted in deforestation and increased risk of downstream flooding. Everywhere we see the effects of fertilizers, pesticides, and herbicides in contaminated water sources. Environmental costs must figure in any evaluation of the effectiveness of a proposed innovation.

The researcher concerned with development must always consider the strengths as well as the weaknesses of the local system of knowledge or practice. In Bali, Indonesia, according to J. Stephen Lansing (1991), an elaborate network of temples dedicated to water goddesses is controlled by priests who regulate and coordinate the irrigation of fields belonging to thousands of farmers. In the 1970s in an effort to modernize farming the government encouraged farmers to irrigate their fields according to whatever schedule they judged would increase their rice production. As a consequence, fields were irrigated according to individual farmers' timetables and unexpectedly this provoked an ecological crisis that resulted in a massive decline in overall yields. When farmers planted and irrigated on their own schedules, pests that were formerly controlled by the coordinated flooding dictated by the temples simply moved from field to field. Coordinated irrigation turned out to be a vital means of crop cycling and pest control. In this case we see a traditional religious institution playing a critical role in resource management. Stephen Lansing, an anthropologist, was instrumental in making government planners aware of the value of this supposedly non-economic and anachronistic cultural system.

Social Ties. Development may have unintended consequences for social relations as well. If these consequences are negative, they must be included among the costs of planned change. Attempts to introduce improved clothes-washing facilities, for instance, may cause women to lose the opportunity to meet and exchange information with their neighbors at a community washing place. Changes in cattle management, as with the Dinka of Sudan, may deprive elders of their special status as camp group leaders (Lako, 1988). The building of modern high-rise apartment houses to replace slum housing may have negative social consequences by breaking down established social networks, patterns of social control, and even pride of residence. Of course, an innovation may have an even more significant impact on traditional social ties, as when a minority or a traditionally subordinate group is placed in an economically competitive position with the majority population. This was the case in Burundi and Rwanda, where the Belgians, during the colonial period, recruited members of the smaller Tutsi ethnic group to the civil service, army, and police forces. They are now locked in deadly ethnic enmity with the numerically superior Hutu population.

Managing Social Change. Any country faces problems when it sets out to manage social change and tries to anticipate the costs. The anthropologist can help at the community level, where detailed knowledge can mean the difference between success and failure. Respect for indigenous solutions and ways of doing things can also make a difference. All too often planners work from the top down, with little interest in or respect for traditional, time-proven methods. Indigenous solutions in the areas of land use and food production are almost always critical to the long-term success of a new strategy. As Della McMillan found in her study of the land-use project in the Sahel (discussed in the case study), the effectiveness of any development plan is dependent on the involvement of the people who are the intended beneficiaries of the project.

Much of the present crisis in food production is attributable to the fact that the growth rates of the populations of many countries in the tropics have outstripped their ability to feed themselves. But most of the techniques that are being imported by such countries are based on farming methods first developed in temperate climates. In the Amazon region, large development schemes involving the clearing of forests, introduction of new food crops, and mechanization have had very poor economic results. Most cleared land in the Brazilian Amazon is used for cattle ranching; 85 percent of recently cleared land is now altogether unproductive because of soil degradation (Posey, Frecchone, Eddins, & DaSilva, 1984, p. 95). Tropical soils are generally thin and subject to rapid erosion and breakdown of nutrients once the protective cover of the rain forest is removed. As a consequence, intensification of agriculture or other uses of once-forested land often result in less rather than more food. Many people who have worked in tropical agricultural systems think the way out of this dilemma is to pay more attention to developing more productive farming based on plants and techniques that are already locally established.

George Appell, who has worked on development projects in Indonesia, offers a set of principles that, in somewhat abridged form, aptly summarize the sorts of negative impacts that planned change occasions and that have to be weighed against possible benefits (Appell, 1988, p. 272):

Every act of development necessarily involves an act of destruction.

Any new activity introduced is likely to displace an indigenous activity.

Each act of change has the potential to cause physiological, nutritional, psychological, and/or behavioral impairment among some segment of the subject population.

Modernization can erode indigenous mechanisms for coping with social stress, such as regulating conflict and solving family problems.

To this list we might add one more caution: The costs and benefits of any innovation or planned changed are not going to be distributed equally throughout the population; some people will benefit

River blindness is a major health hazard in West Africa that has been largely controlled in recent years. Here a young boy leads a blind man so that he can work in his field.

(D. Deriaz/The World Health Organization)

and some will lose. What has to be kept in mind is whether the distribution of costs and benefits is fair or desirable.

The ultimate cost-benefit outcome of any development project or effort to effect some form of desired social change can be influenced by many factors. Some of the most important are environmental and ecological factors, traditional values and beliefs, and social ties.

CASE STUDY

Sahel Visions

DEVELOPMENT INVOLVES MANY ACTORS WITH many different visions. What implications does this have for the design of foreign development assistance and for anthropological research?

This case study describes the first attempt by a West African government to develop a comprehensive land-use plan for its river basins covered by the Onchocerciasis (meaning "river blindness") Control Program (OCP) (Figure 7–2). The government agency charged with the coordination of this plan was the Volta Valley Authority (or AVV) of Burkina Faso (McMillan, 1995).

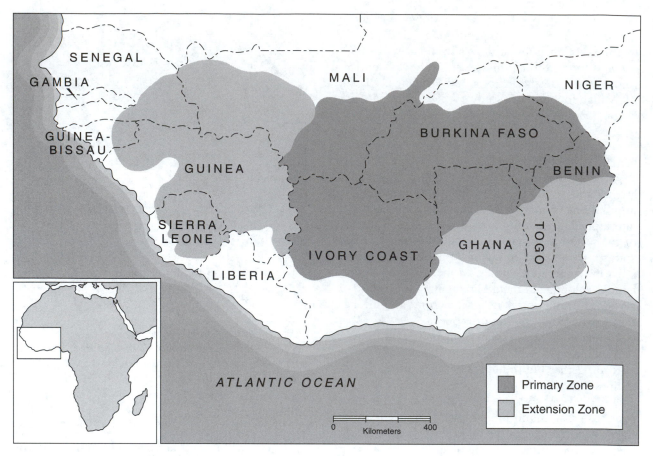

Figure 7–2. *The Sahel*

River blindness control was one of the great development visions to emerge from the 1968–1974 drought in West Africa. The disease river blindness (onchocerciasis) is spread through the bites of female black flies that breed in fast-running water; the disease is caused by threadlike worms that inhabit the subcutaneous tissues of the skin. In its advanced stages, the disease causes serious skin ailments, eye damage, and blindness. In 1974, nearly 700,000 million square kilometers with a population of 10 million were affected in the original seven-country control zone. In 1986, the control program was expanded to cover 1.3. million square kilometers, including additional areas of Benin, Ghana, Mali, and Togo, and parts of Guinea, Guinea-Bissau, Sierra Leone, and Senegal (Figure 7–2).

In 1974, the high incidence of onchocerciasis was considered to be the major reason that large areas of river basin in the Sudano-Sahelian areas of West Africa remained sparsely inhabited despite high population pressure in surrounding zones. Foreign donors like the U.S. Agency for International Development (USAID) and the United Nations Development Program (UNDP) thought that by con-

trolling river blindness, they could create vast new settlement opportunities for impoverished farmers and pastoralists from the areas worst hit by the drought. They also reasoned that the anticipated increase in rainfed and irrigated crop production would reduce trade imbalances, raise rural living standards in the areas being resettled, and minimize the threat of future famines. One attraction of the project for foreign donors was that once disease abatement was underway, they could report success to their headquarters in faraway capitals like Bonn, Riyadh, and Washington.

For Burkina Faso (then known as Upper Volta), the control program appeared to offer an unprecedented opportunity to resettle one-tenth of the country's population on more productive land and at the same time to triple cotton production. To implement this vision, the Burkinabè government created a centralized program of planned settlement and development that restricted the amount of land that individual households could farm and required settlers to adopt a prescribed package for intensive agriculture and new democratic institutions designed to encourage sustainable cropping.

In 1977, Della McMillan, then a second-year graduate student in anthropology, arrived to study the effects of resettlement on villagers who moved from three traditional villages near Kaya to a group of AVV planned settlements that were located in the river basins. She returned to study the home village and the immigrants living in the AVV project villages as part of her doctoral dissertation research (1978–1980), and again in 1983, 1988, and 1989–1990, making her involvement in this project unique for its length. (It is her 1995 book from which this case is drawn.) When she showed up at the compound of the chief of the traditional village that had lost the largest number of immigrants to the project, she did not know how closely her career was to be bound up with the Sahel, the OCP, and the AVV. Accepting the invitation of the chief or *naba*, she constructed a small house attached to his court, signifying to the populace that she was under his protection.

McMillan's vision was to compare the agricultural production patterns and income patterns of farmers remaining in the traditional homelands with those of the settlers who were just beginning to filter into the AVV-sponsored settlements. This form of research is often termed a baseline study, as it can provide a base for later comparison. The chief, in turn, envisioned that the presence of a foreign anthropologist would attract government and donor money to his region, where farming was a precarious venture.

The development theories that guided foreign donor funding and government planning in the AVV changed dramatically in the two decades that followed the start of control in 1974. Initially (1974–1981), the AVV-planned settlement project was managed from the top down and focused on the design and implementation of a project program for intensive farming that could be closely monitored by extension service personnel. Once a site was considered to be suitable for planned settlement (based on aerial photos and soil and water surveys), the AVV was responsible for the creation of all basic infrastructure including roads, wells, schools, and health facilities, as well as the design and implementation of extension programs to promote intensive farming. In return for the right to cultivate a 10–20 hectare project farm, the settlers were to use high-yield seeds and fertilizers, follow a strict crop rotation, practice monoculture rather than polyculture (see Chapter 4), and apply insecticides. The labor potential of each household was evaluated, and land was awarded on the basis of family labor supply—families with more adults getting more land. The new villages were to be organized differently than the traditional ones, which were centered on clan rights

and leadership by a chief. They were to have elected leaders, closely supervised by government extension workers, and were deliberately mixed in terms of clan and even ethnic composition. The underlying assumption behind the project's land tenure, settlement, and government policies was that once removed from their traditional norms and values, the settlers would be freer to experiment and adopt more modern, environmentally sustainable crop and livestock production practices.

McMillan soon found that as the settlements evolved, both the social and economic results began to diverge from the project model. In short, the people themselves had other visions and these visions grew and changed. The first settlers had to face many hardships in claiming their new fields; being strangers in the river basins, they were very dependent on the government's assistance and the leadership of the extension workers. The villagers shared labor and cooperated in house building and numerous activities critical to community survival without consideration of clan or ethnic distinctions. While the first sorghum harvest was poor, the cotton did well, and the settlers could report back to their home villages that things were going well. The first years, in fact, went very well, and most settlements prospered and attracted new settlers, often relatives of the initial families.

One divergence from the planners' model was that money was not being reinvested in intensive farming. Instead of respecting the project policy of cultivating a restricted area intensively, most farmers cleared additional land outside the 10–20 hectare farms that they were authorized to farm. In addition, they invested in more animals, trade, and crafts, and in education for their children. In sum, over time, the settlers' selective nonparticipation in the proposed system of intensive farming led them to abandon the proposed system of monoculture and rotation in favor of a more diversified system of crop, livestock, and nonagricultural employment. The communities came also to increasingly reflect the social realities of kinship and ethnicity; de facto leaders emerged who led by drawing on these ties. None of these deviations from the donor's vision or the government's vision meant that the project failed; it was simply not meeting its original policy goals. In particular, farmers were not producing the quantities of cash crops originally desired. One major problem turned out to be the labor supply. Cotton's demand for labor inputs is such that even low-yielding cereal crops produce more per human investment of labor. In addition, the cotton production required commercial fertilizers that would have to be paid for even if the crop failed.

When McMillan returned in December 1988, she saw how dramatically things had changed in the preceding five years. Especially important, almost all the households who had emerged as highly successful had re-immigrated to a new town that was adjacent to the country's first hydroelectric dam. This new town was located more than 250 kilometers away from the AVV-sponsored settlements where the settlers had lived for periods ranging from eleven to thirteen years. Here again, the settlers' response demonstrated not only their resilience and creativity, but their determination to diversify their subsistence bases. In contrast to the isolated river basins where the AVV-planned settlements were located, the new town offered opportunities to set up shops, find employment, and educate their children, while still farming.

In sum, the AVV planned settlement project did succeed in raising incomes; its failures were in not increasing export crops to the level desired and in the partial adoption of the desired modern farming techniques. In addition, the high costs of developing the planned settlements restricted the number of settlers that could be relocated, so the problem of overcrowding in traditional farming areas was only slightly alleviated. The doors of the AVV closed finally in 1989, but the settlements and their farmers remain.

What are some of the main lessons McMillan draws from her long involvement with the settlers living in the AVV-sponsored settlements? One of the most basic lessons is that people, consciously or not, are interested in building diversity into their resource base in order to avoid dependency on any one natural resource or income stream. The settlers living in the AVV project villages were vividly aware of how dependent the extension workers and the project were on foreign donor countries and organizations. Moreover, they knew better than the anthropologists and the project managers just how fickle these organizations can be, and did not wish to become dependent on their support. McMillan suggests that policy guidelines to promote more diversified social and economic systems should be built into any future planning for resettlement and regional development in the valleys.

Second, planners usually think of rural labor as being abundant—usually overabundant. From the perspective of the settler households living in areas with short-term supplies of "new" land, like the river basins covered by this project, labor is in short supply and is a limiting factor in intensifying farming.

Third, where settlement is envisioned, it should not be planned from the top down, but allowed to develop spontaneously with appropriate direction and assistance. That is, settlers should be largely self-selected and self-organized, but directed and assisted to help avoid economic and ecological problems that often plague completely spontaneous settlement: destruction of forest covers, soil erosion, land tenure disputes, etc. In particular, she points to the paradox arising from donor schedules and the needs of the people involved in the program. Donors usually want prompt results that they can showcase, and they are willing (sometimes required) to spend large amounts of money in relatively short periods of time. Sometimes they are investing money much more rapidly than can be usefully absorbed in the project. Many times, it is in the final stages of a project that good investment opportunities become clear, but as with the AVV, little money is available at that point. For example, the AVV administration tried to establish several market towns but was unsuccessful; when a major market did spring up without any government assistance, there were few funds left to assist its growth.

Finally, she points to the absolute necessity of reconciling the many different visions that ultimately shape the outcome of a development project—including those of foreign donors and the national government, as well as the local beneficiary households. ◗

The Ethics of Development Work

Ethical issues are a major concern in anthropological development work, from the time anthropologists make their initial decisions as to where and how they will do fieldwork through their final evaluations of the effects of their projects. The effort of McMillan and her coworkers is exemplary in making anthropological expertise serve the needs of people who require assistance. In some respects, it combines the traditional role of anthropological advocacy with the role of the modern, socially responsible scientist, as we saw Box 7.1, *Imaging Resource Depletion*.

Some anthropologists consider it unethical to interfere directly in other people's lives. Arturo Escobar, for example, has argued that development projects increase the incorporation of indigenous peoples into the larger economy, hence marginalizing them, and that anthropological assistance on development projects adds legitimacy to this process (1991). The assumption seems to be that participating in national economies is "bad" and that individuals affected by development projects have numerous options. Neither seem valid points. Further, if anthropologists were not involved, would the same people be less marginalized, less dependent? As Horowitz reports, World Bank projects where anthropologists and other social scientists are involved show a 15-percent higher rate of return of investment than comparable projects where they are not (1994). McMillan's study (1995) shows why this occurs; anthropologists not only accumulate factual data, they bring together experience from other areas. McMillan, in studying settlement, drew heavily on previous work by other anthropologists in Africa and Asia on resettlement.

While ethical issues may appear to be more sharply focused in development work, they are present in all kinds of anthropological research. Taking a thoughtful and balanced approach to these issues is essential—even more so when the lives of people are affected. The key question may be, "Is it ethical for anthropologists not to put their expertise to practical use?" Whether involved in an advocacy role, development projects, or just disseminating their knowledge and expertise to others, anthropologists in the next century need to make their voices heard. In concluding his statement of the theme for the 1995 American Anthropological Association meeting, James Peacock states that anthropologists should be involved in "shaping the world as it moves beyond 1999 to the next millennium. Let us—the most interdisciplinary of disciplines—look beyond immediate debates and projects to demonstrate resoundingly and creatively the understanding and guidance we can bring this new—or once-again renewed—world" (1995).

Summary

CHANGE IS CONSTANT IN ALL SOCIETIES, DESPITE A marked human tendency to maintain the status quo. Anthropologists focus on a variety of aspects of social change, but common to all approaches is some measure of costs and benefits, success and failure. The problems facing today's world—food shortages, rapid population growth, depletion of resources, pollution, and the difficulty of adapting to rapid and continuous change—are many and complex.

Over the long term, we see a number of interrelated trends in cultural change or evolution. As societies increase in population size and complexity, their energy budgets must allocate a larger share to maintain infrastructure; to maintain larger populations, food production is intensified; society becomes increasingly differentiated in terms of tasks performed and activities engaged in; production in general becomes more specialized; political and economic power becomes more centralized; settlements become larger and denser; and, socially, populations show increased stratification (division into groups that have unequal access to resources and power). At the same time, as with the Vikings in the North Atlantic, complex societies may succumb to political and demographic collapse.

Today we have moved into yet another era in the organization of production and integration of peoples. This has been termed variously the communications era, the age of the computer, and the high-tech age. The organization of commerce and industry is changing. The historian David Noble (1984) describes this transformation as the triumph of "numerical control" in industry. It has removed control from the factory to the central office; it also has allowed for decentralized production. The long-term significance of these changes will be profound; not only are entire segments of the populations of already-industrialized nations marginalized, but the peoples of many countries that lack an educational infrastructure will not participate fully in the economies of the future.

Much of the present unequal distribution of the benefits of the postindustrial era, together with the attendant environmental degradation as people desperately try to make a living, is not a problem of the relationship of people with their habitats, but of relationships among peoples competing for access to productive resources.

Since World War II, per-capita energy consumption throughout the world has risen at an ever-increasing rate. New technology makes low-cost fossil fuel, nuclear energy, and solar energy widely available. The energy that pulses through human society affects where and how people live, the material goods available to them, and their relations with their physical environment. Cheap energy allows huge cities to emerge because they are sustained by foods grown in distant fields and by water from faraway reservoirs. Because energy is cheap, people are consuming the world's resources at a phenomenal rate.

Energy management, or control over its downstream impacts, is as important as simply securing it. Quite apart from how we will cope with the depletion of our resources, there is the even more urgent problem of how we will dispose of the toxic by-products of what we have already consumed. Global communications and the emergence of cyberculture also have transformed culture. Satellite communications, global television networks, fax machines, and cellular telephones have, within the last decade, become part of world culture. People of all countries are participating in a globally shaped media culture. The good aspects of this are obvious: Free communications are critical to maintaining democracy, human rights, and economic exchange. The negative aspects are not just visible in the extreme cases of pornography and the like, but in a diminishing of regional cultural heterogeneity. Just as world material culture is becoming more homogeneous, so is expressive culture—the arts, dress, and even social conventions.

Closely linked to new developments in computer, information, and biological technology is what some have termed "cyberculture." The term comes from cybernetics, or systems theory, and refers to the emerging importance of computer-mediated communication, including global networks such as the Internet.

Anthropologists have become increasingly interested in analyzing the relationship between general trends and innovations on the one hand and development on the other. In the process of assessing the impact of change on society, some of them become personally involved in efforts to bring about change.

Anthropologists have identified themselves as "development anthropologists" for only about twenty years but have made numerous contributions: providing a critical understanding of the nature of development, including showing that indigenous expertise cannot be ignored; showing the importance of long-term research; increased sensitivity to environmental issues, and the need for an alliance between anthropologists, social scientists, and biophysical ecologists.

Some principles regarding development work have emerged. Every act of development necessarily involves an act of destruction. Any new activity introduced is likely to displace an indigenous activity. Each act of change has the potential to cause physiological, nutritional, psychological, and/or behavioral impairment among some segment of the subject population. Modernization can erode indigenous mechanisms for coping with social stress, such as regulating conflict and solving family problems. And finally, the costs and benefits of any innovation or planned changed are not going to be distributed equally throughout the population; some people will benefit and some will lose. What has to be kept in mind is whether the distribution of costs and benefits is fair or desirable.

Ethical issues are a major concern in development work as well as other areas of anthropology. Many feel that anthropologists should use their expertise to facilitate the planning and modification of development projects so that they will provide the most benefit to the people they are designed to help. Others attribute the marginalization of indigenous groups to development

and believe that any participation in development projects legitimizes that process. In the end, though, the breadth and depth of the expertise that anthropologists can provide should equip them to play a dominant role in shaping the world in the next century.

Key Terms

acculturation	intensification
centralization	Neolithic Revolution
cyberculture	nucleation
development anthropology	postindustrial society
differentiation	specialization
global culture	stratification
impact assessment	sustainable energy

Suggested Readings

Bodley, J. H. (1985). *Anthropology and contemporary human problems.* Palo Alto, CA: Mayfield. An examination of resource depletion, hunger and starvation, and other problems of our industrialized world. The author reexamines tribal cultures and compares their solutions with those of our society.

Chambers, E. (1985). *Applied anthropology: A practical guide.* Englewood Cliffs, NJ: Prentice Hall. A synthesis of the field of applied anthropology that reviews the ways in which the profession has adapted to new career opportunities, the ethical concerns associated with applied work, and the training of applied anthropologists.

Davis, S. H. (1977). *Victims of the miracle: Development and the Indians of Brazil.* New York: Cambridge University Press. This book documents the effects of Brazil's program of development on indigenous populations that have often suffered in the name of economic progress.

Grillo, R. & Rew, A. (Eds.). (1985). Social anthropology and development policy. New York: Tavistock Publications. A collection of papers that examines the role of the anthropologist in different political contexts, the contribution to be made by anthropologists to policy, and what working in the applied field might mean for anthropologists and those who hire them.

Johnston, B. R. (Ed.). (1994). *Who pays the price? The sociocultural context of environmental crisis.* Washington, D.C.: Island Press. This fine collection of articles focuses exclusively on the victims of environmental change. The issues examined include loss of land and contamination of air, water, and soil, to name a few.

McMillan, D. E. (1995). *Sahel visions: Planned settlement and river blindness control in Burkina Faso.* Tucson and London: University of Arizona Press. McMillan's study examines a period of fifteen years in which a development plan was implemented in order to relieve population pressure, increase food production, improve health conditions, and establish communities in areas afflicted with onchocerciasis (river blindness) in Burkina Faso in West Africa. An insightful study on land settlement and human development concerns.

Miller, M. S., Project Director (with the Cultural Survival staff). (1993). *State of the peoples: A global human rights report on societies in danger.* Boston: Beacon Press. This text provides us with contemporary and well-researched data on critical issues such as human rights, endangered societies, and resources for action. A valuable contribution that presents innovative solutions.

Newson, L. A. (1988). Indian survival in colonial Nicaragua. Norman, OK: University of Oklahoma Press. A detailed description of the colonial experiences of Indians in Nicaragua that focuses on the cultural and demographic factors that have resulted in different rates of survival for indigenous populations.

Southwick, C. H. (1996). *Global ecology in human perspective.* New York: Oxford University Press. Written by a well-known ecologist, this book deals with the ecology of planet Earth, focusing on the condition of the global environment and the quality of human life.

Glossary

acculturation Cultural change that occurs in response to extended first-hand contacts between two or more previously autonomous groups.

adaptation The process by which organisms or populations of organisms make biological or behavioral adjustments that facilitate their survival and reproductive success in their environment.

administrative system A twentieth-century system of ownership in which land is owned and managed by the state; found in China, the former Soviet Union, and some parts of Africa and Latin America.

affinal kin Persons related by marriage.

age grade A group of people of the same sex and approximately the same age who share a set of duties and privileges.

age set A named grouping of individuals of approximately the same age; as with age grades, predominantly found in East Africa.

alienation The fragmentation of individuals' relations to their work, the things they produce, and the resources with which they produce them.

animal husbandry The breeding, care, and use of herd animals such as sheep, goats, camels, cattle, and yaks.

archaeology The study of the relationship between material culture and behavior; investigations of the ways of life of earlier peoples and of the processes by which their ways of life changed.

authority The ability to exert influence because of one's personal prestige or the status of one's office.

balanced reciprocity Gift giving that clearly carries the obligation of an eventual and roughly equal return.

band A loosely integrated population sharing a sense of common identity but few specialized institutions.

biological (physical) anthropology The study of the human species, past and present, as a biological phenomenon.

biological race A genetically distinct population within a species.

biological species A group of interbreeding populations that is reproductively isolated from other such groups.

Blue Revolution Modern aquaculture, producing fish, shellfish, and other products.

bride price Payment made by a man or his kin group to the family from whom he takes a daughter in marriage.

bride service Service rendered by a man as payment to a family from whom he takes a daughter in marriage.

bridewealth Property given by the family of the groom to the family of the bride to compensate them for the loss of their daughter's service.

bureaucracy Institutionalized political administration, usually hierarchically organized.

call system A repertoire of sounds, each of which is produced in response to a particular situation.

carrying capacity The point at or below which a population tends to stabilize.

caste A social category in which membership is fixed at birth and usually unchangeable.

cattle complex An East African socioeconomic system in which cattle represent social status as well as wealth.

centralization Concentration of political and economic decisions in the hands of a few individuals or institutions.

chiefdom A society distinguished by the presence of a permanent central political agency to coordinate the activities of multicommunity political units.

clan A group that claims but cannot trace precisely their descent from a common ancestor.

closed corporate community A community that strongly emphasizes community identity and discourages outsiders from settling there by restricting land use to village members and prohibiting the sale or lease of property to outsiders.

cognates Words so similar from one language to the next as to suggest that both are variants of a single ancestral prototype.

commune Collective ownership of land or other factors in production, ostensibly for members to share proceeds and expenses.

consanguineal kin Persons related by birth.

consensual decisions Arriving at decisions that the entire group can accept.

corporate ownership Control of land and other productive resources by a group rather than by individuals.

corporateness The sharing of specific rights by group members.

corvée Unpaid labor in lieu of taxation, usually on road construction and maintenance.

creole A pidgin language that has evolved into a fully developed language, with a complete array of grammatical distinctions and a large vocabulary.

cross cousins Mother's brothers' children and father's sisters' children.

cultural anthropology The study of specific contemporary human cultures (ethnography), and of the underlying patterns of human culture in general (ethnology).

cultural ecology An approach to the study of cultural diversity that requires the simultaneous investigation of technology, culture, and the physical environment.

cultural evolution The idea that human culture has been transformed by regular and cumulative changes in learned behavior.

cultural materialism The theory, espoused by Marvin Harris, that ideas, values, and religious beliefs are the means or products of adaptation to environmental conditions ("material constraints").

cultural relativism The ability to view the beliefs and customs of other peoples within the context of their culture rather than one's own.

culture A system of shared beliefs, values, customs, behaviors, and artifacts that the members of a society use to cope with one another and with their world and that are transmitted from generation to generation through learning.

culture of poverty A self-perpetuating complex of escapism, impulse gratification, despair, and resignation; an adaptation and reaction of the poor to their marginal position in a class-stratified, highly individuated, capitalistic society.

cyberculture The emergent worldwide system of communication via computers.

demographic transition A rapid increase in a society's population with the onset of industrialization, followed by a leveling off of the growth rate due to reduced fertility.

descent group A group of consanguineal kin united by presumed lineal descent from a common ancestor.

descent ideology The concept of kinship as a basis of unambiguous membership in a group and possibly of property rights and political obligations.

descent relationship The ties between mother and child and between father and child.

development anthropology Employment of anthropological theory and findings to have a practical and ameliorating effect on the lives of people.

dialect A distinctive speech community within a language.

differentiation Organization in separate units for various activities and purposes.

diffusion The spread of an aspect of culture from the society in which it originated by migration or imitation.

domestic cycle The changes in household organization that result from a series of demographic events.

domestic herds Animals maintained for domestic consumption.

domestic mode of production The organization of economic production and consumption primarily in the household.

domestication The process by which people try to control the reproductive rates of animals and plants by ordering the environment in such a way as to favor certain species.

dowry Payment made by the bride's family to the groom or to the groom's family.

ecology The study of the interplay between organisms (or the populations to which they belong) and their environment.

economic class A group that is defined by the economic position of its members in relation to the means of production in the society—the wealth and relative economic control they may command.

economic stratification The segmentation of society along lines of access to resources.

economic system The ideas and institutions that people drawn upon and the behaviors in which they engage in order to secure resources to satisfy their needs and desires.

ecosystem The cycle of matter and energy that includes all living things and links them to the nonliving.

ecosystem equilibrium A balance among the components of an ecosystem.

empiricism Reliance on observable and quantifiable data.

enculturation Becoming proficient in the cultural codes of one's society.

endogamy Marriage within a particular group with which one is identified.

entrepreneurship Economic innovation and risk-taking.

ethnicity A basis for social categories that are rooted in socially perceived differences in national origin, language, and/or religion.

ethnocentrism The tendency to judge the customs of other societies by the standards of one's own.

ethnographic present Describes the point in time at which a society or culture is frozen when ethnographic data collected in the field are published in a report.

ethnography Gathering information on contemporary cultures through fieldwork or first-hand study.

ethnology Uncovering general patterns and "rules" that govern social behavior.

evolution The process by which small but cumulative changes in a species can, over time, lead to its transformation; may be divided into two categories: physical evolution (adaptive changes in biological makeup) and cultural evolution (adaptive changes in thought and behavior).

evolutionary ecology The study of living organisms within the context of their total environment, with the aim of discovering how they have adapted.

exchange The distribution of goods and services among members of a society.

exogamy Marriage outside a particular group with which one is identified.

extended family household A multiple-family unit incorporating adults of two or more generations.

extensive agriculture Farming using limited sources of nonhuman energy.

fallow time The time required for soils to regain nutrients following planting; industrial farming has greatly shortened this time leading to increased production.

family household A household formed on the basis of kinship and marriage.

fieldwork The first-hand observation of human societies.

fossils The naturally mineralized remains of earlier forms of plant and animal life.

fraternal polyandry Marriage of one woman with a set of brothers.

freehold Private ownership of property.

gender A cultural construct consisting of the set of distinguishable characteristics associated with each sex.

generalized reciprocity Informal gift giving for which no accounts are kept and no immediate or specific return is expected.

global culture Due to recent developments in communication and transportation, people all over the world are coming to share similar aspirations, cultural codes, and patterns of consumption.

grammar The formal structure of a language, comprising phonology, morphology, and syntax.

Green Revolution Use of recently developed new genetic strains of major food crops, which has transformed agriculture since the 1970s.

habitat The specific area where a species lives.

headmen Leaders in tribal- or band-organized societies, usually informally selected with limited formal coercive power.

holism The philosophical view that no complex entity can be considered to be only the sum of its parts; as a principle of anthropology, the assumption that any given aspect of human life is to be studied with an eye to its relation to other aspects of human life.

Homo sapiens The human species.

horizontal migration A nomadic pattern characterized by regular movement over a large area in search of grass.

horticulture A simple form of agriculture based on the working of small plots of land without draft animals, plows, or irrigation; also called *extensive agriculture*.

household A domestic residential group whose members live together in intimate contact, rear children, share the proceeds of labor and other resources held in common, and in general cooperate on a day-to-day basis.

hypothesis A statement that stipulates a relationship between a phenomenon for which the researcher seeks to account and one or more other phenomena.

impact assessment Measuring the social, economic, or cultural impacts of development efforts.

independent family household A single-family unit that resides by itself, apart from relatives or adults of other generations.

industrial agriculture Farming using large inputs of fossil fuel and industrial technology.

institutions A society's recurrent patterns of activity, such as religion, art, a kinship system, law, and family life.

intensification An increase in the product derived from a unit of land or labor.

intensive agriculture A form of agriculture that involves the use of draft animals or tractors, plows, and often some form of irrigation.

jati Occupational categories or groupings within the Indian caste system.

joint family household A complex family unit formed through polygyny or polyandry or through the decision of married siblings to live together in the absence of their parents.

lineage A unilineal descent group composed of people who trace their genealogies through specified links to a common ancestor.

lineal relatives Direct ascendants and descendants.

lingua franca Any language used as a common tongue by people who do not speak one another's native language.

linguistic anthropology A subdivision of anthropology that is concerned primarily with unwritten languages (both prehistoric and modern), with variation within languages, and with the social uses of language; traditionally divided into three branches: *descriptive linguistics,* the systematic study of the way language is constructed and used; *historical linguistics,* the study of the origin of language in general and of the evolution of the languages people speak today; and *sociolinguistics,* the study of the relationship between language and social relations.

low-energy budget An adaptive strategy by which a minimum of energy is used to extract sufficient resources from the environment for survival.

market exchange Trading goods and services through a common medium of value.

material culture The technology and all material artifacts of a society; used primarily by archaeologists.

matrilateral Relatives on the mother's side in a genealogy or kinship system.

matrilineage A lineage whose members trace their genealogies through specified female links to a common female ancestor.

matrilineal descent Descent traced through the female line.

matrilineal descent group A unilineal descent group in which membership is inherited through the maternal line.

matrilocal residence Residence of a married couple with or near the wife's kin.

mechanization The replacement of human and animal labor by mechanical devices.

mediation Intervention by an outside party in a dispute.

medical anthropology Specialization within anthropology focusing on medical knowledge and practice; often related to practical efforts in health care delivery.

moiety One of the two subdivisions of a society with a dual organizational structure.

monogamy An exclusive union of one man and one woman.

nationalism The feeling or belief that a people and land are inherently linked, and using this belief to legitimize a particular state or nation.

natural selection The process whereby members of a species who have more surviving offspring than others pass their traits on to the next generation, whereas the less favored do not do so to the same degree.

negative reciprocity An exchange between enemies or strangers in which each side tries to get the better end of the bargain.

Neolithic Revolution Refers to the development of agriculture and consequent cultural changes that occurred at different times and places in the Old and New Worlds.

neolocal residence Residence of a married couple in a new household established apart from both the husband's and the wife's kin.

niche The environmental requirements and tolerances of a species; sometimes seen as a species' "profession" or what it does to survive.

nomadic pastoralism The strategy of moving the herds that are one's livelihood from pasture to pasture as the seasons and circumstances require.

nonunilineal descent A way of looking at kinship in which descent may be traced through either parent or through both.

nuclear family household An independent family unit formed by a monogamous union.

nucleation The tendency of populations to cluster in settlements of increasing size and density.

paleontologists Experts on animal life of the distant past.

parallel cousins Mother's sisters' children and father's brothers' children.

participant observation Actual participation in a culture by an investigator, who seeks to gain social acceptance in the society as a means to acquire understanding of her or his observations.

pastoralism A form of social organization based on herding.

patriclan A group that claims but cannot trace their descent through the male line from a common male ancestor.

patrilineage A lineage whose members trace their genealogies through specified male links to a common male ancestor.

patrilineal descent Descent traced through the male line.

patrilineal descent group A unilineal descent group in which membership is inherited through the paternal line.

patrilocal residence Residence of a married couple with or near the husband's kin.

patron-client relationship A mutually obligatory arrangement between an individual who has authority, social status, wealth, or some other personal resource (the "patron") and another person who benefits from his or her support or influence (the "client").

peasants Farmers who lack control over the means of their production—the land, the other resources, the capital they need to grow their crops, and the labor they contribute to the process.

pidgin A language based on a simplified grammar and lexicon taken from one or more fully developed languages.

political ecology Focuses on the ecological consequences of the distribution of power.

politics The process by which a community's decisions are made, rules for group behavior are established, competition for positions of leadership is regulated, and the disruptive effects of disputes are minimized.

polyandry Marriage between one woman and two or more men simultaneously.

polyculture Closely associated with horticulture, the planting of many species or strains of plants in close proximity.

polygamy Plural marriage.

polygyny Marriage between one man and two or more women simultaneously.

power The ability to exert influence because one's directives are backed by negative sanctions of some sort.

primates A grouping of mammals that includes humans, apes, and New and Old World monkeys.

primatology The study of living nonhuman primates.

production The conversion of natural resources to usable forms.

productive life span The period bounded by the culturally established ages at which a person ideally enters and retires from the work force.

productivity The amount of work a person accomplishes in a given period of time.

racism Acting upon the belief that different races have different capacities for culture.

random sample A sample in which each individual in a population has the same chance of being selected as any other.

rational economic decisions Weighing available alternatives and calculating which will provide the most benefit at the least cost.

reciprocity Mutual giving and taking between people who are often bound by social ties and obligations.

redistribution Reallocation of a society's wealth by means of obligatory payments or services.

regulation of access to resources Control over the use of land, water, and raw materials.

resilience The ability of an ecosystem to undergo change while still maintaining its basic elements or relationships.

revitalization movements Conscious efforts to build an ideology that will be relevant to changing cultural needs.

rites of intensification Rituals intended either to bolster a natural process necessary to survival or to reaffirm the society's commitment to a particular set of values and beliefs.

rites of passage Rituals that mark a person's transition from one set of socially identified circumstances to another.

ritual Behavior that has become highly formalized and stereotyped.

role A set of behavioral expectations appropriate to an individual's social position.

sampling bias The tendency of a sample to exclude some members of the sampling universe and overrepresent others.

sampling universe The largest entity to be described, of which the sample is a part.

scarce resources A central concept of Western economics that assumes that people have more wants than they have resources to satisfy them.

scientific theory A statement that postulates ordered relationships among natural phenomena.

sedentary pastoralism Animal husbandry that does not involve mobility.

sedentism The practice of establishing a permanent, year-round settlement.

segmentary lineage A descent group in which minimal lineages are encompassed as segments of minor lineages, minor lineages as segments of major lineages, and so on.

shaman A medium of the supernatural who acts as a person in possession of unique curing, divining, or witchcraft capabilities.

sharecropping Working land owned by others for a share of the yield.

slash-and-burn agriculture A method of farming, also called *swidden agriculture*, by which fields are cleared, trees and brush are burned, and the soil, fertilized by the ash, is then planted.

social class A category of people who have generally similar educational histories, job opportunities, and social standing and who are conscious of their membership in a social group that is ranked in relation to others and is replicated over generations.

social control A framework of rewards and sanctions that channel behavior.

social division of labor The process by which a society is formed by the integration of its smaller groups or subsets.

socialization The process by which a person acquires the technical skills of his or her society, the knowledge of the kinds of behavior that are understood and acceptable in that society, and the attitudes and values that make conformity with social rules personally meaningful, even gratifying; also termed *enculturation*.

sociolinguistics The study of the interrelationship of social variables and language.

specialization The limited range of activities in which a single individual is likely to be engaged.

specialized pastoralism The adaptive strategy of exclusive reliance on animal husbandry.

spheres of exchange The modes of exchange—reciprocity, redistribution, and market exchange—that apply to particular goods or in particular situations.

stability The ability of an ecosystem to return to equilibrium after disturbances.

state A complex of institutions that transcend kinship in the organization of power.

status A position in a pattern of reciprocal behavior.

stratification The division of a society into groups that have varying degrees of access to resources and power.

stratified sample A sample obtained by the process of dividing a population into categories representing distinctive characteristics and then selecting a random sample from each category.

stratified society A society in which extensive subpopulations are accorded differential treatment.

subsistence agriculture Farming directed to domestic consumption with limited nonhuman energy sources.

swidden agriculture See *slash-and-burn agriculture*.

taboo A supernaturally justified prohibition on certain activities.

time allocation A method of collecting data by making observations according to a systematic schedule.

tontine A group of people who agree to collect and pool funds, and then use the pot in an agreed-upon order.

totem A plant or animal whose name is adopted by a clan and that holds a special significance for its members, usually related to their mythical ancestry.

transhumance Seasonal movement of livestock between upland and lowland pastures.

tribe A descent- and kinship-based group in which subgroups are clearly linked to one another, with the potential of uniting a large number of local groups for common defense or warfare.

unilineal descent A way of reckoning kin in which membership is inherited only through either the paternal or the maternal line, as the society dictates.

vengeance A form of social control arising from shared responsibility and the idea that each offense will be met with comparable and automatic retaliation.

water table The level of water under the earth.

witchcraft Use of religious ritual to control, exploit, or injure unsuspecting, or at least uncooperating, other persons.

workday The culturally established number of hours that a person ideally spends at work each day.

Bibliography

Aberle, D. F., Bronfenbrenner, U., Hess, E. H., Miller, D.R., Schneider, D. H., Spuhler, J. N. (1963). The incest taboo and the mating patterns of animals. *American Anthropologist, 65*, 253–265.

Abramson, A. (1987). Beyond the Samoan controversy in anthropology: A history of sexuality in the eastern interior of Fiji. In P. Caplan (Ed.), *The cultural construction of sexuality* (pp. 193–216). New York: Tavistock.

Abruzzi, W. (1987). Ecological stability and community diversity during Mormon colonization of the Little Colorado River Basin. *Human Ecology, 15*, 317–338.

———. (1993). *Dam that river! Ecology and Mormon settlement in the Little Colorado River basin.* New York: Penn State University Press.

Abu Lughod, L. (1988). *Veiled sentiments.* Berkeley: University of California Press.

———. (1993). *Writing women's worlds: Bedouin stories.* Berkeley: University of California Press.

Abu-Rabia, A. (1994). *The Negev Bedouin and livestock rearing: Social, economic and political aspects.* Providence, RI: Berg Publishers.

Adams, J. W., & Kasakoff, A. B. (1976). Factors underlying endogamous group size. In C. Smith (Ed.), *Regional analysis: Social systems* (Vol. 2, pp. 149–172). New York: Academic Press.

Adams, R. M. (1966). *The evolution of urban society: Early Mesopotamia and prehispanic Mexico.* Chicago: Aldine.

Agrawal, A. (1994). Mobility and control among nomadic shepherds: The case of the Raikas II. *Human Ecology, 22*, 131–144.

Alcock, J. (1995). The belief engine. *Skeptical Inquirer, 19*(3), 14–18.

Anderson, B. (1991). *Imagined communities.* London: Verso.

Angeloni, E. (Ed.). (1994). *Annual editions: Anthropology 94–95* (17th rev. ed.). Guilford, CT: Dushkin Publishing.

Angier, N. (1995, January 3). Heredity's more than genes, new theory proposes. *New York Times,* pp. B13, B22.

———. "Sexual identity not pliable after all." *New York Times,* (Fri., Mar 14, 1997) pp. A1, A18.

Annis, S. (1988). *God and production in a Guatemalan town.* Austin: University of Texas Press.

Antoun, R. T. (1968). On the significance of names in an Arab village. *Ethnology, 7,* 158–170.

Appell, G. N. (1988). Casting social change. In M. R. Dove (Ed.), *The real and imagined role of culture in development: Case studies from Indonesia* (pp. 271–284). Boulder, CO: Westview.

Armelagos, G. (1987). Biocultural aspects of food choice. In M. Harris & E. B. Ross (Eds.), *Food and evolution: Towards a theory of human food habits* (pp. 565–578). Philadelphia: Temple University Press.

Atkinson, J. M. (1992). Shamanism today. *Annual Review of Anthropology, 21,* 307–330.

Bailey, R. C., & Peacock, N. R. (1990). Efe Pygmies of Northeast Zaire: Subsistence strategies in the Ituri Forest. In I. DeGarine & G. A. Harrison (Eds.), *Uncertainty in the food supply.* New York: Cambridge University Press.

Balee, W. (1994). *Footprints of the forest: Ka'apor ethnobotany-historical ecology of plant utilization by an Amazonian people.* New York: Columbia University Press.

Balikci, A. (1970). *The Netsilik Eskimo.* New York: Natural History Press.

Barfield, T. J. (1993). *The nomadic alternative.* Englewood Cliffs, NJ: Prentice Hall.

Barnet, R. J., & Muller, R. E. (1974). *Global reach: The power of the multinational corporations.* New York: Simon & Schuster.

Barry, H., III, Child, I. L., & Bacon, M. K. (1959). Relation of child training to subsistence economy. *American Anthropologist, 61,* 51–63.

Barry, J. W. (1965). *A study of Temne and Eskimo visual perception: Preliminary report.* (Psychology Laboratory Report No. 28). Edinburgh: University of Edinburgh

Barth, F. (1959). Political leadership among Swat Pathans. *Monographs on Social Anthropology, 19,* London School of Economics.

———. (1961). *The nomads of south Persia: The Basseri tribe of the Kamseh confederacy.* New York: Humanities Press.

———. (1963). *Role of the entrepreneur in social change in Northern Norway.* Bergen: Norwegian Universities Press.

———. (1966). The problem of comparison. *Royal Anthropological Institute* (Occasional Paper No. 23, pp. 22–23).

———. (1969). *Ethnic groups and boundaries: The social organization of cultural difference*. Boston: Little, Brown.

———. (1981). *Process and form in social life*. London: Routledge & Kegan Paul.

———. (1994). Brief comment. *Anthropology Newsletter, 34*(4), 1.

Bates, D. G. (1973). *Nomads and farmers: The Yörük of Southeastern Turkey*. (University of Michigan Museum of Anthropology Monograph, p. 52). Ann Arbor: University of Michigan Press.

———. (1974). Normative and alternative systems of marriage among the Yörük of Southeastern Turkey. *Anthropological Quarterly, 47*, 270–287.

———. (1994). What's in a name? Minorities, identity and politics in Bulgaria. *Identities, 1*(2–3), 201–225.

Bates, D. G., & Lees, S. H. (1977). The role of exchange in production specialization. *American Anthropologist, 79*, 824–841.

———. (1979). The myth of population regulation. In N. A. Chagnon & W. Irons (Eds.), *Evolutionary biology and human social behavior: An anthropological perspective* (pp. 273–289). North Scituate, MA: Duxbury Press.

Bates, D. G., & Plog, F. (1990) *Cultural anthropology* (3rd ed.). New York: McGraw-Hill.

Bates, D. G., & Rassam, A. (1983). *Peoples and cultures of the Middle East*. Englewood Cliffs, NJ: Prentice Hall.

Beals, A. R. (1962). *Gopalpur: A south Indian village*. New York: Holt, Rinehart & Winston.

Beattie, J. (1964). *Other cultures*. New York: Free Press.

Beck, L. (1986). *The Qashqa'i of Iran*. New Haven, CT: Yale University Press.

———. (1991). *Nomad: A year in the life of a Qashqa'i tribesman in Iran*. Berkeley and Los Angeles: University of California Press.

Beckerman, S. (1983). Does the swidden ape the forest? *Human Ecology, 11*, 1–12.

Bell, D. (1975). Ethnicity and social change. In N. Glazer & D. P. Moynihan (Eds.), *Ethnicity*. Cambridge, MA: Harvard University Press.

Benedict, R. (1959). *Patterns of culture*. New York: New American Library. (First published 1934.)

Bentley, G. (1985). Hunter-gatherer energetics and fertility: A reassessment of !Kung San. *Human Ecology, 13*, 79–110.

Berleant-Schiller, R., & Shanklin, E. (Eds.). (1983). *The keeping of animals*. Totowa, NJ: Allenheld, Osmun.

Bernard, H. R. (1988). *Research methods in cultural anthropology*. Beverly Hills, CA: Sage.

———. (1994). *Research methods in anthropology: Qualitative and quantitative approaches* (2nd ed.). Thousand Oaks, CA: Sage.

Berreby, D. (1995, April 9). Unabsolute truths: Clifford Geertz. *New York Times Magazine*, pp. 44–47.

Berreman, G. D. (1972). Race, caste, and other invidious distinctions in social stratification. *Race, 13*, 500–536. London: Institute of Race Relations.

Bettinger, R. L. (1987). Archaeological approaches to hunter-gatherers. *Annual Review of Anthropology, 16*, 121–142.

Bicketon, D. (1995). *Language and Human Behavior*. Seattle: University of Washington Press.

Binford, L. R. (1968). Post-Pleistocene adaptations. In S. R. Binford & L. R. Binford (Eds.), *New perspectives in archaeology*. Chicago: Aldine.

———. (1983). *Working at Archaeology*. New York: Academic Press.

———. (1989). Ancestral lifeways: The faunal record. In A. Podolefski & P. J. Brown (Eds.), *Applying anthropology: An introductory reader*. Mountain View, CA: Mayfield Press.

Bird, G., & Melville, K. (1994). *Families and intimate relationships*. New York: McGraw-Hill.

Blackwood, E. (1984). Sexuality and gender in certain Native American tribes: The case of cross-gender females. *Signs, 10*, 27–42.

Blanton, R. E. (1994). *Houses and households: A comparative study*. New York: Plenum.

Bloomfield, L. (1965). Language history. In H. Hoijer (Ed.), *Language*. New York: Holt, Rinehart & Winston.

Board of Education of the City of New York, Division of Bilingual Education. (1994). *Facts and figures*.

Boas, F. (1940). *Race, language and culture*. New York: Macmillan.

———. (1966). *The limitations of the comparative method of anthropology*. New York: Free Press. (First published 1896.)

Boddy, J. P. (1988). Spirits and selves in Northern Sudan: The cultural therapeutics of possession and trance. *American Ethnologist, 15*, 2–27.

———. (1994). *Aman: The story of a Somali girl*. New York: Pantheon.

Boehm, C. (1984). *Blood revenge: The anthropology of feuding in Montenegro and other tribal societies*. Lawrence: University Press of Kansas.

Bogen, J. E. (1969). The other side of the brain: An oppositional mind. *Bulletin of the Los Angeles Neurological Societies, 34*, 135–162.

Bohannan, P. (1960). Africa's land. *Centennial Review, 4*, 439–449.

———. 1965. The Tiv of Nigeria. In J. L. Gibbs, Jr. (Ed.), *Peoples of Africa*. New York: Holt, Rinehart & Winston.

Bongarts, J. (1988). Modeling the demographic impact of AIDS in Africa. In R. Kulstad (Ed.), *AIDS 1988: American Association for the Advancement of Science Symposia Papers* (pp. 85–94). Washington, DC: AAAS.

Boone, J. (1992). Competition, conflict and development of social hierarchies. In E. R. Smith & B. Winterhalder (Eds.), *Evolutionary ecology and human behavior* (pp. 301–338). Hawthorne, NY: Aldine de Grutyer.

Borofsky, R. (Ed.). (1994). *Assessing cultural anthropology*. New York: McGraw-Hill.

Boserup, E. (1970). *Women's role in economic development*. Chicago: Aldine.

Boster, J. (1983). A comparison of the diversity of Jivaroan gardens with that of the tropical forest. *Human Ecology, 11*, 47–68.

Bott, E. (1957). *Family and Social Networks*. London: Tavistock.

Boulding, K. (1961). *Economic analysis* (4th ed.). New York: Harper & Row.

Bourguignon, E., & Greenbaum, L. (1973). *Diversity and homogeneity*. New Haven, CT: HRAF Press.

Bowen, E. S. (1964). *Return to laughter: An anthropological novel*. New York: Doubleday/American Museum of Natural History.

Bowlby, J. (1969). Attachment. *Attachment and loss series* (Vol. 1). New York: Basic Books.

Boyd, R., & Richerson, P. J. (1985). *Culture and the evolutionary process*. Chicago: University of Chicago Press.

———. (1991). Punishment allows the evolution of cooperation (or anything else) in sizable groups. *Ethology and Sociobiology, 13,* 171–196

Brace, C., Brace, M. L., & Leonard, W. R. (1989). Reflections on the face of Japan: A multivariate craniofacial and odontometric perspective. *American Journal of Physical Anthropology, 78,* 93–114.

Bradburd, D. (1980). Never give a shepherd an even break: Class and labor among the Komanchi of Kerman, Iran. *American Ethnologist, 7,* 604–620.

———. (1984). The rules and the game: The practice of Komanchi marriage. *American Ethnologist, 11,* 738–754.

———. (1990). *Ambiguous relations: Kin, class and conflict among Komachi pastoralists*. Washington, DC: Smithsonian Institution Press.

Brandes, S. (1980). *Metaphors of masculinity: Sex and status in Andalusian folklore*. Philadelphia: University of Pennsylvania Press.

Bray, F. (1994). *The rice economies: Technology and development in Asian societies*. Berkeley and Los Angeles: University of California Press.

Briggs, J. L. (1970). *Never in anger: Portrait of an Eskimo family*. Cambridge, MA: Harvard University Press.

Brondizio, E., Moran, E., Mausel, P., & Wu, Y. (1994). Land use change in the Amazon estuary: Patterns of Caboclo settlement and landscape management. *Human Ecology, 22*(3), 243–248.

Brooke, J. (1987, November 30). Informal capitalism grows in Cameroon. *New York Times*, p. 8.

Brown, D. (1991). *Human universals*. New York: McGraw-Hill.

Browne, M. W. (1994, October 16). What is intelligence? And who has it? *New York Times Book Review*, pp. 3ff.

Buchler, I., & Selby, H. A. (1968). *Kinship and social organization: An introduction to theory and method*. New York: Macmillan.

Burbank, V. K. (1994). *Fighting women: Anger and aggression in Aboriginal Australia*. Berkeley and Los Angeles: University of California Press.

Burch, E. S., Jr. (1994). North Alaskan Eskimos: A changing way of life. In M. Ember, C. Ember, & D. Levinson (Eds.), *Portraits of a culture* (pp. 1–36). Englewood Cliffs, NJ: Prentice Hall.

———. (1994). The future of hunter-gatherer research. In E. S. Burch, Jr. & L. J. Ellanna (Eds.), *Key issues in hunter-gatherer research* (pp. 441–455). Providence, RI: Berg Publishers.

Burch, E. S., Jr., & Ellanna, L. J. (Eds.) (1994). *Key issues in hunter-gatherer research*. Providence, RI: Berg Publishers.

———. (1994). Introduction. In E. S. Burch, Jr. & L. J. Ellanna (Eds.), *Key issues in hunter-gatherer research*. Providence, RI: Berg Publishers.

Burling, R. (1970). *Man's many voices: Language in its cultural context*. New York: Holt, Rinehart & Winston.

———. (1974). *The passage of power*. New York: Academic Press.

Button, G. (1995). What you don't know can't hurt you: The right to know and the Shetland oil spill. *Human Ecology, 23,* 31.

Cairo Population Conference. (1994, September 11). *New York Times*, p. 10.

Calhoun, C., Light, D., & Keller, S. (1994). *Sociology* (6th ed.). New York: McGraw-Hill.

Campbell, B. K. (1995). *Human ecology* (2nd ed.). Hawthorne, NY: Aldine de Gruyter.

Cane, S. (1996). Australian aboriginal subsistence in the western desert. In Bates, D. G. & Lees, S. H. (Eds.), *Case studies in human ecology* (pp. 17–54). New York: Plenum.

Cann, R. L. (1988). DNA and human origins. *Annual Review of Anthropology* (Vol. 17, pp. 127–143). Palo Alto, CA: Annual Reviews.

Caplan, P. (Ed.). (1987). *The cultural construction of sexuality*. New York: Tavistock.

Carneiro, R. L. (1981). The chiefdom: Precursor to the state. In G. D. Jones & R. R. Kautz (Eds.), *The Transition to Statehood in the New World* (pp. 37–77). New York: Cambridge University Press.

Carrington, J. F. (1949). *Talking drums of Africa*. London: Carey Kingsgate Press.

———. (1971). The talking drums of Africa. *Scientific American, 255,* 90–94.

Cashdan, E. (1992). Spatial organization and habitat use. In E.A. Smith & B. Winterhalter (Eds.), *Evolutionary ecology and human behavior*. New York: Walter de Gruyter.

Castells, M. (1996a). The net and the self: Working note for a critical theory of the informational society. *Critique of Anthropology, 16*(1), 11–39.

Castells, M. (1996b). *The rise of the network society: The informational age,* vol. 1. Oxford: Blackwell Press.

Cavalli-Sforza, P., & Piazza, A. (1994). *The history and geography of human genes*. Princeton, NJ: Princeton University Press.

Chagnon, N. A. (1967). Yanomamö social organization and warfare. In M. Fried, M. Harris, & R. Murphy (Eds.), *War: The anthropology of armed conflict and aggression*. New York: Natural History Press.

———. (1983) *Yanomamö: The fierce people* (3rd ed.). New York: Holt, Rinehart & Winston.

———. (1992). *Yanomamö: The last days of Eden*. San Diego: Harcourt Brace Jovanovich.

———. (1993, October 23). Covering up the Yanomamö massacre. *New York Times*, Op. Ed.

———. (1995). L'Ethnologie du déshonneur: Brief response to Lizot. *American Ethnologist, 22*(1), 187–189.

———. (1997). *Yanomamö: The last days of Eden* (5th ed.). San Diego: Harcourt Brace Jovanovich.

Chagnon, N. A. & Hames, R. (1979). Protein deficiency and tribal warfare in Amazonia: New Data. *Science, 203* (4383), 10–15.

Chagnon, N. A., & Irons, W. (Eds.). (1979). *Evolutionary biology and human social behavior: An anthropological perspective*. North Scituate, MA: Duxbury Press.

Chagnon, N. A., & Melancon, T. (1983). Epidemics in a tribal population. In *The impact of contact: Two Yanomamö cases*, Report No. 11 (pp. 53–75). Cambridge, MA: Cultural Survival International.

Chance, N. A. (1990). *The Inupiat and Arctic Alaska: An ethnography of development.* Fort Worth, TX: Harcourt Brace College.

Cheal, D. (1993). Changing household financial strategies: Canadian couples today. *Human Ecology, 21*(2), 197–213.

Chibnik, M. (Ed.). (1987). *Farm work and fieldwork: American agriculture in anthropological perspective.* Ithaca, NY: Cornell University Press.

Chira, S. (1995). Struggling to find stability when divorce is a pattern. *New York Times*, pp. 1, 42.

Chomsky, N. (1972). *Language and mind.* New York: Harcourt Brace Jovanovich.

Clark, K., & Uhl, C. (1987). Farming, fishing, and fire in the history of the upper Rio Negro region of Venezuela. *Human Ecology, 15*, 1–26.

Clarke, K. B. (1993). Racial progress & retreat: A personal memoir. In H. Hill & J. E. Jones (Eds.), *Race in America: The struggle for equality* (pp. 3–18). Madison: University of Wisconsin Press.

Clarke, L. (1989). *Acceptable risk? Making decisions in a toxic environment.* Berkeley and Los Angeles: University of California Press.

Colchester, M. (1985). *The health and survival of the Venezuelan Yanomamö* (IGWA Document No. 53). Cambridge, MA: Cultural Survival International.

Cole, J. B. (Ed.). (1988). *Anthropology for the nineties: Introductory readings.* New York: Free Press.

Collier, J., Jr. (1967). *Visual anthropology: Photography as a research method.* New York: Holt, Rinehart & Winston.

Collins, W. T. (1974). An analysis of the Memphis garbage strike of 1968. *Public Affairs Forum, 3*, 1–6. Memphis State University.

Colson, E. (1954). Ancestral spirits and social structure among the plateau Tonga. *International Archives of Ethnography, 1*, 21–68.

Conant, F. P. (1965). Korok: A variable unit of physical and social space among the Pokot of East Africa. *American Anthropologist, 67*, 429–434.

———. (1982). Thorns paired sharply recurved: Cultural controls and rangeland quality in East Africa. In B. Spooner & H. Mann (Eds.), *Anthropology and desertification: Dryland ecology in social perspective* (pp. 111–122). London: Academic Press.

———. (1984). Remote sensing, discovery, and generalizations in human ecology. In E. Moran (Ed.), *The ecosystem concept in anthropology.* Boulder, CO: Westview Press.

———. (1988). Social Consequences of AIDS: Implications for East Africa and the Eastern United States. In R. Kulstad (Ed.), *AIDS 1988: American Association for the Advancement of Science Symposia Papers* (pp. 147–156). Washington, DC: AAAS.

———. (1994). Human ecology and space age technology: Some predictions. *Human Ecology, 22*(3), 405–413.

Cook, S. (1966). The obsolete anti-market mentality: A critique of the substantive approach to economic anthropology. *American Anthropologist, 68*, 323–345.

Coughenour, M. B., Ellis, J. E., Swift, D. M., Coppock, D. L., Galvin, K., McCabe, J. T., & Hart, T. C. (1985). Energy extraction and use in a nomadic pastoral ecosystem. *Science, 230*, 619–625.

Coult, A. D., & Habenstein, R. W. (1965). *Gross tabulations of Murdock's world ethnographic sample.* Columbia: University of Missouri Press.

Cowell, A. (1994, September 11). Cairo parley hits anew on migrants. *New York Times*, p. 10.

Craige, B. J. (Ed.). (1988). *Literature, language and politics.* Athens: University of Georgia Press.

Creed, G. W. (1994). Bulgaria: Anthropological corrections to cold war stereotypes. In M. Ember, C. Ember, & D. Levinson (Eds.), *Portraits of culture.* Englewood Cliffs, NJ: Prentice Hall.

Cronk, L. (1991). Human behavioral ecology. *Annual Review of Anthropology, 20*, 25–53.

Cunningham, W. P., & Saigo, B. W. (1995). *Environmental science, a global concern.* Dubuque, IA: William C Brown.

Curran, J. W., Jaffe, H. W., Hardy, A. M., Morgan, W. M., Selik, R. M., & Dondero, T. J. (1988). Epidemiology of AIDS and HIV infection in the United States. In R. Kulstad (Ed.), *AIDS 1988: American Association for the Advancement of Science Symposia Papers* (pp. 19–34). Washington, DC: AAAS.

Cyriax, R. J. (1939). *Sir John Franklin's last Arctic expedition.* London: Methuen.

Dalton, G. (1962). Traditional production in primitive African economies. *Quarterly Journal of Economics, 76*, 360–378.

———. (1972). Peasantries in anthropology and history. *Current Anthropology, 13*, 385–415.

D'Andrade, R. G. (1973). Cultural constructions of reality. In L. Nader & T. W. Maretski (Eds.), *Cultural illness and health: Essays in human adaptation.* Washington, DC: American Anthropological Association.

D'Aquili, E. (1972). *The biopsychological determinants of culture.* McCaleb Modulein Anthropology. Reading, MA: Addison-Wesley.

Davis, W. (1988). *Passage of darkness: The ethnobiology of the Haitian Zombie.* Chapel Hill: University of North Carolina Press.

———. (1993). Death of a people. Logging in the Penan homeland. *Cultural Survival Quarterly, 17*(3), 15–20.

Dawson, J. L. M. (1967). Cultural and psychological influences upon spatial perceptual processes in West Africa. *International Journal of Psychology, 2*, 115–128, 171–185.

Deb, D. (1996). Of cast net and caste identity: Memetic differentiation between two fishing communities of Karnataka. *Human Ecology 24*(1), 109–124.

Denevan, W., Treacy, J., Alcorn, J., Paddoch, C., Denslow, J., & Paitan, S. (1984). Indigenous agroforestry in the Peruvian Amazon: Bora Indian management of swidden fallows. *Interciencia, 9*, 346–357.

Denich, B. (1994). Dismembering Yugoslavia: Nationalist ideologies and the symbolic revival of genocide. *American Ethnologist, 21*(2), 367–390.

Dennett, D. C. (1994). *Darwin's dangerous idea: Evolution and the meaning of life.* New York: Simon & Schuster.

Diamond, J. (1994). Race without color. *Discover, 15*(11), 82–91.

Dietz, T. (1987). *Pastoralists in dire straits.* Netherlands Geographical Studies (No. 49). Amsterdam: University of Amsterdam, Institute for Social Geography.

Divale, W., & Harris, M. (1978). The male supremacist complex: Discovery of a cultural invention. *American Anthropologist, 80*, 668–671.

Dore, R. P. (1994). *Shinohata: A portrait of a Japanese village.* Berkeley and Los Angeles: University of California Press.

Douglas, M. (1962). The Lele resistance to change. In E. E. LeClair, Jr., & H. K. Schneider (Eds.), *Economic anthropology: Readings in theory and analysis.* New York: Holt, Rinehart & Winston.

Dove, M. R. (1984). The Chayanov slope in a Swidden society: Household demography and extensive agriculture in Western Kalimantan. In P. Durrenburger (Ed.), *Chayanov, peasants, and economic anthropology* (pp. 97–132). Orlando, FL: Academic Press.

———. (1988). Introduction. In M. R. Dove (Ed.), *The real and imagined role of culture in development: Case studies from Indonesia* (pp. 1–37). Honolulu: University of Hawaii Press.

Downs, J. F. (1965). The social consequences of a dry well. *American Anthropologist, 67,* 1387–1417.

Dozier, E. P. (1970). *The Pueblo Indians of North America.* New York: Holt, Rinehart & Winston.

Draper, P. (1976). Social and economic constraints on child life among the !Kung. In R. B. Lee & I. DeVore (Eds.), *Kalahari hunter-gatherers* (pp. 199–217). Cambridge, MA: Harvard University Press.

Duben, A. (1986). The significance of family and kinship in urban Turkey. In C. Kaˉitcibasi (Ed.), *Sex roles, family and community in Turkey.* Indiana University Turkish Studies No. 3. Bloomington: Indiana University Press.

Dunbar, R. (1997). *Grooming, gossip, and the evolution of language.* Cambridge, MA: Harvard University Press.

Duranti, A. (1994). *From grammar to politics: Linguistic anthropology in a Western Samoan village.* Berkeley and Los Angeles: University of California Press.

Durham, E. (1987). *High Albania.* Boston: Beacon.

Durham, W. H. (1991). *Coevolution: Genes, Culture, and Human Diversity.* Stanford, CA: Stanford University Press.

Durkheim, E. (1961). *The elementary forms of the religious life.* New York: Collier. (First published 1912.)

———. (1964). *The division of labor in society.* New York: Free Press.

Durrenberger, P. (Ed.). (1984). *Chayanov, Peasants, and Economic Anthropology.* Orlando, FL: Academic Press.

Dyson-Hudson, N., & Dyson-Hudson, R. (1982). The structure of East African herds and the future of East African herders. *Development and Change, 13,* 213–-238.

Dyson-Hudson, R. (1988). Ecology of nomadic Turkana pastoralists: A discussion. In E. Whitehead, C. Hutchinson, B. Timmerman, & R. Varady (Eds.), *Arid lands: Today and tomorrow* (pp. 701–703). Boulder, CO: Westview.

Dyson-Hudson, R., & Little, M. A. (Eds.). (1983). *Rethinking human adaptation: Cultural and biological models.* Boulder, CO: Westview.

Dyson-Hudson, R., & Smith, E. A. (1978). Human territoriality. *American Anthropologist, 80,* 21–42.

Earle, T. (Ed.). (1991). *Chiefdoms: Power, economy and ideology.* Cambridge: Cambridge University Press.

Eder, J. F. (1996). Batak foraging camps today: A window to the history of a hunting-gathering economy. In Bates, D. G. & Lees, S. H. (Eds.), *Case Studies in human ecology* (pp. 85–102). New York: Plenum.

Edgerton, R. B. (1971). *The individual in cultural adaptation: A study of four East African peoples.* Berkeley and Los Angeles: University of California Press.

Eggan, F. (1950). *Social organization of the Western Pueblo.* Chicago: University of Chicago Press.

Ehrlich, P., & Ehrlich, A. H. (1972). *Population, resources, environment: Issues in human ecology* (2nd ed.). San Francisco: Freeman.

Eicher, M. (1988). *Nonsexist research methods: A practical guide.* London: Allen & Unwin.

Eliade, M. (1975). In W. C. Beane & W. G. (Eds.), *Myths, rites, symbols: A Mircea Eliade reader* (Vol. 2). New York: Harper & Row.

Ember, C. R. (1978). Myths about hunter-gatherers. *Ethnology, 17*(4), 439–448.

———. (1983). The relative decline in woman's contribution to agriculture with intensification. *American Anthropologist, 85,* 285–304.

———. (1992). Resource unpredictability, mistrust & war. *Journal of Conflict Resolution, 36*(2), 242–262.

Ember, C. R., & Ember, M. (1992). Peace between participatory polities: A cross-cultural test of the "democracies rarely fight each other" hypothesis. *World Politics, 44*(4), 573–599.

Ember, C. R., Ember, M. & Pasternak, B. (1974). On the development of unilineal descent. *Journal of Anthropological Research, 30,* 69–94.

Ember, M., & Ember, C. R. (1971). The conditions favoring matrilocal versus patrilocal residence. *American Anthropologist, 73,* 571–594.

Ember, M., Ember, C., & Levinson, D. (Eds.). (1994). *Portraits of culture.* Englewood Cliffs, NJ: Prentice Hall.

Eminov, A. (1990). There are no Turks in Bulgaria: Rewriting history by administrative fiat. In K. Karpat (Ed.), *The Turks of Bulgaria: The History, Culture and Political Fate of a Minority.* Istanbul: Isis Press.

Engels, F. (1972). In E. B. Leacock (Ed.), *The origin of the family, private property, and the state.* New York: International Publishers. (First published 1884.)

Escobar, A. (1991). Anthropology and the development encounter: The making and marketing of development anthropology. *American Ethnologist, 18*(4), 658–682.

———. (1994). Welcome to "Cyberia." *Current Anthropology 18*(3). 38–45.

Estioko-Griffin, A., & Griffin, P. B. (1981). Woman the hunter: The Agta. In F. Dahlberg (Ed.), *Woman the Gatherer* (pp. 121–151). New Haven, CT: Yale University Press.

Etienne, M., & Leacock, E. (Eds.). (1988). *Women and colonization: Anthropological perspectives.* South Hadley, MA: Bergin & Garvey.

Evans-Pritchard, E. E. (1940). *The Nuer: A description of the modes of livelihood and political institutions of a Nilotic people.* Oxford: Clarendon Press.

Fagan, B. M. (1992). *People of the Earth: An introduction to world prehistory* (7th ed.). New York: HarperCollins College.

Farb, P. (1974). *Word play: What happens when people talk.* New York: Knopf.

Farley, R. (1993). The common destiny of blacks and whites: Observations about social and economic status of the race. In H. Hill & J. E. Jones (Eds.), *Race in America: The struggle for equality* (pp. 197–233). Madison: University of Wisconsin Press.

Fay, R. E., Turner, C. F., Klassen, A. D, & Gagnon, J. H. (1989). Prevalence and patterns of same-gender sexual contact among men. *Science, 243,* 338–348.

Feder, B. J. (1994, March 7). Big decisions before spring planting. *New York Times*, p. D1.

Feinberg, R. (1988). Margaret Mead and Samoa: Coming of age in fact and fiction. *American Anthropologist, 90,* 656–663.

Feinman, G., & Nicholas, P. (1992). Prehispanic interregional interaction in southern Mexico: The Valley of Oaxaca and the Ejutla Valley. In E. M. Schortman & P. A. Urban (Eds.), *Resources, power, and interregional interaction* (pp. 77–114). New York: Plenum.

Feinmen, G. & Neitzel, J. (1984). Too many types: An overview of sedentary prestate societies in the Americas. *Advances in Archaeological Methods and Theory, 7,* 39–102. Orlando, FL: Academic Press.

Feit, H. A. (1973). The ethno-ecology of the Waswanipi Cree; or how hunters can manage their resources. In B. Cox (Ed.), *Cultural ecology: Readings on the Canadian native peoples.* Toronto: McClelland & Stewart.

———. (1994). The enduring pursuit: Land, time and social relationships in anthropological models of hunter-gatherers and in Subarctic hunters' images. In E. S. Burch, Jr. & L. J. Ellanna (Eds.), *Key issues in Hunter-gatherer research* (pp. 421–439). Providence, RI: Berg Publishers.

Ferguson, B. R. (Ed.). (1984). *Warfare, culture, and environment.* New York: Academic Press.

———. (1992). Tribal warfare. *Scientific American, 256*(1), 108–113

———. (1995). A reputation for war. *Natural History, 104*(4).

———. (1995). *Yanomamö warfare: A political history.* Santa Fe, NM: SAR Press.

Ferraro, G. P. (1990). *The cultural dimension of international business.* Englewood Cliffs, NJ: Prentice Hall.

Fischer, J. L. (1958). Social influences on the choice of a linguistic variant. *Word, 14,* 47–56.

Fisher, H. E. (1987). The four-year itch: Do divorce patterns reflect our evolutionary heritage? *Natural History, 10,* 22–33.

Fisher, M. (1980). *Iran: From religious dispute to revolution.* Cambridge, MA: Harvard University Press.

Flinn, M. (1986). Correlates of reproductive success in a Caribbean village. *Human Ecology, 14,* 225–245.

Flowers, N. M. (1988). The Spread of AIDS in rural Brazil. In R. Kulstad (Ed.), *AIDS 1988: American Association for the Advancement of Science Symposia Papers* (pp. 159–168). Washington, DC: AAAS.

Flowers, N., Gross, D., Ritter, M., & Werner, D. (1975). Protein capture and cultural development in the Amazon. *American Anthropologist, 3,* 526–549.

———. (1982). Variation in Swidden practices in four central Brazilian Indian Societies. *Human Ecology, 10,* 203–217.

Ford, R. I. (1972). An ecological perspective on the Eastern Pueblos. In A. Ortiz (Ed.), *New Perspectives on the Pueblos.* Albuquerque: University of New Mexico Press.

Foster, B. (1974). Ethnicity and commerce. *American Ethnologist, 1,* 437–448.

Foster, B., & Scidman, S. (1982). Urban structures derived from collections of overlapping subsets. *Urban Anthropology, 11,* 171–182.

Foster, G. M. (1969). *Applied anthropology.* Boston: Little, Brown.

Fox, R. (1994). Evil wrought in the name of good. *Anthropology Newsletter* (March), 2.

———. (1994). *The challenge of anthropology: Old encounters and new excursions.* New Brunswick, NJ: Transaction Publishers.

Frank, A. G. (1969). *Capitalism and underdevelopment in Latin America.* New York: Monthly Review Press.

Frank, R. H. (1988). *Passion within reason: The strategic role of the emotions.* New York: Norton.

Fratkin, E. (1991a). *Surviving drought and development: Ariaal pastoralists of Northern Kenya.* Boulder, CO: Westview Press.

———. (1991b). Surviving drought and development. Ariaal pastoralists of Kenya. *Human Ecology, 23*(3).

Fratkin, E., Galvin, K., & Roth, E. A. (1994). *African pastoralist systems: An integrated approach.* Boulder, CO: L. Reinner Publishers.

Fratkin, E., & Roth, E. A. (1996). Who survives drought? Measuring winners and losers among the Ariaal Rendille pastoralists of Kenya. In Bates, D. G. & Lees, S. H. (Eds.), *Case studies in human ecology* (pp. 159–174). New York: Plenum.

Frayer, D. W., Wolpoff, M. H., Thorne, A. G., & Pope, G. G. (1994). Getting it straight. *American Anthropologist, 96*(2), 424–438.

Frayser, S. (1985). *Varieties of sexual experience.* New Haven, CT: HRAF Press.

Frazer, J. (1959). *The new golden bough* (Abr. ed.). New York: Criterion. (First published 1900.)

Freeman, D. (1983). *Margaret Mead and Samoa: The making and unmaking of an anthropological myth.* Cambridge, MA: Harvard University Press.

Freeman, J. D. (1961). On the concept of the Kindred. *Journal of the Royal Anthropological Institute, 91,* 192–220.

Freeman, M. M. R. (1971). A social and ecological analysis of systematic female infanticide among the Netsilik Eskimo. *American Anthropologist, 73,* 1011–1019.

Freilich, M. (1971). *Meaning of culture: A reader in cultural anthropology.* Lexington, MA: Xerox College.

Fricke, T. (1994). *Himalayan households.* New York: Columbia University Press.

Fried, M. (1967). *The evolution of political society: An essay in political anthropology.* New York: Random House.

Fromkin, V., & Rodman, R. (1988). *An introduction to linguistics* (4th ed.). New York: Holt, Rinehart & Winston.

Gailey, C. W. (1987). *Kinship to kingship: Gender hierarchy and state formation in the Tongan Islands.* Austin: University of Texas Press.

Galvin, K. A. (1988). Nutritional status as an indicator of impending food stress. *Disasters, 12,* 147–156.

Gardner, A., & Gardner, B. (1969). Teaching sign language to a chimpanzee. *Science, 165,* 664–672.

Geertz, C. (1966). Religion as a cultural System. In M. Banton (Ed.), *Anthropological approaches to the study of religion.* New York: Praeger.

———. (1969). Two types of ecosystems. In A. P. Vayda (Ed.), *Environment and cultural behavior.* New York: Natural History Press.

Giampietro, M., Bukkens, S. F., & Pimientel, D. (1993). Labor productivity: A biophysical definition and assessment. *Human Ecology, 21,* 229–260.

Gibbs, J. L., Jr. (1963). The Kpelle Moot. *Africa, 33,* 1–10.

Gilmore, D. D. (1987). *Aggression and community: Paradoxes of Andalusian culture*. New Haven, CT: Yale University Press.

———. (1990). *Manhood in the making: The cultural construction of masculinity*. New Haven, CT: Yale University Press.

———. (1991). Subjectivity and subjugation: Fieldwork in the stratified community. *Human Organization, 50*, 215–224.

———. (1994). The "mayete" as object and stereotype in Andalusian proletarian poetry. *Ethnology, 33*(4), 353–365.

Gladwin, C., & Butler, J. (1982). Gardening: A survival strategy for the small, part-time Florida farm. *Proceedings Florida State Horticultural Society, 95*, 264–268.

Glenny, M. (1992). *The fall of Yugoslavia: The third Balkan war*. London: Penguin.

Gluckman, M. (1965). *Politics, law, and ritual in tribal society*. Chicago: Aldine.

Goldberg, J. (1995, January 22). A war without purpose in a community without identity. *New York Times Magazine*, pp. 36–39.

Goldschmidt, W. (1947). *As you saw*. New York: Harcourt, Brace.

———. (1971). *Exploring the ways of mankind*. New York: Holt, Rinehart & Winston.

Goldsmith, E., & Hildyard, N. (1984). *The social and environmental effects of large dams*. San Francisco: Sierra Club.

Goleman, D. (1988, August 13). Sex roles reign powerful as ever in the emotions. *New York Times*, pp. C1-C2.

———. (1988, April 10). An emerging theory on Blacks' IQ scores. *New York Times*, Education Supplement, pp. 22–24.

Good, K. (1995). The Yanomamö keep on trekking. *Natural History, 104*(4).

Goodall, J. Van L. (1971). *In the shadow of man*. Boston: Houghton Mifflin.

Goodenough, W. H. (1955). A problem in Malayo-Polynesian social organization. *American Anthropologist, 57*, 71–83.

———. (1970). *Description and comparison in cultural anthropology*. Chicago: Aldine.

Gorkin, M. (1993). *Days of honey, days of onion: The story of a Palestinian family in Israel*. Berkeley and Los Angeles: University of California Press.

Gorman, E. M. (1989). The AIDS epidemic in San Francisco: Epidemiological and anthropological perspectives. In A. Podolefsky & P. J. Brown (Eds.), *Applying anthropology* (pp. 192–201). Mountain View, CA: Mayfield Press.

Gorman, P. (1994). A people at risk. In E. Angeloni (Ed.), *Annual editions: Anthropology*. Guilford, CT: Dushkin Publishers.

Gossen, G. H. (1972). Temporal and spatial equivalents in Chamula ritual symbolism. In W. A. Lessa & E. S. Vogt, *Reader in comparative religion: An anthropological approach*. New York: Harper & Row.

Gottesfeld Johnson, L. M. (1994). Aboriginal burning for vegetation management in Northwest British Columbia. *Human Ecology, 22*, 171–188.

Gough, E. K. (1959). The Nayars and the definition of marriage. *Journal of the Royal Anthropological Institute, 89*, 23–34.

———. (1971). Nuer kinship: A Reexamination. In T. O. Beidelman (Ed.), *The translation of culture* (pp. 79–122). London: Tavistock.

Gould, J. L., & Marler, P. (1987). Learning by instinct. *Scientific American, 256*, 74–85.

Gould, S. J. (1986). Cardboard Darwinism: This view of life. *Natural History, 95*, 14–21.

———. (1989). Tires to sandals: This view of life. *Natural History 98*, 8–16.

———. (1994, October 20). So near and yet so far. *New York Review of Books*, pp. 229–260.

———. (1996). The Diet of Worms and the defenestration of Prague. *Natural History* (Dec. 1996), 18–65.

Graves, T. D. (1970). The personal adjustment of Navajo Indian migrants to Denver, Colorado. *American Anthropologist, 72*, 35–54.

Greenberg, J. (1993). *Language in America*. Palo Alto, CA: Stanford University Press.

Gregor, T. (1985). *Anxious pleasures: The sexual lives of an Amazonian people*. Chicago: University of Chicago Press.

———. (1988). *Culture, people, nature: An introduction to general anthropology* (5th ed.). New York: Harper & Row.

Grigg, D. B. (1974). *The agricultural systems of the world: An evolutionary approach*. Cambridge: Cambridge University Press.

Gross, D. R. (1983). Village movement in relation to resources in Amazonia. In R. B. Hames & W. T. Vickers (Eds.), *Adaptive responses of Native Amazonians* (pp. 429–499). New York: Academic Press.

———. (1984). Time allocation: A tool for the study of cultural behavior. *Annual Review of Anthropology, 13*, 519–558.

Gross, D. R., & Underwood, B. A. (1971). Technological change and caloric costs: Sisal agriculture in Northeastern Brazil. *American Anthropologist, 73*, 725–740.

Hackenberg, R. (1962). Economic alternatives in arid lands: A case study of the Pima and Papago Indians. *Ethnology, 1*, 186–195.

Hames, R. (1983). Monoculture, polyculture, and polyvariety in tropical forest Swidden cultivation. *Human Ecology, 11*, 13–34.

Hammel, H. A. (1994). Meeting the Minotaur. *Anthropology Newsletter, 36*(4).

Harris, M. (1966). The cultural ecology of India's sacred cattle. *Current Anthropology, 7*, 51–66.

———. (1974). *Patterns of race in the Americas*. New York: Norton.

———. (1984). A cultural materialist theory of band and village warfare: The Yanomamö test. In B. R. Ferguson (Ed.), *Warfare, culture, and environment* (pp. 111–140). New York: Academic Press.

———. (1985). *Good to eat: Riddles of food and culture*. New York: Simon & Schuster.

———. (1987). Comment on Vayda's review of good to eat: Riddles of food and culture. *Human Ecology, 15*, 511–518.

———. (1988). *Culture, people, nature: An introduction to general anthropology* (5th ed.). New York: Harper & Row.

Hart, C. W., & Pilling, A. R. (1960). *The Tiwi of North Australia*. New York: Holt, Rinehart & Winston.

Hart, T. B., & Hart, J. A. (1996). The ecological basis of hunter-gatherer subsistence in African rain forests: The Mbuti of eastern Zaire. In Bates, D. G. & Lees, S. H. (Eds.), *Cast studies in human ecology* (pp. 55–83). New York: Plenum.

Hayden, B. (1994). Competition, labor and complex hunter-gatherers. In E. S. Burch, Jr. & L. J. Ellanna (Eds.), *Key issues in hunter-gatherer research* (pp. 223–239). Providence, RI: Berg Publishers.

Headland, T. (1987). The wild yam question: How well could independent hunter-gatherers live in a tropical forest ecosystem? *Human Ecology, 15,* 463–492.

Hemming, J. (Ed.). (1985). *Change in the Amazon Basin: Vol. 2: Man's impact on forests and rivers*. Manchester, Eng.: Manchester University Press.

Herdt, G. (1987). AIDS and anthropology. *Anthropology Today, 3,* 1–3.

Hernstein, R. J., & Murray, C. (1994). *The bell curve: Intelligence and class structure in American life.* New York: Free Press.

Herskovits, M. (1924). A preliminary consideration of the cultural areas of Africa. *American Anthropologist, 26,* 50–63.

Hertzberg, H. T. E. (1989). Engineering anthropology: Past, present, and potential. In A. Podolefsky & P. J. Brown (Eds.), *Applying anthropology: An introductory reader*. Mountain View, CA: Mayfield Press.

Hiatt, L. R. (1980). Polyandry in Sri Lanka: A test case for parental investment. *Man, 15,* 583–598.

Hill, K., Hawkes, K., Hurtado, M., & Kaplan, H. (1984). Seasonal variance in the diet of the Ache hunter-gatherers in eastern Paraguay. *Human Ecology, 12,* 101–136.

Hockett, C. F., & Ascher, R. (1964). The human revolution. *Current Anthropology, 5,* 135–168.

Hoebel, E. A. (1954). *The law of primitive man.* Cambridge, MA: Harvard University Press.

Hoijer, H. (1954). The Sapir-Whorf hypothesis. In H. Hoijer (Ed.), *Language in culture* (No. 79). Washington, DC: American Anthropological Association.

Holling, C. S. (1973). Resilience and stability of ecological systems. *Annual Review of Ecology and Systematics, 4,* 1–23.

Holmberg, A. (1958). Research and development approach to the study of change. *Human Organization, 17,* 12–16.

Holmes, R. (1984). Non-dietary modifiers of nutritional status in tropical forest populations of Venezuela. *Interciencia 9,* 386–391.

———. (1985). Nutritional status and cultural change in Venezuela's Amazon Territory. In J. Heming (Ed.), *Change in the Amazon Basin: Vol. 2. Man's impact on forests and rivers.* Manchester Eng.: Manchester University Press.

Hopkins, N. (1983). The social impact of mechanization. In A. Richards & P. L. Martin (Eds.), *Migration, mechanization, and agricultural labor markets in Egypt* (pp. 181–197). Boulder, CO: Westview Press.

Horgan, J. (1988). The violent Yanomamö: Science and citizen. *Scientific American, 255,* 17–18.

Horowitz, D. (1985). *Ethnic groups in conflict.* Berkeley and Los Angeles: University of California Press.

Horowitz, M. (1988). Anthropology and the new development agenda. In Bulletin of the Institute for Development Anthropology, *Development Anthropology Network, 6,* 1–4.

———. (1994). Development anthropology in the mid-1990s. *Development Anthropology Newsletter, 12*(1, 2), 1–14.

Howell, N. (1976). *Normal selection rates of the demographic patterns of the !Kung San.* Paper presented at the 1976 meeting of the American Anthropological Association, Washington, DC.

———. (1979). *Demography of the Dobe !Kung.* New York: Academic Press.

Hughes, A. L. (1988). *Evolution and human kinship.* New York: Oxford University Press.

Hultkrantz, A. (1994). Religion and ecology of Northern Eurasian/Siberian peoples. In T. Irimoto & T. Yamada (Eds.), *Circumpolar religion and ecology* (pp. 347–374). Tokyo: University of Tokyo Press.

Humphries, S. (1993). The intensification of traditional agriculture among Yucatec Maya farmers: Facing up to the dilemma of livelihood sustainability. *Human Ecology, 21,* 87–102.

Hurd, J. P. (Ed.). (In press). *The significance of evolutionary biology for research on human altruism.* Lewiston, NY: Edwin Mellen Press.

Ingold, T. (1980). *Hunters, pastoralists, and ranchers.* Cambridge: Cambridge University Press.

Irons, W. (1975). The Yomut Turkmen: A study of social organization among a Central Asian Turkic-speaking population. Anthropological Papers (No. 58). Ann Arbor: University of Michigan, Museum of Anthropology.

———. (1979). Natural selection, adaptation and human social behavior. Chagnon, N.A. & Irons, W. G. (Eds.) 1979. *Evolution, Biology and Human Social Behavior.* North Scituat, MA. Duxsbury Press.

———. (1991). How did morality evolve? *Zygon: Journal of Religion and Science, 26,* 49–89.

———. (1995). Morality as an evolved adaptation. In James P. Hurd (Ed.), *The Biology of Morality.* Lewiston, NY: Edwin Mellen Press.

Jablonka, E., & Avital, E. (1995, January 3). Heredity's more than genes, new theory proposes. *New York Times,* pp. B13ff.

Johnson, G. A. (1983). Decision-making organization and pastoral nomad camp size. *Human Ecology, 11,* 175–200.

Johnson, P. L. (1988). Women and development: A highland New Guinea example. *Human Ecology, 16,* 105–122.

Johnson, P. L. (1996). Changing household composition, labor patters, and gertility of a highland New Guinea population. In Bates, D. G. & Lees, S. H. (Eds.), *Case studies in human ecology* (pp. 237–250). New York: Plenum.

Johnson, T. M., & Sargent, C. F. (Eds.). (1990). *Medical anthropology: Contemporary theory and method.* New York: Praeger.

Johnston, B. R. (1994). *Who pays the price: The sociocultural context of environmental crisis.* Washington, DC: Island Press.

Jolly, C. J., & White, R. (1995). *Physical anthropology* (5th ed.). New York: McGraw-Hill.

Jorgenson, J. (1971) Indians and the Metropolis. In J. O. Waddell & O. M. Watson (Eds.), *The American Indian in urban society*. Boston: Little, Brown.

Katz, S. H., Hediger, M. L., & Valleroy, L. A. (1974). Traditional maize processing in the new world. *Science, 17,* 765–773.

Keesing, R. M. (1975). *Kin groups and social structure.* New York: Holt, Rinehart & Winston.

Kelly, R. (1985). *The Nuer conquest.* Ann Arbor: University of Michigan Press.

Kemp, W. B. (1971). The flow of energy in a hunting society. *Scientific American, 225,* 104–115.

Khaldun, I. (1958). Franz Rosenthal (Trans.), *The Mugaddimah: An introduction to history* (Vol. 1). London: Kegan Paul. (Original work published in 1377 A. D.)

Kili, S. (1991). *Modernity and tradition: Dilemmas concerning women's rights in Turkey*. Paper presented at the annual meeting of the International Society of Political Psychology, Helsinki.

Kimball, J. C. (1984). *The Arabs 1984-85: An atlas and almanac*. Washington, DC: The American Educational Trust.

Kirch, P. V. (1994). *The wet and the dry: Irrigation and agricultural intensification*. Chicago: University of Chicago Press.

Kirkby, A. V. (1973). *The use of land and water resources in the past and present, Valley of Oaxaca, Mexico*. Ann Arbor: Museum of Anthropology, University of Michigan.

Konner, M. (1983). *The tangled web*. New York: Harper & Row.

———. (1988, August 14). Body and mind: The aggressors. *New York Times Magazine*, pp. 33–34.

Konstantinov, Y. (1992). "Nation-state" and "minority" types of discourse problems of communication between the majority and Islamic minorities in contemporary Bulgaria. *Innovation in Social Science Research, 5*(3), 75–89.

Konstantinov, Y., Gulbrand, A., & Igla, B. (1991). Names of the Bulgarian Pomaks. *Nordlyd, 17*, 8–118.

Koop, C. E. (1988). Foreword: Current issues in AIDS. In R. Kulstad (Ed.), *AIDS 1988: American Association for the Advancement of Science Symposia Papers* (pp. vii–viii). Washington, DC: AAAS.

Kopytoff, I. (1977). Matrilineality, residence, and residential zone. *American Ethnology, 4*, 539–558.

Korte, C., & Milgram, S. (1970). Acquaintance networks between racial groups: Application of the small world method. *Journal of Personality and Social Psychology, 15*, 101–108.

Kramer, M. (1987). *Three farms: Making milk, meat, and money from the American soil*. Cambridge, MA: Harvard University Press.

Kroeber, A. L., & Kluckhohn, C. (1952). *Culture: A critical review of concepts and definitions*. New York: Knopf.

Kwong, P. (1994, October 17). China's human traffickers. *The Nation*, pp. 422–425.

Labov, W. (1964). Phonological correlates of social stratifications. *American Anthropologist, 66* (Special Issue, Pt. 2), 164–176.

Laderman, C. (1983). *Wives and midwives: Childbirth and nutrition in rural Malaysia*. Berkeley and Los Angeles: University of California Press.

Lako, G. T. (1988). The impact of the Jonglei scheme on the economy of the Dinka. In J. H. Bodley (Ed.), *Tribal peoples and development issues: A global overview*. Palo Alto, CA: Mayfield Press.

Lansing, S. J. (1991). *Priests and programmers: Technologies of power in the engineered landscape of Bali*. Princeton, NJ: Princeton University Press.

———. (1995). The Balinese. In G. Spindler & L. Spindler (Eds.), *Case studies in cultural anthropology*. Fort Worth, TX: Harcourt Brace College.

Lardy, N. R. (1985). State intervention and peasant opportunities. In W. L. Parish (Ed.), *Chinese rural development: The great transformation* (pp. 33–56). Armonk, NY: M. E. Sharpe.

Laswell, H. (1936). *Politics: Who gets what, when, and how*. New York: McGraw-Hill.

Lawrence, P. (1964). *The road belong Cargo: A study of the Cargo movement in the Southern Madang District, New Guinea*. Manchester, Eng.: University of Manchester Press.

Leach, E. R. (1954). *Political systems of highland Burma*. New York: Humanities Press.

———. (1965). *Political systems of highland Burma*. Boston: Beacon Press.

———. (1982). *Social anthropology*. Glasgow: Fontana Paperbacks.

Leaf, M. J. (1972). *Information and behavior in a Sikh village: Social organization reconsidered*. Berkeley and Los Angeles: University of California Press.

Leavitt, G. C. (1989). The disappearance of the incest taboo. *American Anthropologist, 91*, 116–131.

Lee, R. B. (1968). What hunters do for a living, or, how to make out on scarce resources. In R. B. Lee & I. DeVore (Eds.), *Man the hunter*. Chicago: Aldine.

———. (1969). !Kung Bushmen subsistence: An input-output analysis. In A. P. Vayda (Ed.), *Environment and cultural behavior*. New York: Natural History Press.

———. (1979). *The !Kung San*. Cambridge: Cambridge University Press.

———. (1993). *The Dobe Ju/'hoansi*. Fort Worth, TX: Harcourt Brace College.

Lee, R. B., & DeVore, I. (Eds.). (1968). *Man the hunter*. Chicago: Aldine.

———. (1976). *Kalahari hunter-gatherers: Studies of the !Kung-San and their neighbors*. Cambridge, MA: Harvard University Press.

Lees, S. H. (1994). Irrigation and society. *Journal of Archeological Research, 2*(4), 361–378.

Lennihan, L. (1988). Wages of change: The unseen transformation in Northern Nigeria. *Human Organization 18*(3), 45–56.

Lepowsky, M. (1994). *Fruit of the motherland: Gender in an egalitarian society*. New York: Columbia University Press.

Leslie, P. W., & Fry, P. H. (1989). Extreme seasonality of births among nomadic Turkana pastoralists. *American Journal of Physical Anthropology 16*(2), 126–135.

Leslie, P. W., Fry, P. H., Galvin, K., & McCabe, J. T. (1988). Biological, behavioral, and ecological influences on fertility in Turkana pastoralists. In E. Whitehead & C. Hutchinson (Eds.), *Arid lands: Today and tomorrow* (pp. 705–726). Boulder, CO: Westview.

Lessa, W. A., & Vogt, E. Z. (1962). *Reader in comparative religion: An anthropological approach* (2nd ed). New York: Harper & Row.

Levi-Strauss, C. (1943). The social use of kinship terms among Brazilian Indians. *American Anthropologist, 45*, 398–409.

———. (1955). The structural study of myth. *Journal of American Folklore, 67*, 428–444.

———. (1969). *The raw and the cooked*. J. and D. Weightman (Trans.). New York: Harper Torch Book.

———. (1988). *The jealous potter*. Benedicte Chorier (Trans). Chicago: University of Chicago Press.

Levine, N. E. (1988). *The dynamics of polyandry: Kinship, domesticity, and population on the Tibetan border*. Chicago: University of Chicago Press.

Levinson, D., & Malone, M. J. (1980). *Toward explaining human culture*. New Haven, CT: HRAF Press.

Lewellen, T. C. (1992). *Political anthropology: An introduction* (2nd ed.). Westport, CT: Bergin & Garvey.

Lewis, H. T., & Ferguson, T. A. (1988). Yards, corridors, and mosaics: How to burn a boreal forest. *Human Ecology, 16*, 57–78.

Lewis, O. (1959). *Five families.* New York: Basic Books.

———. (1960). *Tepoztlán: A village in Mexico.* New York: Holt, Rinehart & Winston.

———. (1961). *The children of Sánchez.* New York: Random House.

———. (1966). *La vida: Puerto Rican family in the culture of poverty—San Juan and New York.* New York: Random House.

Lewis, P. (1993, November 10). Stoked by ethnic conflict: Refugee numbers swell. *New York Times*, p. A6.

Lewis, R. L. (1987). *Black coal miners in America: Race, class, and community conflict, 1790–1980.* Lexington: University Press of Kentucky.

Lieberman, P., & Crelin, E. (1971). On the speech of Neanderthal. *Linguistic Inquiry, 2*, 203–222.

Lightfoot, D. (1993). The cultural ecology of Puebloan Pebble-Mulch gardens. *Human Ecology, 21*(2), 115–144.

Lincoln, B. (1981). *Emerging from the chrysalis: Rituals of women's initiation.* New York: Oxford University Press.

Linton, R. (1937). One hundred percent American. *The American Mercury, 40*, 427–429. Reprinted in J. P. Spradley & M. A. Rynkiewich (Eds.), *The Nacerima* (pp. 405–406). Boston: Little, Brown.

Little, M. A. (1988). Introduction to the symposium: The Ecology of the nomadic Turkana pastoralists. In E. E. Whitehead, C. F. Hutchinson, B. N. Timmerman, & R. G. Vardy (Eds.), *Arid Lands today and tomorrow: Proceedings of an international research and development conference* (pp. 696–734). Boulder, CO: Westview Press.

Little, M. A., Dyson-Hudson, R., Ellis, J. E., Galvin, K. A., Leslie, P. W., & Swift, D. M. (1990). Ecosystem approaches in human biology: Their history & a case study of the South Turkana Ecosystem project. In E. F. Moran (Ed.), *The ecosystem approach in anthropology: From concept to practice* (pp. 389–434). Ann Arbor: University of Michigan Press.

Little, M. A., Galvin, K., & Leslie, P. W. (1988). Health and energy requirements of nomadic Turkana pastoralists. In I. de-Garine & G. A. Harrison (Eds.), *Coping with uncertainty in food supply* (pp. 288–315). Oxford: Oxford University Press.

Livingstone, F. B. (1968). The effects of warfare on the biology of the human species. In M. Fried, M. Harris, & R. Murphy, *War: The anthropology of armed conflict and aggression.* New York: Natural History Press.

Lizot, J. (1994). On warfare: An answer to N. A. Chagnon. *American Ethnologist, 21*, 841–858.

Lorenz, K. (1965). *Evolution and modification of behavior.* Chicago: University of Chicago Press.

Lowie, R. H. (1954). *Indians of the Plains.* New York: Mc-Graw-Hill.

Mageo, J. M. (1992). Male transvestism and cultural change in Samoa. *American Ethnologist, 19*, 443–459.

Magnarella, P. (1993). *Human materialism: A model of sociocultural systems and a strategy for analysis.* Gainesville: University of Florida Press.

Mahdi, M. (1971). *Ibn Khaldun's philosophy of history.* Chicago: University of Chicago Press.

Mair, L. (1965). *Introduction to social anthropology.* New York: Oxford University Press.

Malinowski, B. (1927). *Sex and repression in savage society.* London: Routledge & Kegan Paul.

———. (1931). Culture. In *Encyclopedia of the social sciences* (Vol. 4). New York: Macmillan.

———. (1954). *Magic, science, and religion and other essays.* Garden City, NY: Anchor/Doubleday.

———. (1961). *Argonauts of the Western Pacific.* New York: Dutton. (First published 1922.)

Manners, R. (1956). Tabara: Subculture of a tobacco and mixed crop municipality. In J. Steward (Ed.), *The people of Puerto Rico.* Urbana: University of Illinois Press.

Marett, R. R. (1909). *The threshold of religion.* London: Methuen.

Marks, J. (1994). Black, white, other. *Natural History, 103*, 32–35.

———. (1995). *Human biodiversity: Genes, race and history.* Hawthorne, NY: Aldine de Gruyter.

Marshall, L. (1960). !Kung Bushman bands. *Africa, 30*, 325–354.

———. (1961). Sharing, talking, and giving: Relief of social tensions among !Kung Bushmen. *Africa, 31*, 233–249.

———. (1965). The !Kung Bushman of the Kalahari Desert. In J. L.Gibbs, Jr. (Ed.), *Peoples of Africa.* New York: Holt, Rinehart & Winston.

Maybury-Lewis, D. (1992). *Millennium: Tribal wisdom and the modern world.* New York: Viking Penguin.

Mayer, A. C. (1968). The Indian caste system. *International Encyclopedia of the Social Sciences, 2*, 339–344.

Mayr, E. (1963). *Animal species and evolution.* Cambridge, MA: Harvard University Press.

McMillan, D. E. (1995). *Sahel visions: Planned settlement and river blindness control in Burkina Faso.* Tucson: University of Arizona Press.

McGovern, T., Bigelow, G., Amorosi, T., & Russell, D. (1996). Northern islands, human error, and environmental degradation. In Bates, D. G. & Lees, S. H. (Eds.), *Case studies in human ecology* (pp. 103–152). New York: Plenum.

McGovern, T. H. (1980). Cows, harp seals, and churchbells: Adaptation and extinction on Norse Greenland. *Human Ecology, 8*, 245–276.

Mead, M. (1935). *Sex and temperament in three primitive societies.* New York: William Morrow.

———. (1949). *Male and female.* New York: Morrow.

———. (1956). *New lives for old: Cultural transformation—Manus, 1928–1953.* New York: Morrow.

———. (1971). *Coming of age in Samoa.* New York: Morrow. (First published 1928.)

———. (1975). *Blackberry winter.* New York: Random House.

Meggars, B. J. (1971). *Amazonia: Man and culture in a counterfeit paradise.* Chicago: Aldine.

Meggitt, M. J. (1964). Male-female relationship in the highlands of Australian New Guinea. *American Anthropologist, 66* (Special Issue, Pt. 2), 204–224.

Meir, A. (1997). *As nomadism ends: The Israeli Bedouin of the Negev.* Boulder, CO: Westview Press.

Micklin, P. P. (1988). Desiccation of the Aral Sea: A water management disaster in the Soviet Union. *Science, 241*(1), 170–171, 175.

Middleton, J. (1960). *Lugbara religion: Ritual and authority among an East African people*. London: Oxford University Press.

Milan, F. (1970). The demography of an Alaskan Eskimo village. *Arctic Anthropology, 71*, 26–43.

Mills, C. W. (1959). *The power elite*. New York: Oxford University Press.

Milton, K. (1985). Ecological foundations for subsistence strategies among the Mbuti Pygmies. *Human Ecology, 13*, 71–78.

Mintz, S. W. (1986). *Sweetness and power: The place of sugar in modern history*. Harmondsworth, Eng.: Penguin.

Moghadam, V. (1993). *Modernizing women: Gender and social change in the Middle East*. Boulder, CO: Lynne Rienner.

Mooney, J. (1965). *The ghost dance religion and the Sioux outbreak of 1890*. Chicago: University of Chicago Press. (First published 1896.)

Mooney, K. A. (1978). The effect of rank and wealth on exchange among the Coast Salish. *Ethnology, 17*, 391–406.

Moore, O. K. (1957). Divination—A new perspective. *American Anthropologist, 59*, 69–74.

Moorehead, A. (1963). *Cooper's creek*. New York: Harper & Row.

Moran, E. F. (1990). Ecosystem ecology in biology and anthropology: A critical assessment. In E. F. Moran (Ed.), *The ecosystem approach in anthropology: From concept to practice* (pp. 3–40). Ann Arbor: University of Michigan Press.

———. (1990). Levels of analysis & analytical level shifting: Examples from Amazonian ecosystem research. In E. F. Moran (Ed.), *The ecosystem approach in anthropology: From concept to practice* (pp. 279–308). Ann Arbor: University of Michigan Press.

———. (1993). Deforestation and land use in the Brazilian Amazon. *Human Ecology, 21*, 1–21.

Morgan, L. H. (1963). *Ancient society*. New York: World. (First published 1877)

Morren, G. E. B., & Hyndam, D. C. (1987). The Taro monoculture of Central New Guinea. *Human Ecology, 15*, 301–315.

Moynihan, D. P. (1993). *Pandaemonium: Ethnicity in international politics*. New York: Oxford University Press.

Munson, H., Jr. (1988). *Islam and revolution in the Middle East*. New Haven, CT: Yale University Press.

Murdock, G. P. (1949). *Social Structure*. New York: Macmillan.

———. (1967). *The Ethnographic Atlas*. Pittsburgh, PA: University of Pittsburgh Press.

Murphy, R. F. (1986). *Cultural and social anthropology: An overture* (2nd ed.). Englewood Cliffs, NJ: Prentice Hall.

Murphy, Y., & Murphy, R. F. (1985). *Women of the forest* (2nd ed.). New York: Columbia University Press.

Mydans, S. (1997). Scientists developing "super rice" to feed Asia. *New York Times* International edition, April 6, p. 9.

Nadel, S. F. (1935). Nupe state and community. *Africa, 8*, 257–303.

Nader, L. (Ed.). (1965). The ethnology of law. *American Anthropologist, 67* (Special Issue, Pt. 2).

Nash. J. (n.d.). The revindication of indigenous identity: Mayan responses to state intervention in Mexico. Unpublished paper.

Nash, M. (1966). *Primitive and peasant economic systems*. San Francisco: Chandler.

Nations, J. D. (1994). Zapatism and nationalism. *Cultural Survival Quarterly, 18*(1), 31–33.

Navarro, M. (1989). The personal is political: Las madres de la Plaza de Mayo. In S. Eckstein (Ed.), *Protest and resistance: Latin American experience*. Berkeley and Los Angeles: University of California Press.

Newson, L. A. (1988). *Indian survival in colonial Nicaragua*. Norman: University of Oklahoma Press.

Nietschmann, B. (1995). Defending the Miskito Reefs with maps & GPS. *Cultural Survival Quarterly* (Winter), 34–37.

Nimkoff, M. F., & Middleton, R. (1960). Types of family and types of economy. *American Journal of Sociology, 66*, 215–225.

Noble, D. (1984). *The forces of production*. New York: Knopf.

Nugent, D. (1994). Building the state, making the nation: The bases and limits of state centralization in "Modern Peru." *American Ethnologist, 96*, 333–369.

Obbo, C. (1988). Is AIDS just another disease? In R. Kulstad (Ed.), *AIDS 1988: American Association for the Advancement of Science Symposia Papers* (pp. 191–198). Washington, DC: AAAS.

Obler, R. S. (1996). Whose cows are they anyway? Ideology and behavior in Nandi cattle ownership and control. *Human Ecology, 24*(2) (June 1996), 255–272.

O'Brien, D. (1984). Women never hunt: The portrayal of women in Melanesian ethnography. In D. O'Brien & S. Tiffany (Eds.), *Rethinking women's roles: Perspectives from the Pacific*. Berkeley and Los Angeles: University of California Press.

Odum, H. T. (1971). *Environment, power, and society*. New York: Wiley-Interscience.

———. (1992). *Energy and Public Policy*. New York: Wiley-Interscience.

Oliver, D. L. (1955). *A Solomon Island society: Kinship and leadership among the Siuai of Bougainville*. Cambridge, MA: Harvard University Press.

Ortner, S. B. (1989). *High religion: A cultural and political history of Sherpa Buddhism*. Princeton, NJ: Princeton University Press.

Otterbein, K. F. (1970). *The evolution of war: A cross-cultural study*. New Haven, CT: HRAF Press.

Parish, W. L. (1985). Introduction: Historical background and current issues. In W. L. Parish (Ed.), *Chinese Rural Development: The great transformation* (pp. 3–32). Armonk, NY: M.E. Sharpe.

Parker, R. G. (1987). Acquired immunodeficiency syndrome in urban Brazil. *Medical Anthropology Quarterly, 1*, 155–175.

———. (1988). Sexual culture and AIDS education in urban Brazil. In R. Kulstad (Ed.), *AIDS 1988: American Association for the Advancement of Science Symposia Papers* (pp. 169–174). Washington, DC: AAAS.

Parker, S. (1976). The precultural basis of the incest taboo: Toward a biosocial theory. *American Anthropologist, 78*, 285–301.

Pasternak, B. (1972). *Kinship and community in two Chinese villages*. Stanford, CA: Stanford University Press.

———. (1976). *Introduction to kinship and social organization*. Englewood Cliffs, NJ: Prentice Hall.

———. (1978). Seasons of birth and marriage in two Chinese localities. *Human Ecology, 6*, 299–324.

———. (1983). *Guests in the dragon: Social demography of a Chinese District, 1895–1946*. New York: Columbia University Press.

———. (1985). On the causes and consequences of uxorilocal marriage in China. In S. Hanley & A. Wolf (Eds.), *Family and population in East Asian history* (pp. 310–335). Stanford, CA: Stanford University Press.

Pasternak, B., & Wang Ching. (1985). Breastfeeding decline in urban China: An exploratory study. *Human Ecology, 13,* 433–465.

Pasternak, B., & Salaff, J. (1993). *Cowboys and Cultivators: The Chinese of Inner Mongolia.* Boulder, CO: Westview.

Peacock, J. (1995). Claiming common ground. *Anthropology Newsletter, 36*(4), 1, 3.

Peacock, N. (1984). The Mbuti of Northeast Zaire: Women and subsistence exchange. *Cultural Survival Quarterly, 8,* 15–17.

Peet, R., & Watts, M. (1994). Introduction: Development theory & environmentalism in an age of market triumphalism. *Economic Geography, 69*(3), 227–253.

Pehrson, R. (1957). *The bilateral network of social relations in Kön Kämä Lapp District.* Bloomington: Indiana University Press.

Perlmutter, D. (1986). No nearer to the soul. *Natural Language and Linguistic Theory, 4,* 515–523.

Petkov, K., & Fotev, G. (1990). *Ethnic conflict in Bulgaria, 1989: Sociological archive.* (In Bulgarian with English summary.) Sofia: Profizdat.

Piaget, J. (1954). *The construction of reality in the child.* New York: Basic Books.

Pianka, E. R. (1974). *Evolutionary biology.* New York: Harper & Row.

Pinker, S. (1994). *The language instinct: How the mind creates language.* New York: HarperCollins.

Poggie, J. J., DeWalt, B. R., & Dressler, W. W. (1992). *Anthropological research: Process and application.* Albany: State University of New York Press.

Pojman, L. P. (1995). *Ethics: Discovering right and wrong.* Belmont, CA: Wadsworth.

Poole, P. (1995). Geomatics: Who needs it? *Cultural Survival Quarterly, 18*(4), 1.

Popkin, S. (1979). *The Rational Peasant.* Berkeley and Los Angeles: University of California Press.

Posey, D. (1983). Indigenous ecological knowledge and development. In E. Moran (Ed.), *The dilemma of Amazonian development* (pp. 225–257). Boulder, CO: Westview Press.

———. (1984). Ethnoecology as applied anthropology in Amazonian development. *Human Organization, 43,* 95–107.

Pospisil, L. J. (1963). *The Kapauku Papuans of West New Guinea.* New York: Holt, Rinehart & Winston.

Powdermaker, H. (1966). *Stranger and friend: The way of an anthropologist.* New York: Norton.

Price, D. (1981). Complexity in non-complex societies. In S. E. van der Leeuw (Ed.), *Archaeological approaches to the study of complex society* (pp. 57–97). Amsterdam: University of Amsterdam's Albert van Giffen Institute for Prehistory.

Prince, A., & Smolensky, P. (1997). Optimality: From neural net to universal grammar. *Science, 275* (March 14), 1604–1610.

Pringle, H. (1997). Death in Norse Greenland. *Science 175* (Feb. 14), 924–926.

Putterman, L. (1981). Is a democratic collective agriculture possible? *Journal of Development Economics, 9,* 375–403.

Rabben, L. (1993). Demarcation and then what? *Cultural Survival Quarterly, 17*(2), 12–14.

Radcliffe-Brown, A. R. (1952). *Structure and functions in primitive society.* New York: Free Press.

Rapoport, A. (1981). "Realism" and "relevance" in gaming simulations. *Human Ecology, 9,* 137–150.

Rappaport, R. A. (1967). Ritual regulation of environmental relations among a New Guinea people. *Ethnology, 6,* 17–30.

———. (1968). *Pigs for the ancestors: Ritual in the ecology of a New Guinea people.* New Haven, CT: Yale University Press.

———. (1979). *Ecology, meaning, and religion.* Berkeley, CA: North Atlantic Books.

———. (1993). The anthropology of trouble. *American Anthropologist, 95,* 295–303.

Rasmussen, K. (1929). *Report of the fifth Thule expedition, 1921-1924* (Vol. 7, No. 1). *Intellectual Culture of the Iglulik Eskimos.* Copenhagen: Glydendalske Boghandel.

Redman, C. L. (1978). *The rise of civilization: From early farmers to urban society in the ancient Middle East.* San Francisco: Freeman.

Rensberger, B. (1989). Racial odyssey. In A. Podelefski & P. J. Brown (Eds.), *Applying anthropology: An introductory reader.* Mountain View, CA: Mayfield Press.

Reyna, S. P. (1994). Literary anthropology and the case against science. *Man, 29*(3), 555–581.

Reynolds, V., & Tanner, R. (1995). *The social ecology of religion.* Oxford: Oxford University Press.

Riegelhaupt, J. (1967). Saloio women: An analysis of informal and formal political and economic roles of Portuguese peasant women. *Anthropology Quarterly, 40,* 109–126.

Rigdon, S. M. (1988). *The culture facade: Art, science, and politics in the work of Oscar Lewis.* Urbana: University of Illinois Press.

Rindos, D. (1980). Symbiosis, instability, and the origins and spread of agriculture. *Current Anthropology, 21,* 751–765.

Rogers, E. M. (1962). *Diffusion of innovations.* New York: Free Press.

Rogers, E. M., & Shoemaker, F. F. (1971). *Communication of innovations: A cross-cultural approach.* New York: Free Press.

Romaine, S. (1994). *Language in society: An introduction to sociolinguistics.* New York: Oxford University Press.

Romanucci-Ross, L., Moerman, D. E., & Tancredi, L. R. (Eds.). (1991). *The anthropology of medicine: From culture to method* (2nd ed). Westport, CT: Bergin & Garvey.

Roosevelt, A. (1987). The evolution of human subsistence. In M. Harris and E. B. Ross (Eds.), *Food and evolution: Towards a theory of human food habits* (pp. 565–578). Philadelphia: Temple University Press.

Rostow, W. (1960). *The stages of economic growth: A Non-Communist manifesto.* Cambridge: Cambridge University Press.

Rubin, J., Flowers, N., & Gross, D. R. (1986). The adaptive dimensions of leisure time. *American Anthropologist, 13,* 524–536.

Rushforth, S., & Upham, S. (1993). *A Hopi social history.* Austin: University of Texas Press.

Rumbaugh, S. S., & Lewis, R. (1994). *The ape at the brink of the human mind.* New York: Wiley.

Rutz, H. J. (Ed.). (1992). The politics of time. *American Ethnographic Society Monograph Series*, No. 4.

Safa, H. I. (1974). *The urban poor of Puerto Rico: A study in development and inequality*. New York: Holt, Rinehart & Winston.

Safa, H. I. (1995). *The myth of the male breadwinner*. Boulder, CO: Westview.

Saffirio, J., & Hammer, R. (1983). The forest and the highway. In *The impact of contact: Two Yanomamö case studies*. (Report No. 11), pp. 3–48. Cambridge, MA: Cultural Survival.

Sahlins, M. D. (1961). The segmentary lineage: An organization of predatory expansion. *American Anthropologist, 63*, 332–345.

———. (1963). Poor man, rich man, big man, chief: Political types in Melanesia and Polynesia. *Comparative Studies in Society and History, 5*, 285–303.

———. (1965). On the sociology of primitive exchange. In *The relevance of models for social anthropology*. Association of Social Anthropologist (Monograph No. 1). New York: Praeger.

———. (1968). *Tribesmen*. Englewood Cliffs, NJ: Prentice Hall.

———. (1972). *Stone Age economics*. Chicago: Aldine.

Salamon, S. (1992). *Prairie patrimony: Family, farming and community in the Midwest*. Chapel Hill: University of North Carolina Press.

Salzman, P. C. (1971). Movement and resource extraction among pastoral nomads: The case of the Shah Nawazi Baluch. *Anthropological Quarterly, 44*, 185–197.

———. (1980). *When nomads settle: Processes of adaptation and response*. New York: Praeger.

Sanjek, R. (1977). Cognitive maps of the ethnic domain in urban Ghana: Reflections on variability and change. *American Ethnologist, 4*, 603–622.

Sankoff, G. (1972). *A quantitative paradigm for the study of communicative competence*. Paper prepared for the Conference on the Ethnography of Speaking, Austin, Texas, April 20–23.

Sapir, E. (1921). *Language: An introduction to the study of speech*. New York: Harcourt Brace and World.

———. (1929). The status of linguistics as a science. *Language, 5*, 207–214.

Sargent, C., & Harris, M. (1992). Gender ideology, child rearing, and child health in Jamaica. *American Ethnologist, 19*, 523–537.

Saunders, L., & Mehenna, S. (1986). Village entrepreneurs: An Egyptian case. *Ethnology, 25*, 75–8.

Schama, S. (1987). *An embarrassment of riches*. New York: Knopf.

Scheper-Hughes, N. (1979). The Margaret Mead controversy: Culture, biology, and anthropological inquiry. *Human Organization, 43*, 443–454.

Schick, K. D., & Toth, N. (1993). *Making silent stones speak: Human evolution and the dawn of technology*. New York: Simon & Schuster.

Schimmer, B. (1996). Anthropology on the Internet: A review and evaluation of networked resources. *Current Anthropology, 37*(3), 561.

Schneider, B. E. (1988). Gender and AIDS. In R. Kulstad (Ed.), *AIDS 1988: American Association for the Advancement of Science Symposia Papers* (pp. 97–106). Washington, DC: AAAS.

Schneider, D. M., & Gough, K. (Eds.). (1961). *Matrilineal kinship*. Berkeley and Los Angeles: University of California Press.

Schneider, H. K. (1970). *The Wahi Wanyaturu: Economics in an African society*. Viking Fund Publications in Anthropology (No. 48). Chicago: Aldine.

———. (1974). *Economic man: The anthropology of economics*. New York: Free Press.

Schoepf, B. G., wa Nkera, R., Ntsomo, P., Engundu, W., & Schoepf, C. (1988). AIDS, women, and society in Central Africa. In R. Kulstad (Ed.), *AIDS 1988: American Association for the Advancement of Science Symposia Papers* (pp. 175–182). Washington, DC: AAAS.

Schrire, C. (1984). Wild surmises in savage thoughts. In C. Schrire (Ed.), *Past and present in hunter-gatherer societies*. Orlando, FL: Academic Press.

Scott, J. C. (1976). *The moral economy of the peasant*. New Haven, CT: Yale University Press.

Service, E. R. (1971). *Primitive social organization: An evolutionary perspective* (2nd ed). New York: Random House.

Sheets, P. (1989). Dawn of a new Stone Age. In A. Podolefsky & P. J. Brown (Eds.), *Applying anthropology: An introductory reader*. Mountain View, CA: Mayfield Press.

Shepher, J. (1983). *Incest: A biosocial view*. New York: Academic Press.

Sheridan, T. E. (1988). *Where the dove calls: The political ecology of a peasant corporate community in Northwestern Mexico*. Tucson: University of Arizona Press.

Shreeve, J. (1994). Terms of estrangement. *Discover, 15*(11), 56–63.

Sidel, R. (1986). *Women and children lost*. New York: Viking-Penguin.

Simon, H. A. (1966). *Models of man: Social and rational; Mathematical essays on rational human behavior in a social setting*. New York: Wiley.

Sims, C. (1995, March 25). Argentina to issue new list of missing in "Dirty War." *New York Times*, p. 4.

Slobodkin, L. B. (1968). Toward a predictive theory of evolution. In R. C. Lewontin (Ed.), *Population biology and evolution*. Syracuse, NY: Syracuse University Press.

Smil, V. (1984). *The bad earth*. Armonk, NY: M. E. Sharpe.

———. (1994, May 30). A land stretching to support its people. *Herald Tribune* (international ed.), p. 8.

Smith, A. (1994). For all those who were Indian in a former life. *Cultural Survival Quarterly* (Winter), 70–72.

Smith, E. A., & Winterhalder, B. (Eds.). (1992). *Evolutionary ecology and human behavior*. New York: Aldine de Gruyter.

Smith, R. (1984). Social class. In *Annual review of anthropology* (pp. 467–494). Palo Alto, CA: Annual Reviews.

Soffer, O., Vandiver, P., & Klima, B. (1995). Paleolithic ceramics and clay objects from Pavlov I. Paper presented to Society for American Anthropology, May 4, Minneapolis.

Sorensen, C. W. (1988). *Over the mountains are mountains: Korean peasant households and their adaptation to rapid industrialization*. Seattle: University of Washington Press.

Southwick, C. H. (1996). *Global ecology in human perspective*. New York: Oxford University Press.

Southwold, M. (1965). The Ganda of Uganda. In J. L. Gibbs, Jr. (Ed.), *Peoples of Africa*. New York: Holt, Rinehart & Winston.

Spears, A. K. (1991). Teaching race, racism and ideology. *Transforming Anthropology,* 2, 16–18.

Spence, J. (1988). *The question of Hu.* New York: Knopf.

Speth, J. D. (1988). *Seasonality, resource stress, and food sharing in egalitarian foraging societies.* Paper presented at the Symposium Coping with Seasonal Constraints, 86th Annual Meeting of the American Anthropological Association, Chicago, 1987.

Spiro, M. (1992). Cultural relativism and the future of anthropology. In G. Marcus (Ed.), *Rereading cultural anthropology.* Durham, NC: Duke University Press.

Spiro, M. E. (1952). Ghosts, Ifaluk, and teleological functionalism. *American Anthropologist,* 54, 495–503.

Stacey, J. (1991). *Brave new families: Stories of domestic upheaval in late twentieth century America.* New York: Basic Books.

Stephan, C. W., & Stephan, W. C. (1985). *Two social psychologies.* Homewood, IL: Dorsey Press.

Stevens, W. K. (1994, January 18). Threat of encroaching deserts may be more myth than fact. *New York Times,* pp. C1–C10.

Steward, J. (1953). Evolution and process. In A. L. Kroeber (Ed.), *Anthropology today.* Chicago: University of Chicago Press.

———. (1972). *Theory of culture change: The methodology of multilinear evolution.* Urbana: University of Illinois Press.

Stoffle, R. W., Halmo, D. B., Wagner, T. W., & Luczkovich, J. L. (1994). Reefs from space: Satellite imagery, marine ecology, and ethnography in the Dominican Republic. *Human Ecology,* 22(3), 355–378.

Stoller, P. (1996). Spaces, places, and fields: The politics of West African trading in New York City's informal economy. *American Anthropologist* 88(4) (Dec.), 777–788.

Stone, P. M., Stone G. D., & Netting, R. M. C. (1995). The sexual division of labor in Kofyar agriculture. *American Ethnologist,* 22(1), 165–186.

Stringer, C., & Bauer, G. (1994). Methods, misreading and bias. *American Anthropologist,* 96(2), 416–424.

Stringer, C., & Gamble, C. (1994). *In search of the Neanderthals: Solving the puzzle of human origins.* London: Thames & Hudson.

Stringer, C., & McKie, R. (1997). *African exodus: The origin of modern humanity.* New York: Henry Holt.

Sturtevant, W. C., & Damas, D. (Eds.). *1984 Handbook of North American Indians, Vol. 5: Arctic.* Washington, DC: Smithsonian Institution.

Susser, I. (1986). Work and reproduction: Sociologic context. *Occupational Medicine: State of the Art Reviews,* 1, 517–530.

———. (1989). Gender in the anthropology of the United States. In S. Morgan (Ed.), *Gender and anthropology: Critical reviews for research and teaching* (pp. 343–358). Washington, DC: American Anthropological Association.

Susser, I. (1996). The construction of poverty and homelessness in U.S. cities. *Annual Review of Anthropology,* 25, pp. 411–435. Palo Alto: Annual Reviews, Inc.

Sussman, R. W., Green, G. M., & Sussman, L. K. (1994). Satellite imagery, human ecology, anthropology, and deforestation in Madagascar. *Human Ecology,* 22(3), 333–354.

Swanson, G. E. (1960). *The birth of the gods: The origin of primitive beliefs.* Ann Arbor: University of Michigan Press.

Sweet, L. E. (1965). Camel pastoralism in North Arabia and the minimal camping unit. In A. Leeds & A. P. Vayda (Eds.), *Man, culture, and animals: The role of animals in human ecological adjustment* (Publication No. 78). Washington, DC: American Association for the Advancement of Science.

Swift, J. (1974). The future of Tuareg pastoral nomadism in the Malian Sahel. Paper presented at the SSRC Symposium on the Future of Traditional Societies.

Tainter, J. (1988). *The collapse of civilization.* Cambridge: Cambridge University Press.

Tannen, D. (1994). *Talking from 9 to 5: How women's and men's conversational styles affect who gets heard, who gets credit, and what work gets done.* New York: Morrow.

Tapper, R. (1979). *Pasture and politics.* London: Academic Press.

Tattersal, I. (1995). *The fossil trail: How we know what we think we know about human evolution.* Oxford: Oxford University Press.

Tekeli, S. (Ed.). (1994). *Women in modern Turkish society.* London: Zed Books.

Thomas, D. H. (1986). *Refiguring anthropology.* Prospect Heights, IL: Waveland Press.

Thompson, L. (1950). *Culture in crisis: A study of the Hopi Indians.* New York: Harper & Row.

Thompson, L., & Joseph, A. (1947). *The Hopi way.* Chicago: University of Chicago Press.

Tierney, J., Wright, L., & Springen, K. (1988, January 11). The search for Adam and Eve. *Newsweek.*

Trevathan, W. R. (1987). *Human birth: An evolutionary perspective.* Hawthorne, NY: Aldine.

Tsiang, H. (1884). S. Bell (trans.), *Buddhist records of the Western world* (Vol. 1). London: Trubner. Reprinted in and cited from C. Coon (Ed.), *A reader in general anthropology* (pp. 452–463). New York: Holt, 1948.

Turnbull, C. (1961). *The forest people.* New York: Simon & Schuster.

———. (1965). The Mbuti Pygmies of the Congo. In J. L. Gibbs, Jr. (Ed.), *Peoples of Africa.* New York: Holt, Rinehart & Winston.

Turner, V. W. (1967). *The forest of symbols: Aspects of Ndembu ritual.* Ithaca, NY: Cornell University Press.

Tyler, P. E. (1994, March 27). Nature and economic boom devouring China's farmland. *New York Times,* pp. A1–A8.

———. (1995, April 10). On the farms, China could be sowing disaster. *New York Times,* p. A4.

Tyler, S. (1987). *The unspeakable: Discourse, dialogue, and rhetoric in the postmodern world.* Madison: University of Wisconsin Press.

Tylor, E. B. (1871). *Primitive culture: Researches into the development of mythology, philosophy, religion, language, art, and custom* (2 vols., 2nd ed.). London: John Murray.

USAID. (1982). Sudan: The Rahad irrigation project. Impact Evaluation Report No. 31. Washington, DC.

U.S. Public Health Service. (1986). *The Coolfont Report. Public Health Report 101.*

Van Gennep, A. (1960). *The rites of passage.* Chicago: University of Chicago Press.

Vayda, A. P. (1974). Warfare in an ecological perspective. *Annual Review of Ecology and Systematics,* 5, 183–193.

————. (1976). *Warfare in ecological perspective*. New York: Plenum.

————. (1987). Explaining what people eat: A review article. *Human Ecology, 15*, 493–510.

Verdery, K. (1992). The etatization of time in Ceausescu's Romania. In H. J. Ruts (Ed.) *The politics of time* (pp. 37–61). *American Ethnological Society Monograph Series, No. 4*. Washington, DC: American Anthropological Association.

Vondal, P. J. (1987). Intensification through diversified resource use: The human ecology of a successful agricultural industry in Indonesian Borneo. *Human Ecology, 15*, 27–52.

Wallace, A. F. C. (1966). *Religion: An anthropological view*. New York: Random House.

————. (1970). *The death and rebirth of the Seneca*. New York: Knopf.

Washabaugh, W. (1986). *Five fingers for survival*. Ann Arbor, MI: Karoma.

Weiner, A. B. (1976). *Women of value, men of renown: New perspectives in Trobriand exchange*. Austin: University of Texas Press.

————. (1988). *The Trobrianders of Papua New Guinea*. New York: Holt, Rinehart & Winston.

————. (1992). *Inalienable possessions*. Berkeley and Los Angeles: University of California Press.

Weisman, S. (1988, January 29). Where births are kept down and aren't. *New York Times*, p. 4.

Wells, M. (1987). Sharecropping in the United States: A political economy perspective. In M. Chibnik (Ed.), *Farm work and fieldwork: American agriculture in anthropological perspective* (pp. 211–243). Ithaca, NY: Cornell University Press.

Werner, D., Flowers, N., Ritter, M., & Gross, G, (1979). Subsistence productivity and hunting effort in native South America. *Human Ecology, 7*, 303–315.

Westermarck, E. A. (1922). *The history of human marriage* (3 vols.). New York: Allerton. (First published 1889.)

Weston, K. (1991). *Families we chose: Lesbians, gays, kinship*. New York: Columbia University Press.

White, J. (1994). *Money makes us relatives: Women's labor in urban Turkey*. Austin: University of Texas Press.

White, L. (1949). *The Science of culture*. New York: Farrar, Straus & Cudahy.

Whiteley, P. M. (1985). Unpacking Hopi clans: Another vintage model out of Africa. *Journal of Anthropological Research, 41*, 359–374.

————. (1988). *Deliberate acts: Changing Hopi culture through the Oraibi Split*. Tucson: University of Arizona Press.

Whiting, B. B. (Ed.). (1963). *Six cultures: Studies of child bearing*. New York: Wiley.

Whiting, B. B., & Whiting, J. W. (1973). Methods for observing and recording behavior. In R. Naroll & R. Cohen (Eds.), *A handbook of method in cultural anthropology*. New York: Columbia University Press.

————. (1974). *Children of six cultures: A psycho-cultural analysis*. Cambridge, MA: Harvard University Press.

Whiting, J. W., & Child, I. L. (1953). *Child training and personality: A cross-cultural study*. New Haven, CT: Yale University Press.

Whorf, B. L. (1956). The relation of habitual thought and behavior to language. In *Language, thought, and reality: Selected writings of Benjamin Lee Whorf*. Cambridge, MA: MIT Press.

Wikan, U. (1992). Beyond the words: The power of resonance. *American Ethnologist, 19*, 460–482.

Wilcox, S., Wilbers, S. (1987). The case for academic acceptance of American sign language. *Chronicle of Higher Education, 33*, 1.

Wilford, John N. (May 7, 1996). Mummies, textiles offer evidence of Europeans in Far East. *New York Times*, p. C1.

Wilk, R. R. (1991). *Household ecology: Economic change and domestic life among the Kekchi Maya of Belize*. Tucson: University of Arizona Press.

Wilkie, D., & Curran, B. (1993). Historical trends in forager and farmer exchange in the Ituri rain forest of Northeastern Zaire. *Human Ecology, 21*, 389–417.

Williams, T. R. (1967). *Field methods in the study of culture*. New York: Holt, Rinehart & Winston.

Williams, W. L. (1986). *The spirit and the flesh: Sexual diversity in American Indian culture*. Boston: Beacon.

Wilmsen, E. N. (1989a). *Land filled with flies: A political economy of the Kalahari*. Chicago: University of Chicago Press.

————. (1989b). *We are here: Politics of Aboriginal land tenure*. Berkeley and Los Angeles: University of California Press.

Wilson, A., Ochman, H., & Prager, M. E. (1987). Molecular time scale for evolution. *Trends in Genetics, 3*, 241–247.

Wilson, E. O. (1993, May 30). Is humanity suicidal? *New York Times Magazine*, pp. 24ff.

Wisner, B. The reconstruction of environmental rights in South Africa. *Human Ecology, 23*(3).

Wolf, E. R. (1966). *Peasants*. Englewood Cliffs, NJ: Prentice Hall.

————. (1982). *Europe and the people without history*. Berkeley and Los Angeles: University of California Press.

————. (1990). Facing power: Old insights, new questions. *American Anthropologist, 92*, 586–596.

————. (1994). Demonization of anthropologist in the Amazon. *Anthropology Newsletter* (March), 2.

Woods, C. M., & Graves, T. D. (1973). *The process of medical change in a highland Guatemalan town*. Los Angeles: Latin American Center, University of California.

Worsley, P. (1968). *The trumpet shall sound: A study of cargo cults in Melanesia*. New York: Schocken.

Worthman, C. M. (1995). Hormones, sex and gender. *Annual Review of Anthropology*, 593–618.

Wrangham, R., & Peterson, D. (1996). *Demonic males: Apes and the origins of human violence*. New York: Houghton Mifflin.

Wright, H. T., & Johnson, G. A. (1975). Population, exchange, and early state formation in Southwestern Iran. *American Anthropologist, 77*, 267–289.

Wright, R. (1994). *The moral animal*. New York: Pantheon.

Yellen, J. E., & Lee, R. B. (1976). The Dobe-/Du/da environment: Background to a hunting and gathering way of life. In R. B. Lee (Ed.), *Kalahari hunter-gatherers*. Cambridge, MA: Harvard University Press.

Zentella, A. C. (1988). Language politics in the USA: The English only movement. In *Literature, language and politics* (pp. 39-53). Athens: University of Georgia Press.

Index